HENRY FIELDING

GARLAND REFERENCE LIBRARY
OF THE HUMANITIES
(VOL. 147)

HENRY FIELDING
An Annotated Bibliography of Twentieth-Century Criticism, 1900–1977

John A. Stoler
Richard D. Fulton

GARLAND PUBLISHING, INC. • NEW YORK & LONDON
1980

© 1980 John A. Stoler and Richard D. Fulton

Library of Congress Cataloging in Publication Data

Stoler, John A   1935–
   Henry Fielding : an annotated bibliography of
twentieth-century criticism, 1900–1977.

   (Garland reference library of the humanities ; v. 147)
   Includes index.
   1. Fielding, Henry, 1707–1754—Bibliography.
I. Fulton, Richard D., 1945– joint author.
Z8293.72.S76   [PR3456]   016.823'5   78-68276
ISBN 0-8240-9796-3

Printed on acid-free, 250-year-life paper
Manufactured in the United States of America

For Mandy: My Sophia and Amelia
—J.A.S.

For My Wife: Suzanne
—R.D.F.

CONTENTS

V. The Novels

VI. Miscellaneous Writings

ACKNOWLEDGMENTS

There are too many individuals who helped me with my share in this work for me to thank them all by name. However, I would like to single out four people who contributed greatly to the completion of this project. Professor Henry Knight Miller, whose erudition and profound knowledge of Fielding are recorded in the bibliography, read the manuscript—saving the compilers from several embarrassing errors—and offered numerous suggestions which greatly improved the final version. Lawrence Davidow of Garland Publishing, Inc., also made many sound suggestions concerning the manuscript and showed great patience during the two years it took to bring it to completion. I would also like to thank Dr. Alan Craven, Division Director for English, Classics, and Philosophy at the University of Texas at San Antonio, for providing both advice and financial assistance in the preparation of the bibliography. My greatest debt of gratitude is owed to Mandy Stoler, who began her married life with me as a "scholar's widow" and who cheerfully listened to annotations in progress, patiently helped cross-reference, and painstakingly proofread the manuscript.

J.A.S.
San Antonio, Texas
May 1979

To my colleague's acknowledgments above, I would like to add my thanks to Suzanne Fulton, who researched, proofread, typed, and indexed for long hours with unfailing cheerfulness and good grace. I would also like to thank the interlibrary loan staff of Washington State University's Holland Library, and Roberta Stokes, who helped us with the foreign-language materials.

R.D.F.
Pullman, Washington
May 1979

INTRODUCTION

This bibliography attempts a comprehensive, although not exhaustive, listing of critical materials on Henry Fielding published from 1900 to 1977. A few 1978 and 1979 items that came to our attention also are included, but no thorough search of journals published after 1977 was attempted. Works published prior to 1900 are included only if they constitute part of an exchange that carries over into the twentieth century or if they have been republished since 1900. In listing reprinted works, we have given first the publication information of the edition we used for our annotation; in some cases this is the original edition, in others it is the reprint. We have chosen this method in order to be entirely accurate and because some reprints add supplementary information to the original.

Unless otherwise noted, all works listed in the first six sections have been seen by at least one of the compilers or by Professor Henry Knight Miller. Foreign-language materials and dissertations are generally not annotated because of the difficulty of obtaining and translating the former, many of which are not available in the United States, and the prohibitive cost of purchasing copies of the latter in order to review them. Additionally, it seemed futile to annotate from the abstracts of dissertations since most of those abstracts are available in complete form in *Dissertation Abstracts* or *Dissertation Abstracts International* (abbreviated in the bibliography as *DA* and *DAI*).

We have tried to be objective in our annotations. Where controversy has arisen over a work, we have referred the reader to appropriate commentary. As a further aid to the reader's assessment of a given work, reviews have been listed after the work reviewed. In order to enable the researcher to follow controversies and to group closely related items, we have included extensive cross-references within the annotations. The researcher who is pursuing a particular subject, however, should not limit himself to these cross-references but should also consult the subject index. We have cross-listed those books and essays which treat more than one of Fielding's works, but to avoid padding the bibliography, such materials are annotated only once and the reader is referred to the section in which the annotation is printed.

Each section of the bibliography has its own principles of selection and organization. Section I, "Selected Bibliographies," excludes bibliographies printed in critical books on Fielding or in editions of his works, except when those bibliographies are particularly valuable for pre–1900 criticism. In addition to the bibliographies listed here, the researcher should consult the standard annual guides, particularly the *MLA International Bibliography*, *The Annual Bibliography for English Language and Literature*, and *The Eighteenth-Century: A Current Bibliography*.

Section II, "Selected Collections and Editions," does not attempt to be comprehensive. The collections and editions listed were selected on the following principles: (1) they represent authoritative texts; (2) they contain important critical materials such as introductions, essays, or explanatory notes; (3) they are editions accessible to the general reader; or (4) they are the only editions in print. We have deliberately violated these principles only in the "Specialized Collections" section, which consists of various kinds of anthologies such as *Wise Sayings*, a work which does not fit the above-stated principles but which may be of use to someone seeking a well-known quotation from Fielding without knowing the specific work from which it comes. Because neither of the compilers of this work is a textual scholar, we have relied heavily on other, more informed, opinions to help us make our selections of editions. The decisions made, however, are solely ours, so the blame for any significant errors or omissions must also be solely ours. This section is divided into several subsections: Complete Works, Specialized Collections, Plays, Novels, and Miscellaneous Works. The subsections on Plays and Novels have a double chronological order; for example, *Shamela*, because published first, is listed first among the novels, and the various editions of *Shamela* are arranged according to the date published, from the earliest to the most recent. The subdivision for Plays is organized the same way. The other subsections are alphabetized by title.

No matter what subject or work the researcher is pursuing, he should carefully check the items listed in Section III, "General Works on Fielding's Life and Art." Many of these materials are cross-listed, but some that are not may still contain valuable commentary on the topic under investigation. The items here are listed alphabetically by the author's last name, but the next three sections are somewhat differently organized.

Section IV, "The Dramatic Works," appears after the section on general works because Fielding began his literary career as a playwright. Within this section, the plays are listed in the order of their production (or, when unproduced, in the order of publication). Each play is listed with its date, and the criticism on that play follows, alphabetized by the author's last name. A section of general criticism on Fielding's drama precedes the individual plays. The organization of Section V, "The Novels," follows the same principle: a section on Fielding's novels in general is followed by sections on the five novels in order of their publication.

Because of the problems of dating Fielding's miscellaneous writings and the desirability of grouping together some kinds of works (letters and verse, for example), Section VI, "Miscellaneous Writings," is organized to make it as useful as possible. After the subsections on the letters and verse, the miscellaneous prose pieces are listed alphabetically by title. Listing in order of publication dates, as was done with the plays and novels, was undesirable because so many of these works, like the *Champion* essays, are studied together, although they were published over a long period of time. The listings of foreign-language materials and dissertations (Sections VII and VIII) follow. No attempt was made to subdivide these sections, because few of them were seen by the compilers; they are simply listed alphabetically by author.

The bibliography concludes with author, title, and subject indices. The first two of these are designed to aid the reader who may know, for example, that Battestin wrote on Fielding but who may not have the title or titles of his studies, as well as the researcher who may have a title in mind but who has forgotten its author. The author index also enables the researcher to check all the studies of Fielding made by a particular scholar. The subject index is designed to supplement the cross-references in the bibliography. It is limited, however, to the subjects mentioned in the annotations and does not necessarily cover all of the material in every work listed herein. Our guiding principle in the indices, as well as in the rest of the bibliography, is that of usefulness to both the scholar and the novice researcher. We hope we have succeeded in combining these two interests.

No overview of the criticism contained in this bibliography has been attempted, because of the ready availability and excellence of two such overviews: C.J. Rawson's edited collection of Fielding criticism (see item 272) and Martin C. Battestin's "Fielding," in *The English Novel* (see item 2). The compilers felt that we could add little if anything to these insightful and thorough surveys of criticism.

HENRY FIELDING

SELECTED BIBLIOGRAPHIES

1. Bateson, F.W. *A Guide to English Literature*. Garden City, N.Y.: Doubleday Anchor Books, 1965.

   Offers a very brief bibliographical comment on editions of Fielding's works and major criticisms of them.

2. Battestin, Martin C. "Fielding," in *The English Novel: Select Bibliographical Guides*, ed. A.E. Dyson. London: Oxford University Press, 1974. Pp. 71-89.

   Surveys Fielding scholarship with essay and bibliographic sections on Texts, Critical Studies and Commentary, Biographies and Letters, Bibliography, and Background Reading. The overview provided presents a detailed but succinct picture of the history of Fielding criticism.

3. ————. "Henry Fielding," in *The New Cambridge Bibliography of English Literature*, Vol. 2, ed. George Watson. Cambridge: The University Press, 1971. Cols. 925-48.

   An extensive listing, briefly annotated, of bibliographies, collections, selections, works (first editions), editions, and critical studies arranged by year of publication through 1968. Also see Rice-Oxley, item 19.

4. Beasley, Jerry C. "Henry Fielding (1707-54)," in his *English Fiction, 1660-1800*. Detroit: Gale Research Co., 1978. Pp. 111-33.

   Lists and annotates 145 items, including editions, biographies, and critical studies.

5. Bell, Inglis F., and Donald Baird. "Henry Fielding," in their *The English Novel, 1578-1956: A Checklist of Twentieth-Century Criticism*. Denver and Chicago: Swallow, 1958. Pp. 45-49.

   Provides a basic listing of works through 1957 on *Amelia*, *Jonathan Wild*, *Joseph Andrews*, and *Tom Jones*.

6. Cordasco, Francesco. *Henry Fielding: A List of Critical Studies Published from 1895 to 1946*. Brooklyn: Long Island University Press, 1948. Reprinted in *Eighteenth-Century Bibliographies: Handlists of Critical Studies Relating to Smollett, Richardson, Sterne, Fielding, Dibdin, Eighteenth-Century Medicine, the Eighteenth-Century Novel, Godwin, Gibbon, Young, and Burke. To Which is Added John P. Anderson's Bibliography of Smollett*. Metuchen, N.J.: Scarecrow Press, 1970.

   This listing was long the standard bibliography of secondary materials on Fielding, but it is poorly organized (the extensive references to *Notes and Queries*, for example, often give neither title nor author and hence cannot be alphabetized) and frequently inaccurate (corrections and additions are made in *Philological Quarterly*, 29 [1950], 273–75). Nonetheless, it is useful for its listings of items published around the turn of the century.

7. Dickson, Frederick S., compiler. [Articles and Clippings by and about Henry Fielding.] Library of Congress: Fielding Collection, Trays 13–18.

   A collection of material from periodicals, newspapers, and books dating from Fielding's day to the early twentieth century.

8. ―――――, compiler. [Bibliographical References to Fielding.] Library of Congress: Fielding Collection, Trays 10–11.

   An alphabetical arrangement--by name of journal--of periodical references to Fielding from his own time to the early twentieth century.

9. ―――――. "Biographies of Fielding," added to *The Life and Writings of Henry Fielding* by Thomas Keightley. Cleveland: The Rowfant Club, 1907. Pp. 115–28.

   Lists ninety-two items, mostly from the eighteenth and nineteenth centuries, which treat Fielding's life and works.

10. ―――――. *Fielding's Dramatic Works: A List of the Different Editions of His Plays*. Philadelphia, 1929.

   An unpublished manuscript listed in *The National Union Catalog*, Vol. 143 (pre-1956), p. 199, and by Battestin in *The New Cambridge Bibliography of English Literature*.

11. ————, compiler. [Miscellaneous Notes.] Library of Congress: Fielding Collection, Trays 1-4.

    Contains various clippings from sales catalogs and other bibliographical publications relating to Fielding's works.

12. ————, compiler. [Miscellaneous Notes on Fielding Iconography.] Library of Congress: Fielding Collection, Tray 4.

    A compilation of material on iconography and illustrations of Fielding's works.

13. ————, compiler. [Miscellaneous References.] Library of Congress: Fielding Collection, Trays 5-9.

    A collection, alphabetized by author's name, of miscellaneous bibliographical references to works relating to Fielding from his own time to the 1920's.

14. Dyson, H.V.D., and John Butt. *Augustans and Romantics, 1689-1830*. London: Cresset, 1940. Rev. ed., 1950.

    Contains a brief and outdated bibliography of both primary and secondary works and a short evaluation of Fielding's fiction. Fielding is characterized by an ironic detachment, a worldly morality, and a brilliant presentation of characters through speech and action.

15. *English Literature from the 16th Century to the Present: A Select List of Editions*. Published for the British Council. Rev. ed. London: Longmans, Green, 1965.

    Lists several editions plus ten critical works.

*   Fulton, Richard, and John A. Stoler. "Henry Fielding: A Checklist of Criticism, 1946-1975." *Bulletin of Bibliography and Magazine Notes*, 33 (1976), 193-211.

    See under Stoler, item 20.

16. Jobe, Alice. "Fielding's Novels: Selected Criticism (1940-1969)." *Studies in the Novel*, 2 (1970), 246-59.

    A checklist of 252 items divided into five sections, one on each novel, and one section of general criticism.

17. Kyle, Linda Davis. "'Amelia' by Henry Fielding: A Selective Bibliography." *Notes and Queries*, n.s. 24 (1977), 255-58.

    Contains eighty-four items, including editions.

18. Paulson, Ronald, and Thomas Lockwood, eds. *Henry Field-ing: The Critical Heritage*. London: Routledge & Kegan Paul and New York: Barnes and Noble, 1969.

An extensive collection (180 items) of eighteenth-century commentary on Fielding's works, including remarks by Swift, Gray, Shenstone, Richardson, and Johnson.

Review: Times Literary Supplement (Jan. 29, 1970), p. 103.

19. Rice-Oxley, L. "Henry Fielding (1707-1754)," in *The Cambridge Bibliography of English Literature*, Vol. 2, ed. F.W. Bateson. New York: Macmillan and Cambridge: The University Press, 1941. Pp. 517-20.

Important editions, biographies, and critical works pub-lished from the eighteenth century through 1937 are listed. See the updated *New Cambridge Bibliography* by Battestin, item 3.

20. Stoler, John A., and Richard Fulton. "Henry Fielding: A Checklist of Criticism, 1946-1975." *Bulletin of Bibliog-raphy and Magazine Notes*, 33 (1976), 193-211.

Divides 705 items, including reviews, into three sec-tions: books on Fielding and editions of his works with critical commentary; articles and essays; and disserta-tions.

21. Tobin, James E. *Eighteenth Century English Literature and Its Cultural Background: A Bibliography*. New York: Fordham University Press, 1939.

Lists a number of Fielding items, some of which are not listed in Cordasco and Rice-Oxley.

II

SELECTED COLLECTIONS AND EDITIONS

A. Complete Works

22. *Complete Works: With an Essay on the Life, Genius, and Achievement of the Author.* 16 Vols. Ed. William E. Henley. New York: Barnes and Noble, 1967. Originally published London: Heinemann, 1903.

Although Henley probably did not do the editing himself (no one is sure who did), he apparently was in charge of the edition, known as the "Henley edition." It is based on Leslie Stephen's 1882 edition, but with some additional poems and pamphlets and an edited version of *A Journal of a Voyage to Lisbon.* (*Shamela* is omitted.) Although this edition perpetuates previous textual errors and inaccuracies, it has long been considered the "standard" complete works of Fielding. It is, however, being gradually replaced by the "Wesleyan Fielding" (sixteen volumes projected). Henley's critical assessment of Fielding is annotated separately; see item 200.

23. *The Works of Henry Fielding.* 12 vols. Ed. G.H. Maynadier. Cambridge, Mass.: Harvard University Press, 1903.

Omits many of the plays and miscellaneous writings, including *Shamela.* The texts in this edition are perhaps inferior to those in the Henley edition, item 22, but it is nonetheless a useable edition available in many libraries. A brief essay, usually quite general, precedes each individual work (see items 692, 746, 901, 1008, and 1125).

B. Specialized Collections

24. Barnett, George L., ed. *Eighteenth-Century British
     Novelists on the Novel*. New York: Appleton-Century
     Crofts, 1968.

     Includes a brief introduction, excerpts from *Joseph
     Andrews*, and prefaces to *David Simple* and *Familiar Let-
     ters* (see pp. 40–58).

25. *The Fielding Calendar: A Quotation from the Works of
     Fielding for Every Day in the Year*. Selected by John
     Kirkby. London: Frank Palmer, 1913.

     Battestin cites this item in *The New Cambridge Bibliog-
     raphy of English Literature*, but the compilers were un-
     able to locate a copy of it.

26. *Fielding: Selections, With Essays by Hazlitt, Scott,
     Thackeray*. Ed. L. Rice-Oxley. Oxford: The Clarendon
     Press, 1923.

     The compilers have not seen this work, listed in *The New
     Cambridge Bibliography of English Literature*.

27. *The Genius of Fielding*. Ed. H.H. Harper. Boston: Bib-
     liophile Society, 1919.

     The compilers have not personally seen this collection.

28. *Henry Fielding: Scenes and Characters*. Ed. John Hadfield.
     London: Falcon Press, 1950.

     Extracts passages from *Jonathan Wild*, *Joseph Andrews*, and
     Tom Jones and contains a brief assessment of Fielding's
     contributions to literature.

     Review: Times Literary Supplement (18 August 1950), p.
     522.

29. *The Literary and Social Criticism of Henry Fielding*. Ed.
     Ioan M. Williams. London: Routledge and Kegan Paul and
     New York: Barnes and Noble, 1970.

     Reprints seventy-two selections from Fielding's social
     and literary criticism. Items are taken from his letters,
     prefaces, journals, and novels, and are arranged under
     the following headings: "The Theatre," "Colley Cibber,"
     "The Art of Criticism," "Grub Street," "The Laws of
     Good Writing," "Wit and Humour," "Approbations," "*The
     Jacobite's Journal*," and "The 'New Province' of Writing."

Appendices include the "Preface" to the *Miscellanies*, Cibber's "Preface" to *The Provok'd Husband*, and two essays from *Common Sense*.

Review: Howard Erskine-Hill, *Notes and Queries*, n.s. 19 (1972), 393.

30. *Selected Essays of Henry Fielding*. Ed. G.H. Gerould. Boston: Ginn and Co., 1905.

Contains thirty-two essays from the novels, the journals, and the *Miscellanies*--with still useful notes. For the critical introduction, see item 1035.

31. *Wise Sayings and Favorite Passages from the Works of Fielding, Including His "Essay on Conversation."* Ed. C.W. Bingham. Cedar Rapids, Iowa: The Torch Press, 1909.

This work is listed in *The New Cambridge Bibliography of English Literature*, but the compilers have not seen a copy.

C. Plays

32. *The Author's Farce*. Ed. Charles B. Woods. Lincoln: University of Nebraska Press, 1966.

Reprints for the first time Fielding's original version of 1730; the text is collated with the second impression and the second edition. The text is modernized and annotated. There are four appendices: the extensive revision of 1750; the individuals mentioned in the play; the tunes used; and a chronology of major publications and events from 1631 through 1754. Woods' introduction is annotated in Section IV, item 390.

Reviews: Joseph A. Byrnes, *Seventeenth-Century News*, 35 (1968), 34-35; Dean L. Morgan, *Personalist*, 48 (1968), 430; A.H. Scouten, *Philological Quarterly*, 46 (1967), 344-45.

33. *The Tragedy of Tragedies, or The Life and Death of Tom Thumb the Great*. Ed. James T. Hillhouse. New Haven: Yale University Press, 1918.

Prints both the *Tom Thumb* of 1730 and the 1731 revision entitled *The Tragedy of Tragedies*. The book includes a lengthy introduction (see item 396); a long section of notes and comments; two appendices which discuss "The

Battle of the Poets" (an act added anonymously to *Tom Thumb*) and various adaptations of the play; and a bibliography which includes a list of plays specifically parodied by Fielding. The text of *Tom Thumb* is based on the first reprint of the 1730 edition and that of the *Tragedy of Tragedies* is a reprint of the edition of 1731 collated with a later 1731 impression and with the third, fourth, and fifth editions. For a brief comment on the problems with Hillhouse's source texts, see page 12 of the Morrissey edition (item 400).

Reviews: J.P. de Castro, *Notes and Queries*, 12th series, 5 (1919), 54-56; Helen Sard Hughes, *Journal of English and Germanic Philology*, 18 (1919), 464-67.

34. *Tom Thumb*, in *Burlesque Plays of the Eighteenth Century*, ed. Simon Trussler. London: Oxford University Press, 1969. Pp. 143-70.

   Printed from the second edition of 1730.

35. *"Tom Thumb" and "The Tragedy of Tragedies."* Ed. L.J. Morrissey. Berkeley and Los Angeles: University of California Press and Edinburgh: Oliver and Boyd, 1970.

   A thoroughly annotated edition with a glossary and critical introduction (see item 400 for the latter). The edition is based on a collation of two copies of the first version, two copies of the first edition of the second version, and copies of the second and third editions of the second version. The first edition of the second version is the copy-text. All variations from the copy-text, except for a few silent emendations, are recorded in the Textual Notes. This edition is more carefully collated than that of Hillhouse (item 33) because the latter did not collate the first edition of the revised play.

36. *The Tragedy of Tragedies (Tom Thumb)*. A Scolar Facsimile. Intro.: Anthony J. Hassall. London: The Scolar Press, 1973.

   The text is reproduced from a copy in the Edinburgh University Library and is Fielding's final revision, performed on March 24, 1731. It is the third impression of that revision.

37. *The Grub-Street Opera*. Ed. Edgar V. Roberts. Lincoln: University of Nebraska Press, 1967; London: Arnold, 1969.

Includes an Introduction (see item 409) and three appendices: "The Revisions," "The Music," and "Chronology"
(the latter records important publications and historical
events from 1631 through 1754). The copy-text is the
1731 edition in the British Museum which is collated
with copies in the Bodleian, Folger, and Huntington Libraries. Stage directions and annotations are supplied.

38. *The Grub-Street Opera*. Ed. L.J. Morrissey. Fountain-
well Drama Texts, 25. Edinburgh: Oliver & Boyd, 1973.

Provides a brief history of the play from Rayner's two
pirated editions, *The Welsh Opera* and *The Original Grub-
Street Opera*, to Millar's authorized edition. Morrissey
has collated five copies of *The Grub-Street Opera* as well
as two copies of *The Welsh Opera* and *The Original Grub-
Street Opera*. Variations from the copy-text, in the
Yale Library, have been recorded in textual notes.

39. *Covent-Garden Tragedy*, in *Burlesque Plays of the Eighteenth
Century*, ed. Simon Trussler. London: Oxford University
Press, 1969. Pp. 171-208.

Reprints the first and only edition of 1732.

40. *Pasquin*. Eds. O.M. Brack, Jr., William Kupersmith, and
Curt A. Zimansky. Iowa City: University of Iowa Press,
1973.

This first modern critical text is accompanied by explanatory and textual notes.

41. *The Historical Register for the Year 1736 and Eurydice
Hissed*. Ed. William Appleton. Lincoln: University of
Nebraska Press, 1967.

A thoroughly annotated text with Introduction (see item
437). The copy-text for this edition is the 48-page
edition of May 12, 1737. The 41-page edition thought by
Cross (item 126, III, 301-02) to be the true first edition
is, in fact, a piracy.

D. Novels

42. *An Apology for the Life of Mrs. Shamela Andrews*. Ed.
Sheridan Baker. Berkeley and Los Angeles: University of
California Press, 1953.

This edition transcribes the first edition copy at the
Huntington Library, corrected from the second edition
at Yale. Several small errors in proof, untouched in the
second edition, are silently corrected. The introduction
is annotated in item 614.

Review: Charles B. Woods, *Philological Quarterly*, 33
(1954), 272-74.

43. *An Apology for the Life of Mrs. Shamela Andrews (1741)*.
    Ed. Ian Watt. Augustan Reprint Society, No. 57. Los
    Angeles: Clark Memorial Library, 1956.

    Watt's Introduction is reprinted as "*Shamela*" in Paulson
    (item 258). For annotation, see item 633. This volume
    is a photographic reprint of the second edition of
    November 3, 1741.

44. *Shamela* in "*Joseph Andrews*" and "*Shamela*." Ed. Martin C.
    Battestin. Boston: Houghton Mifflin, 1961.

    See under item 49.

45. *Shamela* in "*The History of the Adventures of Joseph
    Andrews and of His Friend Mr. Abraham Adams*" and "*An
    Apology for the Life of Mrs. Shamela Andrews*." Ed.
    Douglas Brooks. London and New York: Oxford University
    Press, 1970.

    See under item 51.

46. *Shamela* in "*Joseph Andrews*" and "*Shamela*." Ed. Sheridan
    Baker. New York: Crowell, 1972.

    See under item 52.

47. *The Adventures of Joseph Andrews*. Ed. J. Paul de Castro.
    London: Scholartis Press, 1929.

    An annotated edition with an index and a brief introduc-
    tion (see item 659). The notes are still of interest,
    but the text has been superseded by more recent editions,
    especially that of Martin C. Battestin.

    Reviews: Aurélien Digeon, *Revue Anglo-Americaine*, 7 (1930),
    263; *Notes and Queries*, 156 (1929), 342; *Times Literary
    Supplement* (April 25, 1929), p. 343.

48. *Joseph Andrews*. Ed. Maynard Mack. New York: Rinehart,
    1948.

    Mack's introduction is reprinted as "*Joseph Andrews* and
    Pamela" in Paulson, item 258, and in Iser, item 507. For
    annotation, see item 688.

49. *"Joseph Andrews"* and *"Shamela."* Ed. Martin C. Battestin.
     Boston: Houghton Mifflin, 1961.

     The text of *Joseph Andrews* is based on the fourth edition
     and that of *Shamela* on the second edition. The volume
     includes a long introduction, pp. v-xl (see item 616),
     and explanatory notes printed at the back of the book.

     Reviews: David Lodge, *Modern Language Review*, 62 (1967),
     317-18; *Times Literary Supplement* (Jan. 6, 1966), p. 5;
     Terence Wright, *Notes and Queries*, n.s. 13 (1966), 231.

50. *Joseph Andrews*. Ed. Martin Battestin. Middletown, Conn.:
     Wesleyan University Press and Oxford: The Clarendon
     Press, 1967.

     This "standard" edition is based on the first four edi-
     tions that appeared in Fielding's lifetime; the copy-
     text is the first edition. The book includes a General
     Introduction by Battestin (see item 640) and a Textual
     Introduction by Fredson Bowers (see item 645). The text
     is footnoted throughout and there are six appendices on
     emendations, historical collation, bibliographical des-
     criptions of the first five editions, and the Murphy
     editions.

     Reviews: Sheridan Baker, *Michigan Quarterly Review*, 6
     (1967), 298; Douglas Brooks, *Modern Language Review*, 66
     (1969), 146-47; H.W. Drescher, *Anglia*, 87 (1969), 101-03;
     J.D. Fleeman, *Review of English Studies*, 19 (1968), 208-
     09; F.W. Hilles, *Yale Review*, 57 (1967), 278-82; *Times
     Literary Supplement* (April 20, 1968), p. 334; Arthur
     Sherbo, *Journal of English and Germanic Philology*, 67
     (1968), 520-22; Niels Jørgen Skydsgaard, *English Studies*,
     50 (1969), 409-10; Ian Watt, *Philological Quarterly*, 47
     (1968), 379-81.

51. *"The History of the Adventures of Joseph Andrews"* and
     "An Apology for the Life of Mrs. Shamela Andrews." Ed.
     Douglas Brooks. London and New York: Oxford University
     Press, 1970.

     Includes an Introduction (see item 651), a Note on the
     Texts, a short Bibliography, and a Chronology of Henry
     Fielding. An appendix prints the Dedication to Conyers
     Middleton's *History of the Life of Marcus Tullius Cicero*.
     Textual and explanatory notes conclude the book. The
     text of *Joseph Andrews* is that established by Martin C.
     Battestin for the Wesleyan edition (see item 50). The
     text of *Shamela* is based on the copy of the first edition
     in the Harold Cohen Library, University of Liverpool,
     collated with the second edition.

52. *"Joseph Andrews" and "Shamela."* Ed. Sheridan Baker.
     New York: Crowell, 1972.

     A "Crowell Critical Edition" with scholarly texts and
     critical essays. The text of *Shamela* follows the first
     edition, although those changes presumed to be Fielding's
     in the second edition have been incorporated. *Joseph
     Andrews* follows the first edition, but Baker has marked
     in the margins those changes from the second, third,
     and fourth editions that seem to be Fielding's. Baker's
     lengthy introduction covers Fielding's career and pre-
     sents overviews of both novels (see item 615). The
     "Essays in Criticism" section contains the following:
     Mark Spilka, "Comic Resolution in Fielding's *Joseph
     Andrews*" (item 712); Dick Taylor, Jr., "Joseph as Hero
     in *Joseph Andrews*" (item 717); Martin C. Battestin, "The
     Moral Basis of Fielding's Art: A Study of *Joseph Andrews*"
     (item 643); Sheridan Baker, "Henry Fielding's Comic Ro-
     mances" (item 637); Eric Rothstein, "The Framework of
     Shamela" (item 629); Patricia Meyer Spacks, "Some Re-
     flections on Satire" (item 711); Douglas Brooks, "Richard-
     son's *Pamela* and Fielding's *Joseph Andrews*" (item 653);
     "Objections [to Brooks] by A.M. Kearney" (item 680); and
     "A Rebuttal [to Kearney] by Mr. Brooks" (item 654).

53. *The Life of Mr. Jonathan Wild the Great.* Ed. J.H. Plumb.
     New York: New American Library, 1962.

     A modernized version of the second edition (1754).
     Plumb's Foreword is annotated at item 749.

54. *"Jonathan Wild the Great" and "The Journal of a Voyage
     to Lisbon."* Ed. Douglas Brooks. Intro. A.R. Humphreys.
     London: J.M. Dent and New York: Dutton, 1973.

     The text of *Jonathan Wild* is based on Fielding's 1754
     revision. The text of *Voyage* follows the longer version
     of December 1755. For the discussion that determined
     that the longer text of the latter is Fielding's own,
     see the following: de Castro, "Henry Fielding's Last
     Voyage," item 1116; Dickson, "The Early Editions," item
     1118; Pollard, items 1128 and 1129; and Prideaux, "Field-
     ing's *Journal*," item 1130. Humphreys' introduction is
     annotated at item 740.

55. *Tom Jones.* Ed. George Sherburn. New York: Random House,
     1950.

     A popular edition with an introduction by George Sherburn
     (see item 953).

56. *The History of Tom Jones.* Ed. R.P.C. Mutter. Harmonds-
     worth, Middlesex: Penguin, 1966.

     Based on the third edition, this text is accompanied by
     explanatory annotations. Although this is still a use-
     ful edition, it has been superseded as a scholarly text
     by Battestin's edition (see item 58).

57. *Tom Jones: An Authoritative Text, Contemporary Reactions,
     Criticism.* Ed. Sheridan Baker. New York: Norton, 1973.

     Baker's text follows Andrew Millar's fourth printing of
     1749. A "Textual Appendix" discusses the early printings
     of the novel and the revisions of "The Man of the Hill's
     Tale." A section of "Contemporary Reactions," including
     commentary by Richardson and Johnson, follows the Appen-
     dix. The "Criticism" section includes the following
     (all of which, except for the Coleridge material, are
     annotated in this work): Samuel Taylor Coleridge, "Notes
     on *Tom Jones*"; Samuel Taylor Coleridge, "A Master of Com-
     position"; David Goldknopf, "The Failure of Plot in *Tom
     Jones*," item 847; John Preston, "Plot as Irony: The
     Reader's Role in *Tom Jones*," item 930; Martin C. Battestin,
     "Fielding's Definition of Wisdom: Some Functions of Am-
     biguity and Emblem in *Tom Jones*," item 773; R.S. Crane,
     "The Plot of *Tom Jones*," item 808; William Empson, "*Tom
     Jones*," item 839; Wayne C. Booth, "'Fielding' in *Tom
     Jones*," item 789; Lyall H. Powers, "*Tom Jones* and Jacob
     de la Vallée," item 928; Kenneth Rexroth, "Tom Jones,"
     item 940; Sheridan Baker, "Bridget Allworthy: The Creative
     Pressures of Fielding's Plot," item 770; Frederick W.
     Hilles, "Art and Artifice in *Tom Jones*," item 859.

58. *The History of Tom Jones, a Foundling.* 2 vols. Intro-
     duction and Commentary by Martin C. Battestin. Text
     edited by Fredson Bowers. Middletown, Conn.: Wesleyan
     University Press and Oxford: The Clarendon Press, 1975.
     Reprinted in a one-volume, paperback edition: Middletown,
     1977.

     Establishes an authoritative text--based on the first
     edition and collated with the other three editions issued
     during Fielding's lifetime--and replaces all previous
     editions as the "standard" edition. Battestin provides
     a General Introduction (see item 774) and Bowers presents
     a Textual Introduction (see item 793). The text is foot-
     noted throughout; six appendices include a list of emen-
     dations, textual notes, and bibliographical descriptions;
     an index of names and places concludes the book.

Reviews: Paul-Gabriel Boucé, *Études anglaises*, 29 (1976), 97-98; Clive Probyn, *Times Literary Supplement* (April 16, 1976), p. 472; Eric Rothstein, *The Eighteenth Century: A Current Bibliography*, n.s. 1 (1978), 289-90.

59. *Amelia*. 2 Vols. Intro. A.R. Humphreys. London: Dent and New York: Dutton, 1962.

Included here as the most accessible edition of the novel. See Humphreys' introduction, item 999.

E. Miscellaneous Works

60. *Covent-Garden Journal*. 2 Vols. Ed. Gerard E. Jensen. New Haven: Yale University Press, 1915.

Includes a lengthy (129 pages) introduction--for annotation see item 1094. Jensen bases his text on the original folio issues in the Burney and Wrenn collections.

61. *The Female Husband and Other Writings*. Ed. Claude E. Jones. English Reprint Series, 17. Liverpool: Liverpool University Press, 1960.

Includes several minor writings, including a selection of Fielding's epilogues and his poem *The Masquerade*. The editing of the texts has been called into question; for commentary on this issue, see the reviews listed below.

Reviews: John Graham, *Journal of English and Germanic Philology*, 61 (1962), 189-90; C.J. Rawson, *Notes and Queries*, 207 (1962), 158-59; Andrew Wright, *Modern Language Review*, 56 (1961), 631.

62. *The History of the Present Rebellion in Scotland*. Ed. I.K. Fletcher. Newport, Monmouthshire: J.K. Fletcher, 1934.

The compilers were unable to review a copy of this edition.

63. *The Jacobite's Journal and Related Writings*. Ed. W.B. Coley. Middletown, Conn.: Wesleyan University Press and Oxford: The Clarendon Press, 1975.

Contains--in addition to *The Jacobite's Journal*--A *Dialogue Between a Gentleman from London ... and an Honest*

Alderman of the Country Party and *A Proper Answer to a Late Scurrilous Libel*. This edition establishes a "standard" text for the three works and includes a General Introduction by Coley (see item 467); a Textual Introduction by Fredson Bowers (see item 1113); six appendices on emendations, bibliographical descriptions, the Murphy editions, and doubtful attributions to Fielding from *The Jacobite's Journal*; and an index of names, places, and topics. The introductions and texts are copiously annotated.

Reviews: John Cannon, *Essays in Criticism*, 25 (1975), 452-56; Thomas R. Cleary, *The Eighteenth Century: A Current Bibliography*, n.s. 1 (1978), 290-92; Gela Curtis, *Times Literary Supplement* (Sept. 12, 1975), p. 1029; Frederick W. Hilles, *Yale Review*, 64 (1975), 128-33; Clarence Tracy, *Queen's Quarterly*, 83 (1976), 127-28.

64. *The Journal of a Voyage to Lisbon*. Ed. Austin Dobson. London: Oxford University Press, 1907.

Reprints the first and shorter version of the *Voyage* (published in February of 1755). For a discussion of the two 1755 versions of the *Voyage*, see the following: de Castro, "Henry Fielding's Last Voyage," item 1116; Dickson, "The Early Editions," item 1118; Pollard, items 1128 and 1129; and Prideaux, "Fielding's *Journal*," item 1130. The best edition is that of Pagliaro, item 65.

65. *The Journal of a Voyage to Lisbon*. Ed. Harold Pagliaro. New York: Nardon Press, 1963.

The editor's introduction is annotated in item 1127. The text is based on the original, unedited version of the *Journal*, published in December 1755. (For the story behind the textual problems involved with the *Journal*, see: de Castro, "Henry Fielding's Last Voyage," item 1116; Dickson, "The Early Editions," item 1118; Pollard, items 1128 and 1129; amd Prideaux, "Fielding's *Journal*," item 1130.) The text retains eighteenth-century spelling forms and is thoroughly annotated.

Reviews: W.B. Coley, *College English*, 25 (1964), 640; C.J. Rawson, *Notes and Queries*, n.s. 11 (1964), 460; Charles B. Woods, *Philological Quarterly*, 43 (1964), 360-61; Andrew Wright, *Modern Language Review*, 59 (1964), 460.

66. *Journey from This World to the Next*. Berkshire: Golden Cockerell Press, 1930.

A non-scholarly edition made more interesting by the in-
clusion of six etchings on copper by Denis Tegetmeir.

67. *A Journey from This World to the Next*. Ed. Claude J.
     Rawson. London: Dent and New York: Dutton, 1973.

     See the critical introduction at item 1135.

68. *The Lovers Assistant, or The New Art of Love (1760)*. Ed.
     Claude E. Jones. Augustan Reprint Society, No. 89. Los
     Angeles: Clark Memorial Library, 1961.

     The text is printed from the 1760 edition collated with
     a copy of the 1759 edition. The Latin text, which in
     the original faces the English, is omitted. This work
     is properly *Ovid's Art of Love* (1747), copies of which
     do exist (see Jarvis, item 1037), but of which Jones was
     unaware.

     Review: Charles B. Woods, *Philological Quarterly*, 40
     (1961), 390.

69. *Miscellanies by Henry Fielding, Esq*. Vol. I. Ed. Henry
     Knight Miller. Middletown, Conn.: Wesleyan University
     Press and Oxford: The Clarendon Press, 1972.

     Based on the first edition, this volume establishes a
     "standard" text for its contents (thirty-eight poems and
     eight prose pieces, including "An Essay on Conversation"
     and "An Essay on Nothing"). The book contains a General
     Introduction by Miller (see item 1043); a Textual Intro-
     duction by Fredson Bowers (see item 1030); four appendices
     (Preface to *Of True Greatness*, "To Sir R. W___le,"
     verses from *The Champion*, and selections from the *Philo-
     sophical Transactions* of the Royal Society); and five
     textual appendices on emendations, collation, and bib-
     liographical descriptions. An index of names and places
     also is included, and the introductions, texts, and ap-
     pendices are thoroughly footnoted.

     Reviews: Douglas Brooks, *Critical Quarterly* (1973), 187-
     88; A.R. Humphreys, *Review of English Studies*, 25 (1974),
     212-14; Ronald Paulson, *Philological Quarterly*, 52 (1973),
     501-03; C.J. Rawson, *Notes and Queries*, n.s. 22 (1975),
     31-32; *Times Literary Supplement* (29 June 1973), p. 740.

70. *The True Patriot: and The History of Our Times*. Ed.
     Miriam Austin Locke. University: University of Alabama
     Press, 1964.

     This fully annotated edition is a reduced photographic
     facsimile of the thirty-two numbers extant in the Burney

Collection in the British Museum; the thirty-third and
final number, no copy of which is known to exist, is
printed in a summary version as it appeared in the June
1746 *London Magazine*. This is the first complete re-
printing of the journal, all previous editors having
reprinted only the ten numbers presumed by Murphy to
have been written by Fielding.

Reviews: Richmond P. Bond, *English Language Notes*, 2
(1965), 307-08; W.B. Coley, *Philological Quarterly*, 44
(1965), 348-49; Frank Kermode, *New York Review of Books*
(Oct. 28, 1965), pp. 5-6.

71. *The Voyages of Mr. Job Vinegar from "The Champion" (1740)*.
    Ed. S.J. Sackett. Augustan Reprint Society, 67. Los
    Angeles: Clark Memorial Library, 1958.

    Because of the condition of the original *Champion* essays,
    this text is printed in typescript instead of being
    photographically reproduced. However, all the printers'
    errors are retained in order to come as close as possible
    to the original text. Sackett's Introduction is annotated
    in item 1078.

III

GENERAL WORKS ON FIELDING'S LIFE AND ART

*   Amory, Hugh. "Fielding's Lisbon Letters." (See item
      1051.)

72.   ————. "Henry Fielding," in *Four Oaks Library*, ed.
      Gabriel Austin. Somerville, N.J.: n.p., 1967. Pp.
      29-40.

      Describes the famous Hyde collection, which--among other
      things--contains almost one-third of Fielding's autograph
      manuscripts.

73.   ————. "Henry Fielding and the Criminal Legislation of
      1751-52." *Philological Quarterly*, 50 (1971), 175-92.

      It has long been assumed--mostly due to references by
      Horace Walpole and Sir John Fielding, Henry's half
      brother--that Henry Fielding was in great part responsible
      for much of the criminal legislation of 1751-52. By com-
      paring Fielding's views, as expressed in his social
      pamphlets, with those of the Committee of 1751, charged
      with the task of recommending criminal legislation, Amory
      concludes that instead of being influential on the com-
      mittee's recommendations, Fielding was in disagreement
      with most of them. Although Fielding and the committee
      agreed that greater severity of punishment was needed as
      a deterrent to crime, they strongly disagreed about the
      ways in which added severity could be effected. Fielding
      made some concrete suggestions concerning such matters
      as the gin problem, but Parliament rejected them. Also
      see Radzinowicz, item 267, and Zirker, item 1100.

74.   ————, ed. *Poets and Men of Letters*. Vol. 7 of *Sale
      Catalogues of Libraries of Eminent Persons*, gen ed.
      A.N.L. Munby. London: Mansell, with Sotheby Parke Bernet,
      1973.

Contains an analysis (pp. 123-39) of Fielding's personal
library. Also see *A Catalogue of the Entire and Valuable
Library of Books of the Late Henry Fielding*, item 109,
and Dobson, "Fielding's Library," item 160.

Review: Paul J. Korshin, *Philological Quarterly*, 53 (1974),
453-54.

75. —————. "A Preliminary Census of Henry Fielding's Legal
Manuscripts." *Papers of the Bibliographical Society of
America*, 62 (1968), 587-601.

In his *Complete Works of Henry Fielding* (London, 1760),
Arthur Murphy describes two volumes of unpublished law
manuscripts written by Fielding and at that time in the
hands of Sir John Fielding, Henry's half brother. All
traceable fragments of Fielding's legal papers seem to
come from these two volumes.

76. —————. "Two Lost Fielding Manuscripts." *Notes and
Queries*, n.s. 14 (1967), 183-84.

Notes references in auction catalogues to a brief Fielding
letter and a bond for 1,892 pounds made out to Andrew
Millar, Fielding's publisher; these documents, now lost,
would be of great interest to Fielding's biographers.

77. Antal, Frederick. *Hogarth and His Place in European Art*.
London: Routledge and Kegan Paul, 1962.

Apparently demonstrates Hogarth's similarities to and
influences on Fielding, but the compilers have not been
able to confirm this assessment personally.

78. —————. "The Moral Purpose of Hogarth's Art." *Journal
of the Warbug and Courtald Institutes*, 15 (1952), 169-97.

Shows an almost identical moral development in Fielding
and Hogarth from their early, "Restoration-like," satire
to later, more mature moral work. Their development
parallels middle-class societal changes in viewing
morality.

79. Armitage, Gilbert. *The History of the Bow Street Runners,
1729-1829*. London: Wishart, 1932.

Deals with Fielding's role in the history of the British
police system.

80. Armstrong, T. Percy. "Fieldingiana." *Notes and Queries*,
Twelfth Series, 10 (1922), 7.

Leslie Stephen mistranslates Taine's "*un bon Buffle*" (an often repeated reference to Fielding, supposedly made by his cousin, Lady Mary Wortley Montagu) as "amiable buffalo." The phrase translates best as "good buffalo." Also see de Castro, "Fieldingiana," item 141.

81. Atkins, J.W.H. "Critical Cross Currents: Fielding, Sheridan, Cowper, Shaftesbury, Hume, Burke, Kames, Reynolds, and Beattie," in his *English Literary Criticism: 17th and 18th Centuries*. London: Methuen, 1951. Pp. 314-55.

Distills Fielding's critical principles from *The Tragedy of Tragedies* and *Tom Jones*. The former implicitly reveals his views of heroic drama, which he sees as too unrealistic, and the latter shows his concern with a realistic portrayal of life rather than an adherence to pre-determined "rules" of art.

82. Austen-Leigh, R.A. *The Eton College Register, 1698-1752*. Eton: Spottiswoode, 1927.

Notes some of Fielding's Eton companions: George and Richard Grenville, William and Thomas Pitt, Charles Wyndham, and George Lyttleton.

Review: Times Literary Supplement (9 June 1927), p. 401.

83. Babington, Anthony. *A House at Bow Street: Crime and the Magistracy, London, 1740-1881*. London: McDonald and Co., 1969.

Should deal with Fielding, but the compilers have not read the book.

84. Baker, Sheridan. "Henry Fielding and the Cliché." *Criticism*, I (1959), 354-61.

Notes that Fielding uses clichés more than any of his contemporaries and argues that this usage is deliberate. Fielding's desire to deal with durable and typical ideas leads him to employ the frozen metaphors that constitute most clichés. However, he often revitalizes these metaphors and gives them a new twist, thus comically frustrating the reader's expectations.

85. Balderston, Katharine C. "Goldsmith's Supposed Attack on Fielding." *Modern Language Notes*, 42 (1927), 165-68.

Argues that Goldsmith's supposed attack on Fielding in Letter 83 of the *Citizen of the World* is really a reprint

from Du Halde's *Description of the Empire of China* and
therefore could not be a conscious attack on any particular writer.

86. Banerji, Hiran Kumar. *Henry Fielding: Playwright, Jour-
nalist, and Master of the Art of Fiction, His Life and
His Works*. Oxford: Basil Blackwell, 1929. Reprinted
New York: Russell and Russell, 1962.

Mixes biography and critical analysis, discussing
Fielding's works in their order of publication. Although
the minor works are summarized rather than analyzed, the
novels are analytically dealt with in some detail.
Joseph Andrews succeeds primarily because of the
brilliant portrait of Adams; *Tom Jones* is "a great
original" in plot; *Amelia* fails because it lacks "ex-
uberance" due to Fielding's infirmities. Fielding's
strengths are his realistic characterizations (he "describes human nature as it is," not as we would like it
to be); the importance he gives to minor and "low"
figures, a method seldom before used; and his genial and
sympathetic nature. The latter trait, however, made him
too tolerant of vices and undermined the morality of his
fiction. Thus, those who see Fielding as a "moralist"
are "wrong."

Reviews: Aurélien Digeon, *Revue Anglo-Americaine*, 7
(1930), 62; George Sherburn, *Philological Quarterly*, 10
(1931), 200-01; *Times Literary Supplement* (April 3, 1930),
p. 293; E.G. Twitchett, *London Mercury*, 21 (1930), 373-
75.

87. Battestin, Martin C. "Fielding and Ralph Allen: Benevolism
and Its Limits as an Eighteenth-Century Ideal." *Modern
Language Quarterly*, 28 (1967), 368-77.

A review article that discusses Benjamin Boyce, *The Benevolent Man: A Life of Ralph Allen of Bath*; Malvin R.
Zirker, Jr., *Fielding's Social Pamphlets*; and Morris
Golden, *Fielding's Moral Psychology*. Although Fielding
was an admirer of Ralph Allen and his benevolist philosophy—an admiration reflected in the characters of Adams,
Allworthy, and Harrison—he felt that benevolism had
certain limits. His pamphlets show that he felt the
stability of the state required a poor class and that
benevolism should not be extended so far as to eliminate
that class.

88. ————, with R.C. Battestin. "Fielding, Bedford, and the
Westminster Election of 1749." *Eighteenth Century Studies*,
11 (1977/78), 143-85.

Uses recent discoveries of documents at the Bedford
Estates Office to tell the story, previously obscure,
of Fielding's relationship with John Russell, fourth
duke of Bedford. Fielding sought and obtained Bedford's
patronage, in return for which he promoted Bedford's interests, especially in the Westminster election of 1749.
Seventeen letters by Fielding and three by members of
his family are reprinted here, nearly doubling the number
of Fielding's letters so far published. Also see Draper,
item 169.

89. Baum, Richard M. "Hogarth and Fielding as Social Critics."
Art Bulletin, 16 (1934), 36-40.

The compilers were not able to locate this issue of the
journal.

90. Bayley, A.R. "Henry Fielding." *Notes and Queries*,
Eleventh Series, 12 (1915), 315.

Responds to T. Cann Hughes (item 207) by noting the
Cambridge History of English Literature article on
Fielding (see Child, item 110) and by remarking that the
only authentic Fielding portrait is Hogarth's. Also see
Bayley, "A Portrait of Fielding," item 91, and Bensly,
"Henry Fielding," item 93.

91. ————. "A Portrait of Fielding." *Notes and Queries*,
178 (1940), 63-4.

Responds to D.C.'s request for information on Hogarth's
picture of Fielding (see item 107). According to Leslie
Stephen, the only picture of Fielding extant is Hogarth's
sketch for Murphy's edition of Fielding's works.

92. Bensly, Edward. "Fielding's Grave." *Notes and Queries*,
Tenth Series, 9 (1908), 134.

The inscription purportedly on Fielding's tomb is actually from Dobson. Also see Hooper, item 203, and Page,
items 255 and 256.

93. ————. "Henry Fielding." *Notes and Queries*, Eleventh
Series, 12 (1915), 408.

Responds to T. Cann Hughes, item 207: a likeness of
Fielding appears in *The Conjurers* and is reproduced in
G.M. Godden's *Henry Fielding: A Memoir* (item 186). Also
see Bayley, "Henry Fielding," item 90, and "A Portrait
of Fielding," item 91.

94. Biron, H.C. "A Famous Magistrate." *National Review*, 74
     (1920), 669-78. Reprinted in his *Pious Opinions*. London:
     Duckworth, 1923.

     From the time he took office as Bow Street Magistrate
     in 1748, Fielding was a dedicated reformer. He broke
     up the street gangs that terrorized London and published
     pamphlets on robbery and the poor. He also brought re-
     spect to his office by remaining completely honest. His
     devotion to his legal work directly contributed to his
     poor health and eventual death. Also see Amory, "Henry
     Fielding and the Criminal Legislation of 1751-52," item
     73; Pringle, item 265; Radzinowicz, item 267; and Zirker,
     item 1099.

95. Birrell, Augustine. "Henry Fielding and the Literary
     Tradition," in his *More Obiter Dicta*. London: William
     Heinemann, 1924. Pp. 105-11. Originally published New
     York, 1896.

     Seeks to establish a "balance" between Cross's totally
     positive views of Fielding and Thackeray's portrait of him
     as a dissolute rake. Lady Mary Wortley Montagu's impres-
     sions of Fielding can be trusted, and even Murphy's opin-
     ions must be respected.

96. Black, Sidney J. "The Peacockian Essence." *Boston Uni-
     versity Studies in English*, 3 (1957), 231-42.

     Declares that Peacock's "satire of contemporary thinking"
     is "guided primarily by Fielding's concept of the ridicu-
     lous...."

97. Blanchard, F.T. "Coleridge's Estimate of Fielding," in
     C.M. Gayley Anniversary Papers. Berkeley: University of
     California Press, 1922. Pp. 153-63.

     Although Battestin lists this work in *The New Cambridge
     Bibliography of English Literature*, the compilers were
     unable to locate a copy before this bibliography was
     readied for publication.

98. Bloch, Tuvia. "Antedatings from Fielding." *Notes and
     Queries*, n.s. 16 (1969), 188-89.

     Lists seventeen words used by Fielding prior to the first
     recorded usage in the O.E.D.

*   Bond, Donald F., and George Sherburn. *The Restoration
     and Eighteenth Century (1660-1789)*, Vol. 3 of *A Literary*

History of England, ed. Albert C. Baugh. 2nd Ed. New York: Appleton-Century-Crofts, 1967. Originally published New York: Appleton-Century-Crofts, 1948.

See under Sherburn, item 291.

99. Boucé, Paul-Gabriel. *The Novels of Tobias Smollett*. London and New York: Longman, 1976. Originally published as *Les Romans de Smollett*. Paris: Didier, 1971.

Comments on Fielding *passim*. Along with frequent comparisons of Fielding's works with Smollett's, there are detailed remarks on Smollett's abusive attacks on Fielding.

100. Boyce, Benjamin. *The Benevolent Man: A Life of Ralph Allen of Bath*. Cambridge, Mass.: Harvard University Press, 1967.

Ralph Allen's life and works are a positive example of the eighteenth-century ideal of benevolism in action. Fielding, who admired Allen greatly, patterns Squire Allworthy in *Tom Jones* after him. Boyce records Allen's relationship with Fielding and notes where Fielding alludes to Allen in his writings.

Reviews: Martin C. Battestin, *Modern Language Quarterly*, 28 (1968), 368-77; Robert E. Kelley, *Philological Quarterly*, 47 (1968), 298; Alison G. Olson, *American Historical Review*, 73 (1968), 135-36; Henry Pettit, *English Language Notes*, 5 (1968), 63; Charles Pullen, *Queen's Quarterly*, 74 (1968), 533-34; A.L. Rowse, *History Today*, 17 (1968), 719-20; Michael F. Shugrue, *Journal of English and Germanic Philology*, 66 (1968), 589-91; *Times Literary Supplement* (7 March 1968), p. 230.

101. Brack, O.M., Jr. and Curt A. Zimansky. "The Charles B. Woods Fielding Collection." *Books at Iowa* (November 1971), pp. 26-32.

The compilers have not seen this item, which is listed in *The Annual Bibliography of English Language and Literature for 1971*, 46 (1973), item 137.

102. Bradley, T.J. "'Fielding' in Dickens." *Notes and Queries*, 170 (1936), 244.

The reference to "Fielding" in the eighth chapter of *The Pickwick Papers* is not to Henry Fielding but to Thomas Fielding's *Select Proverbs*.

103. ————. "The Two Fieldings." *Dickensian*, 32 (1935), 72.

The same note as that in *Notes and Queries*, item 102.

104. Bredvold, Louis I. "The Novel: Fielding, Smollett,
Sterne," in his *The Literature of the Restoration and
the Eighteenth Century, 1660-1798*, Vol. 3 of *A History
of English Literature*, ed Hardin Craig. New York:
Collier Books, 1962. Pp. 148-59. Originally published
New York: Oxford University Press, 1950.

Generalizes about Fielding for the non-specialist, and
in so doing propagates some Fielding myths: *The Historical Register* was the sole impetus for the Licensing
Act of 1737 and *Joseph Andrews* is a consistent parody
of *Pamela*.

105. Brown, Huntington. *Rabelais in English Literature*.
Cambridge, Mass.: Harvard University Press, 1933. Reprinted New York: Octagon Books, 1967.

Says that there are no "traces of Rabelaisian influences"
in any of Fielding's writings because Fielding dismissed
Rabelais on moral grounds.

106. Brown, Jack Richard. "From Aaron Hill to Henry Fielding?" *Philological Quarterly*, 18 (1939), 85-88.

Discusses a letter from Aaron Hill to an unnamed correspondent who may be Fielding. The letter refers to
a play entitled *A Rehearsal of Kings* which the correspondent has written; thus, if the correspondent is
Fielding, that play must be added to the canon of his
drama.

107. C., D. "A Portrait of Fielding." *Notes and Queries*,
178 (1940), 63-4.

Requests information on an apocryphal story about
Garrick dressing up like Fielding and demanding that
Hogarth paint him. Hogarth, who believed in ghosts,
did so, and the painting is now in the National Portrait Gallery. See Bayley, "A Portrait of Fielding,"
item 91.

108. C___n, H. "Fielding Query: 'At Home.'" *Notes and
Queries*, Thirteenth Series, 1 (1923), 270.

Requests a definition of an "at home," mentioned by
Fielding in *Amelia* (XI.iii). See the response, under
the above title, by Bensly, item 987.

109. *A Catalogue of the Entire and Valuable Library of Books of the Late Henry Fielding, Esq. Which Will Be Sold at Auction*. London: [no publisher], 1755.

Lists the volumes from Fielding's library up for Samuel Baker's 1755 auction. Also see Dobson, "Fielding's Library," item 160, and Amory, *Poets and Men of Letters*, item 74. The sale-catalogue is reproduced in Thornbury, item 598.

110. Child, Harold H. "Fielding and Smollett," in *The Cambridge History of English Literature*, Vol. 10, eds. A.W. Ward and A.R. Waller. New York: Macmillan and Cambridge: The University Press, 1933. Pp. 22-50.

Covers Fielding's entire literary output. His plays suffer from his youthful inexperience, the haste with which he had to write because of financial problems, weak characterization, and his use of a dying comedic tradition inherited from Congreve, but with *Joseph Andrews* he found himself as a writer. The novel lives because of its depiction of eighteenth-century life and its portrayal of Adams. *Tom Jones* shows a broadening of scope and even greater realism, but the depiction of coarser aspects of life have led many to condemn the work on moral grounds. Fielding's growing concern with social ills is manifested in *Amelia*, but that concern reduces his ebullience and makes the novel tiresome at points. On the other hand, this last novel shows greater insight into the psychological depths of character than Fielding had before exhibited.

111. Churchill, R.C. "Fielding: To the Novel from the Drama, 1707-1754," in his *English Literature of the Eighteenth Century*. London: University Tutorial Press, 1953. Pp. 114-43.

Contends that Fielding was dissatisfied with the drama as a vehicle for his social criticism long before the Licensing Act drove him from the stage. He turned to the novel and the law as more satisfactory ways of dealing with the vices of his age. *Joseph Andrews* and *Tom Jones* theoretically treat morality and *Jonathan Wild* and *Amelia* specifically deal with crime and the law.

112. ————. "Henry Fielding: The Comic and the Burlesque." *The Library World*, 47 (1944), 6-8.

The compilers have not read this article.

113.   Coley, William B.   "The Background of Fielding's Laugh-
       ter."   *ELH: A Journal of English Literary History*, 26
       (1959), 229-52.

       Objects to the modern emphasis on Fielding's seriousness
       because it distorts his work and obscures the nature of
       the "witty mode" that the Augustans employed to treat
       serious subjects.   This mode evolved from the pulpit
       rhetoricians, like South, who advocated the use of wit
       and humor in sermons; from the aesthetic of Shaftesbury,
       who did not see "the Provinces of Wit and Wisdom" as
       separate; and from Swift's prominence as an "exemplar
       of the witty serious."   Fielding was aware of this
       tradition and consciously attempted to remain within it
       as both a moralist and a witty satirist.

114.   ————.   "Fielding, Hogarth, and Three Italian Masters."
       Modern Language Quarterly, 24 (1963), 386-91.

       Explores Fielding's linking of Hogarth's name with three
       Italian artists--Amigoni, Veronese, and Annibale Carracci
       --in *Joseph Andrews* (III.vi).   Even though the three
       Italians were very popular at the time, Fielding's ref-
       erence to them may be meant to be ironically sympathetic
       to Hogarth, who disliked foreign artists in general and
       Italian artists in particular.   See Shipley, "Ralph,
       Ellys, Hogarth," item 293, and Shipley and Coley,
       "Fielding and the Cabal," item 294.

115.   ————.   "Fielding's Two Appointments to the Magistracy."
       Modern Philology, 63 (1965), 144-49.

       Cites hitherto undisclosed documents and evaluates the
       data from Godden, item 187, and Shepperson, item 288,
       in order to date Fielding's appointments to the magis-
       tracies of Middlesex (June 20, 1747) and Westminster
       (July 30, 1748).

116.   ————.   "Henry Fielding and the Two Walpoles."   *Phil-
       ological Quarterly*, 45 (1966), 157-78.

       Fielding's disaffection with the Opposition does not
       mark him a political turncoat; although his politics and
       views of Robert Walpole underwent a change, so, too, did
       those of many other Opposition members, especially when
       corruption within their own ranks came to their atten-
       tion.   Also see Battestin, "Fielding's Changing Politics,"
       item 638; Goldgar, *Walpole and the Wits*, item 190; and
       Grundy, "New Verse," item 1060.

117. ————. "Henry Fielding's 'Lost' Law Book." *Modern Language Notes*, 76 (1961), 408-13.

It has long been thought that Fielding wrote nothing during the two or three years following the publication of the *Miscellanies* (1743), but a reference in Murphy's biography and journal advertisements make it appear likely that between 1742 and 1745 he was busily engaged in preparing for the press two volumes, never published, on Crown Law.

118. ————. "Hogarth, Fielding, and the Dating of the *March to Finchley*." *Journal of the Warburg and Courtauld Institutes*, 30 (1967), 317-26.

Adduces evidence to show that Hogarth probably painted the *March to Finchley* in 1748 or 1749 and that he did not engrave the headpiece for Fielding's *Jacobite's Journal*.

119. ————. "Notes Toward a 'Class Theory' of Augustan Literature: The Example of Fielding," in *Literary Theory and Structure: Essays in Honor of William B. Wimsatt*, eds. Frank Brady, John Palmer, and Martin Price. New Haven: Yale University Press, 1973. Pp. 131-50.

Contends that Fielding is not as "socially conservative" as is generally thought; he frequently opposed "the system" and treated "the theme of dependence."

120. Collins, Ralph L. "Moore's *The Foundling*—An Intermediary." *Philological Quarterly*, 17 (1938), 139-43.

Notes that Fielding in *The Jacobite's Journal* praised Edward Moore's *The Foundling*, based on the as yet incomplete *Clarissa* and acted on February 13, 1748, for its "natural" characters, especially Belmont.

121. Connely, Willard. "Mr. Justice Fielding." *Folio* (April-June, 1959), 7-11.

General remarks, appreciative of Fielding's labors as a justice of the peace.

122. "Corrigendum." *Notes and Queries*, Eleventh Series, 9 (1914), 520.

Corrects the village name mistakenly spelled "Wotton Wayen" in Dickson, "The Chronology," item 820, to "Wootton Wawen."

123. "Corrigendum." *Notes and Queries*, Eleventh Series, 11
      (1915), 60.

      Corrects a previous article which referred to Mr. G.M.
      Godden instead of Miss G.M. Godden.

124. "Corrigendum." *Notes and Queries*, Twelfth Series, 3
      (1917), 100.

      Corrects a date in Dickson, "Henry Fielding," item 1119.

125. Cross, Wilbur L. "The Fielding Collection." *Yale Uni-
      versity Library Gazette*, 1 (1927), 31-34.

      Primarily an account of Frederick Stoever Dickson, who
      donated a large collection of Fielding materials to the
      Yale library. Also see Cross, item 126.

126. ————. *The History of Henry Fielding*. 3 Vols. New
      Haven: Yale University Press, 1918. Reprinted New York:
      Russell and Russell, 1963.

      Still the standard biography, this study attempts "a
      coherent narrative of what actually occurred [in Field-
      ing's life], with the addition of necessary comment and
      interpretation." The work is highly complimentary to
      Fielding, so much so that Cross is led to some distor-
      tions. For example, his interpretation of Fielding's
      moral doctrine, which was once widely accepted, involves
      a distorted view of his use of Shaftesbury's principles,
      a point not noted until Work's 1949 article (see item
      329). In his study, Cross includes supporting materials
      from newspapers, diaries, letters, and other miscellaneous
      documents, and he provides a detailed picture not only of
      Fielding's life but of eighteenth-century society as well.
      In the chronologically arranged bibliography, Cross tries
      to list accurately the body of Fielding's work, including
      works published anonymously. He includes publishing
      histories, critical apparatus, illustrations, and de-
      tailed indices.

      Reviews: J.P. de Castro, *Modern Language Review*, 15
      (1920), 181-88; Aurélien Digeon, *Revue germanique*, 13
      (1922), 412-17; Helen Sard Hughes, *Dial*, 66 (1919),
      407-09.

127. ————. "The Legend of Henry Fielding." *Yale Review*,
      8 (1918), 107-27.

      Refutes the "legend" of an immoral, profligate Fielding,
      who could not have led the wicked life so many assigned

to him simply because as a full-time justice and a
prolific writer he did not have the time. He was a
dedicated, hard-working, brilliant social reformer who
made many enemies who did not scruple to portray him as
a man similar to the immoral characters he portrayed
in his dramas and novels. Just because he depicted
such figures in his work does not mean he resembled
them.

128. ————. "A New Estimate of Fielding." *Saturday Review
of Literature*, 50 (July 18, 1925), pp. 905-06.

Comments on the changing critical estimate of Fielding.
Where once he was considered a scoundrel and author of
immoral works, now he is seen as a moral man who was
the master of the modern novel. Fielding, in fact,
passed on to us the tradition of the humorous novel.

129. ————. "The New Fielding Collection." *Yale Alumni
Weekly*, February 21, 1913, n.p.

Lists and discusses the Dickson donation of Fielding
materials to the Yale library. Also see item 125.

130. Crouch, Charles H. "Gravelot." *Notes and Queries*, 180
(1941), 107.

Provides information linked to de Castro's "Gravelot,"
item 819, by identifying three bookplates designed by
Henri Gravelot.

131. de Castro, J. Paul. "Edmund Fielding." *Notes and
Queries*, Twelfth Series, 11 (1922), 178.

On March 9, 1740, Lt. Gen. Fielding, Henry's father,
married Elizabeth Sparrye, his fourth wife. See de
Castro, "Fieldingiana," item 140.

132. ————. "Fielding and Lyme Regis." *Times Literary
Supplement* (June 4, 1931), p. 447.

A note in the Lyme Regis town archives, written by
Fielding, reveals two items of biographical interest:
Fielding was attacked by Henry Channery, probably because of Fielding's affair with Sarah Andrew; and Fielding lived in the village of Upton Grey at least as early
as 1725.

133. ————. "Fielding and the Collier Family." *Notes and
Queries*, Twelfth Series, 2 (1916), 104-06.

Notes that Fielding was very close to the family of Rev.
Arthur Collier. He stood bail for Arthur Collier in
1745, and Jane Collier wrote in praise of *Tom Jones* and
Jonathan Wild. Margaret Collier traveled with Fielding's
party to Portugal.

134.   ———. "Fielding as a Publicist." *Notes and Queries*,
        Twelfth Series, 5 (1919), 283-84.

Discusses two actions against corrupt justices while
Fielding served on the bench. The first was successful,
but the second, against Sir Samuel Gower, who was
patently guilty, was not. It is possible that this mis-
carriage of justice prompted Fielding to use Gower as a
model for Justice Thrasher in *Amelia*.

135.   ———. "Fielding as Reformer." *Times Literary Supple-
        ment* (10 August 1933), p. 537.

Quotes Davenport Hill's 1878 assessment of Fielding as
a reformer in connection with the review of B. Maelor
Jones's biography of Fielding (item 219) in *Times
Literary Supplement*, 20 July 1933, p. 493, and Leslie-
Melville's remarks on that review (item 228).

136.   ———. "Fielding at Boswell Court." *Notes and Queries*,
        Twelfth Series, 1 (1916), 264-65.

Refutes the apocryphal story that Fielding lived in
Beaufort Buildings and was often behind in his taxes
during 1744-47. Rate books and other legal documents
show that during this period, Fielding lived at Boswell
Court and was never behind in his taxes.

137.   ———. "Fielding Manuscripts." *Times Literary Supple-
        ment* (June 1, 1940), p. 267.

Rumors of a Fielding commonplace book are probably un-
true. Since Murphy claimed to have published everything
of literary value by Fielding, the stories of novels,
plays, and essays destroyed in the Gordon Riots must be
skeptically received. The manuscripts in the Harvard
Library, composed of law notes, must be presumed to be
a part of a larger collection of law notes only, not
part of a commonplace book. See Wallace, "Fielding
Manuscripts," item 316.

138.   ———. "Fieldingiana." *Notes and Queries*, Twelfth
        Series, 1 (1916), 483-85.

Contains two notes: one identifies the "Miss H" of a poem in Fielding's *Miscellanies* and the other argues that the lawyer served by Partridge in *Tom Jones* was based on one Odber Knapton of Lymington.

139. ———. "Fieldingiana." *Notes and Queries*, Twelfth Series, 3 (1917), 181-83.

Presents four short notes on Fielding: (1) Hogarth probably did not draw the picture on the *Pasquin* theater ticket that is usually attributed to him—the drawing is a fake; (2) responds to Malet, item 243, by proposing that Hogarth's "The Green-Room, Drury Lane" does not picture Fielding; (3) the mention of "Three Letters" in *Amelia* refers to a pamphlet entitled "Three Letters upon the Gin Act and Common Informers, etc."; (4) the reference in the *Voyage to Lisbon* to a public function of lawyers and "the diet that emaciates" is to an entertainment at Lincoln's Inn Hall for Lord Chief Justice Ryder and Justice Bathurst.

140. ———. "Fieldingiana." *Notes and Queries*, Twelfth Series, 3 (1917), 465-68.

Refers to several pieces of previously undiscovered information regarding Fielding, including material on Edmund Fielding's four wives, publishing notes on *Joseph Andrews* and *Amelia*, notes on the originals of some characters in *Tom Jones*, and birth information on Edmund Fielding's children.

141. ———. "Fieldingiana." *Notes and Queries*, Twelfth Series, 10 (1922), 51.

Notes Henley's comment, item 200, that Taine either paid Fielding the highest compliment possible or held the unluckiest of theories of personality when he called Fielding a "good buffalo." Also see Armstrong, "Fieldingiana," item 80.

142. ———. "John Ranby: Henry Fielding." *Notes and Queries*, Twelfth Series, 2 (1916), 11.

John Ranby, a surgeon and friend of Fielding, succeeded Fielding as tenant of Fordhook.

143. ———. "Luke Robinson, M.P." *Notes and Queries*, Eleventh Series, 11 (1915), 55.

Notes that Fielding went bail for William Pentlow in 1751.

144. ————. "Mr. Harris of Salisbury." *National Review*,
      71 (1918), 203-16.

      The compilers were unable to locate a copy of this
      article.

145. ————. [No title available.] *Somerset and Dorset
      Notes and Queries*, 19 (1929), 258-60.

      This item and the next one (item 146) remark on Field-
      ing's "elopement" with Sarah Andrew.

146. ————. [No title available.] *Somerset and Dorset
      Notes and Queries*, 20 (1930), 17-18; 166.

      See previous item.

147. ————. [No title available.] *Somerset and Dorset
      Notes and Queries*, 20 (1931), 130-32.

      Remarks on the charges for assault against Fielding in
      1734 and 1736.

148. ————. "Portrait of Miss Sarah Andrew as Sophia
      Western." *Notes and Queries*, Eleventh Series, 11 (1915),
      301.

      Sarah Andrew had her portrait painted as Sophia Western,
      although it is well-known that Charlotte Cradock was the
      original for Sophia.

149. ————. "A Presentation Inscription by Fielding."
      Notes and Queries, 178 (1940), 337-39.

      Replies to "Olybrius"--who earlier in *Notes and Queries*
      had printed an inscription by Fielding in a book he gave
      to Jane Collier (see item 394)--by identifying her
      through a letter she wrote to a friend; de Castro anno-
      tates several references in the letter. (The content of
      the letter, however, has nothing to do with Fielding.)

150. ————. "The Printing of Fielding's Works." *Library*,
      Fourth Series, 1 (1921), 257-70.

      Lists, from William Strahan's ledgers, specific details
      --such as expenditures and printing dates--relating to
      his printing of Fielding's works for Andrew Millar,
      Fielding's most important publisher.

151. ————. "The Printing of Fielding's Works." *Transac-
      tions of the Bibliographical Society*, Second Series, 1
      (1921), 257-70.

This item actually appears in *Library* (see item 150)
but often is listed as above because of the confusion
that resulted from the Bibliographical Society printing
its transactions both as *Transactions* and as *Library*
at various times.

152.   ————. "Tom Jones." *Notes and Queries*, Twelfth Series,
6 (1920), 118.

The Fieldings signed their name variously "Feilding" or
"Fielding."

153.   ————. "Ursula Fielding and *Tom Jones*." *Notes and
Queries*, 178 (1940), 164-67.

A letter from Ursula Fielding to Mrs. John Barker contains much biographical detail on the Fieldings, their
friends, and their activities in late 1748. Among other
things, it notes that Henry moved from Twickenham earlier
than had previously been thought, and that he composed
the final volumes of *Tom Jones* in his Brownlow Street
residence.

154.   Dewey, Nicholas. "Fielding: 'Justice Dingo.'" *Notes
and Queries*, n.s. 18 (1971), 67.

Notes that Thomas Edwards, in a letter of January 1748/
49, refers to Fielding as "Justice Dingo" and asks why
this term would be applied to Fielding at this time in
his career.

155.   Dickson, Frederick S. "The Author of *Tom Jones*." *Yale
Review*, n.s. 8 (1919), 415-24.

A glowing review of Cross's *History of Henry Fielding*
(item 126) in which Dickson surveys previous Fielding
biographers and concludes that among them only Dobson,
Lowell, and Godden "were really sane"; the rest were
"mendacious." Cross's work is fairer to Fielding and
more accurate than all previous works combined.

156.   ————. "William Makepeace Thackeray and Henry Fielding." *North American Review*, 197 (1913), 522-37.

Finds Thackeray and Fielding amazingly similar, both in
their artistic temperaments and careers, and laments
that Thackeray, a man of so much influence, should have
blackened Fielding's name as he did with biographical
embroiderings on the picture of Fielding the dissolute
rake. Careful research shows that Fielding was not the

immoral man depicted by so many "biographers." In fact,
Fielding was a cheerful, hard-working artist and a loyal,
devoted husband.

157.   Dilworth, E.N. "Fielding and Coleridge: 'Poetic Faith.'"
       Notes and Queries, n.s. 5 (1958), 35-7.

       Confirms Tillett's argument (item 969) that the phrase
       "poetic faith" comes from *Tom Jones*, but argues that
       Coleridge uses it differently than did Fielding. The
       latter used it to refer to "nature," to the "real" world;
       Coleridge used it straightforwardly to refer to the
       supernatural.

158.   Dobson, Austin. "Fielding and Andrew Millar." *Library*,
       Third Series, 3 (1916), 177-90.

       Discusses the relationship of Andrew Millar, Fielding's
       major publisher, with Fielding. Millar published all
       of Fielding's novels, the *Miscellanies*, the *Voyage to
       Lisbon*, and some minor works. Upon his death, he willed
       two hundred pounds each to Fielding's sons, Allen and
       William.

159.   ————. *Fielding and Andrew Millar*. London: A. Morning,
       1916.

       A sixteen-page reprint in limited edition of Dobson's
       article in the July 1916 *Library* (see item 158 for
       annotation).

160.   ————. "Fielding's Library," in his *18th Century
       Vignettes*, Series 3. London: Chatto and Windus and
       New York: Dodd, Mead, 1896. Pp. 64-78. Reprinted Lon-
       don: Oxford University Press, 1951.

       Discusses the auctioning of Fielding's personal library
       in 1755 by Samuel Baker. Dobson cites Baker's list of
       Fielding's books and emphasizes the many volumes of
       classical literature included in order to defend Field-
       ing against Thackeray's charges of poor scholarship.

161.   ————. "Fresh Facts about Fielding," in his *De Libris:
       Prose and Verse*. London: Macmillan, 1911. Pp. 193-203.
       Originally published by Macmillan, 1908.

       Contradicts Murphy's account of Fielding's stay in
       Leyden; Fielding was admitted to the university on March
       16, 1728, and left there before February 8, 1730. Also
       gives the date of Fielding's wedding to Charlotte
       Cradock as November 28, 1734.

162.   ————. "Fresh Facts about Fielding." *Macmillan's Magazine*, 2 (1907), 417-22.

Obviously the same item as the above, although the compilers have not been able to personally confirm this and do not know if the later version contains any changes.

163.   ————. *Henry Fielding.* English Men of Letters. New York: Harper and Brothers, 1901. Originally published New York: Harper and Brothers and London: Macmillan, 1883.

This work was revised, enlarged, and retitled *Henry Fielding, A Memoir.* For annotation, see under the above title, item 164.

164.   ————. *Henry Fielding, A Memoir.* New York: Dodd, Mead, and Co., 1900.

A revised and enlarged version of *Henry Fielding* (item 163), written for the English Men of Letters series. Dobson brings together a large number of biographical anecdotes and attempts to verify them, rejecting most of those stories which show Fielding to be a profligate. Actually, Fielding was a loyal family man who probably worked himself to death pursuing his legal and literary careers and trying to support his family. A great deal of autobiographical material appears in his literary works (for example, the "Letter to Walpole" shows evidence of Fielding's "debts, duns, and dinnerless condition"). In the final assessment, Fielding's plays are second rate and his journal writings of little value. The novels are his finest achievement because of his well-wrought plots and realistic characters. He not only is the originator of the English novel, but he is its greatest practitioner as well.

165.   ————. "Henry Fielding: Two Corrections." *Notes and Queries*, Twelfth Series, 1 (1916), 284.

Notes that Fielding arrived in Portugal on August 6, 1754, and went ashore the next day. See Dickson, "Henry Fielding: Two Corrections," item 1119.

166.   ————. "A New Dialogue of the Dead," in his *Rosalba's Journal.* London: Oxford, 1926. Pp. 263-87. Originally published London: Chatto and Windus, 1915. The essay originally appeared in the *National Review*, 60 (Dec. 1912), 609-17.

A fictitious dialogue between Fielding and his first
biographer, Arthur Murphy, in which Murphy is attacked
for biographical inaccuracy.

167.   Donaldson, Ian.   "High and Low Life: Fielding and the
       Uses of Inversion," in his *The World Upside-Down: Comedy
       from Jonson to Fielding*.   Oxford: The Clarendon Press,
       1970.   Pp. 183-206.   Extract reprinted in Rawson, item
       272.

       Compares Fielding's comedy to that of the Scriblerians
       (Gay, Swift, Pope) from whom Fielding learned many of
       his tactics of irony and satire.   Like his predecessors,
       he uses inversion to show the chaos of society (Tom
       Thumb, eaten by a cow, replaces the Herculean hero of
       "high" tragedy; Jonathan Wild's "greatness" is really
       wickedness).   Fielding, however, is more "genial" than
       the Scriblerians and therefore converts their "despondent
       myth of a civilization falling to ruins to more optimis-
       tic comic ends."   For example, the comic resolutions of
       both the *Author's Farce* and *Joseph Andrews* suggest that
       life is not an absurd farce but is watched over by a
       "benign providence."

168.   Draper, J.W.   "The Theory of the Comic in Eighteenth-
       Century England."   *Journal of English and Germanic
       Philology*, 37 (1938), 207-23.

       Remarks that Fielding's theory of comedy, based on affec-
       tation, is too narrow because it implies that all comedy
       is satiric and thus omits such important works as Shake-
       speare's romances and Goldsmith's *She Stoops to Conquer*.

169.   Draper, M.P.G.   "Letters of the 4th Duke of Bedford."
       Eighteenth Century Studies, 12 (1978/79), 206-08.

       Reprints two hitherto undiscovered letters, dated May 24
       and 29, 1750, from Fielding to the fourth Duke of
       Bedford.   Also see M.C. and R.C. Battestin, item 88.

170.   Dubois, Arthur E.   "A Forgotten Salisbury Surgeon."
       Times Literary Supplement (March 19, 1931), p. 234.

       Disagrees with de Castro's conjecture about the surgeon
       who set Charlotte Cradock's broken nose (see item 992);
       the actual physician probably was Dr. John Barker.

171.   Dudden, F. Homes.   *Henry Fielding: His Life, Works, and
       Times*.   2 Vols.   Oxford: The Clarendon Press, 1952.
       New edition, 2 Vols., London: Archon, 1966.

Argues, along the same lines as Cross (item 126), that
Fielding's character has long been misunderstood, primarily because of the almost slanderous *Life* by Arthur
Murphy (1762). He was not dissipated in his youth nor
was he a frequenter of dens of vice in his later years.
His plays and essays are interesting and skillfully
done, but they show little of the genius he exhibited
in his novels. He shows a consciousness of structure
and style, especially in *Tom Jones*, not found in his
contemporaries. He is superior to them, too, in his
creation of believable characters and realistic scenes
of eighteenth-century life and in his handling of humor.
Rarely, except in *Amelia*, does he allow sentiment to
slip into sentimentality. He influenced almost every
major English novelist to come after him in some way.

Reviews: Cyril Connelly, *Sunday Times* (November 23,
1952), 5; Aurélien Digeon, *Études anglaises*, 7 (1954),
402-04; Frederick W. Hilles, *Yale Review*, 42 (1953),
633-35; George Sherburn, *Sewanee Review*, 61 (1953), 316-
21; *Times Literary Supplement* (January 23, 1953), p. 56;
J.M.S. Tompkins, *Review of English Studies*, 5 (1954),
302-05; R.W., *Twentieth Century*, 156 (1954), 382-83;
Charles B. Woods, *Philological Quarterly*, 32 (1953),
268.

*   Duncan, Jeffrey L. "The Rural Ideal in Eighteenth
      Century Fiction." (See item 663.)

172. Dyson, A.E. "Satiric and Comic Theory in Relation to
      Fielding." *Modern Language Quarterly*, 18 (1957), 225-37.

      Distinguishes between the aims of satire and comedy.
      The former uses ridicule to mock a society that fails
      to live up to ideals and the latter uses ridicule to
      laugh at individuals who deviate from a norm. Fielding
      is more effective as a comic writer in *Tom Jones* because
      his interest lies in persuading people of the value of
      good rather than attacking those elements of society
      who fail to live up to an abstract ideal of good nature.

173. Eaves, T.C. Duncan, and Ben D. Kimpel. "Henry Fielding's
      Son By His First Wife." *Notes and Queries*, n.s. 15
      (1968), 212.

      In addition to the two daughters Fielding had by his
      first wife, he also had a son, Henry, who died in 1750
      at the age of eight.

174.   ————. *Samuel Richardson: A Biography*. Oxford:
        Clarendon Press, 1971.

        Contains, in addition to dozens of scattered references
        to Fielding, a long section (pp. 292-306) on Fielding's
        relationship with Richardson. The authors explain the
        latter's bitterness toward Fielding as primarily due to
        envy, especially over the success of *Tom Jones*.

175.   Elton, Oliver. "Fielding and Smollett," in his *Survey
        of English Literature, 1730-1780*, Vol. I. London: Ed-
        ward Arnold, 1928. Pp. 182-216.

        Surveys the journalism and the plays, concluding that
        the former is of importance primarily as an influence
        on the novels and that among the latter *Tom Thumb* and
        Pasquin make the best reading. The fiction is colored
        by Fielding's interest in law and crime and is marked
        by his ability to preserve "the real proportions of good
        and evil as we find them intermixed in mankind." His
        strengths are his humor, his style, and his characters
        (Tom Jones and Sophia are the first "live" characters
        in English fiction).

176.   Elwes, Winefride. *The Feilding Album*. London: Geoffrey
        Bles, 1950.

        Deals with the nineteenth-century members of the Feilding
        family, relatives of Henry Fielding.

        Reviews: Philological Quarterly, 31 (1952), 233; *Times
        Literary Supplement* (19 January 1951), p. 32.

177.   Elwin, Whitwell. "Fielding," in his *Some XVIII Century
        Men of Letters: Biographical Essays by the Rev. Whitwell
        Elwin, Some Time Editor of "The Quarterly Review," With
        a Memoir*, Vol. 2, ed. Warwick Elwin. London: John
        Murray, 1902. Pp. 83-152. Originally published in *The
        Quarterly Review* for December 1855.

        Mixes biography with discussions of the literary works.
        The plays are dismissed as "unworthy" of Fielding, who
        is judged to be the greatest of English novelists.
        Joseph Andrews is treated primarily as a satire of *Pamela*
        to which it is far superior. The discussion of *Tom Jones*
        focuses on its favorable reception by the reading public.
        Amelia is viewed as inferior to the previous novels in
        everything but "domestic pathos."

178. England, Denzil. "Henry Fielding." *Contemporary Review*, 186 (1954), 218-23.

    Sees Fielding as a "biographical novelist" because his life in London so influenced his fiction and calls him one of the greatest creative artists of his age.

179. *An Essay on the New Species of Writing Founded by Mr. Fielding.* Augustan Reprint Society Publication Number 95, ed. Alan D. McKillop. Los Angeles: Clark Memorial Library, 1962. Originally published London: William Owen, 1751.

    The unknown author of this pamphlet praises Fielding highly for his originality, rhetoric, humor, and characterization, drawing most of his views from the introductory chapters of *Tom Jones*. See McKillop's introduction under item 532.

180. Fitzgerald, Percy. *Chronicles of the Bow Street Police Office.* Montclair, N.J.: Patterson Smith, 1972. Originally published London, 1888.

    Credits Henry and John Fielding with founding the London police, and notes that as a magistrate, Henry was the model of an honest, incorruptible, hard-working justice. His opinions were thoughtful and firmly based in law. Also see Jones, item 219, and Pringle, item 265.

181. George, M. Dorothy. "The Early History of Registry Offices." *Economic History*, 1 (1929), 570-90.

    Traces seventeenth and eighteenth century attempts to establish registry offices. The Fieldings' Universal Register Office was the first to use the name, "Register," and it was the most successful. It concentrated on acting as an employment agency and housing office. Because of its early success, it spawned hundreds of less reputable imitators and eventually collapsed because all register offices lost their reputations by the 1760's.

182. ————. "The Sale of Fielding's Farm." *Times Literary Supplement* (June 26, 1924), p. 404.

    Notes an announcement of the auction of Fielding's farm, with a partial list of the items to be sold, in the *Public Advertiser* of December 26, 1754.

183. Gill, W.W. "Early Fielding Documents." *Notes and Queries*, 171 (1936), 242.

Documents found in the Lyme Regis Town Hall and signed
by Fielding show that he was assaulted at the instiga-
tion of John Tucker after Fielding's attempt to carry
off Sarah Andrew. Also see de Castro, "Fielding and
Lyme Regis," item 132.

184.   Glenn, Sidney Irwin. "Some French Influences on Henry
       Fielding." Urbana: University of Illinois Press, 1932.

       A twenty-page abstract of Dr. Glenn's 1931 dissertation
       (see item 1321). Outside of a very few specific debts
       to Scarron and Molière, the chief debt of Fielding to
       French literature "is the debt of his times." Fielding
       was far too original and English to be a servile imitator
       of French writers and thinkers.

185.   Goad, Caroline. *Horace in the English Literature of the
       Eighteenth Century*. Yale Studies in English, No. 58.
       New Haven: Yale University Press, 1918.

       Fielding's writings, particularly his essays, show his
       vast knowledge and appreciation of Horace. Goad supplies
       a comprehensive list of references to Horace in Field-
       ing's works.

186.   Godden, Gertrude M. *Henry Fielding: A Memoir*. London:
       Sampson Low, Marston and New York: Barse and Hopkins,
       1910.

       Avoids literary criticism to focus on Fielding's life
       and personality. Much previously unpublished material
       is drawn upon, including documents pertaining to Field-
       ing's childhood, archival records of his work as a
       magistrate, and personal letters. Godden corrects many
       of the inaccuracies of Murphy and other early bio-
       graphers, and her work is the most reliable Fielding
       biography prior to Cross (item 126). This work contains
       thirty-five illustrations of people and places in
       Fielding's life.

187.   ————. "Henry Fielding: Some Unpublished Letters and
       Records." *Fortnightly Review*, 92 (1909), 821-32.

       Reviews some hitherto unpublished letters and documents
       to shed new light on Fielding's life and work. In 1738,
       Fielding sold some of his Dorset land, and the money he
       received apparently lasted for some time; he was, then,
       probably a frugal man at this time and not the profligate
       he often is said to have been. He engaged a house in
       London at forty pounds a year in 1739 and, thus, probably

composed, not in a garret as often is said, but in a
pleasant home atmosphere. A letter to the Lord High
Chancellor in 1749, transmitting the draft of a bill to
prevent street crime, indicates his influence and in-
dustry early in his legal career.

188. Golden, Morris. *Fielding's Moral Psychology*. Amherst:
      University of Massachusetts Press, 1966.

      Determines from a study of Fielding's novels that
      Fielding sees man as "self-enclosed," yet striving for
      communication. Fielding's philosophy is derived from
      Shaftesbury, although Fielding does not insist, as does
      Shaftesbury, on the basic goodness of all mankind.
      Fielding believes that much of mankind is good, that
      goodness must be communicated to be worthwhile (thus
      his view that charity is the greatest of virtues), and
      that basic goodness must be combined with prudence and
      tempered with experience.

      Reviews: Martin C. Battestin, *Modern Language Quarterly*,
      28 (1967), 368-77; John A. Dussinger, *Journal of English
      and Germanic Philology*, 66 (1967), 591-94; W.R. Irwin,
      Philological Quarterly, 46 (1967), 345; Maximillian E.
      Novak, *Novel*, 1 (1968), 286-88; Raymond Smith, *Litera-
      ture and Psychology*, 17 (1967), 141-43.

189. Goldgar, Bertrand A. "Fielding, Sir William Yonge, and
      the *Grub Street Journal*." *Notes and Queries*, n.s. 19
      (1972), 226-27.

      The March 1732 performance of *The Modern Husband*, dedi-
      cated to Robert Walpole, precipitated an attack that
      lasted for three months and was motivated by political
      and not literary reasons. It has long been thought
      that Sir William Yonge was behind the attack, but
      actually he supported Fielding's pro-government position
      at the time.

190. ———. *Walpole and the Wits: The Relation of Politics
      to Literature, 1722-42*. Lincoln: University of Nebraska
      Press, 1976.

      Has four sections on Fielding: "Fielding's Early Plays"
      (pp. 98-115); "Fielding, *Common Sense*, and Pope" (pp.
      150-62); "Fielding, the *Champion*, and Cibber" (pp. 189-
      96); and "Fielding's Defection" (pp. 197-208). In his
      early plays--contrary to the received critical view--
      Fielding courted Walpole's favor (see Grundy, item 1060).
      By 1734, however, Fielding had moved to the opposition,

and he continued to oppose Walpole until the spring of
1741 when he dropped out of opposition politics because
he was required to produce distasteful partisan writings
and was not rewarded for his efforts. Also see Amory,
"Henry Fielding's *Epistles to Walpole*," item 1101;
Sheridan Baker, "Political Allusion," item 381;
Battestin, "Fielding's Changing Politics," item 638;
Coley, "Henry Fielding and the Two Walpoles," item 116;
Loftis, *The Politics of Drama*, item 358; and Rizvi,
item 1397.

191.   Gosse, Edmund. "The Character of Fielding," in his
       Books on the Table. London: William Heinemann, 1921.
       Pp. 257-64.

       Seeks to present a better-balanced view of Fielding's
       character than did either Murphy, Fielding's first
       biographer who branded him a dissolute rascal, or Cross
       (item 126), who white-washed Fielding's life. Although
       most of the stories about Fielding's profligacies have
       been proved false, he was certainly no saint, and as a
       man of his time probably indulged in some of his age's
       vices.

192.   Green, Emanuel. *Henry Fielding: His Works*. London:
       Harrison and Sons, 1909.

       A thirty-three page pamphlet--mostly plot summaries of
       Shamela, *Joseph Andrews*, *Tom Jones*, and *Amelia*--which
       attacks Fielding's "indelicacy" and concludes that he
       was a poor scholar and writer with no imagination.

193.   Green, Frederick C. *Literary Ideas in 18th Century
       France and England: A Critical Survey*. New York:
       Frederick Ungar, 1966.

       A reprint, with minor changes, of Green's *Minuet*, item
       194.

194.   ————. *Minuet: A Critical Survey of French and English
       Literary Ideas in the Eighteenth Century*. New York:
       E.P. Dutton and London: J.M. Dent, 1935.

       Refers to Fielding throughout. Green argues that Field-
       ing did not use Marivaux as a source. Marivaux's humor
       is much subtler than Fielding's and his morality is of a
       different order than the English novelist's.

*   Greenberg, Bernard J. "Fielding's 'Humane Surgeon.'"
       (See item 850.)

195. Grinnell, Frank Washburn. *The Legal Careers and In-*
fluence of Henry and Sir John Fielding, an Object Lesson
in the Importance of the Lower Courts. Baltimore and
Chicago: n.p., 1940.

Originally read as a paper before the Massachusetts
Historical Society, this item was reprinted in the
American Bar Association Journal (September 1940) and
then published as a pamphlet. The compilers have not
seen this piece, although copies exist in the Yale and
Harvard libraries.

196. Harrison, Frederic. "Bath--Somerset--Henry Fielding."
Fortnightly Review, 106 (1919), 734-44.

Consists of a review of Cross's *History of Henry Field-*
ing (item 126) and personal remarks on Fielding's life
and literary output. Although he produced some work of
shocking immorality, such as *The Modern Husband*, Fielding in his major works is a moralist. And certainly in
his private life he was not the profligate that tradition
said he was.

197. Hatfield, Glenn W. *Henry Fielding and the Language of*
Irony. Chicago: University of Chicago Press, 1968.
Two extracts from this work are reprinted in Rawson,
item 272.

One of Fielding's lifelong concerns was combatting the
debasement of the English language. Because of mis-
usage by the *beau monde*, words that had once possessed
specific, limited meanings became corrupted to the point
where their meanings were either too vague to be useful
or the direct opposite of what they once meant. Fielding attempts to "purify" the meanings of words he con-
siders important ("honor," "prudence," and "charity,"
among others) through both irony and direct re-defini-
tion. He uses both of these techniques extensively in
Tom Jones to define his conception of true "prudence."

Reviews: Martin C. Battestin, *Modern Language Quarterly*,
30 (1969), 149-51; John A. Dussinger, *Journal of English*
and Germanic Philology, 68 (1969), 599; Michael Irwin,
Review of English Studies, 20 (1969), 507-08; Charles E.
Ledbetter, *Quarterly Journal of Speech*, 55 (1969), 86;
Henry Knight Miller, *Studies in the Novel*, 2 (1970),
230-38; *Times Literary Supplement* (January 2, 1969),
p. 8; Martin Price, *Philological Quarterly*, 48 (1969),
356.

198.   ———. "Quacks, Pettyfoggers, and Parsons: Fielding's
       Case Against the Learned Professions." *Texas Studies
       in Literature and Language*, 9 (1967), 69-83. Reprinted
       in his book, item 197.

       The learned professions themselves are not the objects
       of Fielding's satiric attacks, but only the members of
       those professions who substitute opacity of language for
       learning. Ultimately, Fielding's attack is directed
       toward all debasement of the language from the use of
       jargon in specialized circles to the narrowing of the
       meanings of words in common usage. He sees the common
       understanding of the language as the glue that holds
       society together. The fragmentation of the language by
       learned professions and other groups can only result in
       decreased communication and therefore in the fragmenta-
       tion of society itself.

199.   Heilman, Robert B. "Fielding and 'The First Gothic
       Revival.'" *Modern Language Notes*, 57 (1942), 671-73.

       The first Gothic revival took place in England in the
       1740's and later died out as the tastes of its adherents
       changed. Comments on Gothic architecture in *A Journey
       from This World to the Next* (1743) and *Tom Jones* (1749)
       indicate that Fielding was an admirer of the Gothic when
       that admiration was in vogue. Like many others, he lost
       his taste for the Gothic later in life, as a comment in
       the *Journal of a Voyage to Lisbon* shows.

200.   Henley, William E. "An Essay on the Life, Genius, and
       Achievement of the Author [Henry Fielding]," in *The
       Complete Works of Henry Fielding*, Vol. 1. New York:
       Harper and Brothers, 1902. Pp. v-xlvi.

       Attacks those eighteenth- and nineteenth-century writers
       who blackened Fielding's character and praises Saints-
       bury and Dobson for their attempts to redeem his reputa-
       tion; Henley's own portrait of Fielding is almost totally
       positive. Henley discusses Fielding's literary output
       in the most general terms and remarks that everything
       there is to say about the novels has been said.

201.   Hessler, Mabel Dorothy. *The Literary Opposition to Sir
       Robert Walpole, 1721-1742: Fielding's Attacks on Walpole*.
       Chicago: University of Chicago Libraries, 1936.

       This is Chapter 9 of Ms. Hessler's dissertation, item
       1338.

202. Hill, N.W. "Henry Fielding and the Civil Power." *Notes and Queries*, Eleventh Series, 4 (1911), 534.

Comments that it was probably Henry rather than John Fielding who committed an army officer to jail in October 1751 and that the decision might have been stimulated by a desire to show the precedence of civil over military power. See the following remarks, all under the title, "Henry Fielding and the Civil Power": F.B.M., item 235; Prideaux, item 264; Robbins, items 276 and 277; and St. Swithin, item 283.

203. Hooper, James. "Inscription to Fielding." *Notes and Queries*, Eighth Series, 4 (1893), 164.

An inscription to Fielding, written for his tombstone by Abbé Correa d'Serra, was never placed there. Also see Bensly, "Fielding's Grave," item 92; Page, item 255; and Parker, item 257.

204. Hughes, Helen Sard. "A Vindication of Fielding." *The Dial*, 66 (1919), 407-09.

Primarily a sympathetic review of Cross's *History of Henry Fielding*, item 126. Hughes notes that Cross has produced a significant work with "a fully peopled world reconstructed with the veracity and the imaginative sympathy of the creative scholar."

205. Hughes, Leo. "The Influence of Fielding's Milieu upon His Humor." *Texas Studies in English*, 24 (1944), 269-97.

Surveys Fielding's works in order to demonstrate that he was "far from being ... independent of his age"; he was influenced, "even hampered," by the neoclassic view that the writer must teach as well as entertain. This Horatian requirement led him away from the farces, in which his real dramatic talent lay, and toward the satiric and didactic. He consistently defended his comic writing on moral grounds, never arguing that laughter had social value apart from the moralistic.

206. Hughes, T. Cann. "Henry Fielding." *Manchester Quarterly* (1917), 248-73.

The compilers have not seen this item.

207. ———. "Henry Fielding." *Notes and Queries*, Eleventh Series, 12 (1915), 300.

Requests criticism on plays and novels and information

on portraits of Fielding. See responses by Bayley, item
90, and Bensly, item 93, both under the title, "Henry
Fielding."

208. Hunt, Russell A. "Johnson on Fielding and Richardson:
A Problem in Literary Moralism." *The Humanities Association Review*, 27 (1976), 412-20.

Argues that Johnson's partiality toward Richardson is
based on Johnson's view of the value of reason in man's
life. Richardson's heroines base their actions--and
even their emotions--on reason, while Fielding's heroes,
especially Tom Jones, base their actions on benevolism,
or feeling. Johnson further dislikes Fielding because
of the nature of the latter's characters; they are low,
and therefore they are not instructive.

209. Hunter, J. Paul. *Occasional Form: Henry Fielding and
the Chains of Circumstance*. Baltimore: Johns Hopkins
University Press, 1975.

Places Fielding's works within the milieu from which
they grew. All of his works must be considered in light
of the received modes of thought of his age. The plays,
for example, must be read not only for their political
and social satire, but also as works constructed in the
rhetorical and philosophical forms current in the early
and middle eighteenth century. Fielding is caught
between the old forms of Augustanism and the developing
forms that eventually lead to romanticism. His many
experiments and his use of various masks, particularly
in his novels, reflect his "divided mind," his inability
to remain completely with the "old" and his refusal to
try the completely "new."

Reviews: Martin C. Battestin, *The Eighteenth Century: A
Current Bibliography*, n.s. 1 (1978), 292-93; H.K. Miller
South Atlantic Quarterly, 75 (1976), 525-26.

210. Hunting, Robert S. "Fielding's Revisions of *David
Simple*." *Boston University Studies in English*, 3 (1957)
117-21.

Shows the large number of revisions Fielding made in his
sister's novel, particularly in the following areas:
pronoun usage, sentence structure, diction, and referenc
to law. He also sharpened the irony of several passages

211. Huxley, Aldous. "Tragedy and the Whole Truth," in his
Music at Night and Other Essays. London: Chatto and
Windus, 1931. Pp. 3-18.

Distinguishes between tragedy and "wholly-truthful art." Tragedy limits itself to the description of only those characters and events which directly affect the tragic outcome. Wholly-truthful art, like that of Fielding and Homer, describes all actions of men, even seeming irrelevancies, and thus banishes tragedy. Wholly-truthful art has a more lasting effect than does tragedy.

212. Irwin, William Robert. "An Attack on John Fielding." *Modern Language Notes*, 56 (1941), 523-25.

An anonymous pamphlet entitled *Jonathan Wild's Advice to His Successors* (1758) viciously attacks John Fielding, Henry's brother, by comparing him to the thief-taker, Jonathan Wild.

213. ————. "Satire and Comedy in the Works of Henry Fielding." *ELH: A Journal of English Literary History*, 13 (1946), 168-88.

The apprenticeship that Fielding served in his plays led to his mastery of satire in his novels. In his early works, Fielding had not systematized his views, but his theory of the comic prose epic, expressed in his novels, provided a means for him to systematically incorporate "satirical motifs" into his fiction. Thus, for example, his "shotgun" indictment of writers and critics in the plays becomes subsumed in the novels under the general condemnation of affectation.

214. "Janus." "Saunders Welch: First of Modern Policemen." *Police College Magazine*, 8 (1965), 286-96.

Discusses Welch's relations with Henry and John Fielding and gives Welch credit for many reforms in the police usually credited solely to one of the Fieldings.

215. Jarvis, R.C. "The Death of Walpole: Henry Fielding and a Forgotten Cause Célèbre." *Modern Language Review*, 41 (1946), 113-30.

It is a popular myth that Fielding entered a so-called year of inactivity after the death of his first wife in the late autumn of 1744. In fact, he entered the controversy surrounding Walpole's physicians after Walpole's death and produced a tract entitled "A Charge to the Jury" as part of that controversy.

216.   ———. "Fielding, Dodsley, Marchant, and Ray: Some
        Fugitive Histories of the '45." *Notes and Queries*, 189
        (1945), 90-92, 117-20, and 138-41.

        Speculation that Fielding had a hand in the "Succinct
        History of the Rebellion," published in Dodsley's *Museum*,
        and "A Compleat and Authentick History," which appeared
        as a pamphlet, is unfounded. Internal evidence, plus
        the fact that Fielding did not even have time to keep
        up *The True Patriot*, indicates that he had nothing to
        do with publications on the '45 except for "A History
        of the Present Rebellion," which is certainly his.

217.   Jempson, Keith. "Fielding's Force." *Police College
        Magazine*, 6 (1961), 353-62.

        Views Fielding's plan for a preventative police force
        as still relevant. The social opposition to organized
        police, prevalent in Fielding's day, is still a part of
        society.

218.   Jensen, Gerard E. "Fashionable Society in Fielding's
        Time." *Publications of the Modern Language Association
        of America*, 31 (1916), 79-89.

        Other literature of his time corroborates Fielding's
        contention that the *beau monde*, or high society, was
        incredibly corrupt. Fielding's attacks seem to be
        motivated, at least in part, by his fear that the upper
        classes were corrupting the lower classes.

219.   Jones, Benjamin Maelor. *Henry Fielding, Novelist and
        Magistrate*. London: Allen and Unwin, 1933.

        Provides a thorough picture of Fielding's relationship
        with the law, including references to law in the plays
        and novels, biographical material on Fielding's years
        engaged in legal practice, and a study of his law-related
        writings. Jones includes discussions of the legal sys-
        tem and of the more important acts relating to criminal
        law in Fielding's lifetime. His conclusion is that
        Fielding was well-versed in law and was an able magis-
        trate.

        Reviews: J.P. de Castro, *Times Literary Supplement*
        (August 10, 1933), p. 537; A.R. Leslie-Melville, *Times
        Literary Supplement* (July 27, 1933), p. 572; *Times
        Literary Supplement* (July 20, 1933), p. 493.

220.   Jones, Howard Mumford. "Justice Fielding and the Novel."
        Journal of Public Law, 7 (1958), 162-74.

The compilers were unable to read this article prior to the publication of the bibliography.

221. Kay, Donald, ed. *A Provision of Human Nature: Essays on Fielding and Others In Honor of Miriam Austin Locke.* University, Ala.: University of Alabama Press, 1977.

This *Festschrift* includes the following essays on Fielding: Eugene Williamson, "Guiding Principles in Fielding's Criticism of the Critics," item 326; Jack D. Durant, "The 'Art of Thriving' in Fielding's Comedies," item 342; Eleanor N. Hutchens, "O Attic Shape! The Cornering of Square," item 863; John J. Burke, Jr., "History Without History: Fielding's Theory of Fiction," item 459; George H. Wolfe, "Lessons in Evil: Fielding's Ethics in *The Champion* Essays," item 1089; Susan Miller, "Eighteenth-Century Play and the Game of *Tom Jones*," item 908; and T.C. Duncan Eaves, "Amelia and Clarissa," item 995.

222. Keightley, Thomas. *The Life and Writings of Henry Fielding.* Cleveland: The Rowfant Club, 1907.

Published originally in *Fraser's Magazine* for January, February, and June, 1858, and edited and annotated for this volume by Frederick S. Dickson, who also added a list of biographies of Fielding (see item 9). Keightley's stated purpose "is to vindicate the character of Henry Fielding," who was treated unfairly by his biographers; therefore the bulk of this work is an attempt to disprove statements made by Arthur Murphy in his 1762 biography and by Frederick Lawrence in his 1855 work on Fielding, both of whom view Fielding as dissipated and immoral. Of Fielding's novels, Keightley says that they survive because they are such genuine pictures of eighteenth-century life.

* Kimpel, Ben D., and T.C. Duncan Eaves. "Henry Fielding's Son by His First Wife." *Notes and Queries*, n.s. 15 (1968), 212.

See under Eaves, item 173.

* ————. *Samuel Richardson: A Biography.* Oxford: Clarendon Press, 1971.

See under Eaves, item 174.

223. Knapp, Lewis M. "Fielding's Dinners With Dodington, 1750-1752." *Notes and Queries*, 197 (1952), 565-66.

The ten dinners Fielding had with George Bubb Dodington, dated from the latter's diary, show an apparent intimacy between the two.

224. Kropf, C.R. "Educational Theory and Human Nature in Fielding's Works." *Publications of the Modern Language Association of America*, 89 (1974), 113-20.

Throughout his works, Fielding explores the various eighteenth-century opinions on education and character, finally settling on the theory that while a man's character is predetermined and cannot be entirely transformed, "it can be mended and repaired" by education.

225. La France, Marston. "Fielding's Use of the 'Humor' Tradition." *Bucknell Review*, 17 (1969), 53-63.

Traces Fielding's use of humors characters to Ben Jonson and Congreve. Fielding's humors characters are, by definition, static and incomplete; their humors, whether natural or assumed, make them abnormal. The central figures, such as Tom Jones, Allworthy, and Adams, are not humors characters and therefore have the potential for change. They, too, are imperfect, but their imperfections are a result of too much humanity.

226. Lane, William G. "Relationships Between Some of Fielding's Major and Minor Works." *Boston University Studies in English*, 5 (1961), 219-31.

Points out parallels between such minor works as *The Voyage to Lisbon* and the major novels; Fielding's style, attitudes, and themes change very little throughout his literary career.

227. Lee, W.L. Melville. *A History of Police in England.* London: Methuen, 1901.

States that Henry Fielding provided the impetus for constabulary reform in London with his "Charge to the Grand Jury" and "Late Increase in Robbers"; for an opposing view see Amory, "Henry Fielding and the Criminal Legislation of 1751-52," item 73, and Radzinowicz, item 267. Lee also points out that the famous Bow Street Runners, who formed a model police force for eighteenth-century London, were organized by Henry and improved upon by his brother, John. Also see Pringle, item 265.

228. Leslie-Melville, A.R. "Henry Fielding." *Times Literary Supplement* (27 July 1933), p. 512.

Corrects the review of B. Maelor Jones's biography of
Fielding (item 219) in *Times Literary Supplement* (20
July 1933), p. 493, and discusses Fielding's relationship with the "Philanthropos" who published nine letters
in *The Gentleman's Magazine* and the *Daily Advertiser*
between March 16, 1751, and May 12, 1753.

229. ———. *The Life and Work of Sir John Fielding*. London: Lincoln Williams, 1934.

The first biography of Henry Fielding's half-brother,
with scattered references to Henry.

Review: F.E.B., *Modern Language Review*, 30 (1935), 553.

230. Levine, George R. *Henry Fielding and the Dry Mock: A
Study of the Techniques of Irony in His Early Works*.
Studies in English Literature, No. 30. The Hague:
Mouton, 1967.

Elaborates upon Fielding's use of verbal irony. Fielding
uses most of the techniques of verbal irony popular with
his contemporaries: denotative irony, connotative irony,
understatement, reversal of statement, irony by implication, ironic undercut, and ironic defense. His strength
lies in these verbal techniques; his use of dramatic
irony is undistinguished. He does not use the ironic
mask in the true sense because he never really develops
the character of his narrator-persona.

Review: Malvin R. Zirker, *Philological Quarterly*, 47
(1968), 382-83.

231. Lind, Levi R. "Lucian and Fielding." *Classical Weekly*,
29 (1936), 84-86.

Observes that Fielding owned nine complete sets of
Lucian in various languages and planned a translation
of him. Lind offers some general parallels between
Lucian and Fielding in themes and style. For more complete discussions of Lucian and Fielding, see Miller,
item 1042, and Paulson, item 922.

232. Link, Viktor, ed. *The Life and Adventures of a Cat*.
Braunschweig: Technische Universität Carolo-Wilhelmina,
1973.

The introduction to this anonymous novel (1760), the
second edition of which was published under Fielding's
name, notes that internal evidence proves that it could
not be Fielding's (there are several references, for

instance, to events that transpired in 1759, five years
after Fielding's death). The real author, however,
does employ many of the comic epic devices used by
Fielding: "pseudo-Homeric" passages; the early episodes
dealing with the hero's parentage, birth, and childhood;
the comic exaggeration of details. The author himself
says that he was influenced by Fielding's plot structure and the introductory chapters to each book of *Tom
Jones*.

233. Lobban, J.H. "Henry Fielding." *Blackwood's Magazine*,
181 (1907), 550-65.

Holds to a number of Fielding myths, such as Fielding's
prodigality, the yellow-plush servants in Dorset, and
the miserable life in the garret; Lobban also argues
that Fielding could not have written *Shamela* because it
is too coarse for his style. After dismissing the plays
as being "negligible," Lobban praises Fielding's fiction for its structure, wit, irony, and characterization.
He concludes by placing Fielding in a class with Chaucer,
Shakespeare, and Scott.

234. M., F. "Fielding and Brillat-Savarin." *Notes and Queries*
Ninth Series, 7 (1901), 248-49.

In *Physiologie du Goût*, Brillat-Savarin mistakenly
identifies Fielding as the author of *Pamela*.

235. M., F.B. "Henry Fielding and the Civil Power." *Notes
and Queries*, Eleventh Series, 4 (1911), 58.

The Justice Fielding who committed an army officer to
jail to show the precedence of civil over military power
was probably John Fielding instead of Henry. See the
following discussions, all under the title, "Henry
Fielding and the Civil Power": Hill, item 202; Prideaux,
item 264; Robbins, items 276 and 277; and St. Swithin,
item 283.

236. Mabbott, Thomas O. "A Presentation Inscription by
Fielding." *Notes and Queries*, 178 (1940), 298. Item
published under the pseudonym "Olybrius."

A copy of *The Works of Horace* (Paris, 1660), recently
discovered, includes an inscription from Fielding to
Jane Collyer. Also see de Castro, item 149.

237. Macaulay, Rose. "Lines on Fielding." *Times Literary
Supplement* (October 9, 1943), p. 487.

Requests information about the author of the poem on
Fielding referring to "the green Estrella trees."

238. McBurney, William H. "Mrs. Mary Davys: Forerunner of
      Fielding." *Publications of the Modern Language Associa-
      tion of America*, 74 (1959), 348-55.

      Traces the life and career of Mary Davys (1674-1732), a
      playwright and novelist, whose work shows certain "dis-
      tant" parallels with the later work of Fielding. She
      foreshadowed Fielding's comic prose epics, both in
      theory and practice, and utilized situations and charac-
      ters that were "brilliantly reincarnated" in Fielding
      later.

239. McKillop, Alan D. "The Personal Relations Between
      Fielding and Richardson." *Modern Philology*, 28 (1931),
      423-33.

      Assesses the relationship between Richardson and Field-
      ing and notes that their literary enmity rarely broke
      into the public press. In fact, Fielding praised
      Clarissa in *The Jacobite's Journal*. Richardson's dis-
      like of Fielding appears in several of his letters, but
      the most extreme criticisms of Fielding come not from
      Richardson himself, but from others in his circle,
      especially Thomas Edwards.

240. MacLaurin, Charles. *Mere Mortals: Medico-Historical
      Essays*. New York: George Doran and London: Cape, 1925.

      Peritoneal cancer, a lingering condition, caused Field-
      ing's death in Lisbon (especially see the discussion on
      pages 128-35). For an opposing view of the cause of
      Fielding's death, see Amory, "Fielding's Lisbon Letters,"
      item 1051.

241. MacLean, Kenneth. *John Locke and English Literature of
      the Eighteenth Century*. New Haven: Yale University
      Press, 1936. Reprinted New York: Russell and Russell,
      1966.

      Notes that Fielding owned a three-volume set of Locke's
      Works and valued Locke over all other modern philosophers.
      Scattered remarks throughout demonstrate Fielding's use
      of Locke in his fiction.

242. McSpadden, J. Walker. *Henry Fielding*. Standard Authors'
      Booklets Series. New York: Groscup and Sterling, 1902.

      The compilers were unable to peruse this thirty-two-page

pamphlet, copies of which are in the Yale and Harvard
libraries.

243.   Malet, Harold. "Fieldingiana." *Notes and Queries*,
       Twelfth Series, 3 (1917), 370.

       In his early edition of Fielding's works, Murphy hints
       that a second portrait of Fielding exists. Hogarth's
       "The Green-Room, Drury Lane" is probably that portrait.
       For a view that Fielding is not portrayed in the Hogarth
       engraving, see de Castro, "Fieldingiana," item 139.

244.   Metcalf, John C. "Henry Fielding, Critic." *Sewanee
       Review*, 19 (1911), 138-54.

       Divides Fielding's criticism into three categories:
       ridicule of heroic drama; protest against adaptations
       of Shakespeare; and attacks on foreign "imports."
       Fielding held that humor must necessarily be linked
       with ethics for a work to be considered superior; humor
       without ethics meant the author was little more than a
       buffoon. Above all, formal rules should be avoided be-
       cause all art should be true to nature as it is observed.

245.   Miller, Henry Knight. "Fielding and Lady Mary Wortley
       Montagu: A Parallel." *Notes and Queries*, n.s. 5 (1958),
       442-43.

       Lady Mary Wortley Montagu, in an untitled poem, and
       Fielding, in an untitled travesty of the *Aeneid*, use
       the same couplet: "She said, and turning shew'd her
       wrinkled neck,/In Scales and Colours like a Roach's
       back." The exact parallel indicates that Fielding and
       Lady Mary took a "literary interest in each other."

246.   Milward, Peter. "Shakespeare and Fielding." *Studies
       in English Literature* (English Literary Society of
       Japan), 48 (1972), 33-42.

       Outlines the influence of Shakespeare on Fielding's *Tom
       Thumb*, *Joseph Andrews*, and *Tom Jones*. In the first two
       of these works, lines from Shakespeare's tragedies are
       parodied. In *Tom Jones*, Fielding "evokes the spirit of
       Shakespeare," and *Romeo and Juliet*, *Lear*, and *Othello*
       influence its plot structure, situations, and characters.

247.   Moore, Robert Etheridge. "Dr. Johnson on Fielding and
       Richardson." *Publications of the Modern Language Asso-
       ciation of America*, 66 (1951), 162-81.

       Even though Johnson is often quoted as preferring

Richardson over Fielding, the latter's opinions of
literature are very much like Johnson's; moreover,
Fielding's novels illustrate many of Johnson's most
deeply held principles. That Johnson thought more
highly of Fielding than is generally recognized becomes
clear when one realizes that it is only in comparison
with Richardson, Johnson's good friend, that Fielding
is belittled; when Johnson speaks of Fielding in other
contexts, he often praises him, and he called *Amelia*
"one of the first performances of its kind in the
world."

248. ————. *Hogarth's Literary Relationships*. Minneapolis:
University of Minnesota Press, 1948.

Contains two chapters on Fielding: "Hogarth and Fielding Invade the Theater" (pp. 77-106) and "Hogarth's
Role in Fielding's Novels" (pp. 107-61). Moore shows
the similarities in attitude between the artist and the
novelist, similarities first apparent in Hogarth's
satiric prints mocking the pantomime and opera of the
1720's and 1730's and Fielding's satiric dramas on the
same subjects (particularly *The Tragedy of Tragedies*
to which Hogarth contributed a frontispiece). Much of
Fielding's inspiration for *The Mock Doctor*, *The Lottery*,
and *The Covent-Garden Tragedy* came from Hogarth's first
series of prints, *A Harlot's Progress*. The latter also
influenced *Joseph Andrews*: both tell a simple story with
"truly individual" characters and exuberant humor in
order to make a moral point. In the "Preface" to *Joseph
Andrews*, Fielding compares his art to that of Hogarth
(the former is a comic writer, not a writer of burlesque;
the latter is a comic painter, not a caricaturist).
Further influences can be seen in *Jonathan Wild*, several
incidents of which are drawn from Hogarth's *Rake's
Progress*, and *Tom Jones*, in which three characters—
Bridget Allworthy, Mrs. Partridge, and Thwackum—are
taken from specific Hogarth prints. Hogarth taught
Fielding restraint and how to use comedy to make a
serious moral point.

249. Morse, Charles. "Henry Fielding as a Law Reformer."
Canadian Law Review, 6 (1907), 375-86.

The compilers were unable to obtain a copy of this
item prior to the publication of the bibliography.

250. Murphy, Arthur. *The Lives of Henry Fielding and Samuel
Johnson, together with Essays from the Gray's-Inn
Journal*. Facsimile Reproduction with an Introduction

by Matthew Grace. Gainesville, Fla.: Scholars' Fac-
similes and Reprints, 1968.

The Fielding "life" is from Murphy's 1762 biography; it
is a controversial document because of its unsubstan-
tiated portrait of Fielding as a dissolute reprobate.

251. Nagasawa, Y. "Studies in the Language of Fielding."
      Studies in English Literature (English Literature
      Society of Japan), 13 (1933), 566-75.

      Notes changes in some usages of the principal parts of
      speech from Fielding to the twentieth century.

252. "Notes on Sales: Some Eighteenth-Century Trifles."
      Times Literary Supplement (30 August 1928), p. 620.

      Notes items by Fielding and others sold at recent auc-
      tions, and the prices for those items. Fielding items
      include "The Masquerade" (1728), *Tumble-Down Dick* (1736),
      "A Serious Address to the People of Great Britain"
      (1745), and "The History of Sir Harry Herald and Sir
      Edward Haunch" (1755).

253. Olybrius [Pseud.]. "A Presentation Inscription by
      Fielding." *Notes and Queries*, 178 (1940), 298.

      See annotation under Thomas O. Mabbott, item 236.

254. "Our Immortal Fielding." *Times Literary Supplement*
      (January 24, 1948), p. 50.

      In all his works, but especially in his fiction, Field-
      ing stands for openness, common sense, and genuine
      sentiment. His novels both accurately reflect and
      morally comment on his age. His moral instruction
      never interferes with the sheer entertainment value
      of his works.

255. Page, John T. "Fielding's Grave." *Notes and Queries*,
      Tenth Series, 9 (1908), 277.

      Notes that Austin Dobson paid tribute to Fielding in a
      poem entitled "Henry Fielding: Verses Read at the Un-
      veiling, by Mr. J.R. Lowell, of Miss Margaret Thomas's
      Bust in the Shire Hall, Taunton, September 4, 1883."
      Also see Bensly, "Fielding's Grave," item 92; Hooper,
      item 203; Page, "Inscription to Fielding," item 256;
      and Parker, item 257.

256. ————. "Inscription to Fielding." *Notes and Queries*,
Eighth Series, 4 (1893), 314.

Quotes the long Latin inscription on Fielding's tomb in
full and remarks that the tomb is not neglected. Also
see Bensly, "Fielding's Grave," item 92; Hooper, item
203; Page, "Fielding's Grave," item 256; and Parker,
item 257.

257. Parker, E.M.S. "Fielding's Grave." *Notes and Queries*,
Tenth Series, 9 (1908), 49.

Provides an English translation for the Latin inscription on Fielding's tomb. Also see Bensly, "Fielding's
Grave," item 92; Hooper, item 203; and Page, item 256.

* Passler, Susan Miller. "Coleridge, Fielding, and
Arthur Murphy." (See item 921.)

258. Paulson, Ronald, ed. *Fielding: A Collection of Critical
Essays*. Twentieth Century Views. Englewood Cliffs,
N.J.: Prentice-Hall, 1962.

The introduction by Paulson outlines modern views of
Fielding as moralist, satirist, and ironist. The essays
that comprise this collection are: A.R. Humphreys,
"Fielding's Irony: Its Method and Effect," item 505;
Winifred H. Rogers, "Fielding's Early Aesthetic and
Technique," item 280; Ian Watt, "*Shamela*," item 633;
Maynard Mack, "*Joseph Andrews* and *Pamela*," item 689;
Mark Spilka, "Comic Resolution in Fielding's *Joseph
Andrews*," item 712; Aurélien Digeon, "*Jonathan Wild*,"
item 731; André Gide, "Notes for a Preface to Fielding's
Tom Jones," item 846; Arnold Kettle, "*Tom Jones*," item
874; John Middleton Murry, "Fielding's 'Sexual Ethic' in
Tom Jones," item 912; Ian Watt, "*Tom Jones* and *Clarissa*,"
item 978; William Empson, "*Tom Jones*," item 839; George
Sherburn, "Fielding's *Amelia*: An Interpretation," item
1021; John S. Coolidge, "Fielding and 'Conservation of
Character,'" item 470.

259. ————. *Hogarth: His Life, Art, and Times*. 2 Vols.
New Haven: Yale University Press, 1971. Excerpts reprinted in Rawson, item 272.

Includes a number of anecdotes about Hogarth's relationship with Fielding, perhaps the most important of which
is an explanation of the events surrounding Hogarth's
portrait of the novelist.

260.   Plumb, J.H.   "Henry Fielding and the Rise of the Novel,"
       in his *In the Light of History*.   London: Penguin Press,
       1972.   Pp. 37-51.

       Deals more with Fielding's life and character than with
       his writing; he was a virile writer with "charity, com-
       passion, gentleness."   He strengthened the structure
       of the novel by depicting character through events
       rather than through the analysis of feeling and he is
       "the first great novelist of social criticism," a pre-
       cursor of Dickens.

261.   ————.   "Henry Fielding: The Journey Through Gin Lane."
       Horizon, 6 (1964), 75-83.

       Sees Fielding as a biographical writer—that is, as one
       who writes out of his own experiences.   His books accu-
       rately portray London low life, making him the first
       realistic novelist in England.

262.   Pope, F.J.   "Fielding's Ancestors at Sharpham Park,
       Somerset."   *Notes and Queries*, Twelfth Series, 6 (1920),
       34.

       Sharpham Park came into the Fielding family through
       Henry's maternal grandfather, Richard Davidge, a mer-
       chant, who purchased it in 1657.

263.   ————.   "Fielding's Boyhood."   *British Archivist*, 1
       (1914), 85-88.

       Treats the Chancery case over Fielding's guardianship.

264.   Prideaux, W.F.   "Henry Fielding and the Civil Power."
       Notes and Queries, Eleventh Series, 4 (1911), 419.

       Both John and Henry Fielding were justices in 1751, so
       either could be the "Worshipful Justice Fielding" who
       condemned the military man to jail in order to prove
       that the civil power had ascendancy over the military.
       See the following discussions, all under the title,
       "Henry Fielding and the Civil Power," of this topic:
       Hill, item 202; F.B.M., item 235; Robbins, items 276
       and 277; and St. Swithin, item 283.

265.   Pringle, Patrick.   *Hue and Cry: The Story of Henry and
       John Fielding and Their Bow Street Runners*.   New York:
       Morrow, 1955.

       Deals with eighteenth-century crime, focusing on the
       roles played in the development of the English police

system by Henry and John Fielding. Henry founded the
police and is considered to be one of England's greatest
magistrates. He eliminated London's notorious street
gangs with severity, but dealt compassionately with
women, children, and the poor who were accused of crimes.
Pringle's study presents a more complete history of
Fielding's career in the law than previous works. Also
see Amory, "Henry Fielding and the Criminal Legislation
of 1751-52," item 73; Radzinowicz, item 267; and Zirker,
item 1099.

Reviews: Roger Beckett, *New York Herald Tribune Book
Reviews* (January 15, 1956), p. 2; Jacob Korg, *Nation*,
182 (1956), 224-25.

266. Rader, Ralph W. "Thackeray's Injustice to Fielding."
      Journal of English and Germanic Philology, 56 (1957),
      203-12.

Sometime between 1840, when he admitted his indebtedness
to Fielding in a favorable review of the latter's works,
and 1851, when in his lectures on the English humorists
he called Fielding a profligate and Tom Jones an immoral rogue, Thackeray drastically revised his opinion
of Fielding. Rader argues that Thackeray saw himself
in Fielding and because he could not accept himself,
he found it increasingly difficult to follow his literary model; his harsh statements about Fielding are in
reality remarks about himself and attempts to assuage
his guilt. Unfortunately, his comments did great
damage to Fielding's reputation.

267. Radzinowicz, Leon. *A History of English Criminal Law
      and Its Administration from 1750.* 3 Vols. London:
      Stevens and Sons, 1948.

Contains remarks on Fielding's legal career at I, 399-
499; II, 420; and III, 17f. Presents evidence to con-
tradict B. Maelor Jones, item 219, and Cross, item 126,
that Fielding was behind the resolutions of the Commit-
tee of 1750, although he may have written the Murder
Act of 1751. Fielding was often at odds with the Com-
mittee on how to effect greater severity of punishment
for criminal offenses. Also see Amory, "Henry Fielding
and the Criminal Legislation of 1751-52," item 73;
Pringle, item 265; and Zirker, item 1099.

*   Raleigh, Walter. "Richardson and Fielding." (See item
        555.)

268. Ramondt, Marie. "Between Laughter and Humour in the
      Eighteenth Century." *Neophilologus*, 40 (1956), 128-38.

      Places Fielding's theory and practice of comedy in the
      context of the eighteenth century. Fielding distin-
      guishes between burlesque and the ridiculous; the source
      of the latter is affectation, which arises from vanity
      or hypocrisy. Yet, in *Joseph Andrews*, Adams is a comic
      figure without vanity or hypocrisy. With Adams, Field-
      ing created a precursor of Romantic comedy, a humorous
      figure who carries with him the potential for tragedy.

269. Rawson, C.J. "Fielding, Whose Contemporary?" *Essays
      in Criticism*, 25 (1975), 272-76.

      Answers three major criticisms voiced by Marilyn Butler
      in her review of his *Henry Fielding and the Augustan
      Ideal Under Stress* (item 273); Rawson says that Butler's
      allegations are unspecific, sweeping in nature, and "a
      distasteful combination of innuendo, omission and half-
      truth."

270. ————. "Gentlemen and Dancing-Masters: Thoughts on
      Fielding, Chesterfield, and the Genteel." *Eighteenth-
      Century Studies*, 1 (1967), 127-58.

      According to both Fielding and Chesterfield, gentility
      is necessary to separate men from brutes. However, the
      two disagree on how manners function. Chesterfield sees
      them as an external check, saving civilization from
      "collapsing on itself," while Fielding sees them as an
      internal quality possible for all men of good nature to
      attain. Gentility is a necessary and natural part of
      every noble person, but it must also be taught--the
      function of the dancing master. The basic contradiction
      in both Fielding's and Chesterfield's attitudes toward
      gentility lies in their views of the dancing master,
      who must teach others gentility but who is not himself
      genteel.

271. ————. *Henry Fielding*. Profiles in Literature Series.
      London: Routledge and Kegan Paul, and New York: Humanities
      Press, 1968.

      Provides an account of Fielding's works and career
      through a series of extracts which are chosen and in-
      terpreted to emphasize particular aspects of his art.
      The selections and commentaries are arranged under
      subject headings such as "Comic Epic and the True
      Ridiculous," "Mock-Heroic: Three Treatments of Heroines,"

"Ironic Climaxes," and "Snobbery and Class," among
several others.

Review: Times Literary Supplement (May 23, 1968), p.
529.

272.   ————, ed. *Henry Fielding: A Critical Anthology.*
Harmondsworth, Middlesex: Penguin, 1973.

Consists of a brief biography, over three hundred pages
of eighteenth- and nineteenth-century commentary, and
fifty-five twentieth-century items. The modern criticism, prefaced by an overview of modern Fielding scholarship, ranges from single-sentence journal entries to
complete essays. Significant shorter remarks and all
of the longer items are annotated. See Chesterton,
item 800; Gide, item 846; Ford, items 480 and 481;
Humphreys, item 505; Leavis, item 524; West, item 609;
Bland, item 455; Price, item 549; Paulson, item 259;
Donaldson, item 167; Kettle, item 874; Dyson, item 833;
Hopkins, item 738; Battestin, item 616; Renwick, item
560; Donovan, item 661; Van Ghent, item 975; Watt, item
608; Empson, item 839; Ehrenpreis, item 665; Preston,
item 931; Hatfield, item 197; and Alter, item 443.

Review: A.R. Humphreys, *Review of English Studies*, 25
(1974), 212-14.

273.   ————. *Henry Fielding and the Augustan Ideal Under
Stress.* London: Routledge and Kegan Paul, 1972.

The Augustan ideal of harmony, imaged in Nature, was
threatened by various doubters in Fielding's time. The
threat is reflected in a sense of stress in style and
form and in a crisis in the mock-heroic mode. The stress
in style and form appears in a lack of balance in the
couplet and in descriptions of unnatural people and
events. The crisis in the mock-heroic is reflected in
Jonathan Wild, in which Fielding is not in control of
his material at times. For example, he is unsuccessful
in depicting Wild as a villain; often Wild appears to
be a bumbler and a clown. He also is unsuccessful in
painting a portrait of Heartfree as a totally good man;
the sentimentalism of the latter's portrait makes him
appear at times to be a target of Fielding's satire.

Reviews: Marilyn Butler, *Essays in Criticism*, 24 (1974),
295-300; Howard Erskine-Hill, *Durham University Journal*,
n.s. 36 (1975), 246-49; A.R. Humphreys, *Review of English
Studies*, 25 (1974), 212-14; J. Paul Hunter, *Philological*

Quarterly, 52 (1973), 504-05; George R. Levine, *Journal
of English and Germanic Philology*, 74 (1975), 131-34;
Times Literary Supplement (May 11, 1973), p. 525;
Aubrey Williams, *South Atlantic Quarterly*, 73 (1974),
411-12.

274.   ————. "Nature's Dance of Death, Part I: Urbanity and
Strain in Fielding, Swift, and Pope." *Eighteenth Century Studies*, 3 (1970), 307-38.

In his early works, Fielding sees nature as containing
perfect order, and his art reflects that order in style,
tone, and description. When a character or situation
lacks order, thus defying nature, Fielding creates it
through his art. In his later works, particularly in
the *Voyage to Lisbon*, he shows signs of losing his
belief in natural order through incomplete, or unsym-
metrical, descriptions of unnatural people or events.

275.   Reith, Charles. *The Police Idea. Its History and
Evolution in England in the Eighteenth Century and
After*. London and New York: Oxford University Press,
1938.

The compilers have not read this work.

Review: Times Literary Supplement (11 February 1939),
p. 93.

276.   Robbins, Alfred F. "Henry Fielding and the Civil Power."
Notes and Queries, Eleventh Series, 3 (1911), 486.

When he was a Bow Street magistrate, Fielding committed
an army officer to jail, in part to show him that civil
power took precedence over military power. A lengthy
discussion on this topic ensues; see the following, all
under the above title: Hill, item 202; F.B.M., item
235; Prideaux, item 264; Robbins, item 277; and St.
Swithin, item 283.

277.   ————. "Henry Fielding and the Civil Power." *Notes
and Queries*, Eleventh Series, 4 (1911), 277.

Henry Fielding, not John, committed an army officer to
jail to show the precedence of civil power over military
power. John did not succeed Henry until 1754, and the
incident in question took place in October 1751. See
the following discussion, all under the title above:
Hill, item 202; F.B.M., item 235; Prideaux, item 264;
Robbins, item 276; and St. Swithin, item 283.

278. Rochedieu, Charles A. *Bibliography of French Transla-
     tions of English Works, 1700-1800*. Chicago: University
     of Chicago Press, 1948.

     Lists forty-eight eighteenth-century translations into
     French of various works by Fielding.

279. Rogers, Pat. *Grub Street: Studies in a Sub-Culture*.
     London: Methuen and New York: Barnes and Noble, 1972.

     Discusses the literary views of Grub Street hack writers
     with scattered comments on Fielding's remarks and a
     short section (pp. 327-36) on his plays that treat Grub
     Street. The hack writer or "dunce" was traditionally
     regarded as a pernicious wrongdoer, undermining cul-
     ture, but in Fielding we begin to see a shift to a view
     of the hack as victim, especially of tyrannical book-
     sellers. *The Author's Farce* (1730) is one of the first
     works to depict "the hack as sinned against as well as
     sinning."

280. Rogers, Winfield H. "Fielding's Early Esthetic and
     Technique." *Studies in Philology*, 40 (1943), 529-51.
     Reprinted in Paulson, item 258.

     From 1729 to 1740, Fielding developed the aesthetic and
     the techniques on which his great works were based.
     The most important aspects of his early development
     were: (1) his use of farce as a satiric medium for a
     serious analysis of life; (2) his development of the
     traditional "humors" character as a means of exploring
     human psychology; (3) his use of allegorical symbols to
     interpret experience. Rogers traces the development of
     these techniques through *The Champion* and Fielding's
     plays.

281. Sackett, S.J. "Fielding and Pope." *Notes and Queries*,
     n.s. 6 (1959), 200-04.

     Divides Fielding's published remarks on Pope into four
     phases: (1) remarks made before he met Pope; (2) those
     made between the time he met Pope in 1741 and Pope's
     death in 1744; (3) those published between Pope's death
     and the appearance of *Amelia* in 1751; (4) those made
     during the last years of Fielding's life. In general,
     Fielding praises Pope highly, but—strangely—in the
     third phase above, he criticizes him, sometimes severe-
     ly, before returning in his last years to high praise.
     The most inexplicable aspect of Fielding's shifting at-
     titude is that after Pope's death, he criticized some of

Pope's works that he had praised highly during Pope's lifetime.

282.   ————.` "To Write Like an Angel." *Western Folklore*,
        18 (1959), 250-51.

It has been suggested that the phrase "to write like an angel" was first used by Garrick in 1774, but Fielding uses an expression much like that phrase on two separate occasions, and the manner of his usage indicates that the phrase is proverbial.

283.   St. Swithin. "Henry Fielding and the Civil Power."
        Notes and Queries, Eleventh Series, 4 (1911), 336.

A *Morning Post* article refers to John Fielding as the celebrated Bow Street Magistrate who condemned an army officer to jail to demonstrate the precedence of civil power over the military; *The Times* says Henry Fielding was the magistrate in question. St. Swithin asks here which one it really was. See the following discussions, all under the above title: Hill, item 202; F.B.M., item 235; Prideaux, item 264; and Robbins, items 276 and 277.

284.   Seccombe, Thomas. *The Age of Johnson (1748-1798)*. London: George Bell and Sons, 1907.

Praises Fielding highly: "If a man were restricted to the writings of a single author of the Age of Johnson, he would show both wisdom and taste in naming those of Henry Fielding." The main reason for this judgment is that Fielding seems like "an ordinary man" with whom the reader can identify and he has a "genius for the development of character."

285.   Seymour, William K. "Henry Fielding: Son of Somerset."
        Contemporary Review, 203 (1963), 31-34.

Briefly traces Fielding's life from his birth through his play-writing days, with a detailed description of Sharpham Park, his birthplace. The biography is concluded in a later issue of this journal (see item 286).

286.   ————. "Henry Fielding: The Years of Achievement."
        Contemporary Review, 203 (1963), 154-58.

Concludes the biography begun in an earlier issue of *Contemporary Review*. See item 285.

287.   Shepherd, T.B. *Methodism and the Literature of the Eighteenth Century*. New York: Haskell House, 1966. Originally published London: Epworth Press, 1940.

Cites some passages from Fielding's novels which demonstrate that he viewed the Methodists as hypocrites and
rogues. Especially see pp. 224-25.

288. Shepperson, Archibald B. "Additions and Corrections to
Facts about Fielding." *Modern Philology*, 51 (1954),
217-24.

Accounts for five hitherto unaccounted-for weeks of
Fielding's life (from November 2 to December 8, 1748);
during this period, he was very active as a magistrate,
taking twenty-one recognizances and committing sixty-
four prisoners to the Gatehouse Prison, Westminster.
Shepperson also determines the publication dates of
The Wedding Day (February 23, 1743); *Charge to the Grand
Jury* (July 21, 1749); *A True State of the Case of
Bosavern Penlez* (November 18, 1749); *An Enquiry into
the Causes of the Late Increase of Robbers* (January 19,
1751); and *Amelia* (December 19, 1751). Also see Coley,
"Fielding's Two Appointments to the Magistracy," item
115.

289. ———. "Fielding on Liberty and Democracy," in *English
Studies in Honor of James Southall Wilson*, University
of Virginia Studies, Vol. 4. Richmond, Va.: William
Byrd Press, 1951. Pp. 265-75.

Throughout his writings, Fielding shows his love of the
concept of liberty expressed in the British Constitution
and his hatred of both Republicanism and absolute
monarchy; his hatred of the latter is based on his belief that all men are equal in virtue and fault, and no
man or group of men can ever be perfect.

290. Sherbo, Arthur. "Fielding and Dr. South: A Post Mortem."
Notes and Queries, n.s. 4 (1957), 378-79.

Objects to Wendt's conclusion (see item 320) that near
the end of his career, Fielding had repudiated his tendency to joke about sacred things. As late as the
Journal of a Voyage to Lisbon Fielding is lauding South
for his mixing of levity and gravity. Also see de
Castro, "Did Fielding Write *Shamela*?" item 619; Greene,
item 622; Maxwell, items 626 and 627; and Woods,
"Fielding and the Authorship of *Shamela*," item 635.

291. Sherburn, George, and Donald F. Bond. *The Restoration
and Eighteenth Century (1660-1789)*, Vol. 3 of *A Literary
History of England*, ed. Albert C. Baugh. 2nd Ed. New
York: Appleton-Century-Crofts, 1967. Originally published New York: Appleton-Century-Crofts, 1948.

Contains a section on Fielding's plays, one on his
novels, and extensive bibliographical references.
Fielding was not at home in comedy; his best plays,
hardly surpassed in English, are his farces. He lent
dignity to the art of fiction by imitating the epic
and by cultivating serious criticism of manners.
Moreover, he was a supreme craftsman in integrating apparently disparate elements into a unified plot.

292.   Shipley, John B. "General Edmund Fielding." *Notes
       and Queries*, n.s. 1 (1954), 253-54.

       Prints two previously unknown letters from General
       Edmund Fielding, Henry's father, to Lord Harrington,
       Secretary of State for the Northern department.

293.   ———. "Ralph, Ellys, Hogarth, and Fielding: The
       Cabal Against Jacopo Amigoni." *Eighteenth Century
       Studies*, 1 (1968), 313-31.

       Points out that Ralph, Ellys, Hogarth, and Fielding
       were all good friends, linked by mutual attitudes
       towards the arts, and that they were all engaged in
       the "English vs. foreign" painting controversy which
       swirled around Amigoni's triumphs in the 1730's. Ralph,
       Ellys, and Hogarth actively enlisted in the anti-Amigoni
       faction, and Fielding was sympathetic to their cause, as
       the ironic linking of Hogarth's name with Amigoni's in
       Joseph Andrews suggests. For a rebuttal and reply to
       this article, see item 294. Also see Coley, "Fielding,
       Hogarth, and Three Italian Masters," item 114.

294.   ———, and William B. Coley. "Fielding and the Cabal
       'Against Amigoni': 'A Rebuttal' and 'Reply.'" *Eigh-
       teenth Century Studies*, 2 (1969), 303-11.

       Coley offers a rebuttal to Shipley's "Ralph, Ellys,
       Hogarth, and Fielding," item 293, in which he argues
       that Shipley's conclusion that Fielding was involved
       in a "cabal" is based on too many suppositions. Ac-
       cording to Coley, it cannot be proved that either
       Fielding or Hogarth were involved in Ralph's *Weekly
       Register* campaign against Amigoni. Shipley replies that
       circumstantial evidence points to links among Ralph,
       Hogarth, and Fielding in the early 1730's and that a
       "cabal" can be inferred from the common interests and
       antipathies of this group of friends. Also see Coley,
       "Fielding, Hogarth, and Three Italian Masters," item
       114.

295. Shumuda, Matsuo. "Fielding's Daughter." *The Rising Generation*, 98 (1952), 157-59.

    This work is not available in the United States.

296. ————. *Henry Fielding*. Tokyo: Kenkyusha, 1956.

    Although this work is listed in the *Philological Quarterly* bibliography for 1956, the compilers were unable to locate a copy of it.

297. Smith, J. Oates. "Masquerade and Marriage: Fielding's Comedies of Identity." *Ball State University Forum*, 6 (1965), 10-21.

    Nearly all of Fielding's work is linked by the central metaphor of the masquerade and the theme of marriage. His first publications--the poem "The Masquerade" and the play *Love in Several Masques* (both 1728)--initiate the metaphor and the theme, both of which Fielding continues to use through *Amelia* (1751) to explore questions of appearance versus reality, self-identity, and the elements that constitute a happy marriage.

298. Smith, Leroy W. "Fielding and Mandeville: The 'War Against Virtue.'" *Criticism*, 3 (1961), 7-15.

    Sees similarities in many of Fielding's and Mandeville's observations about society: "false" (self-serving) charity predominates over "true" (altruistic) charity; commercial nations are inevitably corrupted by luxury; self-love is the source of most economic and social disorders. However, in spite of these similarities, Fielding never embraced Mandeville's theories or principles.

299. ————. "Fielding and 'Mr. Bayle's' *Dictionary*." *Texas Studies in Literature and Language*, 4 (1962), 16-20.

    Finds in Bayle's *Dictionary* a source--or at least a support--for many of Fielding's attitudes about the nature of man. In particular, both Bayle and Fielding have the same view of Fortune's influence on men's lives.

300. Starkie, Walter F. "Miguel de Cervantes and the English Novel." *Essays by Divers Hands* (Transactions of the Royal Society of Literature), 34 (1966), 159-79.

    Mentions some parallels between Cervantes' life and Fielding's and notes that Cervantes greatly influenced Fielding's writing.

301. Stewart, Mary M. "A Correction and Further Note Concern-
      ing Henry Fielding as Magistrate." *Notes and Queries*,
      n.s. 20 (1973), 13-15.

      Corrects her previous article on Fielding as magistrate
      (item 302) by citing a series of May 1749 newspaper
      announcements which report on Fielding's election as
      Chairman of the Sessions for Middlesex. Although Field-
      ing was elected to the position, the election was a
      mistake because John Lane had not resigned from the
      position and continued to serve in it for the remainder
      of 1749. Stewart also produces evidence to show that
      Fielding did not succeed Justice John Poulson on Bow
      Street but rather John Green.

302. ————. "Notes on Henry Fielding as Magistrate." *Notes
      and Queries*, n.s. 16 (1969), 348-50.

      Examines *The Whitehall Evening Post*, *The St. James
      Evening Post*, and *The London Evening Post* for 1748 and
      1749 in order to check and correct minor points con-
      cerning Fielding's career as a magistrate. Stewart
      corrects Dudden (item 171) on Fielding's predecessors
      in the magistracy; she adds to Godden's information
      (item 186) on Fielding's being chosen Chairman of the
      Sessions for Middlesex; and she determines that Fielding
      began his activity as a Middlesex justice on February
      17, 1749. Also see Coley, "Fielding's Two Appointments,"
      item 115. Stewart makes some additions to her informa-
      tion in her "A Correction and Further Note," item 301.

303. Swaen, A.E.H. "Fielding and Goldsmith in Leyden."
      Modern Language Review, 1 (1905), 327-28.

      According to the University of Leyden's Rector's records,
      Fielding was registered as a student of literature on
      February 16, 1728. Goldsmith's name is not recorded,
      indicating that he was never a regular student at
      Leyden.

304. Swaminathan, S.R. "Hazlitt, Lamb, and Fielding." *Notes
      and Queries*, n.s. 11 (1964), 180.

      Refers to Maxwell's observation that Hazlitt adapted a
      sentence from Fielding in order to describe Godwin (see
      item 691) and notes that Charles Lamb adapted the same
      Fielding sentence in "The South-Sea House" to describe
      John Tipp.

305. Swann, George R. "Fielding and Empirical Realism," in
      his *Philosophical Parallelism in Six English Novelists*.
      Folcroft, Pa.: Folcroft Press, 1969. Pp. 46-64.

Originally published Philadelphia: University of
Pennsylvania Press, 1929.

Shaftesbury undoubtedly influenced Fielding, but Fielding developed Shaftesbury's philosophy to the point
that he is actually closer to Hume than to Shaftesbury
in key philosophical conceptions. Fielding and Hume
agree that prudence and morality coincide, that a man's
character is determined by his fundamental nature, and
that actions are governed by the passions. Ultimately,
the standard for right actions is governed by what is
best for the public.

306. T____e, W. "Fielding's First Marriage." *Notes and
Queries*, Tenth Series, 6 (1906), 47.

Records an entry in the registers of the Church of St.
Mary, Charlcombe, which notes Fielding's marriage to
Charlotte Cradock on November 28, 1734, and refers to
the same registers for a notation recording the burial
of Fielding's sister, Sarah, in 1768.

307. Item deleted.

308. Taylor, Houghton W. "Fielding Upon Cibber." *Modern
Philology*, 29 (1931), 73-90.

Agrees with C.W. Nichols ("Fielding and the Cibbers,"
item 429) that Fielding's early satire on Cibber was
confined to the latter's theatrical productions and not
his personality. In fact, in *Love in Several Masques*
and *The Mock Doctor*, Fielding actually praises Cibber.
After the publication of Cibber's *Apology*, however,
Fielding's remarks become more personal.

309. Todd, William B. "Three Notes on Fielding." *Papers of
the Bibliographical Society of America*, 47 (1953),
70-75.

Lists the corrections and misprints in the second
edition of *An Apology for the Life of Mr. T[heophilus]
C[ibber]*; records errata in *A Dialogue between a Gentleman of London ... and an Honest Alderman* to demonstrate
that it was rushed through the press; and argues that
the second "edition" of *Amelia*, reportedly printed by
Strahan in January of 1752, was never issued and therefore is a bibliographical "ghost."

310. Tottenham, C.J. "Tom Jones." *Notes and Queries*,
Twelfth Series, 6 (1920), 23.

Notes that Smith's *Student's Manual of English Literature*

credits Fielding's family with being descended from the
Hapsburgs. See White, item 980.

311. Ulanov, Barry. "Sterne and Fielding: The Allegory of
      Irony," in his *Sources and Resources: The Literary Tra-
      ditions of Christian Humanism.* Westminster, Md.:
      Newman Press, 1960. Pp. 206-27.

      Places Fielding in the context of Christian Humanism,
      seen here as a realistic tradition which views man as
      imperfect but capable of rising to great heights.
      Fielding delights in rewarding his good characters and
      punishing his wicked ones, but each time that he seems
      ready to fall "prey to the wiles of guilessness" he
      withdraws to give himself and his readers a lesson on
      the perils of credulity. Underlying such detachment,
      however, is a strain of moral indignation.

312. Van Der Voorde, F.P. *Henry Fielding: Critic and Sati-
      rist.* Gravenhage: Pier Westerbaan, 1931.

      Regards Fielding primarily as a highly patriotic and
      moral satirist whose criticism of literature, politics,
      and society was aimed at making England, especially
      London, a better place in which to live. His genial
      temperament and humanitarianism led him to employ
      ridicule more than castigation in his satire and to
      feel that through the agency of that satire, mankind
      would discover its own follies and amend them. Although
      his attitude changes from the "light and playful" in
      his dramas to that of "the serene teacher" in *Amelia*,
      Fielding's "loving heart" and humane approach to life
      remain constant throughout his literary career.

313. Van Doren, Carl. "The Greatest English Man of Letters."
      Nation, 116 (1923), 659-60.

      Sees Fielding as England's greatest author because he
      was energetic and full of fun, comprehensive in his
      portrayals of English life, wise and learned, honest,
      courageous, and eloquent. The best summation of his
      life and work is to say that he had "magnanimity."

314. Vincent, Howard P. "The Childhood of Henry Fielding."
      Review of English Studies, 16 (1940), 438-44.

      Reviews the depositions of Frances Barber, Bridget
      Penotier, and the Reverend Peter Wiggett in the Fielding
      vs. Fielding trial and finds that they contradict the
      popular supposition that Henry Fielding's father

neglected the children, led them into Catholicism, and
beat them. In fact, the witnesses indicate that Henry
was wild and unruly and often disrespectful to his
family and the servants.

315. ————. "Henry Fielding in Prison." *Modern Language
Review*, 36 (1941), 499-500.

A rare, anonymous pamphlet entitled *An Historical View
of the Principles* ... *Translated from the French* (1740)
mentions that Fielding was imprisoned some time before
1728 and was bailed out by Walpole.

316. Wallace, Robert M. "Fielding Manuscripts." *Times
Literary Supplement* (May 18, 1940), p. 243.

Conjectures that a note attached to two sheets of legal
notes in Fielding's handwriting could indicate that
Fielding kept a commonplace book and that the book may
have survived the Gordon riots. If such a book is
extant, it would be important to Fielding scholars because so little posthumous Fielding material has been
found. Also see de Castro (same title), item 137.

317. ————. "Fielding's Knowledge of History and Biography."
Studies in Philology, 44 (1947), 89-107.

Studies Fielding's library and reviews his essays for
citations and allusions, concluding that his main interests lay in the areas of history and biography. Also
see Burke, item 459, and Stevick, "Fielding and the
Meaning of History," item 592.

318. Wanklyn, Cyril. *Lyme Regis: A Retrospect.* Second
edition. London: Harchards, 1927.

Reproduces in facsimile a holograph Fielding document
and another with two signatures.

319. Wells, John E. "A Few Details of Fielding's Life."
Nation, 94 (April 25, 1912), p. 409.

Not seen by the compilers but listed by Battestin in the
New Cambridge Bibliography of English Literature.

320. Wendt, Allan E. "Fielding and South's 'Luscious Morsel':
A Last Word." *Notes and Queries*, n.s. 4 (1957), 256-57.

Fielding used an epigram from South's *Sermons* ("revenge
is the most luscious morsel the devil can put into the
sinner's mouth") in five of his works: *The Mock Doctor*;

The Champion for February 2, 1739/40; *Shamela*; *An Enquiry into the Causes of the Late Increase in Robbers*; and *Amelia*. This repeated use of the quotation supports Fielding's authorship of *Shamela* and lends credence to the view that he read and was influenced by sermons throughout his life. Also see de Castro, "Did Fielding Write *Shamela*?" item 619; Greene, item 622; Maxwell, items 626 and 627; Sherbo, "Fielding and Dr. South: A Post Mortem," item 290; and Woods, "Fielding and the Authorship of *Shamela*," item 635.

321. Wheatley, Henry B. *Hogarth's London*. New York: E.P. Dutton, 1909.

Contains several anecdotes about Fielding and Hogarth, including the story of how Hogarth came to create the only known portrait of Fielding. There also are brief comments on Fielding the playwright and Fielding the justice.

322. Wheeler, Adrian. "Henry Fielding." *Notes and Queries*, Ninth Series, 12 (1903), 65.

Notes that Fordhook House, which in the *Voyage to Lisbon* Fielding mentions as his home, was demolished in June 1903.

323. Willcocks, Mary P. *A True-Born Englishman, Being the Life of Henry Fielding*. London: Allen and Unwin, 1947. New York: Macmillan, 1948.

Blends biography with criticism in a non-scholarly study which relies heavily on nineteenth- and early twentieth-century criticism (Saintsbury, Dobson, Cross, Blanchard, etc.). Although Fielding's youth was not exemplary, many of his qualities are those valued highly by modern readers: he is realistic, presenting the truth even when it is ugly; he is generous and non-puritanical in his judgments; and he is "tough" in character, laughing through his own pain and hardship. Part of Fielding's continuing popularity is that he is "typically English" in his attitudes.

Reviews: Carlos Baker, *New York Times Book Reviews* (March 7, 1948), p. 6; Howard Mumford Jones, *Saturday Review*, 31 (April 3, 1948), 29-30; C.R.T., *Queen's Quarterly*, 55 (1949), 517-18; *Times Literary Supplement* (November 1, 1947), p. 567; *Times Literary Supplement* (January 24, 1948), p. 50.

324. Williams, Harold. "Henry Fielding (1707–1754)," in his
Two Centuries of the English Novel. London: John
Murray, 1911. Pp. 53–77.

Briefly surveys Fielding's life and career and defends
him against charges of immorality, arguing that he is
realistic, not immoral. He is most successful in his
characterization because, even though he says he deals
with "type" characters, he is a great creator of individuals (Adams, Western, and Amelia, for example),
recognizing that each person is a "medley" of opposing
characteristics.

325. Williams, Murial Brittain. *Marriage: Fielding's Mirror
of Reality*. University: University of Alabama Press,
1973.

Throughout Fielding's plays and novels, courtship and
marriage are devices used to explore morality. Fielding's concept of the "moral marriage" is placed in the
context of the eighteenth-century's "marriage debate"
and is contrasted with that of other writers, particularly Richardson. *The Modern Husband*, *Tom Jones*, and
Amelia receive special consideration.

Review: Jeffrey R. Smitten, *Philological Quarterly*, 53
(1974), 708–09.

326. Williamson, Eugene. "Guiding Principles in Fielding's
Criticism of the Critics," in *A Provision of Human
Nature: Essays on Fielding and Others in Honor of Miriam
Austin Locke*, ed. Donald Kay. University: University
of Alabama Press, 1977. Pp. 1–24.

The adverse reactions to his dramas and novels gave rise
to Fielding's dissatisfaction with the critics of his
day and led to the three main points of his own critical
commentary; most critics are (1) unqualified; (2) pedantic
and mechanical in dealing with texts; and (3) unjust in
dealing with authors. In his own criticism, he tried to
be "informed, genially responsive to creative practice,
and fair"; the latter trait is particularly evident in
Fielding's praise of *Clarissa*.

327. Willy, Margaret. "Portrait of a Man: Henry Fielding,"
in her *Life Was Their Cry*. London: Evans Brothers,
1950. Pp. 98–152.

Mixes biographical fact with interpolations from Fielding's novels to constantly imply that his works are

highly autobiographical. The author contends that Fielding is the father of the modern novel because in *Joseph
Andrews* he became the first novelist to create completely
realistic characters. Parson Adams is the greatest of
these creations, but *Tom Jones* is Fielding's finest
overall work because of its zest and scope. The latter
is not, as generally believed, coarse or immoral; it
simply is frank and realistic.

328.   Wimsatt, W.K.   "Henry Fielding," in his *The Idea of
       Comedy*. Englewood Cliffs, N.J.: Prentice-Hall, 1969.
       Pp. 144-76.

       A brief introduction to Fielding as a humorist and
       theoretician of comedy--noting that he was in the
       Menippean vein of satire--is followed by a selection of
       Fielding's criticism on comedy: "Preface to *Joseph
       Andrews*"; "Book III, Chapter I of *Joseph Andrews*"; "*The
       Covent-Garden Journal*, Number 55"; and "*The Covent-Garden
       Journal*, Number 56."

329.   Work, James A.   "Henry Fielding, Christian Censor," in
       *The Age of Johnson: Essays Presented to Chauncey
       Brewster Tinker*, ed. F.W. Hilles. New Haven: Yale
       University Press, 1949. Pp. 139-48. Reprinted in paper-
       back, 1964.

       Refutes the view, given currency by Cross (item 126) and
       propagated by Digeon (item 474) and Joesten (item 1199),
       that Fielding became converted to Christianity only
       late in life. A re-examination of Fielding's works
       shows that by the time of *The Champion* (late 1739), he
       was in all significant points an orthodox believer in
       the tradition of Tillotson, Clarke, and Barrow, and he
       remained such for the rest of his life. The theme of
       Christian charity dominates all of his major works, and
       he became the most important Christian moralist of his
       generation of writers.

330.   Yardley, E.   "Fielding and Shakespeare." *Notes and
       Queries*, Tenth Series, 7 (1907), 444.

       Notes that Fielding often praised Shakespeare in his
       writings and even paraphrased him in *Tom Jones*.

IV

THE DRAMATIC WORKS

A. General

331. Avery, Emmett L. "Fielding's Last Season with the Hay-
      market Theatre." *Modern Philology*, 36 (1938), 283-92.

      The theater notices in *The Daily Advertiser* offer
      evidence for the contention that Fielding resumed his
      relationship with the Haymarket Theatre in January of
      1737. He probably had a hand in the production of *The
      Defeat of Apollo* and an afterpiece entitled *The Fall of
      Bob*. In late February, Fielding advertised Shakespeare's
      King John in conjunction with Cibber's proposed revision
      of the play. Fielding did not seem to take the possi-
      bility of the Licensing Act very seriously because he
      advertised a full season of drama after the production
      of the *Historical Register*; the Act, of course, resulted
      in the cancellation of the advertised season.

332. ————. "Proposals for a New London Theatre in 1737."
      Notes and Queries, 182 (1942), 286-87.

      Discusses a 1737 proposal, apparently by Fielding, to
      construct a new playhouse for his own company of
      comedians. Also see Avery and Deupree, item 333, and
      de Castro, "Proposals," item 341.

333. ————, and Mildred Avery Deupree. "The New Theatre
      in the Haymarket, 1734 and 1737." *Notes and Queries*,
      171 (1936), 41-42.

      Adds several plays and performances to the lists given
      in Allardyce Nicoll's *A History of the Early Eighteenth
      Century Drama*, item 363. Also see Scouten and Hughes,
      item 373, and de Castro, "Proposals," item 341.

334. Bateson, F.W. "Henry Fielding," in his *English Comic
      Drama, 1700-1750*. New York and Oxford: Clarendon
      Press, 1929. Pp. 115-43. Reprinted New York: Russell
      and Russell, 1963.

      Surveys Fielding's plays and concludes that his skills as
      a dramatist are limited. His best plays are his bur-
      lesques and he is generally more successful in his real-
      istic scenes of contemporary life. Bateson views the
      novels as derived from Fielding's comedies of manners.
      See Goggin, "Development of Techniques," item 344, for
      an opposing view.

335. Battestin, Martin C. "Fielding and 'Master Punch' in
      Panton Street." *Philological Quarterly*, 45 (1966),
      191-208.

      Although Fielding's love of puppet-shows and his use
      of them in *The Author's Farce* and *Tom Jones* is well
      known, his biographers have missed the fact that in
      March 1748, Fielding opened his own puppet theater in
      Panton Street, hiding behind the pseudonym, Madame de
      la Nash. He used his puppet-shows for satiric purposes,
      primarily to attack the mimic and playwright, Samuel
      Foote, and as a result was attacked as a "puppeteer-
      showman" by his many enemies. The theater closed in
      June 1748.

336. Bell, Michael. "A Note on Drama and the Novel: Field-
      ing's Contribution." *Novel*, 3 (1970), 119-28.

      Fielding transplants comic ritual from the drama to the
      novel in such scenes as the final reconciliation be-
      tween Tom and Sophia in *Tom Jones*. The scene's conven-
      tional nature forces the reader to view it as a ritual,
      but because Sophia fully understands the artificiality
      of the situation and uses it to manipulate Tom, it be-
      comes a subtle depiction of her real psychological state.

337. Bernbaum, Ernest. *The Drama of Sensibility*. Gloucester,
      Mass.: P. Smith, 1958. Originally published Boston:
      Ginn and Co., 1915.

      Refers to Fielding occasionally in tracing the develop-
      ment of sentimental drama and remarks that Fielding's
      reluctance to show deep emotion led him to ridicule
      emotional situations that sentimentalists like Lillo
      treated seriously.

338. Boas, Frederick. "Henry Fielding," in his *An Introduction to Eighteenth-Century Drama, 1700-1780*. Oxford: The Clarendon Press, 1953. Pp. 220-38.

Surveys Fielding's plays, mostly through plot summary rather than analysis, and concludes that his dramatic apprenticeship gave edge to the literary tools he employed in *Joseph Andrews*.

*   Brown, Jack Richard. "From Aaron Hill to Henry Fielding?" (See item 106.)

*   Child, Harold H. "Fielding and Smollett." (See item 110.)

*   Churchill, R.C. "Fielding: To the Novel from the Drama." (See item 111.)

339. Clinton-Baddeley, V.C. "Henry Fielding," in *The Burlesque Tradition in the English Theatre After 1660*. London: Methuen and New York: Barnes and Noble, 1952. Pp. 51-65.

Covers all of Fielding's burlesques but sees three of them as especially important in the history of burlesque: *Tom Thumb* successfully combines elements from Buckingham, Swift, Pope, and Gay in one of the most varied comic plays of the century; *The Covent-Garden Tragedy* is vulgar but a masterpiece of sustained burlesque; and *Pasquin* adds political satire to the rehearsal play, thus expanding the boundaries of burlesque.

340. Crean, P.J. "The Stage Licensing Act of 1737." *Modern Philology*, 35 (1938), 239-55.

Traces the attempts to establish a licensing act from 1729 to 1737. Fielding's contribution to the 1737 act was his attack on Walpole in *The Historical Register*, although the final straw for the government was the anonymous *Vision of the Golden Rump*.

341. de Castro, J. Paul. "Proposals for a New Theatre in 1737." *Notes and Queries*, 182 (1942), 346.

Responds to Avery, item 332, arguing that in 1737 Fielding could not have been in a financial position to acquire an interest in a newly constructed theater as he was under an existing lease for the Little Theatre in Haymarket at the time. Also see Avery and Deupree, item 333.

*   Deupree, Mildred Avery, and Emmett L. Avery. "The New
        Theatre in the Haymarket, 1734 and 1737." *Notes and
        Queries*, 171 (1936), 41-42.

        See under Emmett L. Avery, item 333.

342.   Durant, Jack D. "The 'Art of Thriving' in Fielding's
        Comedies," in *A Provision of Human Nature: Essays on
        Fielding and Others in Honor of Miriam Austin Locke,*
        ed. Donald Kay. University: University of Alabama Press,
        1977. Pp. 25-35.

        The organizing principle for Fielding's eight "regular"
        comedies (as opposed to his farces and burlesques) is
        "the art of thriving," defined as "the capacity of each
        individual to sacrifice the interests of others to his
        own advantage." Those who practice the art of thriving
        must disguise their true natures and involve themselves
        in intrigues, stratagems, masquerades, and double-
        dealings of all sorts; because of such people, even
        social institutions become corrupt. The comedies warn
        the "honest undesigning man" to be constantly on his
        guard against the hypocrite.

*   Elton, Oliver. "Fielding and Smollett." (See item 175.)

343.   Gagey, Edmond M. *Ballad Opera*. New York: Benjamin Blom,
        1965. Originally published New York: Columbia University
        Press, 1937.

        Discusses the various types of ballad operas current in
        the eighteenth century and places Fielding's work in
        this larger context. Fielding's major contribution to
        the ballad opera form is his use of it for satiric and
        burlesque purposes.

344.   Goggin, L.P. "Development of Techniques in Fielding's
        Comedies." *Publications of the Modern Language Associa-
        tion of America*, 67 (1952), 769-81.

        A chronological survey of Fielding's comic dramas re-
        veals that they steadily improved as the playwright
        matured. Fielding's characterization becomes more and
        more realistic in both dialogue and motivation; he
        rapidly learned to integrate all elements, especially
        the sub-plots, of his plays; and he becomes more vivid
        as he matures. His comedies, not his farces, are his
        most important plays, and the novels develop from them.
        See Bateson, item 334.

*   Goldgar, Bertrand A. "Fielding's Early Plays," in his
       Walpole and the Wits, pp. 98-115. (See item 190.)

345.   Hammond, Geraldine E. "Evidence of the Dramatist's Tech-
       nique in Henry Fielding's Novels." *Bulletin of the
       University of Wichita*, 16 (1941), 3-27.

       Lists the many dramatic devices Fielding uses in his
       fiction. His people are characterized primarily through
       their speech and he uses dialogue to move the action.
       He suggests "business" through stage directions. His
       settings are only sketched in. Finally, he adapts many
       plot devices from the stage.

346.   Hassall, Anthony J. "The Authorial Dimension in the
       Plays of Henry Fielding." *Komos*, 1 (1967), 4-18.

       In his fiction, Fielding comments on the action as if
       he were a part of the novel. He employs the same tech-
       nique in at least ten of his plays, especially the re-
       hearsal plays. In these dramas, he appears to be speak-
       ing through a character; he often juxtaposes reality
       with the artifice of the play; and he introduces himself
       or other real people into the action. The result of his
       method is to provide his plays with an added dimension
       for satire.

347.   —————. "Fielding's Puppet Image." *Philological Quar-
       terly*, 53 (1974), 71-83.

       The puppet master is used in both the plays and the
       novels as an image of the author.

348.   Hughes, Leo. *A Century of English Farce*. Princeton,
       N.J.: Princeton University Press, 1956.

       Seeks to distinguish "farce" from "burlesque"; frequent
       references to Fielding include the argument that his
       burlesques are not farces (especially see pp. 11-12,
       123-25).

*   —————, and A.H. Scouten. "The New Theatre in the Hay-
       market, 1734 and 1737." *Notes and Queries*, 186 (1944),
       52-53.

       See annotation under Scouten, item 373.

349.   Hunter, J. Paul. "Fielding's Reflexive Plays and the
       Rhetoric of Discovery." *Studies in the Literary Imagi-
       nation*, 5 (1972), 65-100.

Stresses Fielding's plays within plays and discusses
the ways in which they demonstrate a concern with real
identities and with artistic consciousness. These plays
also show that Fielding is almost as concerned with the
audience's consciousness as he is with the artist's.
(This material is reprinted in his *Occasional Form*, item
209.)

*   Irwin, W.R. "Satire and Comedy in the Works of Henry
         Fielding." (See item 213.)

350.   Kern, Jean B. *Dramatic Satire in the Age of Walpole,
         1720-1750*. Ames: The Iowa State University Press, 1976.

         Contains dozens of scattered remarks on Fielding's plays
         but does not generalize about his work. Kern obviously
         sees Fielding as one of the age's most effective satiric
         dramatists.

351.   ————. "Fielding's Dramatic Satire." *Philological
         Quarterly*, 54 (1975), 239-57.

         In the years 1730-37, Fielding moved through a variety
         of dramatic forms--rehearsal plays, parodies, political
         allegories, and ballad operas--to attack literary
         figures such as Pope, Cibber, and Rich and political
         leaders such as Walpole. Because there was no critical
         theory about dramatic satire, Fielding continually ex-
         perimented with the form of his plays; it is also likely
         that he experimented as much as he did in order to avoid
         political reprisals from Walpole's ministry. He was
         always looking for ways to cover his satiric tracks in
         order to prevent the cutting off of his livelihood.
         All of Fielding's comedies are written with more vitality
         than intensity and all fall into Northrup Frye's category
         of satire of the "low norm." Fielding's plays were the
         most successful attempts to adapt satire to the stage in
         the first half of the eighteenth century.

352.   Knapp, Mary E. *Prologues and Epilogues of the Eighteenth
         Century*. New Haven: Yale University Press, 1961.

         Many of Fielding's prologues and epilogues, for both his
         own plays and the plays of others, are used for satiric
         purposes. In them he frequently attacks, through lively
         and coarse humor, the fawning and self-serving nature of
         such devices. He also uses them to criticize the opera
         and pantomime; the taste of an audience which supported
         such entertainments; poor acting; and bad writing.

353. Largmann, Malcolm G. "Stage References as Satiric Weapon: Sir Robert Walpole as Victim." *Restoration and 18th Century Theatre Research*, 9 (1970), 35-43.

     Makes several references to Fielding's satiric portraits of Walpole as a criminal, clown, actor, and puppeteer.

354. Levine, George R. "Henry Fielding's 'Defense' of the Stage Licensing Act." *English Language Notes*, 2 (1965) 193-96.

     In the *Champion* (December 10, 1739/40), Fielding adopts the mask of a bourgeois merchant to attack ironically the Licensing Act. He exposes both the Walpole government and the London merchants by hypocritically defending the Act for moral and political reasons.

355. Lewis, P.E. "Three Notes on Fielding's Plays." *Notes and Queries*, n.s. 21 (1974), 253-55.

     Comments briefly on (1) the influence of *The British Stage* (1724) on Fielding's *The Author's Farce*, *Tom Thumb*, and *Tumble-Down Dick*; (2) the reference in *Pasquin* to "Merlin's Cave," which is intended to mock a spectacular play by William Giffard and a pantomime by Edward Phillips; (3) the figure of Apollo in *The Historical Register for the Year 1736* who is identified as Charles Fleetwood rather than Theophilus Cibber. On the latter issue, see Appleton, item 437.

356. Loftis, John. *Comedy and Society from Congreve to Fielding*. Stanford Studies in Language and Literature, 19. Stanford, Calif.: Stanford University Press, 1959.

     Analyzes the effects of social changes, particularly economic changes, on early eighteenth-century comic drama. Fielding's plays epitomize the dramatic activity in England from 1728 to 1737. He uses all the popular modes--comedy, burlesque, ballad operas, and farces-- and in all his plays he criticizes the depravity of London life and society's preoccupation with money. This emphasis distinguishes his plays from Restoration comedy.

     Reviews: Emmett Avery, *Philological Quarterly*, 19 (1960), 299-301; Benjamin Boyce, *South Atlantic Quarterly*, 59 (1960), 458-59; Arthur M. Eastman, *Critical Quarterly*, 3 (1961), 88-89; John C. Hodges, *Modern Philology*, 58 (1960), 134-35; Leo Hughes, *Modern Language Notes*, 76 (1961), 867-69; Claude E. Jones, *Modern Language Quarterly*, 21 (1960), 270-71; Clifford Leech, *Modern Language*

Review, 56 (1961), 104–05; Sybil Rosenfeld, *Theatre Notebook*, 14 (1960), 135–36; Arthur Sherbo, *Journal of English and Germanic Philology*, 59 (1960), 578–81; John C. Stephens, *Emory University Quarterly*, 16 (1960), 121; W.B.F., *Books Abroad*, 34 (1960), 26–27; Aubrey Williams, *Yale Review*, 49 (1960), 451–57.

357.   ————. "The Limits of Historical Veracity in Neo-classical Drama," in *England in the Restoration and Early Eighteenth Century: Essays in Culture and Society*, ed. H.T. Swedenberg, Jr. Berkeley and Los Angeles: University of California Press, 1972. Pp. 27–50.

In his later five-act comedies, Fielding broke with Restoration tradition by using highly individualized central characters instead of representative types. In *The Modern Husband* (1731), for example, he abandoned the neoclassical conception of decorum in characterization and introduced a serious analysis of contemporary life; these two aspects of his playwrighting technique approximate Shaw's methods over a century and a half later.

358.   ————. *The Politics of Drama in Augustan England*. Oxford: The Clarendon Press, 1963.

Traces the "progressive alienation" of early eighteenth-century English drama from the government, with frequent references to Fielding, including an entire chapter, "Fielding and the Stage Licensing Act of 1737" (pp. 128–53). Fielding's plays were more subtle and vigorous than those of his contemporaries and they were much more effective in castigating Walpole. Although it was Fielding's satires against the government that caused Walpole to wish to censor the drama, the pretext used by the Prime Minister for the Licensing Act was a lewd anonymous play, *The Vision of the Golden Rump*, which directly alluded to both Walpole and the King. See Goldgar, *Walpole and the Wits*, item 190.

359.   MacMillan, Dougald. *Catalogue of the Larpent Plays in the Huntington Library*. San Marino, Calif.: Huntington Library, 1939.

Lists original dramatic manuscripts at the Huntington, including some by Fielding.

*   Moore, Robert E. "Hogarth and Fielding Invade the Theater," in his *Hogarth's Literary Relationships*, pp. 77–106. (See item 248.)

360. Morrissey, L.J. "Henry Fielding and the Ballad Opera." *Eighteenth Century Studies*, 4 (1971), 386-402.

Identifies three main influences on Fielding's selection of music for his ballad operas: (1) the tastes of theater managers and of John Watts, who published most ballad operas with musical scores; (2) the tastes of his public; and (3) the tastes of his friend, James Ralph. Musicians, directors, and composers carried very little influence because Fielding, like most of his contemporaries, borrowed music from already published ballad operas.

361. Moss, Harold Gene. "'Silvia, My Dearest': A Fielding Ballad-Opera Tune and a Biographical Puzzle." *South Atlantic Bulletin*, 38 (1973), 66-71.

Because Fielding received copies of Vol. VI of Watts's *Musical Miscellany* at least seven months before its publication, he and Watts must have had a relationship much closer than Fielding's biographers have observed.

361a. N., A.E. "Revivals of Fielding's Plays." *Notes and Queries*, 179 (1940), 423.

Asks for information on revivals of Fielding's plays. See the following replies, all under the above title: Bayley, item 392; de Castro, items 394 and 395; Jaggard, item 397; and Rolleston, item 372.

362. Nicholson, W. *The Struggle for a Free Stage in London*. New York: Benjamin Blom, 1966. Originally published New York, 1906.

Contrary to popular belief, Fielding was not the cause of the Licensing Act of 1737. The Act was passed for several reasons: the multitude of theaters resulted in a large number of bad plays being presented; widespread political satire had stung the government; and the holders of patents resented the free theaters because the patented theaters were losing money to them. Also see Goldgar, *Walpole and the Wits*, item 190, and Loftis, *The Politics of Drama*, item 358.

363. Nicoll, Allardyce. *A History of Early Eighteenth Century Drama, 1700-1750*. Cambridge: The University Press, 1925. Incorporated into *A History of English Drama, 1660-1900* as Volume II (1952). Cambridge: The University Press, 1952-59.

Makes many scattered remarks on Fielding's plays, mostly of a technical nature, and lists their various performance dates (pp. 323-29).

364.   Price, Lawrence M. "The Works of Fielding on the German
        Stage, 1762-1801." *Journal of English and Germanic
        Philology*, 41 (1942), 257-78.

        Points out that *The Wedding Day* and *The Jealous Wife*
        (Colman's dramatic version of *Tom Jones*) were trans-
        lated and produced on the German stage in the eighteenth
        century. However, adaptations of *Tom Jones*, performed
        several times between 1767 and 1801, were the most
        popular of Fielding's works in Germany.

365.   Raushenbush, Esther M. "Charles Macklin's Lost Play
        about Henry Fielding." *Modern Language Notes*, 51
        (1936), 505-14.

        Discovers a manuscript of Macklin's *The Covent-Garden
        Theatre, or Pasquin Turn'd Drawcansir*, long thought
        lost, which reveals that the play is not a satire
        on Fielding. The plotless play praises Pasquin as a
        just censor of the age.

*   Rawson, C.J. "Some Considerations on Authorial Intrusion
        and Dialogue in Fielding's Novels and Plays." (See
        item 559.)

366.   Regan, Charles Lionel. "Fielding's Stage Career: Repe-
        tition of an Error." *American Notes and Queries*, 6
        (1968), 99-100.

        An obscure actor named Timothy Fielding has often been
        mistaken for Henry Fielding, thus giving rise to a myth
        about Henry Fielding, actor. Although Frederick La-
        treille corrected the error some ninety years ago, it
        persists in some quarters.

367.   Roberts, Edgar V. "Eighteenth-Century Ballad Opera:
        The Contribution of Henry Fielding." *Drama Survey*, 1
        (1961), 77-85.

        The form of the ballad opera was established by Gay's
        Beggar's Opera, but Fielding was the most prolific
        writer of such plays. Characteristic of his eleven
        ballad operas is his use of balance and antithesis,
        dialect, and short, witty speeches. He is unique in
        using the form for both burlesque and satire. Fielding
        is the most important playwright of the 1730's and one
        of the best of his century.

368.   ————. "Henry Fielding and Richard Leveridge: Author-
        ship of 'The Roast Beef of Old England.'" *Huntington
        Library Quarterly*, 27 (1964), 175-81.

        Clarifies the confusing situation surrounding the author-

ship of the song, "The Roast Beef of Old England,"
which Fielding used in his ballad operas *The Grub-Street
Opera* (1731) and *Don Quixote in England* (1734) but
which usually is attributed to Richard Leveridge. It
seems clear that Fielding wrote the first two stanzas
of the song and then Leveridge added five stanzas and
wrote new music for it.

369. ————. "Mr. Seedo's London Career and His Work with
Henry Fielding." *Philological Quarterly*, 45 (1966),
179-90.

The German composer and conductor, Seedo, worked closely
with Fielding on several productions, particularly *The
Lottery*, *The Author's Farce*, and *The Grub-Street Opera*.

370. ————. "The Songs and Tunes in Henry Fielding's Ballad
Operas," in *Essays in the Eighteenth-Century English
Stage*, eds. Kenneth Richards and Peter Thomson. London:
Methuen, 1972. Pp. 29-49.

Provides technical background material for Fielding's
eleven ballad operas, discussing his singing actors,
orchestras, musical preferences, and use of the ballad
tradition. He wrote 206 songs for his ballad operas,
many of them designed to ironically contrast with the
play's subject matter.

371. Roberts, W. "Henry Fielding in French." *National
Review*, 79 (1922), 723-28.

The compilers were not able to read this item prior to
the publication of this bibliography.

*   Rogers, Pat. *Grub Street*. (See item 279.)

372. Rolleston, J.D. "Revivals of Fielding's Plays." *Notes
and Queries*, 180 (1941), 70.

Responds to A.E.N.'s request for information (item 361a)
by listing several dramatized versions of *Tom Jones* in
English, French, and German. Other dramatic versions
of the novel are listed by Dobson, *Henry Fielding*,
item 163.

*   Roy, G. Ross. "French Stage Adaptations of *Tom Jones*."
(See item 946.)

373. Scouten, A.H., and Leo Hughes. "The New Theatre in the
Haymarket, 1734 and 1737." *Notes and Queries*, 186
(1944), 52-53.

Offers corrections to Avery's list of entries designed

to supplement Nicoll's listing of theatrical performances
in 1734 and 1737. See Avery, items 332 and 333.

374. Sellery, J'nan. "Language and Moral Intelligence in the
Enlightenment: Fielding's Plays and Pope's *Dunciad*."
Enlightenment Essays, 1 (1970), 17-26; 108-19.

The play-within-a-play structure so often employed by
Fielding provides an opportunity for him to comment on
the declining standards of taste in his audience. Im-
perceptive viewers will merely be entertained by the
play itself, while perceptive viewers will recognize
his critical comments and react to them. Fielding's
ultimate goal is to point out the stupidity and disorder
of the age and to plead for rationality.

375. Sherburn, George. "*The Dunciad*, Book IV." *Texas
Studies in English*, 24 (1944), 174-90.

The structural pattern of the last *Dunciad*, as well as
the triumph of Dullness, had been made familiar to the
fashionable world by Fielding's popular farces. For
example, in *The Author's Farce*, the scene in which Queen
Nonsense is put to sleep by Sir Farcical Comic's song--
itself a satiric attack on Cibber--parallels the sopo-
rific reading contest in the *Dunciad*, and in *Pasquin*,
Queen Ignorance establishes her rule--much like Pope's
Dullness--with "the plaudits of the Royal Society, Grub-
Street, the learned professions, and the opera."

*   ————, and Donald F. Bond. *The Restoration and
Eighteenth Century (1660-1789)*. (See item 291.)

376. Sokoljanskij, Mark G. "Genre Evolution in Fielding's
Dramaturgy." *Zeitschrift für Anglistik und Amerikanistik*
20 (1972), 280-95.

Although Fielding began his dramatic career under the
influence of Congreve and Vanbrugh, he at once put his
own stamp on his work by deriding the London beaux and
adding political commentary to his plays. As he pro-
gressed in his dramatic writings, he tried to integrate
burlesque, parody, farce, and satire in his plays. At
the end of his dramatic career, he had achieved the integration of these various elements as well as allegory
to successfully and unambiguously juxtapose the theatrical and political worlds in a didactic but highly entertaining manner.

377. Tucker, Joseph E. "The Eighteenth-Century English Translations of Molière." *Modern Language Quarterly*, 3 (1942), 83-103.

     The Select Comedies of Mr. de Moliere, published in July 1732, was translated by Henry Baker and James Miller and not, as thought by Cross (item 126), by Fielding. Stylistic differences between Fielding's adaptations of Molière and the translations make it improbable that Fielding contributed to the *Select Comedies*. See Goggin, "Fielding and *The Select Comedies*," item 416.

378. Woods, Charles B. "Captain B_ _ _ _'s Play." *Harvard Studies and Notes in Philology and Literature*, 15 (1933), 243-55.

     Offers contemporary evidence that Hervey and Prince Frederick actually wrote *The Modish Couple* (1732), for which Fielding wrote an epilogue and which is usually attributed to Charles Boden. The play was hissed off the stage after three performances but it was damned not for artistic, but for political reasons.

379. Wright, Kenneth D. "Henry Fielding and the Theatres Act of 1737." *Quarterly Journal of Speech*, 50 (1964), 252-58.

     Briefly traces the history of theatrical censorship in England and discusses the events that led to the Theatres Act of 1737. Although many playwrights, including John Gay and the anonymous author of *The Vision of the Golden Rump*, had antagonized Walpole's ministry, it was Fielding's consistent and popular attacks on the government which served as a catalyst for the act's passage. Also see Goldgar, *Walpole and the Wits*, item 190, and Loftis, *The Politics of Drama*, item 358.

B. *The Temple Beau* (1730)

380. Rogers, Winifred H. "The Significance of Fielding's *Temple Beau*." *Publications of the Modern Language Association of America*, 55 (1940), 440-44.

     Fielding's concern with ethics is reflected in his characterizations of the pedants in *The Temple Beau*. His

definition of pedantry is derived from Addison (*Spectator*, 105), who sees a pedant as one who has lost his
balance, creating an ethical as well as a social problem.

C. *The Author's Farce* (1730)

381.   Baker, Sheridan. "Political Allusion in Fielding's
        Author's Farce, *Mock Doctor*, and *Tumble-Down Dick*."
        *Publications of the Modern Language Association of
        America*, 77 (1962), 221-31.

        A number of subtle political allusions in Fielding's
        later plays have been overlooked. These allusions
        indicate that Fielding was not a political zealot and
        that political references in his plays were expedient
        and designed to appeal to popular taste. He did not
        detest Walpole and, in fact, felt that most men have
        their prices. Also see Battestin, "Fielding's Changing
        Politics," item 638; Coley, "Henry Fielding and the Two
        Walpoles," item 116; Goldgar, *Walpole and the Wits*,
        item 190; and Grundy, "New Verse," item 1060.

382.   Item deleted.

383.   Folkenflik, Robert. "*The Author's Farce* and *Othello*."
        Notes and Queries, n.s. 23 (1976), 163-64.

        Finds "an early example of Fielding's allusive art" in
        The Author's Farce, in which frequent allusions to
        Othello are used to ridicule Italian Opera.

384.   Hughes, Helen Sard. "Fielding's Indebtedness to James
        Ralph." *Modern Philology*, 20 (1922-23), 19-34.

        Both *The Author's Farce* and *Tom Thumb* show a good deal
        of James Ralph's influence. The use of the puppet
        show, along with other details, shows Ralph's influence
        on *The Author's Farce*. The idea for *Tom Thumb*, as well
        as that for many specific scenes in the play, may have
        come to Fielding from Ralph's *The Touchstone*.

*   Hughes, Leo. *A Century of English Farce*. (See item
        348.)

385. Kinder, Marsha. "The Improved Author's Farce: An
      Analysis of the 1734 Revisions." *Costerus*, 6 (1972),
      35-43.

      Analyzes the 1734 revisions of *The Author's Farce*,
      which show "an increase in the commenting author's
      reliability, an expansion of the range of the satire,
      and a more controlled use of verbal irony." Fielding
      revised Luckless's relationship with Harriot and Mrs.
      Moneywood, and made significant changes in the characters
      of those two females. He also made an attempt to justify
      the incoherence of the "inner" play.

*   Lewis, P.E. "Three Notes on Fielding's Plays." (See
      item 355.)

*   Roberts, Edgar V. "Mr. Seedo's London Career and His
      Work With Henry Fielding." (See item 369.)

*   Rogers, Pat. *Grub Street*. (See item 279.)

386. Rudolph, Valerie C. "People and Puppets: Fielding's
      Burlesque of the 'Recognition Scene' in *The Author's
      Farce*." *Papers on Language and Literature*, 11 (1975),
      31-38.

      Sees Fielding as a better dramatic craftsman than he is
      generally thought to be. His skill is demonstrated by
      the "recognition scene" in *The Author's Farce* in which
      he adroitly blends the real and the fantastic in order
      to satirically comment on the perceptiveness of his
      audience, the Puritan view of the theater, and the
      chaos of aesthetic values.

387. Speaight, George. *The History of the English Puppet
      Theatre*. London: Harrap and New York: De Graff, 1955.

      Alludes to Fielding several times, noting his use of
      puppet shows in *The Author's Farce* and *Tom Jones*.
      Speaight, of course, did not know of Battestin's later
      discovery that Fielding had his own puppet theater (see
      item 335).

      Reviews: David Clay Jenkins, *Philological Quarterly*,
      35 (1956), 271-72; Waldo S. Lanchester, *Theatre Note-
      book*, 10 (1956), 30-31; *Times Literary Supplement* (29
      July 1956), p. 424; H. Sparnay, *Neophilologus*, 38 (1956),

235-36; Th. C. van Stockum, *English Studies*, 35 (1956), 132-34; G. Waterhouse, *Comparative Literature*, 6 (1956), 82-84; Richard F. Wilkie, *Modern Language Quarterly*, 15 (1956), 86-87.

*   Sherburn, George. "*The Dunciad*, Book IV." (See item 375.)

388.   Smith, Dane. *Plays About the Theatre in England from The Rehearsal in 1671 to the Licensing Act in 1737.* London: Oxford University Press, 1936.

Discusses (pp. 220-31) Fielding's use of the play-within-a-play device in *The Historical Register*, *The Author's Farce*, and *Pasquin*, noting that Fielding uses it for satiric rather than burlesque purposes.

389.   Woods, Charles B. "Cibber in Fielding's *Author's Farce*: Three Notes." *Philological Quarterly*, 44 (1965), 145-51.

Discusses the origin of the name "Keyber" as applied to Colley Cibber and equates Marplay in the *Author's Farce* with Cibber. In the latter, Sir Farcical Comick in Act III is identified with Cibber. Also see Tucker, item 632.

390.   ————. "Introduction" to *The Author's Farce* by Henry Fielding. Lincoln: University of Nebraska Press, 1966. Pp. xi-xix.

Covers the various editions and impressions of the play and critically evaluates Fielding as a dramatist, emphasizing the importance of *The Author's Farce* in his dramatic career. Many of the techniques he employed in the latter were developed in later plays (the puppet show, for instance, was used for satiric purposes in *Pasquin* and *The Historical Register*). The play was his first triumph on the stage, running for forty-one performances in 1730.

391.   ————. "Theobald and Fielding's Don Tragedio." *English Language Notes*, 2 (1965), 266-71.

Finds several similarities between lines in Theobald's plays and lines spoken by Don Tragedio in *The Author's Farce*, suggesting that the Don is a parody of Theobald.

D. *Tom Thumb* (1730) /
The Tragedy of Tragedies (1731)

*   Atkins, J.W.H. "Critical Cross Currents." (See item 81.)

*   Banerji, H.K. *Henry Fielding: Playwright, Journalist, and Master of the Art of Fiction, His Life and His Works*. (See item 86.)

392. Bayley, A.R. "Revivals of Fielding's Plays." *Notes and Queries*, 180 (1941), 15.

Responds to a request by A.E.N., item 361a, for information on revivals of Fielding's plays and notes that the Malvern Festival revived *Tom Thumb* in 1907. Other responses are listed under the A.E.N. request.

393. Chase, Lewis Nathaniel. *The English Heroic Play*. New York: Macmillan, 1965.

Notes specific passages from heroic plays that Fielding's *Tom Thumb* and *The Tragedy of Tragedies* mock.

*   Clinton-Baddeley, V.C. "Henry Fielding." (See item 339.)

394. de Castro, J. Paul. "Revivals of Fielding's Plays." *Notes and Queries*, 179 (1940), 461.

Answers A.E.N.'s request, item 361a, for information on revivals of Fielding's plays by listing revivals of *The Letter Writers*, *The Lottery*, and *Tom Thumb*. Other responses are listed under A.E.N.'s request.

395. ————. "Revivals of Fielding's Plays." *Notes and Queries*, 180 (1941), 35.

Notes, in response to A.E.N.'s request for information, item 361a, that *Tom Thumb* was acted at the Malvern Festival in 1932. Other responses are listed under A.E.N.'s request.

396. Hillhouse, James T. "Introduction" to *The Tragedy of Tragedies, or The Life and Death of Tom Thumb the Great* by Henry Fielding. New Haven: Yale University Press, 1918. Pp. 1-39.

Divides his discussion into three parts: composition, production, and burlesque. The models for the play were

primarily *The Rehearsal* and *The Dunciad*. Even though
many critics sneered at it when it was produced, the public flocked to see it and it ran at least thirty-three
nights. Part of the fun for the audience was its recognition of the forty-two plays that Fielding burlesqued.

*   Hughes, Helen Sard. "Fielding's Indebtedness to James
       Ralph." (See item 384.)

*   Hunter, J. Paul. *Occasional Form: Henry Fielding and
       the Chains of Circumstance*. (See item 209.)

397.   Jaggard, William. "Revivals of Fielding's Plays."
       Notes and Queries, 180 (1941), 15.

Does not really provide information about *revivals* of
plays, but notes that *Tom Jones* was adapted as an opera
in 1769 and produced again in 1907 and that *Tom Thumb*
was rewritten as a "burletta" by Kane O'Hara and acted
in 1780.

*   Lewis, P.E. "Three Notes on Fielding's Plays." (See
       item 355.)

398.   Macey, Samuel L. "Fielding's *Tom Thumb* as Heir to Buck-
       ingham's *Rehearsal*." *Texas Studies in Literature and
       Language*, 10 (1968), 405-14.

Views *Tom Thumb* as heir to *The Rehearsal* because like
its predecessor it directly satirizes contemporary
theater. It mocks at least fifteen heroic plays.

399.   Morrissey, L.J. "Fielding's First Political Satire."
       Anglia Zeitschrift für Englische Philologie, 90 (1972),
       325-48.

Discusses the satiric differences between *Tom Thumb* and
its revised version, *The Tragedy of Tragedies*. The
earlier work contains both general burlesque and political satire; the later version eliminates part of the
general satire and sharpens the political commentary so
that its remarks on Walpole's administration are unmis-
takably clear.

400.   ————. "Introduction" to *"Tom Thumb and "The Tragedy
       of Tragedies"* by Henry Fielding. Berkeley and Los
       Angeles: University of California Press and Edinburgh:
       Oliver and Boyd, 1970. Pp. 1-9.

Surveys Fielding's dramatic output and concludes that
his best plays are "*mélanges*," plotless plays in which

songs, dances, verbal parodies, vignettes, and satiric
thrusts at politicians, theater managers, and physicians
are all jumbled together. *Tom Thumb* is such a play and
was Fielding's first great success, running for nearly
forty nights consecutively in the late spring of 1730.
The revised version, retitled *The Tragedy of Tragedies*,
had almost as successful a run a year later. Even though
its topical satire has lost its point, the play con-
tinues to be of interest because of its use of "physical
and verbal bathos" and because its main target, theatrical pretension, is still with us.

401. Prideaux, W.F. "Tom Thumb's First Appearance in London."
Notes and Queries, Tenth Series, 6 (1906), 76.

Listed in some bibliographies as a reference to Fielding's play, *Tom Thumb*, this note actually refers to P.T.
Barnum's famous midget, General Tom Thumb.

402. R., E. "An Advertisement of Fielding's." *Notes and
Queries*, 159 (1930), 315.

Prints a disclaimer from the Monday, November 29, 1730,
Daily Journal in which Fielding denies that he wrote or
even saw a new act, "The Battle of the Poets," introduced anonymously into a performance of *Tom Thumb*.

403. Willson, Robert F. "*The Tragedy of Tragedies* as Literary
Hoax: Fielding's Ironic Style," in his *"Their Form Con-
founded": Studies in the Burlesque Play from Udall to
Sheridan*. The Hague: Mouton, 1975. Pp. 111-37.

Emphasizes Scriblerus's "Preface" and the notes to *The
Tragedy* in order to illustrate Fielding's use of irony
in attacking bad writing and plotting, crude audiences,
poor critics, and unskilled actors. Because the notes
are so important in the satire, the play must be read
as well as seen for full comic impact.

E. *The Coffee-House Politician* (1730) /
Rape Upon Rape (1730)

404. Goldgar, Bertrand A. "The Politics of Fielding's *Coffee-
House Politician*." *Philological Quarterly*, 49 (1970),
424-29.

Finds the original title of the *Coffee-House Politician*--
Rape Upon Rape--highly significant in that it undoubtedly

refers to the famous Charteris rape case, in which
Francis Charteris was convicted of the rape of his
maid but quickly pardoned by the king because of Prime
Minister Walpole's intervention. Fielding uses this
event as a metaphor for injustice and political corruption in the Walpole administration.

405. Masengill, Jeanne Addison. "Variant Forms of Fielding's
      Coffee-House Politician." *Studies in Bibliography*, 5
      (1952), 178-83.

      Only one true edition of *The Coffee-House Politician*
      exists, but it appeared in three issues and the third
      issue exists in two states. The first issue is entitled
      Rape upon Rape: or, the Justice Caught in His Own Trap.

406. Mead, Herman R. "Variant Issues of *The Coffee-House
      Politician* (1730)." *Papers of the Bibliographical
      Society of America*, 35 (1941), 69.

      Notes two issues of *The Coffee-House Politician*, the
      Kemble-Devonshire copy and the Hoe copy. Also see
      Masengill, item 405.

F. *The Welsh Opera* (1731)

407. Brown, Jack Richard. "Henry Fielding's *Grub-Street
      Opera*." *Modern Language Quarterly*, 16 (1955), 32-41.

      Although the *Grub-Street Opera* was never performed, the
      afterpiece on which it was based, *The Welsh Opera*,
      played at least ten times. A study of the two versions
      shows that Fielding softened his satire in moving from
      the original to the *Grub-Street Opera*, which contains
      little political commentary.

408. Moss, Harold Gene. "Satire and Travesty in Fielding's
      The Grub-Street Opera." *Theatre Survey*, 15 (1974),
      38-50.

      Believes that Fielding consciously emphasizes his imita-
      tions of other playwrights and his use of travesty in
      the *Grub-Street Opera* in order to protect himself from
      libel suits for his satire on the Royal Family.

*   Roberts, Edgar V. "Henry Fielding and Richard Leveridge:
       Authorship of 'The Roast Beef of Old England.'" (See
       item 368.)

409.   ————. "Introduction" to *The Grub-Street Opera* by
Henry Fielding. Lincoln: University of Nebraska Press,
1968. Pp. xi-xxv.

Evaluates this play as "the most audacious, ambitious,
and tuneful" of Fielding's nine ballad operas and discusses its performance history. Its political satire
also is discussed and an outline presented which shows
the real person that each principal character in the
drama was designed to portray.

*   ————. "Mr. Seedo's London Career and His Work With
Henry Fielding." (See item 369.)

G. *The Letter Writers* (1731)

*   de Castro, J. Paul. "Revivals of Fielding's Plays."
(See item 394.)

H. *The Lottery* (1732)

*   de Castro, J. Paul. "Revivals of Fielding's Plays."
(See item 394.)

410.   Moss, Harold G. "A Note on Fielding's Selection of
Handel's 'Si Cari' for *The Lottery*." *Notes and Queries*,
n.s. 19 (1972), 225-26.

"Si Cari" from Handel's *Admetus* was used in the *Grub-
Street Opera* (1731); after that ballad opera was suppressed by the government, Fielding used the song again
in *The Lottery* (1732) in an attempt to embarrass the
royal family who had supported a revival of *Admetus*.

411.   Roberts, Edgar V. "Fielding's Ballad Opera *The Lottery*
(1732) and the English State Lottery of 1731." *Huntington Library Quarterly*, 27 (1963), 39-52.

Provides details on the 1731 lottery as background for
a study of Fielding's third ballad opera, which deserves
attention because it was the first Fielding play to be
published with the music "prefixed to each song," it was
his first play that used original music, and it is his
only play for which flute or violin accompaniments have
been preserved entire.

*   ————. "Mr. Seedo's London Career and His Work With
         Henry Fielding." (See item 369.)

412.   ————. "Possible Additions to Airs 6 and 7 of Henry
         Fielding's Ballad Opera *The Lottery* (1732)." *Notes and
         Queries*, n.s. 9 (1962), 455-56.

         Two stanzas to Air 6 and one to Air 7 were silently
         added by editors of song collections during the 1730's
         and 1740's; these stanzas were never printed in any
         edition of *The Lottery* and hence it is not known whether
         or not Fielding wrote them.

413.   Smith, John Harrington. "Tony Lumpkin and the Country
         Booby Type." *Publications of the Modern Language
         Association of America*, 58 (1943), 1038-49.

         Notes that *The Lottery* (which in this article is not at-
         tributed to Fielding) was an important source for Gold-
         smith's *She Stoops to Conquer*. Goldsmith borrowed many
         of Timothy's qualities for his character of Tony Lumpkin.

414.   Woods, Charles B. "Notes on Three of Fielding's Plays."
         *Publications of the Modern Language Association of
         America*, 52 (1937), 359-73.

         Rejects the view, commonly held, that the source of
         Fielding's *The Letter-Writers* is Vanbrugh's *The Con-
         federacy*; rather the central device of the extortion
         letters is drawn from the wave of extortions that swept
         England and Ireland in 1730-31. The object of satire
         in *The Modern Husband* is probably Lord Abergavenny, who
         won a court case in 1730 by using the same tactic as
         that used by the husband in the play. *Eurydice Hiss'd*
         is a double satire: it satirizes the reception of
         Fielding's earlier *Eurydice* and attacks Walpole's Excise
         Bill of 1733.

                    I. *The Grub-Street Opera* (1732)
                       See under *The Welsh Opera*.

                    J. *The Modern Husband* (1732)

*   Goldgar, Bertrand A. "Fielding, Sir William Yonge, and
         the *Grub-Street Journal*." (See item 189.)

* Williams, Murial Brittain. *Marriage: Fielding's Mirror of Reality*. (See item 325.)

* Woods, Charles B. "Notes on Three of Fielding's Plays." (See item 414.)

415. Zaki, Jafar. "Sir Robert Walpole and Fielding's *Modern Husband*." *The Aligarh Journal of English Studies*, 2 (1977), 60-71.

     Listed in the 1977 MLA bibliography, but the compilers have not seen this study.

K. *The Covent-Garden Tragedy* (1732)

* Avery, Emmett L. "Some Notes on Fielding's Plays." (See item 439.)

* Clinton-Baddeley, V.C. "Henry Fielding." (See item 339.)

L. *The Mock Doctor* (1732)

* Baker, Sheridan. "Political Allusion in Fielding's *Author's Farce*, *Mock Doctor*, and *Tumble-Down Dick*." (See item 381.)

416. Goggin, L.P. "Fielding and the *Select Comedies of Mr. de Molière*." *Philological Quarterly*, 31 (1952), 344-50.

     A close comparison of Molière's *Le Médecin malgré lui* and *L'Avare* with the translations of those works in the *Select Comedies* and with Fielding's adaptations in *The Mock Doctor* and *The Miser* indicates that Fielding did not translate the *Select Comedies* and that, in the case of *The Mock Doctor*, he worked from a French text in adapting the play. See Tucker, item 377.

417. Lewis, Peter. "Fielding's *The Covent-Garden Tragedy* and Philips's *The Distrest Mother*." *Durham University Journal*, 37 (1976), 33-46.

     Fielding considered *The Distrest Mother* to be an example of all the worst qualities of contemporary drama with

its barely classical subject matter; unmotivated
characters; stilted, bathetic diction; and cloying
sentimentality. Therefore, in the *Covent-Garden
Tragedy* , Fielding burlesqued several key scenes from
Philips's play, as well as his style and dramatic technique. Fielding also takes random satiric shots at
Rowe and Otway.

M. *The Miser* (1733)

418.   Barrow, Bernard E. "Macklin's Costume and Property
        Notes for the Character of Lovegold: Some Traditional
        Elements in Eighteenth-Century Low-Comedy Acting."
        Theatre Notebook, 13 (1958), 66-7.

        Macklin's supposedly original characterization of Love-
        gold in Fielding's *The Miser* is in fact derived from
        earlier actors' performances of low-comedy character
        types.

*   Goggin, L.P. "Fielding and the *Select Comedies of Mr.
        de Moliere*." (See item 416.)

419.   Milford, R.T. "Cotes's Weekly Journal." *Times Literary
        Supplement* (19 March 1931), p. 234.

        Discusses a journal, begun by Cornelius Cotes in 1734,
        which intended to print "all the plays in the English
        language." Numbers 1-9, of which number 4 is Fielding's
        The Miser, are in the Bodleian Library. Also see
        Stratman, item 422.

420.   Read, Stanley E. "Fielding's *Miser*." *Huntington Library
        Bulletin*, 1 (1931), 211-13.

        The folio edition of the play was carelessly reprinted
        from the octavo. See Stonehill, item 421.

421.   Stonehill, Charles. "Fielding's *The Miser*." *Times
        Literary Supplement* (22 October 1925), p. 698.

        At least one copy of *The Miser* exists that was published
        before the generally accepted date of 1733. Just when,
        where, and by whom it was published remains a mystery.
        See Read, item 420.

422. Stratman, Carl J. "Cotes's Weekly Journal; or, The
English Stage-Player." *Papers of the Bibliographical
Society of America*, 56 (1962), 104-06.

Notes that the fourth issue of Cotes's *Journal*--only
one copy of which exists (at the Bodleian)--prints
Fielding's *The Miser*, but omits the last sheet, thus
ending the play in the middle of scene ten of Act Five.
See Milford, item 419.

423. Woods, Charles B. "The Folio Text of Fielding's *The
Miser*." *Huntington Library Quarterly*, 28 (1964), 59-61.

Shows that the folio *Miser* was published between May 11
and July 16, 1734.

N. *Deborah* (1733)

424. Roberts, Edgar V. "Henry Fielding's Lost Play *Deborah,
or a Wife for You All*." *Bulletin of the New York Public
Library*, 66 (1962), 576-88.

Conjectures that *Deborah*, a "lost" play by Fielding,
was probably a piece of very little substance. From
what is known of the actors and possibly similar pieces
by Fielding, the play can be reconstructed in outline.
It was probably a satirical farce with little originality.

O. *The Intriguing Chambermaid* (1734)

425. Swaen, A.E.H. "Fielding's *The Intriguing Chambermaid*."
Neophilologus, 29 (1944), 117-20.

Says that *The Intriguing Chambermaid* is an adaptation
of Regnard's *Le Retour Imprévu*, which in turn is adapted
from Plautus's *Mostellaria*. In transforming Plautus's
play, Regnard made it thoroughly French; likewise,
Fielding made Regnard quite English. However, certain
incidents and characters remain the same in all three
versions.

P. *Don Quixote in England* (1734)

*   Avery, Emmett L. "Some Notes on Fielding's Plays."
      (See item 439.)

*   Roberts, Edgar V. "Henry Fielding and Richard Lever-
      idge: Authorship of 'The Roast Beef of Old England.'"
      (See item 368.)

426. Thomas, Gordon K. "The Knight Amid the Dunces." *Res-
      toration and Eighteenth Century Theatre Research*, 14
      (1975), 10-22.

      The eight plays published between 1694 and 1742 which
      dealt in some way with Don Quixote (including Fielding's
      Don Quixote in England) reflect the conditions of the
      stage at that time. The plays range from indecent
      farce to political satire.

Q. *The Universal Gallant* (1735)

427. Avery, Emmett L. "Fielding's *Universal Gallant*." *Re-
      search Studies*, 6 (1938), 46.

      Fielding had apparently completed *The Universal Gallant*
      by December 1733 when it was advertised in *The Daily
      Advertiser*. The play, however, was not acted until
      February 1735. It is possible that Fielding recognized
      the play's weaknesses and only produced it when he had
      nothing stronger to offer.

R. *The Virgin Unmasked* (1735)

428. Woods, Charles B. "The 'Miss Lucy' Plays of Fielding
      and Garrick." *Philological Quarterly*, 41 (1962), 294-
      310.

      David Garrick's theatrical afterpiece, *Lethe, or Esop
      in the Shades* (1740), was influenced by Fielding's *The
      Virgin Unmask'd* (1735). Garrick and Fielding also co-
      authored another afterpiece, *Miss Lucy in Town* (1742),
      which was Fielding's last dramatic production.

S. *Pasquin* (1736)

* Clinton-Baddeley, V.C. "Henry Fielding." (See item 339.)

* de Castro, J. Paul. "Fieldingiana." (See item 139.)

* Lewis, P.E. "Three Notes on Fielding's Plays." (See item 355.)

429. Nichols, Charles W. "Fielding and the Cibbers." *Philological Quarterly*, 1 (1922), 278-89.

Colley Cibber, Theophilus Cibber, and the latter's wife were frequently attacked both for their professional activities and their personalities. In *The Historical Register* and *Pasquin*, Fielding also attacks them, but he limits his satire to their professional activities only.

430. ————. "Fielding Notes." *Modern Language Notes*, 34 (1919), 220-24.

Prints three short notes on Fielding: (1) references to contemporary incidents, including the flood of February 16, 1736, prove that *Pasquin* was written in a very short time; (2) March 21, 1737, was probably the first day that *The Historical Register* was presented; and (3) internal evidence and a corroborating contemporary letter indicate that Fielding was the author of a letter in *Common Sense* (May 21, 1737) defending political satire on the stage.

431. ————. "Fielding's Satire on Pantomime." *Publications of the Modern Language Association of America*, 46 (1931), 1107-12.

In attacking pantomime, Fielding ran counter to the general taste of the town. Nevertheless, in *Pasquin* and *Tumble-Down Dick*, Fielding characterized pantomime as a cheat because it raised ticket prices and abridged the main drama; it also lowered the popular taste, to the detriment of legitimate drama.

432. ————. "Social Satire in Fielding's *Pasquin* and *The Historical Register*." *Philological Quarterly*, 3 (1924), 309-17.

The two plays above satirize Farinelli, Italian opera,

polite conversation, auctions, waxworks, and other fads.
These targets were common ones in the journals of the
day.

*   Raushenbush, Esther M. "Charles Macklin's Lost Play
About Henry Fielding." (See item 365.)

*   Sherburn, George. *"The Dunciad*, Book IV." (See item
375.)

*   Smith, Dane. *Plays About the Theatre in England from
The Rehearsal in 1671 to the Licensing Act in 1737.*
(See item 388.)

433.   Wells, John E. "Some New Facts Concerning *Tumble-Down
Dick* and *Pasquin*." *Modern Language Notes*, 28 (1913),
137–42.

Gives the acting dates of the two plays; *Pasquin* was
first staged on March 5, 1736, and *Tumble-Down Dick* was
first acted on April 29 of the same year. The latter
was probably printed near the end of April 1736, shortly
after its first staging.

T. *Tumble-Down Dick* (1736)

*   Baker, Sheridan. "Political Allusion in Fielding's
Author's Farce, *Mock Doctor*, and *Tumble-Down Dick*."
(See item 381.)

*   Lewis, P.E. "Three Notes on Fielding's Plays." (See
item 355.)

434.   Nichols, Charles W. "The Date of *Tumble-Down Dick*."
Modern Language Notes, 36 (1921), 312–13.

Assigns correct dates for the first performance and
publication of *Tumble-Down Dick*. The play was advertised and acted on April 29, 1736, and twenty-one performances followed. It was first published on the same
date; a first edition bearing that date is in the Dickson
Collection at Yale University.

*   ————. "Fielding's Satire on Pantomime." (See item
431.)

435.   ———. "Fielding's *Tumble-Down Dick*." *Modern Language Notes*, 38 (1923), 410-16.

   Tumble-Down Dick satirizes afterpieces in general and *The Fall of Phaeton* in particular; many passages in the latter are closely paralleled in Fielding's play.

*   Wells, John E. "Some New Facts Concerning *Tumble-Down Dick* and *Pasquin*." (See item 433.)

U. *Eurydice* (1736)

*   Peterson, William. "Satire in Fielding's *An Interlude between Jupiter, Juno, Apollo, and Mercury*." (See item 436.)

V. *An Interview Between Jupiter, Juno, Apollo, and Mercury* (1737)

436.   Peterson, William. "Satire in Fielding's *An Interlude between Jupiter, Juno, Apollo, and Mercury*." *Modern Language Notes*, 65 (1950), 200-02.

   The *Interlude*, although only a sketch, is a companion piece to *Eurydice Hissed*; like the latter, it contains satiric thrusts at Walpole's government and the hack writers who supported it.

W. *The Historical Register* (1737)

437.   Appleton, William W. "Introduction" to *"The Historical Register for the Year 1736" and "Eurydice Hissed"* by Henry Fielding. Lincoln: University of Nebraska Press, 1967. Pp. ix-xviii.

   Traces the theatrical history of the two plays and discusses their satiric targets, noting that *The Historical Register*, while not solely responsible, possibly contributed to the Licensing Act of 1737. Although Fielding's topicality makes his plays difficult, much of their satire is still valid and their wit still pleases.

438.   Avery, Emmett L. "An Early Performance of Fielding's
       Historical Register." *Modern Language Notes*, 49 (1934),
       407.

       An entry in the diary of Viscount Percival, first Earl
       of Egmont, refers to a performance of the *Historical
       Register* as early as March 22, 1737.

439.   ————. "Some Notes on Fielding's Plays." *Research
       Studies*, 3 (1935), 48-50.

       Locates in *The Daily Advertiser* announcements for first
       performances of *The Historical Register* (March 21, 1737)
       and *Don Quixote in England* (April 5, 1734). *Advertiser*
       notices also add several acting dates to previously pub-
       lished lists for *The Covent-Garden Tragedy* and *Eurydice
       Hiss'd*.

*   Crean, P.J. "The Stage Licensing Act of 1737." (See
       item 340.)

*   Lewis, P.E. "Three Notes on Fielding's Plays." (See
       item 355.)

*   Nichols, Charles W. "Fielding and the Cibbers." (See
       item 429.)

*   ————. "Fielding Notes." (See item 430.)

440.   ————. "A New Note on Fielding's *Historical Register*."
       Modern Language Notes, 38 (1923), 507-08.

       Both the *St. James Evening-Post* and the *London Evening-
       Post* for March 8-10, 1737, note the upcoming presentation
       of *The Historical Register*, but neither gives dates.

*   ————. "Social Satire in Fielding's *Pasquin* and *The
       Historical Register*." (See item 432.)

*   Smith, Dane. *Plays About the Theatre in England from
       The Rehearsal in 1671 to the Licensing Act in 1737*.
       (See item 388.)

              X. *Eurydice Hissed* (1737)

*   Appleton, William W. "Introduction" to *"The Historical
       Register for the Year 1736" and "Eurydice Hissed."* (See
       item 437.)

*   Avery, Emmett L. "Some Notes on Fielding's Plays."
        (See item 439.)

*   Woods, Charles B. "Notes on Three of Fielding's Plays."
        (See item 414.)

Y. *Miss Lucy in Town* (1743)

*   Woods, Charles B. "The 'Miss Lucy' Plays of Fielding
        and Garrick." (See item 428.)

Z. *The Wedding Day* (1743)

*   Shepperson, Archibald B. "Additions and Corrections to
        Facts About Fielding." (See item 288.)

AA. *The Fathers, or, The
Good Natured Man* (1778)

*   Wallace, Robert M. "Fielding Manuscripts." (See item
        316.)

V

THE NOVELS

A. General

441. Allen, Walter. *The English Novel*. New York: E.P. Dutton, 1954.

Finds Fielding's strength as a novelist in his innovative methods of characterization. He was able to psychologically individualize his "type" characters, and with Tom Jones, he created a new "type," the unheroic hero. Amelia, too, is a rare character: the perfectly good person who is credible. The English novelists' conception of character was derived from Fielding, who established the main tradition of the novel.

442. ————. "Henry Fielding," in his *Six Great Novelists: Defoe, Fielding, Scott, Dickens, Stevenson, and Conrad*. Folcroft, Pa.: Folcroft Library Editions, 1971. Pp. 38-63. Originally published London: Hamish Hamilton, 1955.

Presents a brief biography in which Fielding is defended against charges of immorality. Fielding's strengths in the novel include his skillful use of irony, his ability to portray realistic figures like Tom and Booth, and his success in depicting totally good persons like Adams and Amelia.

443. Alter, Robert. *Fielding and the Nature of the Novel*. Cambridge, Mass.: Harvard University Press, 1968.

Emphasizes three aspects of Fielding's technique: style, character, and structure. Fielding employs a highly artificial and stylized language to maneuver the reader into seeing things from the angle of vision he wants. He develops characters as individuals but also makes them part of a symmetrical whole, often pairing figures

111

to reveal important aspects of their characters. For example, the enthusiasm of Western emphasizes the "starched formality" of Allworthy, while the latter's moderation and reasonableness emphasizes Western's excesses and ignorance. Other such pairings include Square and Thwackum and Tom and Partridge. The structure of Fielding's novels is based on parallels (the interpolated tales, for example, parallel the themes, characters, and events of the main action); repetition (society's reaction to Jenny and Molly's sexual transgressions, for instance); and the development of apparently trivial points into important incidents which help resolve the plot (such as Blifil's manipulation of lawyer Dowling, which later becomes a means of reconciling Tom and Allworthy). Most of the adverse criticism of Fielding comes from a misunderstanding of these three key aspects of Fielding's art.

Reviews: Martin C. Battestin, *Georgia Review*, 23 (1969), 100–103; John A. Dussinger, *Journal of English and Germanic Philology*, 68 (1969), 529–35; Michael Irwin, *Review of English Studies*, 11 (1971), 89–93; Juliet McMaster, *Dalhousie Review*, 49 (1969), 268–70; Martin Price, *Philological Quarterly*, 48 (1969), 354.

444. ———. "Fielding and the Uses of Style." *Novel*, 1 (1967), 53–63. Reprinted in Battestin, item 779.

Fielding contributed to the novel form by fashioning a stylized language which achieves the qualities of precision of reference, complexity of statement, and aesthetically pleasing form. He is adept at controlling tone, rhythm, imagery, and syntax. Style to Fielding is not just the way of telling a story, it is often the story itself; he is able to successfully fuse form and meaning so as to integrate all elements of his work.

445. ———. "On the Critical Dismissal of Fielding," in *Henry Fielding: Tom Jones*, ed. Neil Compson (London: Macmillan, 1970), pp. 220–42. This material originally appeared in Alter's *Fielding and the Nature of the Novel*, item 443.

Reviews the negative criticism of Fielding, particularly that of Dr. Johnson, F.R. Leavis, Frank Kermode, and Ian Watt, and concludes that Fielding has often not been read properly and that many critics fault him for not writing another kind of novel, the kind created by Richardson. Criticism has tended to "canonize" the

Richardsonian novel and to "excommunicate" the Field-
ingesque novel, yet Fielding's intricacies and subtleties
helped shape the novel as a serious form of art.

446. ————. "On the Critical Dismissal of Fielding: Post-
Puritanism in Literary Criticism." *Salmagundi*, 1 (1966),
11-28.

Views *Tom Jones* as more complex than Leavis, Kermode,
and others give it credit for. Many contemporary critics,
including the above two, dismiss the novel and Fielding
because Fielding's moral views in general, and his view
of sex in particular, seem to be over-simplified, over-
intellectualized, and externalized. In fact, however,
Fielding invites the reader to make situational and
moral judgments just as Tom and the other characters
must. The precise structure of the novel provides a
"set of multiple, mutually qualifying perspectives in
which to view the moral action of the novel." Within
those multiple perspectives lies the novel's moral
complexity. (This material was reworked as Chapter V
of *Fielding and the Nature of the Novel*, item 443,
and then was reprinted, in part, in Compson, item 804.)

447. Auty, Susan G. *The Comic Spirit of Eighteenth-Century
Novels*. Port Washington, N.Y.: Kennikat Press, 1975.

Places Fielding in the context of the eighteenth century
and shows his influence on Coventry, Goldsmith, Mrs.
Lennox, and others. Fielding's "new style of writing"
consists of his amiable humor, of his ability to create
balanced characters with whom we can sympathize, of his
consistent comic tone, and of his ability to teach without losing his humor.

448. Baker, Ernest A. *Intellectual Realism from Richardson
to Sterne*, Vol. 4 of *The History of the English Novel*.
London: H.F. and G. Witherby, 1930. Reprinted New York:
Barnes and Noble, 1950.

Treats Fielding in detail in chapters four through eight.
A brief survey of his life and plays is followed by a
lengthy discussion of *Joseph Andrews* in which the focus
is on his realistic methods of characterization and
his debt to Cervantes. The chapter on the *Miscellanies*
concentrates on the ironic methods of *Jonathan Wild*.
The discussion of *Tom Jones* emphasizes the novel's
dependence on accident and its use of antithesis and
irony. *Amelia*'s seriousness is due to Fielding's

experience as a magistrate; Baker views the novel as "a pamphlet, a sermon, and indictment" on the legal system as much as a work of fiction. The final chapter on Fielding discusses *The Covent-Garden Journal* and *The Journal of a Voyage to Lisbon* and concludes that Fielding is "the Shakespeare of English fiction" because of his great variety. He laid the groundwork for the novel of character, of situation, of plot, of intrigue, of comedy, as well as the "slice-of-life" and the "problem" novel.

*   Banerji, H.K. *Henry Fielding: Playwright, Journalist, and Master of the Art of Fiction, His Life and His Works.* (See item 86.)

449.   Battestin, Martin C. "Fielding's Novels and the Wesleyan Edition: Some Principles and Problems," in *Editing Eighteenth-Century Novels*, ed G.E. Bentley, Jr. Toronto: A.M. Hakkert Ltd., 1975. Pp. 9-30.

Argues that any authoritative text of Fielding's novels must retain the eighteenth-century flavor of the accidentals (capitalization, italics, unique spelling, etc.). Battestin also argues that the fourth edition of *Tom Jones* represents Fielding's final intentions.

*   ————. *The Moral Basis of Fielding's Art: A Study of "Joseph Andrews."* (See item 642.)

450.   Beasley, Jerry C. "English Fiction in the 1740's: Some Glances at the Major and Minor Novels." *Studies in the Novel*, 5 (1973), 155-75.

Richardson, Fielding, and Smollett all were influenced heavily by minor novelists writing in the early part of the century. The influences took the form of themes, subjects, and approaches to fiction. Among the many "bits and pieces" characterizing early eighteenth-century fiction that the three major novelists fitted into their own works were: fidelity to both external and moral reality; anti-romanticism; topicality; creation of ordinary protagonists; use of pseudohistory, pseudobiography, and voyage memoirs; sentimentalism (lightly sprinkled with eroticism); and a moral point. Thus, although the three major novelists used their tools in "new" ways and "new" combinations, they did not create "new" tools.

451.   ————. "Romance and the 'New' Novels of Richardson,
        Fielding, and Smollett." *Studies in English Literature*,
        16 (1976), 437-50.

        The literary climate of the 1740's still favored
        romances, but many of the romances of the time contained
        important anti-romantic elements. Even though Oriental
        settings, magic, monsters, and undeveloped heroes and
        villains predominated, several books introduced the
        anti-romantic qualities of topical allusions, political
        satire, and social criticism. Fielding, like Richardson
        and Smollett, did use some romantic devices in charac-
        terization and plotting, but the main thrust of his
        novels is towards realistic characters, familiar settings,
        and ethical themes, all of which are anti-romantic.

452.   Beatty, Richard Croom. "Criticism in Fielding's Narra-
        tives and His Estimate of Critics." *Publications of
        the Modern Language Association of America*, 49 (1934),
        1087-1100.

        Reviews Fielding's philosophy of composition, which is
        expressed throughout his works in the form of asides
        and introductory essays. He comments on the form of
        fiction, character development, plot, and kinds of
        literature (romance, histories, travel literature, etc.).
        His low opinion of critics was based in part on the
        savage treatment which he received at their hands and in
        part on the low, arbitrary state to which criticism had
        fallen in the eighteenth century. Also see Williamson,
        item 326.

*   Bell, Michael. "A Note on Drama and the Novel." (See
        item 336.)

453.   Bissell, Frederick Olds. *Fielding's Theory of the Novel*.
        Ithaca, N.Y.: Cornell University Press, 1933. Reprinted
        New York: Cooper Square, 1969.

        Distills Fielding's theory of the novel from *Joseph
        Andrews* and *Tom Jones*. That theory, which Fielding con-
        sistently puts into practice in his own fiction, re-
        quires believable characters, realistically portrayed
        events, traditional romance elements modified by comedy,
        a moral point or points (gently conveyed), classical
        poetical ornament, and good-hearted sympathy for the
        fictional characters and the reader. The sources for
        Fielding's theory are both classical and contemporary.

        Review: Times Literary Supplement (3 August 1933), p. 526.

454. Blanchard, Frederic T. *Fielding the Novelist: A Study
      in Historical Criticism*. New Haven: Yale University
      Press, 1926.

      Presents an account of Fielding's changing critical
      reputation from the beginnings through the early twen-
      tieth century. In his own lifetime, Fielding was a
      popular, although not a critical, success. Even though
      such early nineteenth century artist/critics as Hunt,
      Lamb, and Byron enthusiastically embraced Fielding, he
      was strongly objected to by moralistic critics. The
      Victorians in particular found his work and his charac-
      ter morally objectionable. Dobson's 1883 work on Field-
      ing (item 163) began the rehabilitation of his reputa-
      tion, both as an individual and as an artist, and by
      the 1920's he was generally regarded as a benevolent
      human being and one of the fathers of the novel.

      Reviews: E.A. Baker, *Review of English Studies*, 3 (1927),
      227-32; F. Baldensperger, *Litteris*, 4 (1927), 222-25;
      Aurélien Digeon, *Revue Anglo-Américaine*, 5 (1927), 57-59;
      Paul Dottin, *RELV*, 43 (1926), 450-55; Oliver Elton,
      Modern Language Review, 22 (1927), 225-28; E.S. Noyes,
      Saturday Review of Literature (October 16, 1926), p.
      198; H. Schojjer, *Beiblatt*, 38 (1927), 345-96.

455. Bland, D.S. "Endangering the Reader's Neck: Background
      Description in the Novel." *Criticism*, 3 (1961), 121-39.
      Partially reprinted in Rawson, item 272.

      Regards Fielding as an important figure in the develop-
      ment of landscape in the novel. In *Joseph Andrews*
      (III.v) there is a description of a wood which is con-
      sciously employed to set a romantic mood for the lovers,
      and in *Tom Jones* (I.iv) we get a picture of Allworthy's
      estate which both places Allworthy in society and dis-
      plays his breeding and good taste. This use of setting
      marked an important step toward the later use of back-
      ground as symbol.

456. Booth, Wayne C. *The Rhetoric of Fiction*. Chicago:
      University of Chicago Press, 1961.

      Contains scattered remarks on Fielding plus a detailed
      discussion of his intrusions into *Tom Jones*; for the
      latter, see item 789.

457. ————. "The Self-Conscious Narrator in Comic Fiction
      Before *Tristram Shandy*." *Publications of the Modern
      Language Association of America*, 67 (1952), 163-85.
      Reprinted in Iser, item 507.

Demonstrates that every form of authorial intrusion in *Tristram Shandy* appears first in Fielding's works. Sterne follows Fielding in using intrusions to manipulate the reader into accepting the author's values, to insure a comic response to scenes which are potentially serious, and to characterize the narrator and discuss his narrative procedures. Also see Booth, item 789.

* Boucé, Paul-Gabriel. *The Novels of Tobias Smollett.* (See item 99.)

458. Brissenden, R.F., ed. *Studies in the Eighteenth Century: Papers Presented at the Second David Nichol Smith Memorial Seminar.* Toronto: University of Toronto Press, 1973.

Contains two essays on Fielding: C.J. Rawson, "The Hero as Clown: Jonathan Wild, Felix Krull, and Others" (item 753) and Roger Robinson, "Henry Fielding and the English Rococo" (item 562).

459. Burke, John J., Jr. "History Without History: Fielding's Theory of Fiction," in *A Provision of Human Nature: Essays on Fielding and Others in Honor of Miriam Austin Locke*, ed. Donald Kay. University, Ala.: University of Alabama Press, 1977. Pp. 45-63.

Traces Fielding's views of historiography from *Jonathan Wild* through *Tom Jones.* Fielding felt that history did a disservice to the public, encouraging people to admire and even imitate the selfishness and ambition that characterize the great. He therefore invited the public to consider his fiction as "a general history of England," one that presented positive moral values for emulation. However, instead of creating a new type of historiography, Fielding really developed a form of idealized autobiography which freed him from the pressures of external fact and allowed him to make events turn out right in order to emphasize his moral view. Also see Stevick, "Fielding and the Meaning of History," item 592, and Wallace, "Fielding's Knowledge of History," item 317.

460. Burton, A.P. "Cervantes the Man Seen through English Eyes in the Seventeenth and Eighteenth Centuries." *Bulletin of Hispanic Studies*, 45 (1968), 1-15.

Says that Fielding, knowing of Cervantes only from his work, merely imitates his use of the *persona*, unlike Sterne, who had a knowledge of the man.

461. Burton, Richard. *Masters of the English Novel*. New
     York: Henry Holt, 1909.

     Although Fielding is able to create realistic characters,
     he has no talent for presenting the softer emotions or
     for creating a "recognizable" plot. His taste and
     morality are always questionable.

462. Butt, John. *Fielding*. Writers and Their Work, No. 57.
     London: Longmans, Green, and Co., 1954.

     Offers a succinct, basic introduction to Fielding's life
     and works, emphasizing *Joseph Andrews*, *Tom Jones*, and
     Amelia. These three novels follow the classic epic
     structure as that structure was understood by Field-
     ing's contemporaries and they also contain one common
     theme—the difference between appearance and reality
     and the necessity of each individual understanding that
     difference.

*   ————, and H.V.D. Dyson. *Augustans and Romantics,
         1689-1830*. London: Cresset, 1940. Rev. ed., 1950.

         See under Dyson, item 14.

463. Champion, Larry S., ed. *Quick Springs of Sense: Studies
     in the Eighteenth Century*. Athens, Ga.: University of
     Georgia Press, 1974.

     Includes the following essays on Fielding: A.S. Knowles,
     Jr., "Defoe, Swift, and Fielding: Notes on the Retirement
     Theme," item 521; C.J. Rawson, "Language, Dialogue, and
     Point of View in Fielding: Some Considerations," item
     558; and J. Paul Hunter, "The Lesson of *Amelia*," item
     1000.

464. Chandler, Frank W. *Literature of Roguery*. 2 Vols.
     Boston and New York: Houghton Mifflin, 1907. Reprinted
     New York: Burt Franklyn, 1958.

     Of all of Fielding's novels, only *Jonathan Wild* is
     thoroughly picaresque. The other novels are influenced
     by the picaresque, but Fielding's genius enabled him to
     transcend his picaresque models.

*   Churchill, R.C. "Fielding: To the Novel from the Drama."
         (See item 111.)

465. Cleary, Thomas R. "Fielding: Style for an Age of Sensi-
     bility." *Transactions of the Samuel Johnson Society of*

the Northwest, Vol. 6. Calgary: Samuel Johnson Society, 1973. Pp. 91-96.

Terms "invalid" Northrop Frye's distinction between Fielding as a "product" novelist and Sterne as a "process" novelist. The eighteenth-century novel does not lend itself to a clear product-process distinction, and Fielding in particular embodies seemingly equal qualities of both. And his narrators certainly are "process" figures.

466. Clifford, James, ed. *Eighteenth Century English Literature*. New York: Oxford University Press, 1959.

Includes George Sherburn's "Fielding's Social Outlook," item 579 (see pp. 251-73).

467. Coley, William B. "Gide and Fielding." *Comparative Literature*, 11 (1959), 1-15. Reprinted in Iser, item 507.

Presents Gide's views of Fielding. He saw Fielding as less realistic than Richardson and as antireligious. Fielding does not reject all moral principles, but he objects to any system based on absolutes; honor and virtue can exist independent of religion, according to Fielding. Gide approves of Fielding's moral views and of his use of "interior parodies" or "paradigms" of his novels; in *Tom Jones* these parodies are found in the interpolated tales of the Man of the Hill and the King of the Gypsies, both of which, like mirrors, reflect the major concerns of the novel.

468. Collins, Norman. "Henry Fielding," in his *The Facts of Fiction*. London: Victor Gollancz, 1932. Pp. 38-55.

Regards Fielding as a "hopeless romantic" and *Joseph Andrews* as his greatest work. Although condemned by many, Fielding avoids offending those readers with senses of humor because his wit and comedy keep his coarser scenes from disgusting his audience.

469. Cooke, Arthur L. "Henry Fielding and the Writers of Heroic Romance." *Publications of the Modern Language Association of America*, 62 (1947), 984-94.

Although there is little similarity between the heroic romances and Fielding's novels, the writers of those romances developed a theory of prose fiction based on classical principles and remarkably like Fielding's

theory. Both the writers of heroic romance and Fielding
claimed that their works should be regarded as "history";
both insisted that fiction should be probable and
"natural"; both advocated a principle of unity but admitted episodes as long as they were related to the
main action; both emphasized the careful differentiation
of characters; and both believed in the moral purpose
of fiction. The similarities in their theories is due
to the fact that both drew their principles from the
theory of the classical epic.

470.   Coolidge, John S. "Fielding and 'Conservation of
       Character.'" *Modern Philology*, 57 (1960), 245-59.
       Reprinted in Iser, item 507, and Paulson, item 258.

       Explores in detail Fielding's method of characteriza-
       tion, which is based on the classical view of nature as
       static. This view underlies his techniques in his
       dramatic productions which he transferred to his fiction.
       His method is to define each person's character on that
       person's first appearance and then to keep the individ-
       ual acting consistently in a way that can be deduced
       from the original portrait of him. On stage this
       method poses few problems when the unity of time is
       adhered to because it is unlikely that an individual
       would significantly change within a few hours, but in
       the novel, where the time span is usually longer, the
       method severely limits the writer. In *Amelia*, Field-
       ing deliberately set out to use a different tech-
       nique; here he does not provide a "preliminary character"
       for his major figures but instead shows them growing
       and changing, a process most evident in the figure of
       Booth. Fielding's new method enables him to explore
       more realistically than he had done before the relation
       of good to evil.

471.   Cowler, Rosemary, ed. *Twentieth-Century Interpretations
       of "Pamela."* Englewood Cliffs, N.J.: Prentice-Hall,
       1969.

       Contains material on Fielding, including selections from
       the following: Sheldon Sacks, "Moralists, Novelists, and
       Unfallacious Intentions" from *Fiction and the Shape of
       Belief* (item 566); Owen Jenkins, "Richardson's *Pamela*
       and Fielding's 'Vile Forgeries'" (item 510); William
       Park, "Fielding *and* Richardson" (item 543); and Bernard
       Kreissman, *Pamela-Shamela* (item 625).

472.   Cross, Wilbur L. "Henry Fielding," in his *The Develop-
       ment of the English Novel*. New York: Macmillan, 1926.

Pp. 42-57. Originally published New York: Macmillan, 1899.

Deals primarily with *Tom Jones* and *Amelia*. The former is significant for its use of a more realistic setting than its predecessors and its high moral aim. It presents a multitude of character types to give a complete picture of human nature. *Amelia* is Fielding's most realistic novel and is designed to attack legal loopholes and incompetency in the administrators of "justice."

473. Dickson, Frederick S. "Fielding and Richardson on the Continent." *Notes and Queries*, Twelfth Series, 3 (1917), 7-8.

Mrs. Barbauld may have started the untruth, accepted for a century, that Richardson was more popular than Fielding on the continent. In fact, not only was Fielding more popular, in the latter half of the eighteenth century more editions of *Joseph Andrews*, *Tom Jones*, and *Amelia* appeared on the continent than in England.

474. Digeon, Aurélien. *The Novels of Fielding*. London: Routledge, 1925. Reprinted New York: Russell and Russell, 1962. Originally published as *Les Romans de Fielding* (see item 1167).

Focuses on Fielding's reaction against the "dissolute" temper of his time and the falseness of Richardson's moral portraits. Fielding moves from sentiment in the early novels (especially in *Tom Jones*) to sentimental (in *Amelia*). Fielding realistically portrays his age and also constructs accurate psychological studies in his novels, studies which are far more accurate than those of Richardson.

Reviews: W.L. Cross, *Saturday Review of Literature* (18 July 1925), pp. 905-06; R.M. Lovett, *New Republic* (26 August 1925), pp. 22-23; George Saintsbury, *Bookman*, 68 (1925), 96-99.

475. Dircks, Richard J. "Cumberland, Richardson, and Fielding: Changing Patterns in the Eighteenth-Century Novel." *Research Studies*, 38 (1970), 291-99.

Traces the changing emphasis in eighteenth-century sentimental fiction. In Richardson, sentimentality deals mainly with love; in Fielding, it deals with benevolence; and in Cumberland, it deals with benevolence tempered with democratic social concerns.

*   Doody, Margaret Anne. *A Natural Passion: A Study of
       the Novels of Samuel Richardson*. (See item 620.)

476.   Dooley, D.J. "Some Uses of Mutations of the Picaresque."
       Dalhousie Review, 37 (1958), 363-77.

       Fielding deviated from the dominant picaresque tradition
       of his time by giving his novels form and by taking
       folly rather than knavery for his subject. His influence
       in these areas lasted for over seventy years, and the
       picaresque did not return as a force in the novel until
       after 1820.

*   Dyson, H.V.D., and John Butt. *Augustans and Romantics,
       1689-1830*. London: Cresset, 1940. Rev. Ed., 1950.

       See annotation under item 14.

*   Elton, Oliver. "Fielding and Smollett." (See item 175.)

477.   Ernle, Lord. "Founders of the Modern Novel: II. Henry
       Fielding." *Edinburgh Review*, 243 (1926), 336-54.

       Characterizes Richardson as full of "spiteful little-
       ness," but sees Fielding as possessed of "bigness of
       nature." Fielding is a realist both in his analysis of
       ethical conduct and in his method of characterization,
       which shows frailties in good men and positive traits
       in bad ones. To him, what a man *is* is at least as im-
       portant as what he does, and his novels emphasize the
       difference between "being" and "seeming." Fielding's
       constant moralizing balances his strain of coarseness
       and his insensitivity to "low" conduct.

478.   Evans, James E. "The English Lineage of Diedrich
       Knickerbocker." *Early American Literature*, 10 (1975),
       3-13.

       Traces the influence of Swift, Sterne, and Fielding
       on Irving's *Knickerbocker's History of New York*.
       Irving uses some of Fielding's narrative devices in
       his work, especially discursive prefatory chapters and
       the mock-heroic.

479.   Farrell, William J. "Fielding's Familiar Style." *ELH:
       A Journal of English Literary History*, 34 (1967), 65-77.

       Contends that Fielding's intrusive narrator and intimate
       style--usually viewed negatively as distancing devices
       designed to provide the reader with the proper comic

perspective--actually reduce "the distance between the artifact and the life it imitates," thus separating his novels from the more eloquent fiction of the past while simultaneously emphasizing their closer correspondence to reality.

480. Ford, Ford Madox. *The English Novel*. Philadelphia and London: Lippincott, 1929. Extracts reprinted in Rawson, item 272.

Condemns Fielding for being a moral hypocrite and *Tom Jones* for being "salacious" and "badly written"; Tom and Sophia are "stupid," and Blifil should have been the hero.

481. ————. *The March of Literature*. New York: Dial Press, 1938. Extracts reprinted in Rawson, item 272.

Indicts Fielding, as he did in his *The English Novel* (item 480), for immorality. The introductory chapters of *Tom Jones* are full of "nauseous prurience and hypocrisy" and the novel is one of the most immoral ever written. *Amelia* is a better novel because it is a more serious story, but it is marred by the intrusive narrator.

482. Forster, E.M. *Aspects of the Novel*. London and New York: Harcourt, Brace and World, 1927.

In the once-famous distinction between "flat" and "round" characters, declares Parson Adams and Tom Jones to be "round" characters. Views *Joseph Andrews* as an "aborted" attempt to parody *Pamela*; with the creation of such "round" characters as Adams and Slipslop, the parody ceases.

483. Forsyth, William. *The Novels and Novelists of the Eighteenth Century in Illustration of the Manners and Morals of the Age*. Port Washington, N.Y.: Kennikat Press, 1970, Originally published London: J. Murray and New York: D. Appleton, 1871.

Presents a typically Victorian view of Fielding: one cannot analyze or describe the plot of *Tom Jones* "without offending against the respect due to female delicacy." Tom's adventures are fit "only for the ale-house." *Amelia* is a realistic portrayal of the times but is marred by its depiction of "licentious manners."

484.   Foster, James R. *History of the Pre-Romantic Novel in
       England*. New York: Modern Language Association and
       London: Oxford University Press, 1949.

       Among the many scattered references to Fielding are
       discussions of the sentimental attitudes in *Amelia* and
       the impact of French literature on Fielding.

       Review: H.S. Hughes, *Philological Quarterly*, 29 (1950),
       253-54.

485.   Fox, Ralph W. *The Novel and the People*. London:
       Lawrence and Wishart, 1937. Reprinted New York: Inter-
       national Publishers, 1945.

       Examines Fielding in a Marxian context. Fielding's
       greatness lies in his humane realism; his weakness is
       his inability to wed that realism with sentiment.

486.   Freedman, Richard. *The Novel*. New York: Newsweek
       Books, 1975.

       Uses outdated materials to generalize about Fielding's
       life and career: Fielding "tired of flailing Richardson"
       in *Joseph Andrews* and so decided to write his own novel,
       Tom Jones; *Amelia* "makes a sad pendant to a glittering
       career."

487.   Galbraith, Lois Hall. *The Established Clergy as Depic-
       ted in English Prose Fiction from 1740 to 1800*. Phila-
       delphia: University of Pennsylvania Press, 1950.

       This work supposedly contains material on Fielding's
       fiction, but the compilers have not perused the work.

488.   Garnett, David. "Samuel Richardson, Henry Fielding,
       and Tobias Smollett," in *The English Novelists: A
       Survey of the Novel by Twenty Contemporary Novelists*,
       ed. Derek Verschoyle. London: Chatto and Windus, 1936.
       Pp. 67-80.

       Presents a negative view of Fielding, who lacks imagina-
       tion and whose style is "humdrum." Fielding's introduc-
       tory essays in *Tom Jones* and his moralizing have been
       pernicious influences on the development of the novel
       because they led to the "vast army of bores" who use
       the novel to lecture on morality.

489.   Gerould, Gordon Hall. *The Patterns of English and
       American Fiction: A History*. New York: Russell and
       Russell, 1966. Originally published Boston: Little,
       Brown, 1942.

Regards *Shamela* as "coarse," "brutal," and "ignoble."
Joseph Andrews is not a mere imitation of *Pamela* but is
a new kind of novel that reflects its author's disgust
at Richardson's morality. The chief merit of *Tom Jones*
is its organization: Fielding adjusts "the space given
an event to its real importance" and increases "the
density of incident" as the story progresses. This
technique lends the novel an aura of reality. *Amelia*
fails because of an inept transference of dramatic
method from the stage. Overall, Fielding's strength
is his style; he had a command of prose greater than
any other English novelist.

490. Golden, Morris. "The Novel as Education." *Husson Review*, 1 (1968), 7-13.

Many eighteenth-century novelists, Fielding among them,
examine contemporary formal education in their works.
Most of these novelists, however, are more concerned
with moral and social education than they are with formal education. Fielding's aim, for example, "is to
educate the reader in the sum of a culture," an aim
which comprehends moral, social, and formal education.

491. Gosse, Edmund. *A History of Eighteenth-Century Literature (1660-1780)*. Freeport, N.Y.: Books for Libraries
Press, 1972. Originally published New York: Macmillan,
1889.

Briefly generalizes about Fielding's fiction: *Joseph
Andrews* is a "beautiful structure of pure comedy"
weakened only by the interpolated tales; *Jonathan Wild*
has "force and originality" but is cynical and gloomy;
Tom Jones, perhaps the greatest English novel, is a
"truly sunny book," marred only by digressive episodes;
Amelia is less "sunny" but more "humane and tender"
than *Tom Jones*.

492. Grant, Damian. *Tobias Smollett: A Study in Style*. Manchester: Manchester University Press and Totowa, N.J.:
Rowman and Littlefield, 1977.

Remarks on Fielding's style *passim*, and concludes that
his constant undercutting and irony results in a "feeble"
and "unnatural" style which greatly flaws *Tom Jones* (see
pp. 74-78 in particular).

493. Greene, Graham. "Fielding and Sterne," in his *The Lost
Childhood and Other Essays*. London: Eyre and Spottis-
wood, 1951. Pp. 58-65. Originally published in *From*

Anne to Victoria: Essays by Various Hands, ed. Bonamy
Dobrée. London: Cassel and Co., 1937. Pp. 279-89.
The latter book was reprinted Freeport, N.Y.: Books for
Libraries Press, 1967.

Even though Sterne is pleasurable to read, he contributed
nothing to the development of the novel. Fielding, on
the other hand, was a great innovator: he gave the novel
its "architecture," showing others how to impose order
on the chaos of the picaresque; he used parody as did
Joyce in *Ulysses*; he employed innumerable sub-plots to
give the novel "the proportions of life."

494. Halsband, Robert. "Fielding: The Hogarth of Fiction."
      Saturday Review, 33 (September 30, 1950), 20-1.

      This item was not reviewed by the compilers.

495. ————. "Lady Mary Wortley Montague and Eighteenth-
      Century Fiction." *Philological Quarterly*, 45 (1966),
      145-56.

      Briefly discusses Lady Mary's attitudes towards Fielding's
      work: *Joseph Andrews* was her favorite Fielding novel, and
      she thought *Tom Jones* was a "sorry scoundrel"; she de-
      plored the lack of realism and didacticism in Fielding's
      work.

*   Hammond, Geraldine E. "Evidences of the Dramatist's
      Technique in Henry Fielding's Novels." (See item 345.)

*   Hassall, Anthony J. "Fielding's Puppet Image." (See
      item 346.)

*   Hatfield, Glenn. *Henry Fielding and the Language of
      Irony*. (See item 197.)

496. Heidler, Joseph B. *History, from 1700-1800, of English
      Criticism of Prose Fiction*. Urbana: University of
      Illinois Press, 1928.

      Refers to Fielding frequently, stressing his rejection
      of unrealistic fiction and emphasizing his theoretical
      commitment to a realistic portrayal of life. Fielding's
      focus on realism helped found the so-called "modern"
      novel.

497. Hibbett, Howard S. "Saikaku and Burlesque Fiction."
      Harvard Journal of Asiatic Studies, 20 (1957), 53-73.

      Compares the burlesque vein in the Japanese writer,

Ihara Saikaku (1642-93), with that in Fielding. Both
authors are primarily wits, rather than novelists of
"illusionistic realism," and both use burlesque to
heighten their satires on manners. They differ in that
Fielding's plots are more dramatic and unified; moreover, Saikaku does not attempt, as does Fielding, to
create sympathetic characters or to satirically attack
particular individuals.

498. Hill, Rowland M. "Setting in the Novels of Henry Fielding." *The Citadel Faculty Studies*, 7 (1943), 26-52.

Sees setting in Fielding's novels as negligible; he
eschews extended descriptions, possibly because of his
dramatic training, but more likely because such lengthy
digressions interrupt the flow of the action. However,
he does occasionally employ mock-heroic settings, in
conformance with the mock-heroic nature of his fiction,
and uses some "gothic mood-settings."

499. Hilles, Frederick W. "More About Fielding." *Yale Review*, 57 (1967), 278-82.

A review-article on Michael Irwin's *Henry Fielding, the
Tentative Realist* (item 506) and Martin C. Battestin's
Wesleyan edition of *Joseph Andrews* (item 50).

500. Holliday, Carl. *English Fiction from the Fifth to the
Twentieth Century*. New York: Century, 1912.

Regards Fielding as the greatest of the eighteenth-century novelists because of his plotting and characterization. His plots are well-constructed, although *Joseph
Andrews* has too many sub-plots, and his characters are
natural and masculine. In addition, Fielding's code
of ethics is admirable because goodness of *being* is more
important than goodness of *doing*.

501. Horn, Andreās. "Social Morality: Fielding," in his *Byron's "Don Juan" and the Eighteenth-Century English
Novel*. Berne: Francke, 1962. Pp. 9-27.

Both *Don Juan* and Fielding's novels are infused with the
moral view that the only sin is doing harm and the only
virtue is doing good. This attitude implies tolerance
on the one hand and active benevolism on the other.
Unlike Byron, however, who is consistently tolerant,
Fielding becomes less tolerant between *Joseph Andrews*
and *Amelia*.

502.   Horne, Charles F. *The Technique of the Novel: The Ele-*
        ments of the Art, Their Evolution and Present Use. New
        York and London: Harper and Brothers, 1908.

        Contrasts Richardson and Fielding, viewing the former
        as an "unconscious artist" and the latter as a "deliber-
        ate student" of his art. Richardson's simplicity keeps
        him from exploring motives, whereas Fielding wishes to
        penetrate beneath the surface to see what a person really
        is and how he actually feels. Richardson's characters
        are idealized, but Fielding employs a wide range of
        characterization techniques. He uses the idealized
        figure (Allworthy), the caricature (Square and Thwackum),
        and the realistic individual (Tom Jones and Booth).
        Fielding's minor characters are more vivid than Richard-
        son's and they play more important roles in his novels.
        In terms of plot, Richardson is superior, but Fielding's
        plots cover a wider range of experience and show a
        greater knowledge of humanity.

503.   Huffman, C.H. *The 18th Century Novel in Theory and*
        Practice. Dayton, Va.: Ruebush-Kieffer Co., 1920.

        Stresses Fielding's use of realistic characters. He was
        the first novelist to fully realize the importance of
        realism in establishing a new kind of prose fiction.

504.   Humphreys, A.R. "Fielding and Smollett," in *From Dryden*
        to Johnson, Vol. 4 of *The Pelican Guide to English*
        Literature. Baltimore: Penguin, 1957. Pp. 313-32.

        Calls *Joseph Andrews* "as sane and attractive a novel as
        there is" and sees it as a "counter" to the emotional
        melodrama of *Pamela.* *Jonathan Wild* overcomes the "weak-
        nesses of propaganda" in its "panoramic survey of cor-
        rupt power." *Tom Jones* is Fielding's masterpiece,
        characterized by its honest portrayal of social fact
        and human nature. *Amelia* serves as an "index" of the
        developing social consciousness of the century. The
        latter novel's seriousness shows that there are "two
        Fieldings," the earlier one expansive, urbane, gently
        rebuking folly through comedy, and the later one thought-
        ful, analytical, and focused on social ills.

505.   ————. "Fielding's Irony: Its Method and Effects."
        Review of English Studies, 18 (1942), 183-96. Reprinted
        in Iser, item 507, and Paulson, item 258. Extracts re-
        printed in Rawson, item 272.

        Unlike Swift's irony, which is profoundly disturbing,

and Butler's irony, which undermines traditional ethics, Fielding's irony attacks deviations from societal norms in an orthodox way; it is an irony of integration rather than disintegration. Because of his use of caricature and exaggeration, Fielding is less ambiguous in his use of irony than is Swift. Fielding is particularly effective in using irony to reduce complex psychological behavior to easily accessible formulas.

* Hunter, J. Paul. *Occasional Form: Henry Fielding and the Chains of Circumstance*. (See item 209.)

506. Irwin, Michael. *Henry Fielding: The Tentative Realist*. Oxford: The Clarendon Press, 1967.

Regards Fielding's novels, which are hailed for their realism, as primarily non-realistic. Fielding's concern with irony and didacticism, through which he drives home his moral points, militates against realism. The didactic episodes in *Joseph Andrews* and *Tom Jones* fragment those novels. Although realistic elements are introduced, few characters are ever realized realistically, few plots are ever resolved realistically, and few actions are ever related realistically.

Reviews: Frederick W. Hilles, *Yale Review*, 57 (1967), 278-82; Priscilla Jenkins, *Review of English Studies*, 20 (1969), 249-50; *Johnsonian Newsletter*, 27 (1967), 13; Juliet McMaster, *Dalhousie Review*, 48 (1968), 266-68; Ronald Paulson, *Novel*, 2 (1968), 79-80; C.J. Rawson, *Notes and Queries*, n.s. 15 (1968), 474-77; *Times Literary Supplement* (October 19, 1967), p. 985; J.A. Wightman, *Southern Review: An Australian Journal of Literary Studies*, 3 (1968), 95-97.

* Irwin, W.R. "Satire and Comedy in the Works of Henry Fielding." (See item 213.)

507. Iser, Wolfgang, ed. *Henry Fielding und der Englische Roman des 18. Jahrhunderts*. Darmstadt: Wissenschaftliche Buchgesellschaft, 1972.

A collection of essays in English, French, and German. Contents: George Sherburn, "Fielding's *Amelia*: An Interpretation," item 1021; A.R. Humphreys, "Fielding's Irony: Its Methods and Effects," item 505; Maynard Mack, "*Joseph Andrews* and *Pamela*," item 689; Arnold Kettle, "*Tom Jones*," item 874; R.S. Crane, "The Concept of Plot and the Plot of *Tom Jones*," item 807; Mark

Spilka, "Comic Resolution in Fielding's *Joseph Andrews*,"
item 712; Dorothy Van Ghent, "On *Tom Jones*," item 975;
George Sherburn, "Fielding's Social Outlook," item 579;
Will Erzgräber, "Das Menschenbild in Henry Fieldings
Roman *Amelia*," item 1176; William Empson, "*Tom Jones*,"
item 839; William B. Coley, "Gide and Fielding," item
1114; John S. Coolidge, "Fielding and 'Conservation of
Character,'" item 470; Irwin Ehrenpreis, "Fielding's Use
of Fiction: The Autonomy of *Joseph Andrews*," item 665;
Sheridan Baker, "Fielding's *Amelia* and the Materials of
Romance," item 985; Michel Cazenave, "A Propos de *Tom
Jones*," item 1157; Mark Spilka, "Fielding and the Epic
Impulse," item 585; Wolfgang Iser, "Die Leserrolle in
Fieldings *Joseph Andrews* und *Tom Jones*," item 1196;
R.S. Crane, "Suggestions Toward a Genealogy of the 'Man
of Feeling'" (not on Fielding and therefore not anno-
tated in this bibliography); Edward C. Mack, "Pamela's
Stepdaughters: The Heroines of Smollett and Fielding,"
item 529; Ian Watt, "The Naming of Characters in Defoe,
Richardson, and Fielding," item 607; Irma Z. Sherwood,
"The Novelists as Commentators," item 1022; Frank Ker-
mode, "Richardson and Fielding," item 517; Wayne C.
Booth, "The Self-Conscious Narrator in Comic Fiction
before *Tristram Shandy*," item 457; Franz Stanzel, "*Tom
Jones* und *Tristram Shandy*," item 1252; Victor Lange,
"Erzählformen im Roman des achtzehnten Jahrhunderts,"
item 1206.

508. Jackson, Holbrook. "Henry Fielding," in his *Great
      English Novelists: with Thirty-Two Illustrations*.
      Philadelphia: George W. Jacobs, 1908. Pp. 64-86.

      Presents a brief biography of Fielding and a general
      survey of his works, emphasizing *Tom Jones*, a "master-
      piece" which demonstrates the complexity of human
      psychology. Fielding's novels are satiric protests
      against the sentimentalism and "moral morbidity" of
      Richardson.

509. Jenkins, Elizabeth. *Henry Fielding*. The English
      Novelists Series. London: Home and Van Thal, 1947;
      Denver: Alan Swallow, 1948. Second edition London:
      Barker, 1966.

      Fielding helped develop the novel "as a work of the
      imagination," influencing his successors through Dickens.
      Fielding was helped greatly in his writing by the age in
      which he lived, an age, unlike the twentieth century,
      which stimulated the imagination. Fielding's strength

lay in his creation of believable characters and scenes. The plot of *Tom Jones* also shows him to be "the greatest craftsman who ever attempted the English novel." Jenkins also praises *Amelia* highly because its characters are perfectly developed; Amelia's character, in particular, is a triumph.

Reviews: John Farrelly, *New Republic* (January 3, 1949), p. 27; *Notes and Queries*, 193 (1948), 65-66; *Times Literary Supplement* (December 27, 1947), p. 678; *Times Literary Supplement* (January 24, 1948), p. 50.

510. Jenkins, Owen. "Richardson's *Pamela* and Fielding's 'Vile Forgeries.'" *Philological Quarterly*, 44 (1965), 200-10.

Contrary to received critical opinion, Richardson did not let Fielding's attacks on *Pamela* go unanswered. Richardson's reply is *II Pamela*, where he attacks Fielding under the guise of Mr. Turner.

511. Johnson, Maurice. *Fielding's Art of Fiction: Eleven Essays on "Shamela," "Joseph Andrews," "Tom Jones," and "Amelia."* Philadelphia: University of Pennsylvania Press and London: Oxford University Press, 1961.

Argues that Fielding's theory of fiction is based on the conviction that literature and life are inextricably related, and "that fiction can assist us in mastering reality." Within his works, he often juxtaposes the artificial (the interpolated tales) with the "real" (the story of the novel), inviting the reader to similarly juxtapose the novel with life. He concentrates on seemingly insignificant details, which grow in importance until they affect the outcome of the novel. He also provides guides for living for the reader in his brief essays as well as in his estimable characters. Throughout his study, Johnson emphasizes Fielding's craftsmanship and use of literary analogues, stressing the Biblical parallels in *Joseph Andrews* and providing a book-by-book comparison of the *Aeneid* and *Amelia*.

Reviews: Martin C. Battestin, *Philological Quarterly*, 41 (1962), 588-90; W.W. Combs, *South Atlantic Quarterly*, 61 (1962), 422-23; *Times Literary Supplement* (August 3, 1962), p. 555; Andrew Wright, *Modern Language Review*, 58 (1963), 464.

* Jones, Benjamin Maelor. *Henry Fielding, Novelist and Magistrate.* (See item 219.)

512. Jordan, Robert M. "The Limits of Illusion: Faulkner,
      Fielding, and Chaucer." *Criticism*, 2 (1960), 278-305.

      Explains that unlike writers of the twentieth century,
      when "it became imperative that artifice appear un-
      artificial," Fielding only pretends that there is no
      division between the "real" and the "fictive" worlds.
      Although he continually moves between these two worlds,
      he never loses the distinction between them. In fact,
      Joseph Andrews is about "ways of seeing the world" and
      the madness inherent in failing to distinguish between
      the real and the unreal.

513. Kahler, Erich. *The Inward Turn of Narrative*. Translated
      by Richard and Clara Winston. Bollingen Series, 83.
      Princeton: Princeton University Press, 1973.

      Contains scattered remarks on Fielding, the most de-
      tailed of which is the discussion (pp. 170-75) of his
      innovations in narrative. Among these are his com-
      bining of satire and sentiment and his development of
      a direct and intimate relationship between the narrator
      and audience.

514. Karl, Frederick R. "Henry Fielding: The Novel, The
      Epic, and the Comic Sense of Life," in his *The Adversary
      Literature. The English Novel in the Eighteenth Century:
      A Study in Genre*. New York: Farrar, Strauss, and Giroux,
      1974. Pp. 146-82.

      Includes detailed discussions of *Joseph Andrews*, *Tom
      Jones*, and *Amelia*. Attempts to demonstrate that Field-
      ing's experiments with narrative, character, plot,
      theme, and language "turned prose fiction away from
      romance and epic...." *Tom Jones* is Fielding's most
      mature novel because all its conflicts are subsumed under
      the dialectic "between primitive 'disorder' and civi-
      lized 'order.'" *Amelia* is weakened by the loss of this
      dialectic and is a precursor of sentimental fiction.

515. Kaul, A.N. "The Adjudication of Fielding's Comedy," in
      his *The Action of English Comedy: Studies in the Encoun-
      ter of Abstraction and Experience from Shakespeare to
      Shaw*. New Haven: Yale University Press, 1970. Pp.
      151-92.

      Identifies the central concept in Fielding's comedies
      as an "adjudicated love." That is, although Fielding
      is condemned by turns as a sentimentalist or a sensual-
      ist and libertine, he is neither; rather, he plays these

ideas off against each other to expose and negate them
as partial and misleading theories. For the sentimentalist, the object of love is material advantage; for
the sensualist, love is an appetite; for Fielding, love
ultimately has "no object but itself." This idea
begins in *Shamela*, in which Richardson's sentimentalist
view is exposed as materialistic, develops through *Tom
Jones*, in which the hero has to subjugate his appetites
to learn the nature and value of true love, and cul-
minates in *Amelia*, in which Booth directly articulates
Fielding's views of true love.

516. Kearney, A.M. *Samuel Richardson*. Profiles in Litera-
      ture Series. London: Routledge and Kegan Paul and
      New York: Humanities Press, 1968.

      Concludes with "A Note on Richardson and Fielding" (pp.
      106-08) in which the two authors are compared. Field-
      ing is more scholarly and self-aware than is Richardson.
      His comic emphasis leads him to develop generalized
      characters lacking the psychological depth of Richard-
      son's figures and causes him to "laugh mankind out of
      its viciousness" rather than "shock it back to the paths
      of virtue" as Richardson tries to do.

517. Kermode, Frank. "Richardson and Fielding." *Cambridge
      Journal*, 4 (1950), 106-14. Reprinted in Iser, item
      507, and Spector, item 584.

      The eighteenth- and nineteenth-century arguments that
      Richardson was a moralist and Fielding was immoral were
      laid to rest by Dobson and Cross. However, it is
      worthwhile to compare Fielding's morality with Richard-
      son's by using considerations of formal and technical
      values. Fielding's idea of morality as conveyed in
      Tom Jones is that morality is equivalent to a "good
      heart," and that all right-thinking people know what
      he means; in other words, Fielding depends on eighteenth-
      century forms to carry his ideas. Richardson, on the
      other hand, painfully develops his moral code throughout
      Clarissa.

518. Kettle, Arnold. *An Introduction to the English Novel*.
      London: Hutchinson University Library, 1951. Reprinted
      New York: Harper and Row, 1960. Kettle's discussion of
      Fielding is reprinted as "*Tom Jones*" in Compson, item
      804; Iser, item 507; and Paulson, item 258. Extracts
      are also printed in Rawson, item 272.

      Focuses on *Tom Jones* as epitomizing Fielding's art. The

novel is overplotted with many scenes that do not arise
from character and motive, and its characters are flat
figures in the "humors" tradition. Nevertheless, the
novel engages the reader's sympathies because Tom and
Sophia, like Clarissa, are rebels fighting against conventional society embodied in Blifil, who while osten-
sibly representing discretion and piety, actually is
the self-seeking, hypocritical villain of the work.
Fielding deliberately keeps the reader at a distance
through his abstract, descriptive style, so that life
is surveyed but not experienced. Fielding's concern
is with the panorama of English society, not with the
precise feelings of individual characters.

519. Kinkead-Weeks, Mark. *Samuel Richardson: Dramatic
      Novelist*. London: Methuen, 1973.

      Refers frequently to Fielding throughout and makes a
      comparison of his work with that of Richardson (pp.
      465-71). The formal differences between the two are
      "radical"; whereas Richardson is a dramatic novelist,
      Fielding is an epic writer, standing between his reader
      and the work.

520. Knight, Grant. *The Novel in English*. New York: R.R.
      Smith, 1931.

      Emphasizes Fielding's adaptation of dramatic techniques,
      such as realistic dialogue and settings, to fiction.
      Most of these devices he successfully employed, but
      along with them he unfortunately used the *deus ex machina*,
      which weakens his work. Because Fielding is a naturalist,
      his morality is merely a "by-product" of his technique.

521. Knowles, A.S., Jr. "Defoe, Swift, and Fielding: Notes
      on the Retirement Theme," in *Quick Springs of Sense:
      Studies in the Eighteenth Century*, ed. Larry S. Cham-
      pion. Athens: University of Georgia Press, 1974. Pp.
      124-36.

      The Horatian ideal of rural retirement as a joyous
      escape from urban corruption and as protection against
      enflamed passions is an important theme in Fielding's
      work. His use of the tradition in *Joseph Andrews* and
      Jonathan Wild takes the form of exemplary tales and is
      thematically effective but unoriginal. In *Tom Jones*,
      however, the retirement ideal is handled more complexly
      in the episode of the Man of the Hill, who, as misan-
      thropic nature-worshipper, finds no joy, only relief,

in his retirement, which serves to alienate him from
his fellow man.

522. Konigsberg, Ira. *Samuel Richardson and the Dramatic
      Novel*. Lexington: University of Kentucky Press, 1968.

      Contends that Richardson began the "character novel"
      which leads to Austen and James and that Fielding began
      the "panoramic novel" which leads to Dickens.

523. Lathrop, Henry Burrowes. *The Art of the Novelist*.
      London: George G. Harrap, 1921.

      The scattered remarks on Fielding emphasize his use of
      coincidence (which goes "beyond the limit of accepta-
      bility") and of characters with "mingled qualities"
      (no basically sympathetic figure is too debased for
      regeneration).

524. Leavis, F.R. *The Great Tradition: George Eliot, Henry
      James, Joseph Conrad*. London: Chatto and Windus, 1948.
      Reprinted New York: New York University Press, 1963.
      Excerpts as reprinted in Battestin, item 779, and
      Rawson, item 272.

      Presents a generally negative view of Fielding, who is
      important historically (his ironic style leads to Jane
      Austen) but unimportant intrinsically (his attitudes
      are simplistic and his novels are monotonous).

525. Lodge, David. *Language of Fiction*. London: Routledge
      and Kegan Paul and New York: Columbia University Press,
      1966.

      Alludes to Fielding *passim*. Although Fielding seems to
      have worked out the action of *Tom Jones* with an almanac,
      he "makes no attempt to disguise the fact that his
      novels are fictions," conducting his narrative with "a
      deliberate display of artifice."

526. Lovett, Robert Morss, and Helen Sard Hughes. "Richardson
      and Fielding," in their *The History of the Novel in
      England*. St. Clair Shores, Mich: Scholarly Press,
      1971. Pp. 52-75. Originally published Boston: Houghton
      Mifflin, 1932.

      A general survey that concludes that Fielding contributed
      to English fiction the satiric novel of manners, the
      standards for managing a complicated plot, and the real-
      istic method of portraying characters through their own
      speech and action.

527.   Lutwack, Leonard.   "Mixed and Uniform Prose Styles in
       the Novel."   *Journal of Aesthetics and Art Criticism*,
       18 (1960), 350-57.

       The mixed prose style in the novel gets its main im-
       petus from Fielding, ends briefly with *Moby Dick*, then
       begins again with *Ulysses*. It provides the author with
       the opportunity to vary his presentation in an inter-
       esting and effective manner.

528.   Macallister, Hamilton.   *Fielding*.   London: Evans Broth-
       ers, 1967.   Reprinted New York: Arco, 1971.

       Attempts to present an overview of Fielding and his work
       in a non-scholarly manner for the general reader.   There
       are chapters on background, Fielding's life, *Joseph
       Andrews*, *Tom Jones*, and other prose works; a bibliography
       and index follow the text.   The advanced student of
       Fielding may be troubled by the author's lack of biblio-
       graphic knowledge (he seems unaware, for instance, of
       the three important editions of *Shamela* published between
       1953 and 1961).   He also contends, in spite of the
       great rebirth of interest in Fielding from the fifties
       until the present, that Fielding does not appeal to
       modern readers.

529.   Mack, Edward C.   "Pamela's Stepdaughters: The Heroines
       of Smollett and Fielding."   *College English*, 8 (1947),
       293-301.   Reprinted in Iser, item 507.

       Defines the ideal eighteenth-century heroine as a vapid
       combination of sexual purity and sensibility; writers,
       like Smollett, who stick closely to this ideal have a
       difficult time creating life-like female figures.   Only
       Richardson and Fielding were able to portray women who
       are more than mere abstractions.

530.   McKillop, Alan D.   "Henry Fielding," in *The Early
       Masters of English Fiction*.   Lawrence: University of
       Kansas Press, 1956.   Pp. 98-146.

       Provides a general introduction to Fielding which sur-
       veys all aspects of the novels, emphasizing Fielding's
       ethics and narrative technique.   Fielding is an ethical
       empiricist, rejecting fine feelings for benevolent ac-
       tions in concrete situations.   He prefers virtuous im-
       pulse to the "virtue" which coldly operates on pre-
       conceived principles and codes set by special interests.
       Thus he sets up moral opposites, pitting spontaneity
       against formalism and altruism against self-serving.

Fielding's stories are held together by the intrusive narrator, who lends them moral significance and who provides a unifying thread for them.

Reviews: Douglas Grant, *Modern Language Review*, 52 (1957), 420-21; F.W. Hilles, *Philological Quarterly*, 36 (1957), 328-30; Martin Price, *Yale Review*, 46 (1957), 303-04; Arthur Sherbo, *Journal of English and Germanic Philology*, 56 (1957), 284-86; Ian Watt, *Modern Philology*, 55 (1957), 132-34; Charles B. Woods, *Modern Language Notes*, 72 (1957), 622-24.

531.   ————. "Henry Fielding," in his *English Literature from Dryden to Burns*. New York and London: Appleton-Century-Crofts, 1948. Pp. 267-71.

An extremely general survey of Fielding's fiction which focuses on its differences from Richardson's work while admitting that in *Amelia*, Fielding moved toward Richardsonian pathos.

532.   ————. "Introduction" to *An Essay on the New Species of Writing Founded by Mr. Fielding* (1751). Augustan Reprint Society, Pub. No. 95. Los Angeles: Clark Memorial Library, 1962.

Briefly analyzes this anonymous pamphlet and points out that its praise of Fielding is little more than a re-hashing of contemporary clichés about Fielding's originality and humor.

533.   ————. *Samuel Richardson, Printer and Novelist*. Chapel Hill: University of North Carolina Press, 1936.

Makes dozens of references to Fielding, focusing on Richardson's malevolence toward his rival. Richardson's attacks failed to hurt Fielding's reputation as much as they did his own.

*   MacLean, Kenneth. *John Locke and English Literature of the Eighteenth Century*. (See item 241.)

534.   Maresca, Thomas E. "Fielding," in his *Epic to Novel*. Columbus: Ohio State University Press, 1974. Pp. 181-233.

Traces the process by which the novel replaced the epic as the major literary form in England. Fielding's role in this transition is an important one because he keeps alive the traditional epic theme of wisdom while re-creating the epic hero as a responsible agent who freely chooses and shapes his own life.

535. Mendilow, A.A. *Time and the Novel*. London: Peter
      Nevil, 1952.

      In developing his thesis about the place of time in the
      unity of the novel, Mendilow often uses Fielding as an
      example (e.g., of the unimportance of causal episodes
      in the picaresque or episodic novel).

536. Minchin, Harry C. "Henry Fielding and His Writings."
      Fortnightly Review, 87 (1907), 620-34.

      Moralizes about Fielding's work. In spite of his moral
      purpose, humor, and excellent female characters,
      Fielding created two characters, Tom Jones and Booth,
      whose actions are so depraved that readers must turn
      away from them in disgust.

537. Monteser, Frederick. *The Picaresque Element in Western
      Literature*. Studies in the Humanities No. 5. Univer-
      sity, Ala.: University of Alabama Press, 1975.

      Asserts that *Joseph Andrews* is in the picaresque tradi-
      tion; both the scenes on the road and Adams' character
      are traceable to the *Siglo de Oro*. Likewise, *Jonathan
      Wild* was consciously influenced by the picaresque, es-
      pecially in Wild's "code of conduct" for attaining
      greatness. With *Tom Jones*, Fielding transcended the
      picaresque, although Books VII-XII, which cover Tom's
      trip to London, place Tom among "the Lazarillos of this
      world" and are firmly in the picaresque tradition.

*   Moore, Robert E. "Hogarth's Role in Fielding's Novels,"
      in his *Hogarth's Literary Relationships*, pp. 107-61.
      (See item 248.)

538. Muir, Edwin. *The Structure of the Novel*. New York:
      Harcourt Brace, 1929.

      Although Fielding's characters do not develop, they
      emerge with more completeness as the story progresses.
      Tom is an authentic character in *Tom Jones*, serving
      both as a guide through the plot and as a fully-developed
      protagonist. Also see Forster, item 482.

539. Murakami, Shiko. "Hardy to Igirisu Shosetsu: Hardy to
      Fielding," in *20 Seiki Bungaku no Senkusha Thomas Hardy*,
      eds. Mamoru Osawa, Michio Yoshikawa, and Shigeru Fujita.
      Tokyo: Shinozaki Shorin, 1977. Pp. 31-47.

      The compilers have been unable to read this essay, listed
      in the MLA bibliography for 1977.

540.   Murry, John Middleton.   "In Defence of Fielding," in
       his *Unprofessional Essays*.   London: Jonathan Cape, 1956.
       Pp. 11-52.   Reprinted Fairlawn, N.J.: Essential Books,
       1956.   Slightly edited versions of this essay appear in
       Compson, item 804, and Paulson, item 258.

       Discusses Fielding's view of class distinction, arguing
       that he regards it as an accident because goodness and
       generosity are traits found in the lower orders as well
       as the higher.   Likewise, the morality of sexual en-
       counters is not dependent on social position.   Tom Jones,
       a good-natured idealist about women, is depicted as a
       moral man--he never takes advantage of women, but rather
       submits to their advances in order to be kind.   Also see
       Murry, "Fielding's Sexual Ethic," item 912.

       Review: Times Literary Supplement (20 April 1956),
       p. 238.

*   Needham, Gwendolyn B., and R.P. Utter.   *Pamela's
       Daughters*.   New York: Macmillan, 1936.

       See under Utter, item 602.

541.   Olshin, Toby A.   "*Pompey the Little*: A Study in Field-
       ing's Influence."   *Revue des Langues Vivantes*, 36 (1970),
       117-24.

       Catalogues the similarities between Fielding's fiction
       and Francis Coventry's *Pompey the Little*, noting that in
       the third edition of the latter work, Coventry made
       several changes which show a growing understanding of
       Fielding's meaning and structure.   The major change is
       to "interconnect" several characters who were not con-
       nected in the earlier editions and to develop major
       figures in more detail in order to tighten the plot.

542.   Pantučková, Lidmila.   "The Relationship of W.M. Thackeray
       to Henry Fielding."   *Sbornik Praci Filosofické Fakulty
       Brněnské University*, 11 (1962), 99-114.

       Explains Thackeray's shift from his early admiration of
       Fielding in terms of his gradually increasing acceptance
       of the standards of "the English bourgeoisie."

543.   Park, William.   "Fielding and Richardson."   *Publications
       of the Modern Language Association of America*, 81 (1966),
       381-88.

       Reverses the usual contrastive approach to Fielding and
       Richardson by showing similarities in attitude.   They
       both believe that the novel should provide a positive

example for others to follow and that this is best accomplished by treating "general nature" rather than the
particular or topical. Both view sexual purity as the
highest female virtue. They are most alike, however, in
their belief in an "absolute deity" who created a moral
universe in which human nature is always the same. Also
see Theo Olivier, item 628.

544.   ————. "What Was New About the 'New Species of Writ-
        ing'?" *Studies in the Novel*, 2 (1970), 112-30.

The newness of Richardson and Fielding was in their arrangement of existing fragments of fiction into whole,
new forms. They took over the stock cast of characters
(virgin, prostitute, rake, good man, etc.) of their
age; the standard plot of movement from the country to
the city and an introduction to vice; the idea of the
hero's or heroine's confinement; and the eventual return to the country. They integrated these into unified,
artistic wholes which influenced most of the novels
which came immediately after them.

*   Parker, A.A. "Fielding and the Structure of *Don Quixote*."
        (See item 920.)

545.   Paulson, Ronald. *Satire and the Novel in Eighteenth-
        Century England*. New Haven: Yale University Press,
        1967.

The significant material on Fielding appears as "Lucianic
Satire in *Tom Jones*," item 922.

Reviews: Wayne C. Booth, *Philological Quarterly*, 47
(1968), 340-42; Morris Golden, *Studies in the Novel*, 2
(1970), 222-28.

*   Penner, A.R. "Fielding's Adaptation of Cervantes' Knight
        and Squire." (See item 698.)

546.   Perry, Bliss. *A Study of Prose Fiction*. Boston and New
        York: Houghton Mifflin, 1920. Originally published
        Boston: Houghton Mifflin, 1902.

The few scattered remarks on Fielding emphasize his
realism and defend him against charges of coarseness and
immorality.

547.   Phelps, William Lyon. "Fielding, Smollett, Sterne," in
        his *The Advance of the English Novel*. St. Clair Shores,
        Mich.: Scholarly Press, 1971. Pp. 53-78. Originally
        published New York: Dodd Mead, 1916.

Discusses Fielding's weaknesses and strengths. He was "constitutionally" unable to comprehend Richardson's artistic merits and he was condescending and insincere in his digressive introductory chapters in *Joseph Andrews* and *Tom Jones*, which "break the continuity of the narrative, destroy the illusion, and discontent the reader." However, Fielding is one of the greatest English humorists and has a keen power of observation which gives his novels realism and variety.

* Plumb, J.H. "Henry Fielding and the Rise of the Novel." (See item 260.)

* ————. "Henry Fielding: The Journey Through Gin Lane." (See item 261.)

548. Price, Lawrence Marsden. *English Literature in Germany*. University of California Publications in Modern Philology No. 37. Berkeley and Los Angeles: University of California Press, 1953.

Regards Fielding's impact on German literature as much more significant than has generally been supposed; for example, "*Wilhelm Meister* owes more to Fielding than to Richardson...."

Reviews: Charles B. Woods, *Philological Quarterly*, 33 (1954), 310; A.E. Zucker, *American-German Review*, 19 (1954), 38-39.

549. Price, Martin. "Fielding: The Comedy of Forms," in his *To the Palace of Wisdom: Studies in Order and Energy from Dryden to Blake*. Carbondale: Southern Illinois University Press, 1964. Pp. 286-312. Reprinted in Rawson, item 272.

Characteristic of Fielding's art is "his constant subversion of forms, his deliberate overturning of rigid stances or systematized attitudes." He opposes such rigidity because it often conceals selfishness and vanity, as in *Pamela*, and true virtue is flexible and dependent upon generous conduct. Fielding is a moralist who does not try to re-order society but who wishes to re-establish the basis of its conduct by making it clear that each man can achieve goodness.

550. Priestley, J.B. "Henry Fielding: Then and Now." *The Listener*, 52 (1954), 609-10.

Not only is Fielding the true "father of the modern novel" in the historical sense, but his skillful plot-

ting, characterization, and irony also make him a very
readable novelist today.

551.   Pritchett, V.S. "The Ancestor," in his *The Living Novel
       and Later Appreciations*. New York: Random House, 1964.
       Pp. 3-11. Originally published in *The Living Novel*.
       London: Chatto and Windus, 1946.

       Asserts that Fielding added to English fiction much of
       its most important matter, such as "social problems,
       middle-class humor, the didactic habit, the club cul-
       ture, the horseplay," as well as the metaphoric use of
       country life. His rising interest in psychology, mani-
       fested in *Amelia*, anticipated "the coming age."

552.   ————. "Books in General." *New Statesman and Nation*,
       22 (1941), 510.

       Praises Fielding for his use of stage techniques to
       break the monotony of the flat, episodic, "reportorial"
       methods of picturesque writers like Defoe, but says that
       Fielding's popularity is declining and will continue
       to decline because his vigorous, "masculine" methods
       have been replaced by the "feminine" emphasis of modern
       novelists on sex and psychology. Moreover, to modern
       readers, Fielding's social views seem outdated and his
       overt moralizing too extensive and superficial.

553.   ————. "Our First Comic Novelist." *Listener*, 43
       (1950), 203-04.

       Generalizes about why Fielding is still enjoyable to
       some readers but waning in popularity with most. Al-
       though his zest and benevolence continue to have some
       appeal, the modern reader is likely to find the scenes
       of drunkenness and brawling dated and pointless and to
       view Fielding's moralizing as commonplace and smug.
       Historically, Fielding "put the novel on its feet," and
       his influence is seen in Austen, Thackeray, Dickens,
       Meredith, and Wodehouse.

554.   Proper, Coenraad Bart Anne. *Social Elements in English
       Prose Fiction Between 1700 and 1832*. Amsterdam: H.J.
       Paris, 1929.

       Pages 49-62 discuss Fielding's contributions to the
       "social," or sociological, novel. By localizing his
       setting and using realistic characters, essential for
       the social novel, Fielding paved the way for later
       writers. He also explored a wide range of social prob-

lems: corrupt elections, bad charity schools, public
executions, prison conditions, the use of sponging
houses, and a corrupt legal system, among many others.

555.   Raleigh, Walter. "Richardson and Fielding," in his
       *The English Novel, Being a Short Sketch from the Earliest
       Times to the Appearance of "Waverley"*. St. Clair Shores,
       Mich.: Scholarly Press, 1972. Pp. 140-79. Originally
       published London: John Murray, 1895.

       Defends Fielding's morality; unlike Richardson, who is
       a "classical moralist" believing in a rigid code of
       conduct which leads to a calculating prudence, Fielding
       is a "romantic moralist" believing that each man should
       be true to himself and emphasizing honesty and generous
       feeling. Fielding made two major advances in the novel
       form: he introduced realism in characterization and
       showed later writers how to manage a complicated plot
       artistically.

*   Ramondt, Marie. "Between Laughter and Humor in the
       Eighteenth Century." (See item 268.)

556.   "Ranger." "Henry Fielding." *The Bookman*, 29 (1906),
       202-04.

       Dwells on the disparity between the critical and popu-
       lar estimates of Fielding; the critics admire both his
       artistry and his morality, but the general public er-
       roneously sees his novels, especially *Tom Jones*, as
       immoral. Fielding's strength lies in his happy blend
       of wit and intellect. His greatness of character is
       demonstrated by the courage seen in his Lisbon journal.

557.   Rawson, C.J. "Fielding and Smollett," in *Dryden to
       Johnson*, ed. Roger Lonsdale, Vol. 4 of the *History of
       Literature in the English Language*. London: Barrie
       and Jenkins, 1971. Pp. 259-301.

       Surveys Fielding's fiction, emphasizing his moral stance
       and the use of mock epic, parody, and authorial intru-
       sion. As Fielding's art progressed, his use of parody
       and epic devices gave way to a more serious and direct
       presentation of an ethical view contrary to that of
       Richardson. The authorial intrusions develop an inti-
       macy between the narrator and reader but at the same
       time create a sense of the narrator's superiority and
       aloofness.

558.   ————. "Language, Dialogue, and Point of View in Field-
        ing: Some Considerations," in *Quick Springs of Sense:
        Studies in the Eighteenth Century*, ed. Larry S. Champion.
        Athens: University of Georgia Press, 1974. Pp. 137-56.

        Even though Fielding does not coin terms to fit the
        singularities of his characters, as does Richardson, he
        has a sharp ear for the cadences of the spoken language.
        He is particularly adept at stringing together clichés
        and cant terms in contexts which give them an original
        and comic force. He also enhances his comedy by using
        indirect speech and past tense ironically.

559.   ————. "Some Considerations on Authorial Intrusion
        and Dialogue in Fielding's Novels and Plays." *Durham
        University Journal*, 64 (1971), 32-44.

        In spite of his early dramatic training, Fielding seldom
        attempts a dramatic rendering of character or situation.
        His playwriting experience shows up in his novels in
        other ways: "well-made" plots; carefully patterned,
        self-contained scenes; a gallery of comic characters;
        and set pieces of repartee. His use of dialogue skill-
        fully blends dramatic and novelistic techniques. He is
        able to present vivid, "dramatic" dialogue, but the
        novel form permits him to control it, to call attention
        to certain things, to keep his reader at a distance from
        others, and to express his own attitude about what the
        characters say or the way they say it. His authorial
        presence in dialogue represents his best writing in the
        novels.

560.   Renwick, W.L. "Comic Epic in Prose," in *Essays and
        Studies by Members of the English Association*, Vol. 32,
        ed. Basil Willey. Oxford: The Clarendon Press, 1947.
        Pp. 40-43. Reprinted in Rawson, item 272.

        Analyzes word by word what Fielding meant by his famous
        phrase, "comic epic in prose." His audience would have
        understood "comic" to include realism as well as humor;
        "comic" also modifies "epic" to cut out much traditional
        paraphernalia, but the juxtaposition of the terms ex-
        tends the ethical content of comedy because "epic"
        carries with it the idea of a narrative of "serious im-
        port." The phrase "in prose" cuts out the stylistic
        implications of "epic" and plants the reader firmly in
        the "real" world.

561.   Richardson, A.E. *Georgian England*. Freeport, N.Y.:
        Books for Libraries Press, 1967. Originally published
        London: B.T. Batsford, 1931.

Discusses the historical, social, and artistic aspects
of the period 1660-1800 and briefly notes, in very
general terms, Fielding's contributions to the novel.

562. Robinson, Roger. "Henry Fielding and the English
Rococo," in *Studies in the Eighteenth Century*, 2, ed.
R.F. Brissenden. Toronto: University of Toronto Press,
1973. Pp. 93-111.

Demonstrates that Fielding blends unity of theme with
diversity of form. His interpolated tales, digressions,
asides, and similes are fully relevant to his central
themes. For example, the theme of "right judgment" is
presented through Allworthy's performance as magistrate,
Black George's treachery, the Man of the Hill's story,
the Gypsy episode, and various similes used when the
main action provides no opportunity to directly advance
the theme.

563. ————. "The Influence of Fielding on *Barnaby Rudge*."
*Journal of the Australasian Universities Language and
Literature Association*, 40 (1973), 183-97.

The justice in *Barnaby Rudge* who commits Barnaby to
Newgate is identified by Dickens as Sir John Fielding,
Henry's half-brother. Actually, given the dates Dickens
uses for this episode, Sir John could not have been the
justice; Dickens used his name because of his interest
in Henry Fielding, which is further shown in several
passages in *Barnaby Rudge* which parallel passages in
Joseph Andrews and *Amelia*.

564. Rogers, Katharine M. "Sensitive Feminism vs. Conventional Sympathy: Richardson and Fielding on Women."
Novel, 9 (1976), 256-70.

Discovers a feminist bias in the view of Richardson's
Pamela, Clarissa, and Harriet, all of whom assert that
women are equal to men and can be happy living independent of men. Richardson's women are intelligent, and
they all reject the romantic, sentimental notion that
love completes a woman and marriage is her highest as-
piration. On the other hand, Fielding's women—Fanny,
Sophia, and Amelia—accept the sexist conventions of
the day. Fielding does not want his women to be intelligent or independent; they rejoice in their subor-
dination to men and they see love and marriage as means
to their completion as individuals.

565. Rogers, Pat. "Fielding," in his *The Augustan Vision*.
New York: Barnes and Noble and London: Weidenfeld and
Nicolson, 1974. Pp. 275-85.

The novel "goes public" with *Shamela* and *Joseph Andrews*.
Whereas Richardson's *Pamela* is "unhealthy, private, ob-
sessive," asking the reader only to feel, Fielding's
first two novels are "healthy" and open, inviting the
reader to think and to become actively engaged in their
moral climates. *Tom Jones* dignifies the romance and
gives it prestige through adding a tight, complex plot
and a refreshing moral frankness.

566.   Sacks, Sheldon. *Fiction and the Shape of Belief: A
       Study of Henry Fielding, With Glances at Swift, Johnson,
       and Richardson*. Berkeley and Los Angeles: University
       of California Press, 1964.

       Divides fiction into three categories: satire, "organized
       so that it ridicules objects external to the world crea-
       ted in it"; apologue, "organized as a fictional example
       of the truth of a formulable statement or a series of
       such statements"; action (or novel), "organized so that
       it introduces characters, about whose fates we are made
       to care, in unstable relationships which are then further
       complicated until the complication in finally resolved
       by the removal of the represented instability." *Joseph
       Andrews*, *Tom Jones*, and *Amelia* are all arranged as novels
       although the interpolated tales may be considered apo-
       logues. These works all have a moral purpose, but the
       arrangement of the works through the creation of charac-
       ters about whom we care makes them novels.

       Reviews: Martin C. Battestin, *College English*, 27 (1966),
       654; Benjamin Boyce, *South Atlantic Quarterly*, 64 (1965),
       568-69; Frank Brady, *Journal of General Education*, 17
       (1966), 332-35; George A. Cevasco, *Library Journal*, 90
       (1965), 249-50; W.B. Coley, *Yale Review*, 55 (1965), 129-
       30; George P. Elliott, *Hudson Review*, 18 (1965), 433-41;
       C.T.P., *American Book Collector* (1966), 5; Ronald Paul-
       son, *Journal of English and Germanic Philology*, 65
       (1966), 602-04.

567.   Saintsbury, George. *Fielding*. London: George Bell and
       Sons, 1909.

       Consists of a general introduction and abridgements of
       Joseph Andrews, *Jonathan Wild*, *Tom Jones*, *Amelia*, and
       A Voyage to Lisbon. Saintsbury's remarks on Fielding
       are "appreciative" rather than critical; he praises
       Fielding for his knowledge of human nature, for his
       humor, and for his ability to blend, as few other
       authors have done, "the spirit of life and the spirit
       of letters."

568. ————. "The Four Wheels of the Novel Wain," in his *The English Novel*. London: J.M. Dent and New York: E.P. Dutton, 1913. Pp. 77-132.

Regards Richardson's *Pamela* as the impetus for Fielding's career as a novelist; Fielding began *Joseph Andrews* as a parody of *Pamela*, but it turned into a great original novel which introduced realistic characters and dialogue into prose fiction. Outside of Blifil, the characters of *Tom Jones* are even more realistic. The latter's much-praised plot deserves its praise, but just as important is the great variety of scene and incident. *Amelia* is weakened by its major characters: Amelia is too perfect to be believable, Booth is too great a fool for a hero, and Dr. Harrison is too unreasonable to carry the moral weight assigned him. On the other hand, the minor characters are well-drawn and many of the scenes are fresh and vivid. Fielding is unsurpassed as a novelist because of his originality and realism.

569. ————. "Henry Fielding." *The Bookman*, 32 (1907), 7-10.

A non-scholarly "appreciation" of Fielding, who is viewed here as the "most essentially English of all great English writers" and as "the King of the English Novel." Fielding's greatness lies in his vast knowledge of human nature and in his treatment of hypocrisy.

570. Scholes, Robert, and Robert Kellogg. *The Nature of Narrative*. New York and London: Oxford University Press, 1966.

Links the Theophrastan Characters to the rise of novelists like Fielding who are primarily concerned with generalized characters in plot-dominated fiction. In spite of his emphasis, however, Fielding employs several kinds of characters, especially in *Tom Jones*, in which we find purely "aesthetic" figures like Sophia and Blifil, whose existence has only a tenuous relationship to "real" life; illustrative or allegorical characters like Square and Thwackum; and representative figures like Squire Western, who is both a psychological type (the choleric man) and a sociological type (the country squire). In addition to his importance in characterization, Fielding also is important for his development of narrative technique. Although he did not do much more in this area than Cervantes had done, he justified his practice theoretically and thus directed critical attention to narration.

571. Schulz, Dieter. "'Novel,' 'Romance,' and Popular Fiction in the First Half of the Eighteenth Century." *Studies in Philology*, 70 (1973), 77-91.

     Suggests that the fiction of Defoe, Richardson, and Fielding should be viewed as a reaction to the romances of Aphra Behn, Mary Manley, and Eliza Haywood, whose works were called "novels." Fielding does not use the term "novel" for his own fiction, calling it "history" to emphasize its realistic qualities.

572. Seccombe, Thomas. "Henry Fielding, 1707-1754." *Cornhill Magazine*, 95 (1907), 789-801.

     Laments Fielding's decline in popularity and presents a brief biography and critical survey in order to praise him both as a man and a writer. Although Fielding belongs to no one school, he is "of the race of Rabelais, Montaigne, Shakespeare, and Cervantes" because his books cover a vast range of human experience.

573. Sen, S.C. "Richardson and Fielding: Moral Sense and Moral Vision." *Bulletin of the Department of English, University of Calcutta*, 2 (1961), 38-40.

     The compilers were not able to locate a copy of the above prior to the publication of this bibliography.

574. Shesgreen, Sean. *Literary Portraits in the Novels of Henry Fielding*. Dekalb: Northern Illinois University Press, 1972.

     Literary portraiture in Fielding's novels has its roots in four traditions: the biographical literary sketch, the idealized literary portrait, the emblematic portrait, and the literary caricature. In *Jonathan Wild* and *Joseph Andrews*, the portraits are very close to classical models. However, Fielding gradually becomes freer in his portraiture until, in *Amelia*, little of the classical model remains. In all of his novels, Fielding applies his own system of ethics in creating his characters.

     Review: H.K. Miller, *Modern Philology*, 72 (1975), 321-24.

575. Sherbo, Arthur. "'Inside' and 'Outside' Readers in Fielding's Novels," in his *Studies in the Eighteenth Century English Novel*. East Lansing: Michigan State University Press, 1969. Pp. 35-57.

     Distinguishes between the real audience (the "outside" reader) and the "implied" or "assumed" audience (the

"inside" reader) in Fielding's fiction and reviews the
criticism on the topic. Much of the irony of the
novels, especially in *Tom Jones*, comes from the
superiority of the "outside" reader and the narrator
to the naive, forgetful, and less sophisticated "inside"
reader. Also see Booth, items 457 and 789, and Miller,
"Some Functions of Rhetoric," item 906.

576. ———. "The Narrator in Fielding's Novels," in his
Studies in the Eighteenth Century English Novel. East
Lansing: Michigan State University Press, 1969. Pp.
1-34.

Reviews the criticism on the intrusive narrator in
Fielding's novels in order to put the subject in a
"proper perspective." Sherbo sees the narrator as a
consistent figure throughout all the novels and charac-
terizes him as "a man with his heart (and his head too)
in the right place," a man who is honest, compassionate,
intelligent, and "delightful." Also see Anderson, item
768; Booth, items 457 and 789; Crane, item 808; Ehrenpreis, item 665; McKillop, item 895; Miller, "The Voices
of Henry Fielding," item 907; Price, item 549; and
Sacks, item 566.

577. ———. "Some Aspects of Fielding's Style," in his
Studies in the Eighteenth Century English Novel. East
Lansing: Michigan State University Press, 1969. Pp.
58-84.

Concludes that there is "relatively little difference"
in Fielding's prose style from the beginning to the end
of his career. He employs, usually for ironic purposes,
the same devices over and over: the "economical statement"; the "omission" (usually of something coarse);
the "reminder," often asking the reader to remember
something he scarcely could have forgotten; and the
parenthetical expression. See Miller, "Some Functions
of Rhetoric," item 906.

578. ———. *Studies in the Eighteenth Century English Novel*.
East Lansing: Michigan State University Press, 1969.

Contains six essays on Fielding, one on Sterne, two on
Defoe, and one on character description in the novel.
The six Fielding pieces are: "The Narrator in Fielding's
Novels" (item 576); "'Inside' and 'Outside' Readers in
Fielding's Novels" (item 575); "Some Aspects of Field-
ing's Style" (item 577); "Fielding's *Amelia*: A Rein-
terpretation" (item 1019); "The 'Moral Basis' of *Joseph*

Andrews" (item 709); and "'Naked' Innocence in *Joseph Andrews*" (item 710). In all of these essays, Sherbo analyzes the major criticism on his topic and then draws his own conclusions, many of which are in conflict with the critical consensus.

579. Sherburn, George. "Fielding's Social Outlook." *Philological Quarterly*, 35 (1956), 1-23. Reprinted in Clifford, item 466, and Iser, item 507.

Sees Fielding's social philosophy as based on the concept of a stratified society and on a belief in the necessity of all classes working for the good of the whole. Virtue is put into social terms; its essence is benevolence, hence Fielding is always on the side of good works in the faith vs. good works controversy which raged in the eighteenth century. Fielding's view of society is analytical and ironic rather than sentimental, but he is not aloof--he likes his characters even when they go wrong. He is a healthy writer, spirited and robust.

Review: Allen Wendt, *Philological Quarterly*, 36 (1957), 364-66.

*   ———— and Donald F. Bond. *The Restoration and Eighteenth Century (1660-1789)*. (See item 291.)

580. Simon, Irène. "Early Theories of Prose Fiction: Congreve and Fielding," in *Imagined Worlds: Essays on Some English Novels and Novelists in Honour of John Butt*, ed. Maynard Mack and Ian Gregor. London: Methuen, 1968. Pp. 19-35.

Traces Fielding's theory of the comic epic in prose to French theories of the *roman comique*. Fielding's theory, unlike that of his predecessors, is designed to encompass a moral end for his art and is "the foundation of his formal realism."

581. Skilton, David. "Richardson and Fielding," in his *The English Novel from Defoe to the Victorians*. New York: Harper and Row, 1977. Pp. 19-31.

Distinguishes between Richardson and Fielding on the basis of their respective "aesthetics of fiction." Richardson tries to conceal the facts of composition, whereas Fielding incorporates those facts into his novels through a self-conscious narrator who not only interprets the action but who also presents a complete theory of fiction.

582. Slagle, K.C. *The English Country Squire as Depicted in English Prose Fiction from 1740 to 1800*. New York: Octagon Books, 1971. Originally published Philadelphia: University of Pennsylvania Press, 1938.

Does not treat Fielding in detail, although mention is made of Allworthy and Western. Slagle finds the depiction of the country squire in eighteenth-century novels one of the most realistic aspects of those works.

583. Spearman, Diana. *The Novel and Society*. New York: Barnes and Noble and London: Routledge and Kegan Paul, 1966.

Links Fielding to the Latitudinarian divines and argues that he reflects his society more realistically than do his contemporaries because he portrays a wider range of characters than they do. He also is realistic in his discussion of the common problems of his day; his originality lies in his judicious solutions to those problems.

584. Spector, Robert D., ed. *Essays on the Eighteenth-Century Novel*. Bloomington: Indiana University Press, 1965.

Reprints articles by Crane (item 807), Kermode (item 517), and Spilka (item 585).

585. Spilka, Mark. "Fielding and the Epic Impulse." *Criticism*, 11 (1969), 68-77. Reprinted in Iser, item 507, and Spector, item 584.

When compared to the traditional epic, the novel shows a reduction in heroic scale and focus. On the other hand, by opening up the novel to the immensity of social, personal, and domestic concerns, Fielding gives it a greater magnitude than traditional epic narrative. Fielding's epic sense of the novel's possibilities influenced Dickens, Thackeray, and Eliot and constitute his major contribution to fiction.

586. Stauffer, Donald A. *The Art of Biography in Eighteenth Century England*. 2 vols. Princeton, N.J.: Princeton University Press and London: Oxford University Press, 1941.

Discusses some biographies indebted to Fielding for their technique and argues that Fielding's influence on eighteenth-century biographers was second only to that of Defoe.

587. Steeves, Harrison R. "A Manly Man (Henry Fielding),"
      in his *Before Jane Austen: The Shaping of the Novel in
      the Eighteenth Century*. New York: Holt, Rinehart and
      Winston, 1965. Pp. 103-30. Also published London: Allen
      and Unwin, 1966.

      Presents a general survey of Fielding's fiction, but
      the bulk of the chapter treats *Tom Jones*. The discussion
      focuses on three aspects of Fielding's art: characteri-
      zation, plot, and authorial intrusion. Fielding's
      main characters are romantic-sentimental figures, but
      his minor characters are unsentimentally portrayed;
      his conception of character was influenced by the drama
      of his time, and thus he attempted no profound character
      analysis. In working out his plot, Fielding also was
      influenced by the theater; therefore his plots are
      mechanistic and filled with coincidence and exciting
      scenes. His authorial intrusions are free from affec-
      tation and give *Tom Jones* a conversational quality.
      Steeves' remarks are accompanied by copious quotations
      from the novels.

588. Stephen, Leslie. "Fielding's Novels," in his *Hours in
      a Library*, Vol. 3. New York: G.P. Putnam's Sons, 1904.
      Pp. 1-43. Originally published London, 1879.

      Defends Fielding's character; he was a moral man who
      struggled to rise above Grub Street and whose high moral
      convictions are seen in his novels. His strength and
      his weakness as a novelist lie in his characters; they
      are well-drawn, but they are drawn from the outside.
      Fielding is more of an observer of character than a man
      who can sympathize with his characters.

589. Stern, Guy. "Fielding and the Sub-Literary German Novel:
      A Study of Opitz' *Wilhelm von Hohenberg*." *Monatshefte*,
      48 (1956), 295-307.

      Examines the large number of eighteenth-century German
      novels which imitate Fielding and contends that while
      they often successfully copied his irony and characters,
      they fail to capture his satiric spirit and ability to
      tightly construct his work.

590. ————. "A German Imitation of Fielding: Musäus' *Grandi-
      son der Zweite*." *Comparative Literature*, 10 (1958),
      335-43.

      Musäus does more than merely imitate Fielding's subjects,
      characters, incidents, and so on; he also is able to

capture Fielding's ironic mood and he makes it into a potent force in eighteenth-century German literature.

591. Stevick, Philip. *The Chapter in Fiction*. Syracuse: Syracuse University Press, 1970.

Mentions Fielding in several contexts. Fielding is the first English author to theorize about chapter division. He uses the chapter for a number of reasons: to provide a break for the reader, to change scenes, to omit irrelevant time, to adjust his tone, and to present a "tableau" much as Hogarth did in his painting.

592. ————. "Fielding and the Meaning of History." *Publications of the Modern Language Association of America*, 79 (1964), 561-68.

Argues that Fielding's fiction is analogous to Aron's "history as development." The "development historian" believes that each historical moment bears within itself its own reason for being and that the historian's task is to seek out an era's singularities and to rejoice in them. This view leads to the celebration of life which marks Fielding's fiction and which Andrew Wright (item 612) calls "festive." Also see Burke, item 459, and Wallace, "Fielding's Knowledge of History and Biography," item 317.

593. ————, ed. *The Theory of the Novel*. New York: The Free Press and London: Collier Macmillan, 1967.

This anthology of commentary on the novel contains an excerpt from R.S. Crane, "The Concept of Plot" (item 807) on pp. 141-44 and a selection from *Joseph Andrews* (I.iii) on pp. 387-88.

594. Stewart, Maaja A. "Techniques of Intellectual Comedy in Meredith and Fielding." *Genre*, 8 (1975), 233-47.

Explores the similarities between Fielding and Meredith and sees them both as possessing a "spirit of joy" in the civilized relationships of society. Their comic spirit is intellectual and they make no attempt to hide the fact that their novels *are* novels or to minimize the artistic distance between narrator and narration. The techniques used by both authors emphasize parody, generalization of characters, and "a shifting and artificially controlled point of view."

595. Tave, Stuart M. *The Amiable Humorist: A Study in the Comic Theory and Criticism of the Eighteenth and Early Nineteenth Centuries*. Chicago: University of Chicago Press, 1960.

Traces the shift in comic theory from the seventeenth century, in which laughter is viewed as an aberration and simple folk are seen as fools, to the nineteenth century, in which laughter is seen as natural and simplicity is lauded. Fielding plays a major role in this shift through his praise of "good humor" and "good nature" as virtues which promote cheerfulness and through his creation of Parson Adams, whose simplicity and innocence are positive qualities and whose idiosyncracies are the source of good-natured mirth instead of scorn.

596. Taylor, Houghton W. "'Particular Character': An Early Phase of a Literary Evolution." *Publications of the Modern Language Association of America*, 60 (1945), 161-74.

Outlines the move away from the neo-classical doctrine of universality in characterization, as espoused by Fielding, Dr. Johnson, and Reynolds, and toward particularization of character, as espoused by Blake, Hazlitt, and the Romantics.

597. Thomson, Clara L. *Richardson: A Biographical and Critical Study*. London: H. Marshall and Son and New York: M.F. Mansfield, 1900.

Accounts for Richardson's frequent derogatory remarks on Fielding as due to the former's jealousy over his rival's success.

598. Thornbury, Ethel M. *Henry Fielding's Theory of the Comic Prose Epic*. University of Wisconsin Studies in Language and Literature, No. 30. Madison: University of Wisconsin Press, 1931. Reprinted New York: Russell and Russell, 1966.

Traces the influence on Fielding of both classical and French commentators on the epic and comedy. The volumes in Fielding's library (the Sale-Catalogue of this library is reprinted) and his comments in journals and in *Joseph Andrews* and *Tom Jones* show Fielding's familiarity with and debt to earlier writers such as Aristotle, Scudéry, Molière, Le Bossu, Addison, and

others. Fielding's theory of comedy, then, is developed
in part by drawing on earlier critics. But his own
creations go far beyond his theory. Parson Adams in
particular does not fit either the theory of humors
or Fielding's conception of the ridiculous as being at
the heart of comedy. In some respects, then, Fielding's
theory of comedy is incomplete.

Reviews: G. Kitchin, *Modern Language Review*, 28 (1933),
110-11; A.W. Secord, *Journal of English and Germanic
Philology*, 32 (1933), 417-18; J.R. Sutherland, *Review
of English Studies*, 9 (1933), 342-43.

599. Tichý, Aleš. "Remarks on the Flow of Time in the Novels
of Henry Fielding." *Brno Studies in English*, 2 (1960),
55-75.

Contends that Fielding is nowhere near as precise in his
conscious control of time in the novels as many critics
believe him to be. For example, he constantly "loses"
Sunday and several characters make mistakes in their
references to times past. In fact, what appears to be
an exact record of the passage of time is merely the
author's dependence on the device of connected incident,
which Fielding borrows from Cervantes and the drama.

600. Touster, Eva Beach. "The Literary Relationship of
Thackeray and Fielding." *Journal of English and Germanic Philology*, 46 (1947), 383-94.

Investigates Thackeray's views of Fielding in order to
determine the extent to which Thackeray followed the
theory and practices of his acknowledged "master."
Thackeray genuinely admired Fielding's work, especially
Jonathan Wild, and in many points of style and method,
he closely resembles his predecessor. However, there
are major differences between the two because Thackeray
was not temperamentally suited for writing sustained
irony, and his Victorian viewpoint prevented his por-
traying life as frankly as did Fielding. Also see Dickson, "William Makepeace Thackeray and Henry Fielding,"
item 156; E.D.H. Johnson, item 1001; and Rader, "Thackeray's Injustice to Fielding," item 266.

601. Traill, Henry Duff. "Richardson and Fielding," in his
The New Lucian: Being a Series of Dialogues of the Dead.
London: Chapman and Hall, 1900. Pp. 200-15. Originally
published London: Chapman and Hall, 1884.

In this fictional debate between Richardson and Fielding,
the two novelists assume their traditional roles:

Fielding as an exuberant, tippling man-about-town and Richardson as a prissy moralist. Fielding wins the debate, but concludes that since no one reads either him or Richardson anymore, the debate is moot.

602. Utter, R.P., and G.B. Needham. *Pamela's Daughters*. New York: The Macmillan Co., 1936.

Traces the heroine in English fiction from Richardson to the twentieth century. Fielding's women characters were not the sentimentalized figures of Richardson and his successors; in fact, to Fielding belongs the credit of creating the kind of woman who would appear most often in twentieth-century novels.

*   Van Doren, Carl. "The Greatest English Man of Letters." (See item 313.)

603. Wagenknecht, Edward. "Fielding and the Prose Epic," in his *Cavalcade of the English Novel from Elizabeth to George VI*. New York: Holt, 1943. Pp. 58-68. Second Edition, New York: Holt, 1954 (with Supplementary Bibliography).

Admires Fielding's achievement but is troubled by his moral position. Fielding is "truly epic" because his novels present the "collective life" of his age. His own good nature and his refusal to insist on Christian dogma and ethics prevent him from condemning his fellow man and lead him into lauding "good intentions," an ethically dangerous tendency, fortunately corrected in *Amelia*.

604. Ward, J.A. "Dining with the Novelists." *Personalist*, 45 (1964), 399-411.

Treats the meal as a significant social index in novels. For example, eating is an important facet of Fielding's novels, indicating "zestful indulgence in the common-place activities of life."

605. Warner, John M. "The Interpolated Narrative in the Fiction of Fielding and Smollett: An Epistemological View." *Studies in the Novel*, 5 (1973), 271-83.

Compares the interpolated tales in Fielding with those of Smollett. Fielding's interpolations set up an anti-thetical balance of epistemological views; ultimately, Fielding never advocates either an inductive or a deductive approach to experience. However, in *Amelia*, he

loses his epistemological balance, using the interpolated
tales to corroborate the formal realism of the main narrative, and the novel suffers as a result.

606. Watt, Ian. "Defoe and Richardson on Homer: A Study of
the Relation of Novel and Epic in the Early Eighteenth
Century." *Review of English Studies*, n.s. 3 (1952),
325-40.

Argues that Fielding's comic epic in prose is more concerned with "phylogeny, with claiming a respectable
pedigree for an unhallowed literary genre, than with
ontogeny, with explaining the nature of the genre itself." In fact, late in his career, Fielding rejects
the idea of recreating the epic in his prose.

607. ———. "The Naming of Characters in Defoe, Richardson, and Fielding." *Review of English Studies*, 25
(1949), 322-38. Reprinted in Iser, item 507.

Defoe and Richardson gave their characters more realistic and individualized names than had previous writers.
Fielding, on the other hand, came to the novel from the
traditions of the classics, comedy, and satire, and he
therefore gave his characters the traditional characteristic names of comedy, reflecting his interest in the
aspects of character which are representative of all
mankind.

608. ———. *The Rise of the Novel: Studies in Defoe,
Richardson, and Fielding*. Berkeley and Los Angeles:
University of California Press and London: Chatto and
Windus, 1957. Sections reprinted in Battestin, item
779; Compson, item 804; Paulson, item 258; and Rawson,
item 272.

Devotes two long chapters (one on the epic theory of the
novel and one on *Tom Jones*), plus other remarks, to
Fielding. Watt's discussion has provoked both considerable praise and violent disagreement (see the reviews
listed below). His method is to contrast Richardson's
"formal" and "psychological" realism with Fielding's
realism of "assessment." Whereas Richardson does not
analyze his characters, preferring to present a detailed and highly individualized behavioral report on
them, Fielding continually assesses his figures and
does not individualize them, preferring to deal with
types in order to convey his broadly-based moral views
on society as a whole. Fielding's use of epic devices,

a contrived and manipulated plot, exaggeration, and
unrealistic dialogue destroys the verisimilitude of
his work. His methods are too eclectic to provide a
direction for the novel or to become a permanent part
of its tradition. On the other hand, by attempting to
broaden our moral sense, he brings to the novel a "responsible wisdom" and a realistic assessment of human
affairs.

Reviews: John Bayley, *National and English Review*,
148 (1957), 148-49; Joan Bennett, *Cambridge Review*,
78 (1957), 597-99; Benjamin Boyce, *Philological Quarter-
ly*, 37 (1958), 304-06; Roy Fuller, *London Magazine*, 4
(1957), 73-76; John Holloway, *Spectator* (March 15, 1957),
p. 353; *Listener*, 57 (1957), 483, 485; Alan D. McKillop,
Modern Philology, 4 (1957), 208-10; John Robert Moore,
Modern Language Quarterly, 21 (1960), 373-75; V.S.
Pritchett, *New Statesman*, 53 (1957), 355-56; Richard
B. Sewall, *Saturday Review* (May 4, 1957), p. 22; F.K.
Stanzel, *Anglia*, 76 (1957), 334-36; *Times Literary
Supplement* (February 15, 1957), p. 98; Charles B. Woods,
Modern Language Notes, 72 (1957), 622-25.

609. West, Rebecca. "The Great Optimist," in her *The Court
      and the Castle*. New Haven: Yale University Press,
      1957. Pp. 87-108. Also published London: Macmillan,
      1958. Extract reprinted in Rawson, item 272.

      Uses Shakespeare, particularly *Hamlet*, as a backdrop
      for a study of several other authors, including Fielding.
      The latter's Pelagianism is reflected in his optimistic
      belief in salvation through "good-nature" and his re-
      jection of the doctrine of total human depravity.

610. Williams, Aubrey. "Interpositions of Providence and the
      Design of Fielding's Novels." *South Atlantic Quarterly*,
      70 (1971), 265-86.

      The coincidences that threaten and the fortuitous acci-
      dents that save Fielding's heroes and heroines are re-
      flections of the author's belief in the ordering hand
      of Divine Providence. The precise structuring of his
      novels also mirrors his belief in this divine order.

611. Williams, G.L. "Henry Fielding and the 'Cheery Voiced
      Stranger.'" *Stephen Crane Newsletter*, 4 (1969), 4-7.

      This article was not read by the compilers.

*   Williams, Harold. "Henry Fielding (1707-1754)." (See
       item 324.)

612. Wright, Andrew. *Henry Fielding: Mask and Feast*. Berke-
      ley: University of California Press and London: Chatto
      and Windus, 1965.

      Unlike the traditional writers of fiction, who pretend
      to be telling the truth, Fielding deliberately stresses
      the artificiality of his novels. He draws a line be-
      tween life and art because "an art founded upon life
      must be artificial or it will be unbearable." Morally,
      Fielding's fiction is true, but his moral view must be
      expressed artificially in order to distance the reader
      from the uglier aspects of life. It is only at a dis-
      tance that Lady Booby, Trulliber, Blifil, and Lady
      Bellaston, among others, are endurable. Fielding's
      art is one of "serious playfulness"--serious because it
      is a moralistic art founded on probability and playful
      because it is a comic celebration of life symbolized
      by the images of the mask and the feast. These images
      represent, in order, the artificial fun of the theater
      and the festive gaiety of celebration.

      Reviews: Sheridan Baker, *English Language Notes*, 4
      (1966), 142-44; Martin C. Battestin, *Journal of English
      and Germanic Philology*, 65 (1966), 196-98; W.B. Coley,
      Yale Review, 55 (1965), 126-28; *Choice*, 2 (1965), 230-31;
      George P. Elliott, *Hudson Review*, 18 (1965), 433-41;
      William J. Farrell, *Modern Philology*, 64 (1966), 81-82;
      Michael Gearin-Tosh, *Review of English Studies*, 17 (1966),
      326-27; Frank Kermode, *New York Review of Books* (October
      28, 1965), pp. 5-6; R.E. Moore, *College English*, 27
      (1966), 515; John Preston, *Modern Language Review*, 61
      (1966), 499-501; V.S. Pritchett, *New Statesman* (February
      26, 1965), p. 324; *Times Literary Supplement* (February
      11, 1965), p. 108; Stephen Wall, *Listener*, 74 (1965),
      352-53.

B. *Shamela*

613. Amory, Hugh. "*Shamela* as Aesopic Satire." *ELH: A
      Journal of English Literary History*, 38 (1971), 239-53.

      Three explicit objects of satire--Cibber's *Apology*,
      Middleton's *Life of Cicero*, and Richardson's *Pamela*--are
      linked in *Shamela* to satirically imply that the three
      works reflect the social and political "corruption" of
      the age and that they are "party pieces," the "real"
      author of which is none other than Robert Walpole.

614.   Baker, Sheridan.   "Introduction" to *An Apology for the Life of Mrs. Shamela Andrews* by Henry Fielding.   Berkeley and Los Angeles: University of California Press, 1953. Pp. xi-xxxiv.

Outlines the build-up, from 1883 on, of evidence pointing to Fielding's authorship of *Shamela* and discusses its various satiric targets--Whitefield, Cibber, Walpole, and Richardson.   *Shamela* is an important work because it introduces the novel of manners and of "panoramic social criticism."

615.   ————.   "Introduction" to *"Joseph Andrews" and "Shamela"* by Henry Fielding.   New York: Crowell, 1972.   Pp. xi-xxx.

Briefly surveys Fielding's career and then presents an overview of *Shamela* and *Joseph Andrews*.   With *Shamela*, English fiction becomes "literate" because the book "generates its ... meaning from other literature as it gets its hold on life."   The work satirizes Cibber, Middleton, and Hervey while brilliantly parodying *Pamela*. Fielding uses the conscious and unconscious hypocrisies of sex as a symbol for mankind's comic self-deceptions. The same impetus that led to *Shamela* carried Fielding to *Joseph Andrews*, the most "confident" book in English. Although the beginning and end of the novel parody *Pamela*, the bulk of it parallels Cervantes, Scarron, and Marivaux but at the same time is fresh and original. Fielding gives us a comic, realistic world which presents a serious moral message.

616.   Battestin, Martin C.   "Introduction" to *"Joseph Andrews" and "Shamela"* by Henry Fielding.   Boston: Houghton Mifflin, 1961.   Pp. v-xl.   Partially reprinted in Rawson, item 272.

Begins with an exploration of Richardson's work and then demonstrates why and how Fielding reacted to it negatively.   Battestin concludes that *Shamela*'s lusty good humor, while offensive to some, is essentially healthier than the pruriency of *Pamela*.   Whereas *Shamela* parodied *Pamela*, *Joseph Andrews* from the start has a spirit and design of its own; it offers an antithetic alternative to Richardson's ethical stance in *Pamela*.   It also presents a sophisticated view of the art of the novel. Battestin concludes with a detailed analysis of *Joseph Andrews* which emphasizes its moral and philosophic foundation.

617.   Bernard, F.V.   "*Shamela* and *Amelia*: An Unnoted Parallel." *Notes and Queries*, n.s. 6 (1959), 78.

Apparently unaware of the many previous comments on this topic, the author notes the parallel use in *Shamela* and *Amelia* of Dr. South's epigram on the sweetness of revenge. See de Castro, "Did Fielding Write *Shamela*?" item 619; Greene, item 622; Woods, "Fielding and the Authorship of *Shamela*," item 635; Maxwell, items 626 and 627; Wendt, item 320; and Sherbo, "Fielding and Dr. South: A Post Mortem," item 290.

*   Brooks, Douglas. "Introduction" to *"The History of the Adventures of Joseph Andrews and of His Friend Mr. Abraham Adams" and "An Apology for the Life of Mrs. Shamela Andrews."* (See item 51.)

618.   Davis, Joe Lee. "Criticism and Parody." *Thought*, 26 (1951), 180-204.

In *Shamela*, Fielding "corrects Richardson's ethics, psychology, and sociology" from *Pamela* in a highly creative parody which shows him the way to *Joseph Andrews*. While Richardson's emphasis is on rewarding virtue, Fielding's is on punishing vice.

619.   de Castro, J. Paul. "Did Fielding Write *Shamela*?" *Notes and Queries*, Twelfth Series, 1 (1916), 24-6.

Argues for Fielding's authorship on the basis of contemporary references to him as the author of *Shamela* and because a comparison of passages in the latter with passages in Fielding's acknowledged work also indicates that Fielding wrote the parody. Also see Greene, item 622; Jensen, item 624; Maxwell, items 626 and 627; Sherbo, "Fielding and Dr. South," item 290; Wendt, item 320; and Woods, "Fielding and the Authorship of *Shamela*," item 635.

*   ————. "Introductory Notes" to *Joseph Andrews*. (See item 659.)

620.   Doody, Margaret Anne. *A Natural Passion: A Study of the Novels of Samuel Richardson*. Oxford: Clarendon Press, 1974.

Alludes to Fielding *passim*. Fielding's dislike of *Pamela* is not so much based on his moral views as on his upper-class perspective, which causes him to see Pamela as an "upstart" meddling with her "betters."

621.   Downs, Brian W. "Introduction" to *An Apology for the Life of Mrs. Shamela Andrews* by Henry Fielding. Cambridge: Gordon Fraser, 1930. Pp. v-xi.

Asserts--rather uncertainly--that Fielding wrote *Shamela*, which attacks the morality, psychology, and realism of *Pamela* and which also is designed to attack Colley Cibber.

*   Gerould, Gordon Hall. *The Patterns of English and American Fiction*. (See item 489.)

622.   Greene, Charles Richard. "A Note on the Authorship of *Shamela*." *Modern Language Notes*, 59 (1944), 571.

A passage on revenge in *The Mock Doctor*, added by Fielding in his translation, closely parallels a passage in *Shamela* and thus indicates that Fielding wrote both works. Also see de Castro, "Did Fielding Write *Shamela*?" item 619; Maxwell, items 626 and 627; Sherbo, "Fielding and Dr. South," item 290; Wendt, "Fielding," item 320; and Woods, "Fielding and the Authorship of *Shamela*," item 635.

623.   Jenkins, Ralph E. "A Note on Hogarth and Fielding's 'Shamela.'" *Notes and Queries*, n.s. 18 (1971), 335.

Letter IV of *Shamela* combines religious hypocrisy and pornography in a scene decidedly similar to Hogarth's two 1736 engravings entitled "Before" and "After"; it is likely that Fielding's conception of Shamela's character was influenced by Hogarth's work.

624.   Jensen, Gerard E. "An Apology for the Life of Mrs. Shamela Andrews, 1741." *Modern Language Notes*, 31 (1916), 310-11.

Argues for Fielding's authorship of *Shamela* on the basis of style (the consistent use of "hath," "doth," and "whilst," for example) and parallels with both the *Covent Garden Journal* and the *Champion*.

*   Johnson, Maurice. *Fielding's Art of Fiction: Eleven Essays on "Shamela," "Joseph Andrews," "Tom Jones," and "Amelia."* (See item 511.)

*   Kaul, A.N. "The Adjudication of Fielding's Comedy." (See item 515.)

625.   Kreissman, Bernard. *Pamela-Shamela: A Study of the Criticisms, Burlesques, Parodies, and Adaptations of Richardson's "Pamela."* Lincoln: University of Nebraska Press, 1960.

Provides a context for the eighteenth-century reaction against *Pamela*. Pages 7-22 deal specifically with *Shamela* and *Joseph Andrews*, which Kreissman sees as the most successful of the *Pamela* parodies. He also agrees with Fielding's view of Pamela as an avaricious schemer.

626. Maxwell, J.C. "Fielding and *Shamela*." *Notes and Queries*, 193 (1948), 364-65.

Cites Fielding's use of the statement "revenge is the sweetest morsel the devil ever dropped into the mouth of a sinner" as evidence of Fielding's authorship of *Shamela* because it appears not only there but also in *The Mock Doctor* and *Amelia*. Although he cannot locate the source, Maxwell says that the statement is in the manner of Dr. South. (Later, Maxwell locates the reference in South's *Sermons*--see item 627.) Also see Woods, "Fielding and the authorship of *Shamela*," item 635.

627. ————. "Fielding and *Shamela*." *Notes and Queries*, 195 (1950), 152.

Adds to his previous note on Fielding's repeated statement on the "sweetness" of revenge (see item 626) by noting that it is also used in *The Champion* and that its source is South's *Sermons*.

628. Olivier, Theo. "'Pamela' and 'Shamela': A Reassessment." *English Studies in Africa*, 17 (1974), 59-70.

Opposes the common view that Richardson and Fielding were poles apart in their techniques and attitudes. In *Pamela*, Richardson seeks to entertain his reader through suspense and to show that virtue eventually triumphs over vice. After *Shamela*, which mocks Richardson, Fielding moves closer to Richardson's methods and aims, entertaining through suspense and rewarding the virtuous.

* Rogers, Pat. "Fielding." (See item 565.)

629. Rothstein, Eric. "The Framework of *Shamela*." *ELH: A Journal of English Literary History*, 35 (1968), 381-402. Reprinted in *"Joseph Andrews" and "Shamela,"* ed. Sheridan Baker, item 52.

The prefatory material to *Shamela* not only sustains the burlesque of the main action, but also functions to

satirize English social, political, and religious life.
Through ironic attacks on Cibber, Middleton, and Hervey,
Fielding shows that each is a false artist and a prostitute, like Shamela herself. The prefatory material and
the text focus on egoism, materialism, and corruption
in all areas of English life. Rothstein explores in
detail the sexual innuendos of the work and shows how
they function to forward Fielding's comic satiric purpose.

630.   Shepperson, Archibald. "Richardson and Fielding: *Shamela*
        and *Shamelia*," in his *The Novel in Motley: A History of
        the Burlesque Novel in English*. New York: Octagon Books,
        1967. Pp. 9–38. Originally published Cambridge, Mass.:
        Harvard University Press, 1936.

        Finds both *Shamela* and *Joseph Andrews* delightful bur-
        lesques of *Pamela* and treats some of the little-known
        burlesque attacks on Fielding's own works.

631.   Stern, Guy. "Saint or Hypocrite? A Study of Wieland's
        'Jacinte Episode.'" *Germanic Review*, 29 (1954), 96–101.

        Argues that the story of Jacinte in Wieland's *Don Sylvio
        von Rosalva* is an anti-Pamela satire in the vein of
        Fielding's *Shamela* and *Joseph Andrews*.

632.   Tucker, Susie I. "A Note on Colley Cibber's Name."
        Notes and Queries, n.s. 6 (1959), 400.

        Cibber's name was sometimes pronounced "*Kib-er*" by his
        contemporaries, a pronunciation which gives added meaning
        to Fielding's calling him "Keyber" in *Shamela*.

633.   Watt, Ian. "Introduction" to *An Apology for the Life
        of Mrs. Shamela Andrews* by Henry Fielding, Augustan
        Reprint Society, No. 57. Los Angeles: Clark Memorial
        Library, 1956. Pp. 1–11. Reprinted in Paulson, item
        258.

        Explains the allusions on the title page and the prefa-
        tory material to *Shamela*, identifying Middleton, Cibber,
        Hervey, Slocock, and Trapp, among others. Watt also
        explores the theme of faith versus good works, arguing
        that Fielding's target is generalized and not directed,
        as often assumed, solely against the Methodists.

*   Wendt, Alan E. "Fielding and South's 'Luscious Morsel':
        A Last Word." (See item 320.)

634. Wood, Carl. "*Shamela*'s Subtle Satire: Fielding's Characterization of Mrs. Jewkes and Mrs. Jervis." *English
Language Notes*, 13 (1976), 266-70.

Although Richardson's stated intent was to portray Mrs.
Jewkes and Mrs. Jervis as moral opposites (for the edi-
fication of servants), enough ambiguities about their
actions and motives exist to blur the distinction that
Richardson sought, and Fielding evidently noticed these
ambiguities. His inversion of the two characters in
Shamela is an obvious attack on Richardson's moral
equivocating, and it shows that *Shamela* is a thoughtful,
complex satire rather than the hurried, simplistic
parody that it has often been called.

635. Woods, Charles B. "Fielding and the Authorship of
Shamela." *Philological Quarterly*, 25 (1946), 248-72.

Convincingly demonstrates that Fielding wrote *Shamela*.
Not only is the style of *Shamela* Fielding's, but the subject matter is similar to that in several of his earlier
essays. The attacks on Birch, Whitefield, Middleton, and
Cibber reflect attitudes expressed by Fielding in *The
Champion*. Woods also analyzes *Shamela*'s satiric methods
and argues that the satire has two main functions: to
ridicule a silly story (*Pamela*) and to reprimand the
clergy for praising such a work. The greatest value
of *Shamela*, however, is that it forms a link between
Pamela and *Joseph Andrews*, the latter of which was
written as a moral and stylistic alternative to the
former. Alse see de Castro, "Did Fielding Write
Shamela?" item 619; Greene, item 622; Maxwell, items
626 and 627; Sherbo, "Fielding and Dr. South: A Post
Mortem," item 290; and Wendt, item 320.

C. *Joseph Andrews*

636. Allott, Miriam. *Novelists on the Novel*. London: Routledge and Kegan Paul and New York: Columbia University
Press, 1959.

Quotes from *Joseph Andrews* and *Tom Jones* to show Fielding's views on such aspects of the novel as the super-
natural, didacticism, probability, structure, characterization, and style.

*   Baker, Ernest A. *History of the English Novel.* (See
        item 448.)

*   Baker, Sheridan. "Fielding and the Irony of Form."
        (See item 771.)

637.   ————. "Henry Fielding's Comic Romances." *Papers of
        the Michigan Academy of Science, Arts, and Letters*, 45
        (1959), 411-19. Reprinted in *"Joseph Andrews" and
        "Shamela,"* ed. Sheridan Baker, item 52.

        Disagrees with the critical cliché that *Joseph Andrews*
        and *Tom Jones* are "comic epics in prose"; both works are
        more accurately described as "comic romances." Like
        Cervantes and Scarron, Fielding bases his novels on
        "romantic fancy" and "comic wisdom," and he consistently
        employs such romantic conventions as the hero's mys-
        terious origins (Joseph and Tom), the exchange of
        babies (Joseph and Fanny), and the identifying straw-
        berry mark (Joseph), among many others. Fielding also
        borrows directly from Scarron at times, drawing some of
        his phrasing and certain incidents (Parson Adams' wrong
        turn into Fanny's bed) from the *Comical Romance*.

*   ————. "Introduction" to *"Joseph Andrews" and "Shamela."*
        (See item 52.)

638.   Battestin, Martin C. "Fielding's Changing Politics and
        Joseph Andrews." *Philological Quarterly*, 39 (1960),
        39-55.

        Fielding's apologists have a difficult time accounting
        for his 1741 pamphlet, *The Opposition: A Vision*, which
        supports Walpole. Battestin argues that Fielding's
        personal circumstances (he was broke, his wife was ill,
        and his daughter was dying) and the ingratitude of the
        Opposition for Fielding's work against Walpole, caused
        him to switch sides and accept Walpole's patronage.
        This political disillusionment is reflected in the
        original version of *Joseph Andrews* (II.7-9) in Adams'
        discourse on politics and conversation with "a man of
        courage." Also see Baker, "Political Allusion," item
        381; Coley, "Henry Fielding and the Two Walpoles,"
        item 116; Goldgar, *Walpole and the Wits*, item 190; and
        Grundy, "New Verse," item 1060.

639.   ————. "Fielding's Revisions of *Joseph Andrews*."
        Studies in Bibliography, 16 (1963), 81-117.

        Lists 128 changes, most of them substantial, made by

Fielding through the four editions of *Joseph Andrews*
published in his lifetime. Fielding's editing shows
his concern with sharpening his characters, cleaning
up his prose, and clarifying his satirical points.

640.   ————. "General Introduction" to *Joseph Andrews* by
Henry Fielding. Middletown, Conn.: Wesleyan University
Press and Oxford: The Clarendon Press, 1967. Pp. xv-
xxxvii.

Reviews the circumstances of the novel's composition;
determines the dates on which it was written; and surveys its history of publication and its early reception.
Included is a discussion of Fielding's additions to the
second edition.

*   ————. "Introduction" to *"Joseph Andrews" and "Shamela."*
(See item 49.)

641.   ————. "Lord Hervey's Role in *Joseph Andrews*." *Philological Quarterly*, 42 (1963), 226-41.

Although the character of Beau Didapper is Fielding's
most extensive comment on Lord Hervey, the Didapper
portrait also is aimed at contemptible courtiers in
general and functions to advance the action in such
scenes as Adams' night adventures near the end of
Joseph Andrews.

642.   ————. *The Moral Basis of Fielding's Art: A Study of
"Joseph Andrews."* Middletown, Conn.: Wesleyan University
Press, 1959.

Joseph Andrews is not, as often argued, merely another
burlesque of *Pamela*, but rather is a highly moral work
which poses an alternative to the ethical foundation of
Richardson's novel. Battestin places Fielding in the
Latitudinarian and benevolist traditions but shows how
Fielding modifies those traditions by bringing to bear
upon them his own attitudes toward good nature, the
good man, the folly of vanity, the function of fortune,
the role of the clergy, and the classical ideals of the
Golden Mean and the Good Life. The ethical center of
the novel is Mr. Wilson's story, which epitomizes Fielding's moral position.

Reviews: Jessie Rhodes Chambers, *Modern Language Notes*,
76 (1961), 464-67; William C. Combs, *South Atlantic
Quarterly*, 59 (1960), 299-300; A.R. Humphreys, *Review of
English Studies*, 12 (1961), 211-12; L.C.B., *Etudes*

Anglaises, 14 (1961), 366-67; C.J. Rawson, *Notes and Queries*, 205 (1960), 154-56; H. Winston Rhodes, *Journal of the Australian Universities Language and Literature Association*, 13 (1960), 81-82; Albrecht B. Strauss, *Books Abroad*, 35 (1961), 388-89; *Times Literary Supplement* (December 25, 1959), p. 756; Ian Watt, *Philological Quarterly*, 39 (1960), 325-26; Aubrey Williams, *Yale Review*, 49 (1960), 454-57.

643.   ———. "[From] *The Moral Basis of Fielding's Art: A Study of 'Joseph Andrews*,'" in *"Joseph Andrews" and "Shamela*," ed. Sheridan Baker. New York: Crowell, 1972. Pp. 435-45.

This material comes from pp. 118-29 of Battestin's book, *The Moral Basis of Fielding's Art*, item 642. Battestin argues that Mr. Wilson's story is not a digression but "completes the panoramic satire of English society" and demonstrates what might have happened to Joseph had he not followed the good advice and good example of Adams. Wilson's pilgrimage from sin in the city to redemption in the country symbolically reinforces the movement of the main action from city to country, from vanity to natural simplicity.

644.   ———. "On the Contemporary Reputations of *Pamela, Joseph Andrews*, and *Roderick Random*: Remarks by an 'Oxford Scholar,' 1748." *Notes and Queries*, n.s. 15 (1968), 450-52.

The scandalous memoirs in 1748 of Laetitia Pilkington and "Con" Phillips produced a number of commentaries, one of which—*The Parallel; or, Pilkington and Phillips Compared. Being Remarks upon the Memories of these two Celebrated Writers. By an Oxford Scholar (1748)*—sheds new light on the reputations of the three greatest novelists of the period. The "Oxford Scholar" compares *Joseph Andrews* favorably to Scarron's *Roman comique* and Le Sage's *Gil Blas* and regards Fielding's first novel as a masterpiece.

*   Bissell, Frederick Olds. *Fielding's Theory of the Novel*. (See item 453.)

*   Bland, D.S. "Endangering the Reader's Neck." (See item 455.)

*   Boas, Frederick. "Henry Fielding." (See item 338.)

*   Booth, Wayne C. "The Self-Conscious Narrator in Comic
        Fiction Before *Tristram Shandy*." (See item 457.)

645.   Bowers, Fredson. "Textual Introduction" to *Joseph
        Andrews* by Henry Fielding. Middletown, Conn.: Wesleyan
        University Press and Oxford: The Clarendon Press, 1967.
        Pp. xxxix-xlvii.

        Divides his erudite and technical discussion into three
        sections: the copy-text and its treatment, the apparatus,
        and collation.

646.   Boyce, Benjamin. "Introduction" to *The Comical Romance*
        by Paul Scarron. Translator, Tom Brown. New York:
        Benjamin Blom, 1967.

        Points out parallels between Scarron's work and *Joseph
        Andrews*. The narrators are much alike in tone and per-
        sonality, and there are similarities in the adventures
        along the road, the inn scenes, the realism of the
        characters, and the interpolated tales.

647.   Bradbury, Malcolm. "Fielding, Sterne, and the Comic
        Modes of Fiction," in his *Possibilities: Essays on the
        State of the Novel*. London and New York: Oxford Univer-
        sity Press, 1973. Pp. 31-40. Originally published as
        "The Comic Novel in Sterne and Fielding," in *The Winged
        Skull: Papers from the Laurence Sterne Bicentenary
        Conference*, eds. Arthur Cash and John M. Stedmond.
        London: Methuen, 1971. Pp. 124-31.

        The "Preface" to *Joseph Andrews*, which provides a
        "poetics" with which to explore the early novel, sug-
        gests a strong relationship between the novel form and
        the comic mode. By "comic" Fielding implied several
        things about his new form of fiction: anti-heroic dic-
        tion; an inclusiveness of social range; and the treat-
        ment of social and ethical experience in a comprehen-
        sive action or structure. This new fictional form
        brings, as does stage comedy, order to chaos and demon-
        strates, especially in *Tom Jones*, that what appears to
        be episodic is really coherent.

648.   Braudy, Leo. "Fielding: Public History and Individual
        Perception," in his *Narrative Form in History and Fic-
        tion: Hume, Fielding, and Gibbon*. Princeton, N.J.:
        Princeton University Press, 1970. Pp. 91-212.

        Sees the eighteenth-century novel as drawing its sus-
        tenance from the writing of history. Novelists, like

historians, wished to present a realistic world relevant
to the reader's life and to couch the "truth," as they
perceived it, in the language of general moral precepts.
Although Fielding shares this approach, he also believes
that public history is "bankrupt" as a source for moral
values and a knowledge of human nature; only a study in
private life can provide such values and knowledge.
Hence, Fielding's novels use different methods to arrive
at the same ends. Braudy presents an analysis of the
four major novels to illuminate and support his thesis,
giving more emphasis to *Amelia* than that novel is usually accorded.

649. Brooks, Douglas. "Abraham Adams and Parson Trulliber:
The Meaning of *Joseph Andrews*, Book II, Chapter 14."
Modern Language Review, 63 (1968), 794–801.

Treats two previously undiscussed aspects of *Joseph
Andrews*, II.xiv. First, through the characters of Adams
and Trulliber, Fielding draws ironic parallels with
Book 14 of the *Odyssey*; second, a close study of the
characterization of Trulliber reveals a number of possible symbolic meanings that can be attached to him
through his name.

650. ———. "The Interpolated Tales in *Joseph Andrews*
Again." *Modern Philology*, 65 (1968), 208–13.

Agrees with Cauthen, item 657, and Goldberg, item 673,
that the interpolated tales are integral parts of
Joseph Andrews and adds detail to their arguments in
order to more adequately show the function of "The Un-
fortunate Jilt" and "The History of Two Friends." These
stories at times parallel the main narrative and at
times contrast with it; for example, Leonora is very
much like Fanny in many respects, but her vanity contrasts with Fanny's humility. Both interpolations emphasize the novel's theme of vanity and hypocrisy.
Also see Driskell, item 662.

651. ———. "Introduction" to *"The History of the Adven-
tures of Joseph Andrews and of His Friend Mr. Abraham
Adams" and "An Apology for the Life of Mrs. Shamela
Andrews"* by Henry Fielding. London and New York:
Oxford University Press, 1970. Pp. vii–xviii.

Attempts to answer the question, "Why was Fielding so
troubled by *Pamela* as to write two replies to it?" A
close reading of *Shamela* and *Joseph Andrews* shows that
they are more than attacks on disparate topical subjects

their targets are all emblems of political (Walpole), literary (Cibber), and religious (Methodism) corruption and disorder. The overriding purpose of the two works is to expose the Richardsonian notion of virtue as a sham and to offer in its place the Pelagian doctrine that salvation can be earned through good works.

652.   ————. *Number and Pattern in the Eighteenth-Century Novel: Defoe, Fielding, Smollett, and Sterne*. London and Boston: Routledge and Kegan Paul, 1973.

Contains two chapters on Fielding in which the symmetry of *Joseph Andrews*, *Tom Jones*, and *Amelia* is analyzed in terms of numerological theory and the number-symbolism of the novels is discussed. Brooks' thesis is highly controversial and should be considered in conjunction with two important reviews: Eric Rothstein, *Philological Quarterly*, 53 (1974), 587-88, and Robert W. Uphaus, *Eighteenth-Century Studies*, 8 (1974), 116-19.

653.   ————. "Richardson's *Pamela* and Fielding's *Joseph Andrews*." *Essays in Criticism*, 17 (1967), 158-68.

Argues that *Joseph Andrews* is not a parody of *Pamela* but rather is an imitation of it. In addition to the traditionally noted parallels between the two novels, Brooks sees the clothing imagery that pervades Fielding's novel as designed to remind the reader of *Pamela* In effect, Fielding rewrites *Pamela*, and *Joseph Andrews* stands as "a symbol of Augustanism" in opposition to Richardson's work. See A.M. Kearney's original objections to this article, item 680. Following Kearney's piece, there ensued a lengthy debate between him and Brooks. To follow this exchange, see the following items in the order listed: 654, 681, and 655.

654.   ————. "*Pamela* and *Joseph Andrews*." *Essays in Criticism*, 18 (1968), 348-49. Reprinted as "Rebuttal by Douglas Brooks" in *"Joseph Andrews" and "Shamela,"* ed. Sheridan Baker, item 52.

Replies to Kearney's objections to his article, "Richardson's *Pamela* and Fielding's *Joseph Andrews*," item 653. The author reiterates his original arguments and remains "unrepentant." See Kearney's further objections, item 681.

655.   ————. "*Joseph Andrews* and *Pamela*." *Essays in Criticism*, 19 (1969), 348-51.

The final statement in the debate between Brooks and
Kearney over the former's "Richardson's *Pamela* and
Fielding's *Joseph Andrews*," item 653.

656.   ————. "Symbolic Numbers in Fielding's *Joseph Andrews*,"
in *Silent Poetry: Essays in Numerological Analysis*, ed.
Alastair Fowler. London: Routledge and Kegan Paul,
1970. Pp. 234-60.

Seeks to demonstrate, through numerological analysis,
that Fielding's first novel is so highly patterned that
it possesses a mathematically precise structure. Also
see Brooks' *Number and Pattern*, item 652.

*   Butt, John. *Fielding*. (See item 462.)

657.   Cauthen, I.B. "Fielding's Digressions in *Joseph Andrews*."
College English, 17 (1956), 379-82.

Defends the interpolated tales of Leonora, Mr. Wilson,
and Paul and Leonard against the traditional criticism
that they are digressive. All three stories emphasize
the dire consequences of vanity and hypocrisy and thus
fit into Fielding's moral design of exposing affectation.
Also see Brooks, "The Interpolated Tales," item 650;
Goldberg, "The Interpolated Tales," item 673; and
Driskell, item 662.

*   Child, Harold H. "Fielding and Smollett." (See item
110.)

*   Churchill, R.C. "Fielding: To the Novel from the Drama."
(See item 111.)

*   Collins, Norman. "Henry Fielding." (See item 468.)

*   Davis, Joe Lee. "Criticism and Parody." (See item 618.)

*   de Castro, J. Paul. "Fieldingiana." (See item 140.)

658.   ————. "Fielding's Parson Adams." *Notes and Queries*,
Twelfth Series, 1 (1916), 224-25.

A previously undiscovered manuscript contains information
which confirms that the Rev. William Young was the model
for Parson Adams.

659.   ————. "Introductory Note" to *The Adventures of Joseph
Andrews* by Henry Fielding. London: Scholartis Press,
1929. Pp. 7-15.

Ranks Richardson far below Fielding as a novelist and discusses *Shamela* and *Joseph Andrews* as reactions to *Pamela*. A short section is devoted to defending Fielding against charges that he lacked learning.

660. Dickson, Frederick S. *An Index to "Joseph Andrews"* by Henry Fielding. 1911.

This unpublished manuscript in The Library of Congress lists characters and identifies persons mentioned in the novel.

661. Donovan, Robert Alan. *"Joseph Andrews* as Parody," in his *The Shaping Vision: Imagination in the English Novel from Defoe to Dickens*. Ithaca, N.Y.: Cornell University Press, 1966. Pp. 68-88. Reprinted in Rawson, item 272.

Contrary to received opinion, *Joseph Andrews* is a consistent parody of *Pamela*; at the same time, however, it is an original comic masterpiece. The novel is a "searching critique" of Pamela's morality, which works only in Richardson's unreal world and is, unlike that of Parson Adams, purely self-regarding.

662. Driskell, Leon V. "Interpolated Tales in *Joseph Andrews* and *Don Quixote*: The Dramatic Method as Instruction." *South Atlantic Bulletin*, 33 (1968), 5-8.

Sees the interpolated tales in both Fielding and Cervantes as exempla designed to instruct various characters in proper behavior. Due to the characters' particular weaknesses, however, they miss the points of the tales, but the reader is expected to understand the interpolations and to apply their lessons to the novels' characters in order to more fully understand them. Also see Brooks, "The Interpolated Tales," item 650, Cauthen, item 657; and Goldberg, item 673.

663. Duncan, Jeffrey L. "The Rural Ideal in Eighteenth Century Fiction." *Studies in English Literature*, 8 (1968), 517-37.

Focuses on Fielding, Smollett, Goldsmith, and Sterne as authors who used "the rural ideal of pastoral and georgic tradition" as symbols of moral and religious order. This ideal is at the center of the Wilson episode in *Joseph Andrews*, where the rural life is viewed as morally superior to city life because the former is simple enough to render it "subject to reason and good nature" so that "the intellect can fashion the institutions appropriate to the practice of virtue."

664.   Eaves, T.C. Duncan, and Ben D. Kimpel. "Two Names in
       Joseph Andrews." *Modern Philology*, 72 (1975), 408-09.

       Points out that the name "Slipslop" means kissing and
       that "Tow-wouse" comes from "tow-wow," meaning the
       "female pudendum."

665.   Ehrenpreis, Irwin. "Fielding's Use of Fiction: The
       Autonomy of *Joseph Andrews*," in *Twelve Original Essays
       on Great English Novels*, ed. Charles Shapiro. Detroit:
       Wayne State University Press, 1960. Pp. 23-41. Re-
       printed in Iser, item 507.

       Instead of an organic or cumulative plot, the structure
       of *Joseph Andrews* depends on a series of reversals. A
       typical reversal occurs when Lady Booby, who has been
       pursuing Joseph, decides to protect her reputation and
       give up the lowly footman; however, when she is informed
       that Joseph can't marry Fanny because she is his sister,
       her ladyship reverses herself and decides to marry
       Joseph after all. Such a reversal reveals Lady Booby's
       true character, showing her to be dominated by "low"
       (i.e., sexual) impulses. In addition to using reversals
       to unmask characters, Fielding also employs them, along
       with coincidence and digression, to express his moral
       views.

*   Elwin, Whitwell. "Fielding." (See item 177.)

666.   Esdaile, Katherine A. "Fielding's Danish Translator:
       Simon Charles Stanley, the Sculptor." *Times Literary
       Supplement* (April 3, 1937), p. 252.

       Stanley translated *Joseph Andrews* into Danish in 1749.
       It is likely that he also translated into Danish
       Jonathan Wild and *A Journey from this World to the Next*
       in 1759.

667.   Evans, James E. "Fielding's Lady Booby and Fénelon's
       Calypso." *Studies in the Novel*, 8 (1976), 210-13.

       Points out several parallels between Lady Booby in
       Joseph Andrews and Calypso in *Télémaque*. Fielding, who
       refers to Fénelon in his Preface to the novel, enhances
       his comedy by using a serious epic model for his ridicu-
       lous seductress.

668.   Forman, H. Buxton. "Fielding and the Andrews Family."
       Fortnightly Review, 76 (1901), 949-59.

       Calls Richardson's tone in *Pamela* "sanctimonious" and his

values "distorted." Fielding, a well-adjusted realist, began *Joseph Andrews* as an attempt to correct that tone and lay bare those distortions. Without Richardson, we may never have enjoyed the novelistic genius of Fielding.

*   Forster, E.M. *Aspects of the Novel*. (See item 482.)

669.   Freedman, William A. "*Joseph Andrews*: Clothing and the Concretization of Character." *Discourse*, 4 (1961), 304-10.

The condition of a man's clothing in *Joseph Andrews* is usually an inverse indication of his character: the humbler the clothing, the finer the man. Adams' torn and filthy cassock hides a totally positive character, for example; and the finery of the coach's passengers, who would not allow entrance to the naked and bleeding Joseph, reveals their self-serving natures.

670.   ———. "*Joseph Andrews*: Fielding's Garden of the Perverse." *Tennessee Studies in Literature*, 16 (1971), 35-45.

To Fielding, good nature is the essential nature of man, while ill-nature is an "unhuman," or bestial, distortion of that nature. Thus Fielding uses animal imagery to describe his characters who deviate from the norm of good nature. Furthermore, bestial characters tend to regard and describe their fellow humans as beasts.

*   Gerould, Gordon Hall. *The Patterns of English and American Fiction*. (See item 489.)

671.   Goldberg, Homer. *The Art of "Joseph Andrews."* Chicago: University of Chicago Press, 1969.

Most of Fielding's comic devices--his characters, many of his scenes, and some of his dialogue--are heavily indebted to Cervantes, Scarron, Lesage, and Marivaux. Fielding's comic art also is indirectly indebted to Homer since it is often the epic style and form, as well as epic diction, which Fielding burlesques. In his discussion of *Joseph Andrews*, Goldberg focuses on Parson Adams, who is viewed as the real comic protagonist of the novel. Joseph is merely a foil for Adams. Adams provides the opportunity for Fielding to operate on several levels of irony, and it is through the parson that Fielding makes his comic thrusts at society.

Reviews: Howard Anderson, *Philological Quarterly*, 49

(1970), 349-50; Sheridan Baker, *College English*, 32
(1971), 817-22; Michael Irwin, *Review of English Studies*,
11 (1971), 89-93.

672.   ————. "Comic Prose Epic or Comic Romance: The Argu-
        ment of the Preface to *Joseph Andrews*." *Philological
        Quarterly*, 43 (1964), 193-215.

        Aristotle's *Poetics* influenced Fielding's reasoning in
        the Preface to *Joseph Andrews*. Fielding did not attempt
        to write a treatise on art, but rather he simply wished
        to formulate for his reader his conception of his novel's
        basic form, a form new in English but established in
        other languages. The *Poetics* gave him a model for so
        doing. Goldberg clarifies Fielding's complicated dis-
        tinctions between "Epic" as a particular species or as
        a general high narrative mode, and "Romance" as a prose-
        epic or as a sub-literary form.

673.   ————. "The Interpolated Stories in *Joseph Andrews*,
        or 'The History of the World in General' Satirically
        Revised." *Modern Philology*, 63 (1966), 295-310.

        Discovers the antecedents of Fielding's interpolated
        tales in three episodes of *Don Quixote*--the goatherd's
        tale, the adventure of "the Knight of the Green Coat,"
        and "The Curious Impertinent"--revealing the great in-
        fluence Cervantes had on Fielding's comic imagination.
        Also see Cauthen, item 657; Brooks, "The Interpolated
        Tales," item 650; and Driskell, item 662.

674.   Gottfried, Leon. "The Odyssean Form: An Exploratory
        Essay," in *Essays on European Literature in Honor of
        Liselotte Dieckmann*, eds. Peter Uwe Hohendahl, Herbert
        Lindenberger, and Egon Schwartz. St. Louis: Washington
        University Press, 1972. Pp. 19-43.

        Considers *Joseph Andrews* as "odyssey," defined as a
        literary sub-genre derived from Homer and Cervantes.
        By calling his novel "a new kind of writing," Fielding
        was indicating that he had combined the "manner" of
        Cervantes with the "form" of the classical epic exempli-
        fied in the *Odyssey*. *Joseph Andrews* has a Quixotic
        character in Adams and utilizes the Homeric three-part
        structure, with fixed points of action at the beginning
        and end and with "peripatetic episodes" in between.

675.   Harder, Kelsie B. "The Preacher's Seat." *Tennessee
        Folklore Society Bulletin*, 23 (1957), 38-9.

The practical joke which resulted in Parson Adams' dunk-
ing (*Joseph Andrews*, III.vii) was still being practiced
in Tennessee as late as the 1930's. The local name for
the trick is "the preacher's seat."

676. Hartwig, Robert J. "*Pharsamon* and *Joseph Andrews*."
Texas Studies in Literature and Language, 14 (1972),
45-52.

Notes several similarities between *Joseph Andrews* and
Marivaux's *Pharsamon*. The protagonists resemble each
other in their physical appearance and their histories,
several other characters behave in similar manners.
and certain scenes are very much alike. The most important similarity, however, is that both authors use
comic irony and employ the intrusive narrator.

677. Iser, Wolfgang. "The Role of the Reader in Fielding's
Joseph Andrews and *Tom Jones*," in *English Studies Today*,
Fifth Series. Istanbul: Matbaasi, 1973. Pp. 289-325.

Fielding involves the reader in his novels by forcing
him to provide descriptions and make value judgments.
Often the reader is forced to examine his own prejudices
and to re-evaluate his own values in light of Fielding's
views. Also see Preston, item 930.

678. Jason, Philip K. "Samuel Jackson Pratt's Unpublished
Comedy of *Joseph Andrews*." *Notes and Queries*, n.s. 14
(1967), 416-18.

Announces the discovery of a manuscript of Pratt's
dramatization of *Joseph Andrews*, written as an after-
piece to *Jane Shore* for the benefit of Robert Bensley
and performed only that one time (on April 20, 1778).
Jason argues that the play is better than any of Pratt's
published dramas and is a skillful adaptation of the
novel that deserves a renewal of interest.

* Johnson, Maurice. *Fielding's Art of Fiction: Eleven
Essays on "Shamela," "Joseph Andrews," "Tom Jones,"
and "Amelia."* (See item 511.)

679. Johnston, Arthur. "Fielding, Hearne and Merry-Andrews."
Notes and Queries, n.s. 7 (1960), 295-97.

The reference to Joseph's ancestry in the second chapter
of *Joseph Andrews* includes a reference to "that sect of
laughing philosophers called Merry Andrews." The point
of the reference is to mock antiquarianism in general

and probably Thomas Hearne (fourteen of whose books
Fielding owned) in particular.

*   Jordan, Robert M. "The Limits of Illusion: Faulkner,
    Fielding, and Chaucer." (See item 512.)

*   Karl, Frederick R. "Henry Fielding: The Novel, the
    Epic, and the Comic Sense of Life." (See item 514.)

680. Kearney, A.M. "Pamela and Joseph Andrews." *Essays in
     Criticism*, 18 (1968), 105-07. Reprinted as "Objections
     by A.M. Kearney" in *"Joseph Andrews" and "Shamela,"* ed.
     Sheridan Baker, item 52.

     Objects to Douglas Brooks' "Richardson's *Pamela* and
     Fielding's *Joseph Andrews*," item 653. Brooks' parallels
     between the two novels are too ingenious, especially
     the identification of Joseph with Mr. B. because
     Booby's clothes fit Joseph perfectly; actually Joseph
     merely needed to dress as a gentleman and so was forced
     to borrow the clothes. Kearney also strongly objects
     to Brooks' thesis "that Fielding was handing out some
     kind of lesson to Richardson." See Brooks' rebuttal,
     item 654.

681. ———. "Pamela and Joseph Andrews." *Essays in Crit-
     icism*, 18 (1968), 479-80.

     Raises further objections to Brooks' "Richardson's
     Pamela and Fielding's *Joseph Andrews*," item 653. See
     Brooks' rejoinder, item 655.

682. Ker, W.P. *On Modern Literature: Lectures and Addresses*.
     Eds. Terence Spencer and James Sutherland. Oxford:
     Clarendon Press, 1955.

     Compares Fielding with Richardson as a novelist and
     notes that nature is not important in Fielding's novels.

*   Kimpel, Ben D., and T.C. Duncan Eaves. "Two Names in
    Joseph Andrews." *Modern Philology*, 72 (1975), 408-09.

    See under Eaves, item 664.

*   Kreissman, Bernard. *Pamela-Shamela*. (See item 625.)

683. Kurrelmeyer, W. "A German Version of *Joseph Andrews*."
     Modern Language Notes, 33 (1918), 469-71.

     Reports that J.H. Rüdiger's *Fieldings komischer Roman
     in vier Theilen* (1765) is actually a fairly close trans-

lation of *Joseph Andrews*. Many of the characters' names have been changed, and the changes indicate that Rüdiger translated a French version of the novel rather than the English original.

* Macallister, Hamilton. *Fielding*. (See item 528.)

684. MacAndrew, M. Elizabeth. "Fielding's Use of Names in *Joseph Andrews*." *Names*, 16 (1968), 362-70.

Points out that Fielding gives his characters names which signal something about them. Joseph Andrews and Parson Adams, for example, have first names of Biblical import and surnames which connect them with *Pamela*.

685. McCullen, J.T. "Fielding's Beau Didapper." *English Language Notes*, 2 (1964), 98-100.

Beau Didapper fits H.C. Agrippa's description of "a thing of the moon." Fielding has given Beau "lunary qualities."

686. McCullough, Bruce. "Introduction" to *Joseph Andrews* by Henry Fielding. New York: Scribner's, 1930. Pp. xvii-xlix.

Consists of a brief biography, a lengthy critique of the morality of *Pamela* (the heroine is viewed as an ignoble schemer), a positive discussion of the wit and energy of *Shamela*, and a detailed analysis of *Joseph Andrews* which links it to the picaresque tradition. *Joseph Andrews*, an epic of the modern world, gave direction to the English novel.

687. McDowell, Alfred. "Fielding's Rendering of Speech in *Joseph Andrews* and *Tom Jones*." *Language and Style*, 6 (1973), 83-96.

In order to control and direct dialogue, Fielding uses the method of "free indirect speech" in which he combines dialogue with the narrator's interpolations. This technique makes his novels more dramatic than traditionally has been thought.

688. Mack, Maynard. "Introduction" to *Joseph Andrews* by Henry Fielding. New York: Holt, Rinehart and Winston, 1948. Pp. ii-xxiv. Reprinted as "*Joseph Andrews* and *Pamela*" in Iser, item 507, and Paulson, item 258.

Although *Joseph Andrews* is, in part, a parody of *Pamela*, it really responds to Richardson's moral position not

as much through parody as through creating an entirely
different world, one that is more inclusive and realistic than Richardson's. Moreover, Fielding's techniques
derive not at all from Richardson's but rather from his
early dramatic training and from *Don Quixote*, both of
which influence his methods of characterization and his
intellectual use of humor.

689.   —————. "*Joseph Andrews* and *Pamela*," in *Fielding: A
Collection of Critical Essays*, ed. Ronald Paulson.
Englewood Cliffs, N.J.: Prentice-Hall, 1962. Pp. 52-
58. Also published in Iser, item 507.

See annotation under "Introduction" to *Joseph Andrews*,
item 688.

690.   Mavrocordato, Alexandre. "The Picaresque Novel as a
Variation on the 'Game of the Goose,'" in *Le Voyage
dans la littérature anglo-saxonne*. Paris: Didier, 1972.
Pp. 71-81.

The ancient Game of the Goose (Monopoly is a modern version) supplies the pattern for the picaresque novel.
Joseph Andrews provides an example of the affinities
between the two: the novel is a linear progression, the
characters meet several hazards which set them back on
their journey, the impelling agent is chance, and the
elusive goal is marriage, or a settled state. In addition, the actual journey in *Joseph* occupies 63 chapters,
the same number as there are squares on the Goose board.

691.   Maxwell, J.C. "Hazlitt and Fielding." *Notes and
Queries*, n.s. 11 (1964), 25.

A comment on Godwin by Hazlitt is an adaptation of a
Fielding passage on Parson Adams (*Joseph Andrews*, IV.v).
See Swaminathan, item 304.

692.   Maynadier, G.H. "Introduction" to *The Adventures of
Joseph Andrews and His Friend Mr. Abraham Adams* by
Henry Fielding. Cambridge, Mass.: Harvard University
Press, 1903. Pp. xv-xxviii.

The main influences on *Joseph Andrews* are *Pamela*, *Don
Quixote*, the *Roman Comique*, and *Paysan Parvenu*. In
spite of the fact that its structure is marred by
digressive episodes, *Joseph Andrews* gave direction to
the English novel because of its realism.

*   Monteser, Frederick. *The Picaresque Element in Western
Literature*. (See item 537.)

693. Odo, Minoru. "*Joseph Andrews* as a Literary Experiment." *Memoirs of Osaka Kyoiku University*, 17 (1968), 69-80.

    This item apparently is unavailable in the United States.

694. Olsen, Flemming. "Notes on the Structure of *Joseph Andrews*." *English Studies*, 50 (1969), 340-51.

    The overall structure of *Joseph Andrews* often appears to be chaotic because the characters are divided into two groups, the dramatic characters and Fielding, the narrator. Holding the novel together are the various themes, which revolve around Joseph, Adams, and Fielding's sociological concerns.

695. Palmer, Eustace T. "Fielding's *Joseph Andrews*: A Comic Epic in Prose." *English Studies*, 52 (1971), 331-39.

    In the seventeenth-century sense of the word, *Joseph Andrews* is an epic; that is, it is a quest tale with adventures and a moral. The novel is also comic in its satire of both society and the naiveté of its protagonists.

696. Paulson, Ronald. *The Fictions of Satire*. Baltimore: Johns Hopkins University Press, 1967.

    Contains general remarks on *Joseph Andrews* as part of the Quixotic tradition.

697. ————. "Models and Paradigms: *Joseph Andrews*, Hogarth's *Good Samaritan*, and Fénelon's *Télémaque*." *Modern Language Notes*, 91 (1976), 1186-1207.

    Argues that the structure of *Joseph Andrews* is based on that of *Télémaque* and both the Biblical parable of the Good Samaritan and Hogarth's engraving of the same name. The Good Samaritan is mentioned several times in the novel and helps to structure the benevolence theme. *Télémaque* provides the narrative structure for Joseph's wandering.

698. Penner, A.R. "Fielding's Adaptation of Cervantes' Knight and Squire." *Revue de Littérature Comparée*, 41 (1967), 508-14.

    Adams and Joseph in *Joseph Andrews* owe the basis of their characterization and their adventures to *Don Quixote*, but Fielding draws his figures more naturally than did Cervantes.

699.   Perry, Thomas Sergeant. *English Literature in the*
       Eighteenth Century. Freeport, N.Y.: Books for Libraries
       Press, 1972. Originally published New York: Harper and
       Brothers, 1883.

       Quotes extensively from *Joseph Andrews* to illustrate
       Fielding's humor; largely ignores *Tom Jones* and com-
       pletely ignores the other novels.

700.   Priestley, J.B. "Parson Adams," in his *The English*
       Comic Characters. London: The Bodley Head, 1963. Pp.
       91-110. Originally published London: John Lane, 1925.

       Adams is not the kind of comic character, the mere butt
       of jokes, that Fielding describes in his Preface to
       Joseph Andrews. Although he is based on the stock ab-
       sent-minded figure and also is the butt of some jokes,
       he is a realistic figure who forms the moral center of
       the novel. Also see Priestley's "Three Novelists,"
       item 701.

701.   ————. "Three Novelists," in his *English Humour.* Lon-
       don and New York: Longmans, Green, 1930. Pp. 119-37.

       Sees Fielding's crowning achievement as Parson Adams in
       Joseph Andrews. Nowhere is the influence of *Don Quixote*
       on Fielding so apparent as in the portrayal of the comic-
       heroic parson who ranks among the greatest characters
       in fiction. Also see Priestley's "Parson Adams," item
       700.

*   Ramondt, Marie. "Between Laughter and Humour in the
       Eighteenth Century." (See item 268.)

702.   Reid, B.L. "Utmost Merriment, Strictest Decency:
       Joseph Andrews." *Sewanee Review*, 75 (1967), 559-84.
       Reprinted in the author's *The Long Boy and Others.*
       Athens, Ga.: University of Georgia Press, 1969. Pp.
       52-77.

       Sees the journey from town to country as the novel's
       central metaphor: it is a moral- pilgrimage during which
       temptations are posed and opportunities for good works
       are offered Joseph and Adams; it employs modes of travel
       --pedestrian, equestrian, and vehicular--to indicate
       moral distinctions (walking is wholesome and morally
       healthy and coach travel is indicative of the corruption
       of Lady Booby and Peter Pounce); it marks the movement
       from confusion and corruption in the city to simplicity
       and positive morality in the country. The novel ends

with another metaphor in which simplicity of clothing represents moral worth.

* Robinson, Roger. "The Influence of Fielding on Barnaby Rudge." (See item 563.)

* Rogers, Pat. "Fielding." (See item 565.)

703. Roscoe, Adrian A. "Fielding and the Problem of All-worthy." *Texas Studies in Literature and Language*, 7 (1965), 169-72.

Uncovers a dilemma that Fielding faces in his portrait of Allworthy. On the one hand, Fielding cannot present Allworthy too unfavorably because he does not wish to show ingratitude to Ralph Allen, Allworthy's original; on the other hand, the novel requires Allworthy to be human and to make key misjudgments of character. Fielding's solution is to make Allworthy representative of a good man trapped in a bad situation--the lawless rural retreats of the landed gentry.

* Saintsbury, George. "The Four Wheels of the Novel Wain." (See item 568.)

704. Schilling, Bernard N. *The Comic Spirit: Boccaccio to Thomas Mann*. Detroit: Wayne State University Press, 1965.

Contains two essays on *Joseph Andrews*: "Fielding's 'Preface' and *Joseph Andrews*" (item 705) and "Slipslop, Lady Booby, and the Ladder of Dependence" (item 706).

705. ————. "Fielding's 'Preface' and *Joseph Andrews*," in his *The Comic Spirit: Boccaccio to Thomas Mann*. Detroit: Wayne State University Press, 1965. Pp. 43-70.

Takes Fielding's view of affectation, made up of vanity and hypocrisy, from the Preface to *Joseph Andrews* and then explores the various comic means he uses to treat this theme throughout the novel. Fielding is an important influence on the comic spirit of his time because his compassion modifies the typical harshness of Augustan satire. Like his contemporary satirists, he sees things as they are, but he affirms the good and the genuine as much as he condemns their opposites; nowhere can this be seen more clearly than in his positive portrait of Parson Adams and his negative pictures of Trulliber and Lady Booby.

706.   ————. "Slipslop, Lady Booby, and the Ladder of De-
        pendence," in his *The Comic Spirit: Boccaccio to Thomas
        Mann*. Detroit: Wayne State University Press, 1965. Pp.
        71-97.

        An important aspect of Fielding's treatment of affecta-
        tion is his ridicule of "the idea of superiority," the
        view that one person is better than another because he
        stands higher on the social ladder. In *Joseph Andrews*,
        Slipslop thinks she is better than others because of
        her closeness to Lady Booby, but actually she is a
        fool, far inferior in terms of virtue and mentality to
        those "below" her like the illiterate Fanny and the
        lowly footman, Joseph. Lady Booby, too, feels that to
        marry Joseph would be a "condescension," whereas in
        reality, Joseph is above her morally; by having her
        "condescend" to marry Joseph, who rejects her, Fielding
        shows the shallowness of her pretended superiority.

707.   Shapiro, Charles, ed. *Twelve Original Essays on Great
        English Novels*. Detroit: Wayne State University Press,
        1960.

        Includes Ehrenpreis's "Fielding's Use of Fiction" (item
        665).

*   Shepperson, Archibald. "Richardson and Fielding:
        Shamela and *Shamelia*." (See item 630.)

708.   Sherbo, Arthur. "Fielding's Dogs." *Notes and Queries*,
        17 (1970), 302-03.

        The source for most of the dogs' names in *Joseph Andrews*
        (III.vi) is Thomas D'Urfey's *Marriage-Hater Match'd*
        (II.i).

709.   ————. "The 'Moral Basis' of *Joseph Andrews*," in his
        Studies in the Eighteenth Century English Novel. East
        Lansing: Michigan State University Press, 1969. Pp.
        104-19.

        Objects to Battestin's argument (see *The Moral Basis of
        Fielding's Art*, item 642, pp. 86 and 93) that *Joseph
        Andrews* has a solid philosophical core located in Wil-
        son's story; actually, the latter is an "excrescence."
        In fact, all the interpolated tales are "unnecessary";
        the novel gains its force, its verve, and makes its
        point in the main narrative, especially with the
        figures of Slipslop and Adams. For opposing views, see
        Brooks, item 650; Cauthen, item 657; Driskell, item
        662; and Goldberg, item 673.

710.   ————. "'Naked' Innocence in *Joseph Andrews*," in his
        Studies in the Eighteenth Century English Novel. East
        Lansing: Michigan State University Press, 1969. Pp.
        120-27.

        Argues against Spilka's view (see "Comic Resolution in
        Fielding's *Joseph Andrews*," item 712) that the "lust-
        chastity theme" dominates the novel and that the central
        symbol of that theme is nakedness (which, to Spilka,
        equals innocence). Spilka does not fully comprehend
        all the nuances of the eighteenth-century use of the
        term "naked" and, in fact, most of the characters he
        refers to as "naked" are partly clothed.

*   ————. "The Narrator in Fielding's Novels." (See item
        576.)

711.   Spacks, Patricia Meyer. "Some Reflections on Satire."
        Genre, 1 (1968), 22-30. Reprinted in *"Joseph Andrews"*
        and "Shamela," ed. Sheridan Baker, item 52.

        The main satiric target of *Joseph Andrews* "is the
        human tendency to be sure of oneself in exactly the
        situations where one should doubt"; not only are the
        "bad" characters involved in this satire, but so too
        are Joseph and Adams. In Fielding's universe the cer-
        tainty that man seeks is not present, and the reader's
        recognition of this produces in him the "uneasiness"
        that is the desired satiric response.

712.   Spilka, Mark. "Comic Resolution in Fielding's *Joseph
        Andrews*." *College English*, 15 (1953), 11-19. Reprinted
        in Iser, item 507; *"Joseph Andrews" and "Shamela,"* ed.,
        Sheridan Baker, item 52; Paulson, item 258; and Spector,
        item 584.

        Analyzes the night scenes at Booby Hall in *Joseph Andrews*,
        seeing them as more than just comic interludes. They form
        a comic resolution to the action and serve as a parody
        of the whole novel. The lust-chastity theme is ironical-
        ly resolved when Adams, indifferent to a sexual liaison
        with Fanny, becomes by mistake the first and only man
        to gain her bed, although many others, far from indif-
        ferent to Fanny's sexual charms, have unsuccessfully
        endeavored to gain "the paradise" of her boudoir. The
        novel ends on a theme of benevolent humor when Fanny and
        Joseph indulgently forgive Adams for his blunder.

713.   Staves, Susan. "Don Quixote in Eighteenth-Century
        England." *Comparative Literature*, 24 (1972), 193-215.

Attitudes toward Quixote completely reversed in the eighteenth century, moving from satiric laughter at the buffoon to romantic embrace of the idealistic hero. Fielding's quixotic character, Parson Adams, represents a midpoint in this changing attitude. Readers may laugh at Adams, but they are always in sympathy with him. See Tave, item 595, whose earlier work argues the same points, but in much more detail.

714.   [Stead, P.J.] "The Trial of Mary Blandy." *The Police College Magazine*, 7 (1963), 433-34.

Traces the original of Beau Didapper in *Joseph Andrews* to a Captain Cranstoun, who was involved in the sensational murder of Francis Blandy by the latter's daughter, Mary. The guilt or innocence of Mary and the depth of involvement of Cranstoun are still subjects for debate.

*   Stern, Guy. "Saint or Hypocrite? A Study of Wieland's 'Jacinte Episode.'" (See item 631.)

715.   Stevenson, Lionel. *The English Novel: A Panorama*. Boston: Houghton Mifflin, 1960.

Initially, Fielding's approach to the novel was "unplanned"; thus, he combined exaggeration, coincidence, and realism in the intellectually complex plot of *Joseph Andrews*, into which he interpolated essays and short tales. When he came to write *Tom Jones*, he was more conscious of his craft and therefore more successfully blended the eclectic elements of his art. His intrusive narration and realistic characterizations were original and they continue to give his novels their power.

716.   Sutherland, James R. *English Satire*. Cambridge: The University Press, 1958.

Assesses Fielding's historical importance in the development of English satire as his having contributed incidental satire to the novel form in *Joseph Andrews* and his having created the first purely satirical novel in *Jonathan Wild*. The source of Fielding's satiric impulse was his "outraged sense of truth" which led him to attack Richardson's values as false and to extend his satire to all forms of affectation and hypocrisy. Many later novelists, particularly Thackeray, were influenced by Fielding's satiric targets and methods.

*   Tave, Stuart M. *The Amiable Humorist*. (See item 595.)

717. Taylor, Dick, Jr. "Joseph As Hero in *Joseph Andrews*."
      Tulane Studies in English, 7 (1957), 91-109. Reprinted
      in *"Joseph Andrews" and "Shamela,"* ed. Sheridan Baker,
      item 52.

      Most commentators make little mention of Joseph in their
      discussions of *Joseph Andrews*, but his evolution of
      character throughout the novel shows him to be its real
      hero. He moves from Joey, the naive footman, to the
      mature Joseph who acts as a counterbalance to Adams and
      who often speaks for Fielding in presenting the serious
      moral of the novel.

718. Troughton, Marion. "Parsons in English Literature."
      Contemporary Review, 187 (1955), 39-43.

      Says that Fielding's portrayal of Parson Adams is
      probably true-to-life and that the eighteenth-century
      parson is more like the twentieth-century country clergy-
      man than is his Victorian counterpart.

719. Weinbrot, Howard D. "Chastity and Interpolation: Two
      Aspects of *Joseph Andrews*." *Journal of English and
      Germanic Philology*, 69 (1970), 14-31.

      Deals with Fielding's attitudes toward Joseph's virginity
      and the function of the interpolated tales. Joseph,
      who acts as Pamela should have, is the novel's sexual
      norm, set off against Lady Booby's licentiousness and
      Mr. Wilson's London exploits. The three interpolated
      tales provide "a grimly realistic backbone" for the
      novel, reinforcing the themes embodied in the main nar-
      rative. The tales of Leonora and Mr. Wilson, for ex-
      ample, show the serious results of not accepting Fanny
      and Joseph as models of behavior, and the Leonora and
      Paul story shows the dangers of interfering with "part-
      ners," just as Mr. Booby interferes with Joseph and
      Fanny's relationship. The narrative technique of the
      interpolations is designed to contrast with the benevolent
      intrusive narration of the main story.

720. Item deleted.

721. Weston, Harold. *Form in Literature: A Theory of Tech-
      nique and Construction*. London: Rich and Cowan, 1934.

      Stresses the picaresque element in *Joseph Andrews* and
      Tom Jones.

722.   Whittuck, Charles A. *The Good Man of the Eighteenth Century*. London: Grant Allen, 1901.

Battestin, in the *New Cambridge Bibliography of English Literature*, remarks that this book treats Parson Adams and Allworthy, but the compilers have been unable to confirm this information personally.

723.   Wiesenfarth, Joseph. "'High' People and 'Low' in *Joseph Andrews*: A Study of Structure and Style." *College Language Association Journal*, 16 (1973), 357-65.

Generally Fielding's low characters are morally superior to his upper class figures. He signals this comic inversion by using classical language to describe the low people and low language to describe the high people.

724.   Williams, R.W. "Fielding's 'Joseph Andrews.'" *Teaching of English*, 25 (1973), 18-25.

The compilers have not seen this essay, listed by Battestin in *The New Cambridge Bibliography of English Literature*.

*   Willy, Margaret. "Portrait of a Man: Henry Fielding." (See item 327.)

*   Wright, Andrew. *Henry Fielding: Mask and Feast*. (See item 612.)

725.   ————. "*Joseph Andrews*, Mask and Feast." *Essays in Criticism*, 13 (1963), 209-21.

This essay, printed here as a "work in progress," forms part of Chapter One of the author's *Henry Fielding: Mask and Feast* (item 612). It focuses on Fielding's deliberate attempts, through the introductory chapters and intrusive narration, to make *Joseph Andrews* artificial. Fielding wishes to distance the reader in order to make "bearable the human condition" and to celebrate life.

D. *Jonathan Wild*

* Baker, Ernest A. *History of the English Novel.* (See item 448.)

726. Bispham, G.T. "Fielding's *Jonathan Wild*," in *Eighteenth-Century Literature: An Oxford Miscellany.* Oxford: The Clarendon Press, 1909. Pp. 56-75.

    Provides background on the real Jonathan Wild and links Fielding's legal career to his motivation for writing the novel. Fielding was a sincere reformer who used both his writing and his legal position to benefit society.

* Braudy, Leo. "Fielding: Public History and Individual Perception." (See item 648.)

* Chandler, Frank W. *Literature of Roguery.* (See item 464.)

* Churchill, R.C. "Fielding: To the Novel from the Drama." (See item 111.)

727. de Castro, J. Paul. "Fieldingiana." *Notes and Queries*, Twelfth Series, 2 (1916), 441-43.

    Replies to Robbins, "*Jonathan Wild the Great*: Its Germ," item 755, by arguing that Fielding probably did not write the articles in *Mist's Weekly Journal* (June 12 and 19, 1725) which appear to be similar to *Jonathan Wild*. Also see Robbins, "*Jonathan Wild the Great*," item 756.

728. ———. "Fielding's *Jonathan Wild*." *Times Literary Supplement* (August 6, 1931), p. 609.

    Requests information about an obscure phrase apparently referring to a lottery in *Jonathan Wild* (III.vii).

729. ———. "Jonathan Wild, the Great." *Notes and Queries*, Twelfth Series, 3 (1917), 74.

    Claims that Robbins' arguments (items 755 and 756) that Fielding wrote the *Mist's* articles on Jonathan Wild are unsubstantiated and asks if Robbins knows who wrote two 1758 essays on Wild, published in the appendix of the 1840 Daly edition of Fielding's works and highly critical of Fielding.

730. Dickson, Frederick S. *An Index to "Jonathan Wild, the
      Great"* by Henry Fielding. 1911.

      This unpublished manuscript in the Library of Congress
      contains lists of characters and persons referred to
      in the novel.

731. Digeon, Aurélien. *"Jonathan Wild,"* in *Fielding: A Col-
      lection of Critical Essays*, ed. Ronald Paulson. Engle-
      wood Cliffs, N.J.: Prentice-Hall, 1962. Pp. 69-80.
      This material originally appeared as part of pp. 96-128
      of Digeon's *The Novels of Fielding*, item 474.

      Finds Jonathan Wild, because he was so well known by
      the general public, an ideal figure to mask Fielding's
      attack on Walpole. The attack was violent and heavily
      ironic, so Fielding, who apparently feared that Wild's
      continuous villainy and the unremitting irony of the
      work might weary his audience, introduced the parallel
      story of Heartfree. This perfectly honest man serves
      as both a counterweight and a foil to Wild, giving the
      novel balance and symmetrical form.

732. Dircks, Richard J. "The Perils of Heartfree: A Socio-
      logical Review of Fielding's Adaptation of Dramatic
      Convention." *Texas Studies in Literature and Language*,
      8 (1966), 5-13.

      Disputes the contention that *Jonathan Wild* is primarily
      a political satire. Although some of the satire is
      political, its main thrust is toward the social evils
      threatening the merchant middle class. Fielding drama-
      tizes the middle class struggle against the depreda-
      tions of the "omnipresent" Wilds of the world by show-
      ing Heartfree, his family, and Friendly as helpless in
      the conflict with self-serving schemers like Wild.

733. Downs, Brian W. "Jonathan Wild." *Times Literary Sup-
      plement* (September 11, 1943), p. 444.

      Argues on the basis of internal evidence, including al-
      lusions to events that took place in 1742, that *Jonathan
      Wild* was written in that year following *Joseph Andrews*.

*   Dyson, A.E. "Satiric and Comic Theory in Relation to
      Fielding." (See item 172.)

*   Esdaile, Katharine A. "Fielding's Danish Translator."
      (See item 666.)

734. Evans, David L. "The Theme of Liberty in *Jonathan Wild*." *Papers on Language and Literature*, 3 (1967), 302-13.

     Notes that all discussions of theme in *Jonathan Wild* focus on the "goodness-greatness conflict," which, although important, is actually subsumed by the conflict between "moral imprisonment" and "moral freedom." Reading the novel in this light accounts for such apparent "irrelevancies" as Mrs. Heartfree's report on her many misfortunes.

735. Farrell, William J. "The Mock-Heroic Form of *Jonathan Wild*." *Modern Philology*, 63 (1966), 216-26.

     Demonstrates that the form of *Jonathan Wild* is more closely related to the traditional biography of a hero than it is to the contemporary criminal biography with which it is usually associated. By applying a "high" form to a "low" character, Fielding is able to mock not only Wild but also his counterparts in the "respectable" world.

736. Hatfield, Glenn W. "Puffs and Pollitricks: *Jonathan Wild* and the Political Corruption of Language." *Philological Quarterly*, 46 (1967), 248-67. Reprinted in his book, item 197.

     A concern with the way in which language is corrupted by politicians is reflected throughout Fielding's work, but it is most clearly demonstrated by his use of "greatness" and "goodness" in *Jonathan Wild*, terms which become ironic because they are separated from their essential or core meanings.

737. Hill, Rowland M. "*Jonathan Wild*." *Times Literary Supplement* (August 14, 1943), p. 396.

     Believes that *A Journey from This World to the Next* and *Jonathan Wild* were written before *Joseph Andrews*. For an opposing view, see Downs, "*Jonathan Wild*," item 733.

738. Hopkins, Robert H. "Language and Comic Play in Fielding's *Jonathan Wild*." *Criticism*, 8 (1966), 213-28. An extract is reprinted in Rawson, item 272.

     Argues against those who see *Jonathan Wild* as a moral allegory (in particular Wendt's "The Moral Allegory of *Jonathan Wild*," item 761a) because to view the novel in this light is "to stifle its comic possibilities."

Wild is a "first-rate" satire which uses puns, linguistic allusions, and comic word play to ridicule the "extremes" of language. The language of the confidence man is material, bestial, obscene, and particular; the language of the Heartfrees is full of platitudes, clichés, and abstractions. Also see Irwin, *The Making of Jonathan Wild*, item 741, and Sheridan Baker, "Henry Fielding and the Cliché," item 84.

739.   Howson, Gerald. *Thief-Taker General: The Rise and Fall of Jonathan Wild*. London: Hutchinson and New York: St. Martin's Press, 1970.

An historical and biographical account of Jonathan Wild. Howson notes that Fielding and others used Wild as a symbol and in so doing, distorted the historical personage. Unfortunately, many later readers took Fielding's account of the London underworld literally, but Wild and the real underworld bore little relation to the descriptions in Fielding's novel.

740.   Humphreys, A.R. "Introduction" to *Jonathan Wild the Great and The Journal of a Voyage to Lisbon*, ed. Douglas Brooks. London: Dent and New York: Dutton, 1973. Pp. v-xiv.

With the careers of Wild and the Heartfrees, Fielding makes his most decisive confrontation between the evil and good in human nature. Unfortunately (for Fielding's purposes), the conflict is unbalanced in Wild's favor because he is portrayed so realistically and vigorously while the Heartfrees are rather foolishly passive. Fielding's satire goes beyond the topical target of Walpole in condemning all the Alexanders and Caesars of world history. The *Voyage* is deeply moving because of Fielding's superiority to painful personal circumstances, and it is made vividly interesting by its detailed portraits of the figures that populate its pages.

741.   Irwin, Robert William. *The Making of Jonathan Wild*. New York: Columbia University Press, 1941. Reprinted New York: Archon, 1966.

Discovers Fielding's sources for the life of Jonathan Wild in Defoe and other of Wild's biographers and pseudo-biographers. The ethical problems that Fielding dealt with in the novel--greatness, goodness, self-love, and benevolence--were reworked in his later fiction. The form of the book owes something to the tale of low-life, the picaresque novel, and the traditional English

criminal biography, but Fielding shapes these forms
into something new, almost a comic epic in prose.

742. Kishler, Thomas C. "Heartfree's Function in *Jonathan
Wild*." *Satire Newsletter*, 1 (1964), 32-4.

Heartfree is not meant to be a rounded character, but
is rather a flat conceptualization of "good," necessary
to show the reader the desirable opposite of Wild's
"great."

743. Kronenberger, Louis. "Fielding: *Jonathan Wild*," in
his *The Republic of Letters*. New York: Alfred Knopf,
1955. Pp. 81-88.

Even though the novel is flawed by Fielding's constant
reminders that he is being ironic, by his excessive
personal commentary, and by his open sympathy for the
Heartfrees, it nevertheless is a unique achievement
because the author is able to sustain his ironic comparison between goodness and greatness at such great
length.

744. Lyons, Frederick J.   *Jonathan Wild: Prince of Robbers*.
London: Michael Joseph, 1936.

The compilers have not seen this book.

Review: Times Literary Supplement (31 October 1936),
p. 889.

745. McCusher, H.   "*The Life of Jonathan Wild the Great*."
More Books: The Bulletin of the Boston Public Library,
13 (1938), 72-73.

Announces the library purchase of a first edition of
Fielding's *Miscellanies* and briefly comments on
Jonathan Wild, calling it "the masterpiece of the
Miscellanies."

746. Maynadier, G.H.   "Introduction" to *The History of the
Late Mr. Jonathan Wild the Great* by Henry Fielding.
Cambridge, Mass.: Harvard University Press, 1903. Pp.
xvii-xxiii.

Sees the strength of *Jonathan Wild* as its sustained
irony, but the work is seriously flawed by the Heartfrees who are "silly" and less realistic than the vil-
lains. Fielding's attempt to blend sentimentalized,
virtuous characters with the ironically depicted Wild
ruins the unity of the book so that it is neither novel
nor consistent satire.

747.   Miles, Kathleen.   "Richardson's Response to Fielding's
       Felon." *Studies in the Novel*, 1 (1969), 373-74.

       In *Clarissa* (Vol. I, letter xxxvi), Richardson has
       Clarissa rebut Fielding's contention in *Jonathan Wild*
       that goodness and greatness are not necessarily allied
       qualities.

*   Monteser, Frederick. *The Picaresque Element in Western
       Literature*. (See item 537.)

748.   Newton, William. *The Poetics of the Rogue-Ruined*.
       Humanities Series No. 1. *Bulletin of the Oklahoma A&M
       College*, 48 (1951).

       Defines the "Rogue-Ruined" as a distinct literary form in
       which an unsympathetic protagonist moves from undeserved
       good fortune to deserved ill fortune; comedy constantly
       borders on the tragic; and the protagonist's escapades
       more and more carry the potential for tragedy. *Jonathan
       Wild* is an example of the form.

749.   Plumb, J.H.   "Foreword" to *Jonathan Wild* by Henry Field-
       ing. New York: New American Library, 1962. Pp. xi-xvii.

       Mostly biographical, this essay also presents some
       critical generalizations about the novel. As a compound
       of fact and fiction, it resembles Defoe's work. It is
       a brilliant political satire of Walpole but transcends
       its topicality by functioning as "a morality" which
       ironically condemns human folly and wickedness.

750.   ————.   "Henry Fielding and *Jonathan Wild*" in his *Men
       and Centuries*. Boston: Houghton Mifflin, 1963. Pp.
       281-87.

       A brief biography, emphasizing Fielding's "lust for
       life" and humanitarianism, is followed by a short dis-
       cussion of *Jonathan Wild*. The novel is not only a
       "brilliant" political satire but also presents a real-
       istic picture of London low life.

       Reviews: John Brooks, *Listener*, 69 (1963), 386-89;
       Betty Kemp, *New Statesman*, 65 (1963), 681-82; *Times
       Literary Supplement* (March 28, 1963), p. 214.

751.   Preston, John. "The Ironic Mode: A Comparison of *Jona-
       than Wild* and *The Beggar's Opera*." *Essays in Criticism*,
       16 (1966), 268-80.

       Although the theme of *The Beggar's Opera* is similar to
       that of *Jonathan Wild*, there are great differences in

the ways in which Gay and Fielding use irony. The former's "structural irony" is "a way of thinking"; the latter's rhetorical irony is "a way of speaking." Gay's irony is subtle and complex, whereas Fielding's is superficial because it is based on the single joke of inverting terms to call vice "greatness."

752. Rawson, C.J. "Fielding's 'Good' Merchant: The Problem of Heartfree in *Jonathan Wild* (with Comments on other 'Good' Characters in Fielding)." *Modern Philology*, 69 (1972), 292-313.

Regards the central conflict in *Jonathan Wild* as between "goodness" and "greatness" and explores the various uses of the terms in the novel. The word "great" oscillates "between implications of rank, of 'heroic' prowess, and of moral excellence," but *true* greatness always includes an idea of moral goodness. This moral goodness is embodied in Heartfree and wickedness is embodied in Wild through the ironic application of "greatness" to him; however, the contrast between the two, which is the heart of the novel's irony, is so "polarized" that it is too formulaic. The rigid antitheses between Heartfree and Wild makes the former a failure in characterization because he can only serve as a foil to the more exuberantly portrayed Wild and because frequently Wild is depicted as a "comic clumsy rogue" which makes Heartfree seem "silly" for being duped by him.

* ————. *Henry Fielding and the Augustan Ideal Under Stress*. (See item 273.)

753. ————. "The Hero as Clown: Jonathan Wild, Felix Krull, and Others," in *Studies in the Eighteenth Century*, 2, ed. R.F. Brissenden. Toronto: University of Toronto Press, 1973. Pp. 17-52.

Opposes the widely-held view that Jonathan Wild is a figure of unrelieved viciousness in a "mordant" novel. This view has arisen because readers focus on the "formulaic ironies about 'greatness'" in the novel and fail to perceive the difference between what is said of Wild and what the action reveals about him. Actually, Wild's wickedness is undercut by the comic action which often shows him as an unsuccessful bumbler who is tricked by La Ruse, robbed by Molly, and humiliated by Laetitia.

754. Rinehart, Hollis. "*Jonathan Wild* and the Cant Dictionary." *Philological Quarterly*, 48 (1969), 220-25.

Discovers the source for the cant terms in *Jonathan Wild*

in *A New Canting Dictionary* (1725). Fielding uses such
terms in dialogue for purposes of characterization, but
even more important, he applies "low" terminology to
"fashionable" actions in order to deflate false greatness. Thus, when Fielding says that the fashionable
habit of leaving a theater before the last act of a play
to avoid paying for a seat is a "sneaking-budge," he
is reducing the act to the level of a common criminal
action.

755.   Robbins, Alfred F. "*Jonathan Wild the Great*: Its Germ."
       Notes and Queries, Eleventh Series, 2 (1910), 261.

       An article, in *Mist's Weekly Journal* for June 12 and
       June 19, 1725, describes Jonathan Wild in terms much
       like those Fielding used in his novel, *Jonathan Wild*.
       The article, if not by Fielding himself, certainly must
       have influenced him. On this topic, also see: de Castro,
       "Fieldingiana," item 727, and "Jonathan Wild, the
       Great," item 729; and Robbins, "Jonathan Wild, the
       Great," item 756.

756.   ————. "Jonathan Wild, the Great." *Notes and Queries*,
       Twelfth Series, 3 (1917), 38.

       Argues that Fielding probably wrote the *Mist's* articles
       on Jonathan Wild in 1725; Fielding's knowledge of Roger
       Johnson seems to be as complete as that of the *Mist's*
       author. See the following discussion on this topic: de
       Castro, "Fieldingiana," item 727, and "Jonathan Wild,
       the Great," item 729; and Robbins, "*Jonathan Wild the
       Great*: Its Germ," item 755.

757.   Seamon, Roger G. "The Rhetorical Pattern of Mock-
       Heroic Satire." *The Humanities Association Bulletin*
       (Canada), 17 (1966), 37-41.

       Finds *Jonathan Wild* characteristic of the pattern of
       mock-heroic satire because it moves from a stage of
       non-judgmental comedy, through a stage in which standards
       of heroic action are used to pass judgment on the "low"
       obsession with money and in which low reality is used
       to criticize heroic ideals, to a final stage in which
       all heroes become Jonathan Wilds. In mock-heroic
       satire there is a constant tension between comedic norms,
       in which high and low are juxtaposed with no satiric
       point, and novelistic values, in which everything is
       seen as equal, at least potentially.

758. Shea, Bernard. "Machiavelli and Fielding's *Jonathan Wild*." *Publications of the Modern Language Association of America*, 72 (1957), 55-73.

Sees *Jonathan Wild* as at once an imitation, a parody, and a criticism of Machiavelli, drawing heavily upon Henry Nevile's translations of *The Prince*, *Discourses on the First Ten Books of Titus Livius*, and the *Life of Castruccio Castracani of Lucca* for much of its material. For example, Nevile's ironic use of "great" and "greatness" is similar to Fielding's use of the terms, and the biographical portions of *Jonathan Wild* almost certainly are derived from the *Life of Castraconi*.

Review: R.S. Crane, *Philological Quarterly*, 37 (1958), 328-33.

759. Smith, Raymond. "The Ironic Structure of Fielding's *Jonathan Wild*." *Ball State University Forum*, 6 (1965), 3-9.

The classical device of the *eiron*--"the character who appears to be inferior to his antagonist" but who eventually proves to be superior--generates structural irony in *Jonathan Wild* when the apparently weak benevolist, Heartfree, finally triumphs over the apparently powerful self-interested man, Wild. The *eiron* device links *Jonathan Wild* with *Joseph Andrews* and *Tom Jones*, both of which employ it.

760. Smith, Robert A. "The 'Great Man' Motif in *Jonathan Wild* and *The Beggar's Opera*." *College Language Association Journal*, 2 (1959), 183-84.

Like Gay in *The Beggar's Opera*, Fielding presents his "great" man through contrast as well as exposition. The ultimate point of Fielding's novel is that Wild's death works as a purgative for society.

*   Sutherland, James. *English Satire*. (See item 716.)

761. Wells, John E. "Fielding's Political Purpose in *Jonathan Wild*." *Publications of the Modern Language Association of America*, 28 (1913), 1-55.

Contends that *Jonathan Wild* is clearly a satire on Walpole and his administration. Wild represents Walpole and most of the characters (including the Heartfrees) can be identified with characters surrounding Walpole;

many of the events in the novel are likewise parallels
of real events in which Walpole was involved. The fact
that Fielding inserted three chapters (IV.iii, III.xi,
and II.vi) for political rather than literary purposes
is the most important of several pieces of evidence
which support the contention that the book is primarily
a political satire.

761a. Wendt, Allan. "The Moral Allegory of *Jonathan Wild*."
ELH: A Journal of English Literary History, 24 (1957),
306-20.

Jonathan Wild is an allegory in which Wild represents
greatness without goodness and Heartfree represents
goodness without greatness. Neither one is adequate
by itself because the former results in wickedness and
the latter in foolishness. The ideal, of course, is a
combination of the two qualities.

762. Woolf, Leonard. "The World of Books: Fielding's Novels."
The Nation and Athenaeum, 39 (1926), 503.

Reviews the Shakespeare Head edition of *Jonathan Wild*
and says that Fielding, like other eighteenth-century
writers, tended to create rather uninteresting two-
dimensional characters. His saving grace is his mastery
of the English language.

E. *Tom Jones*

763. Aldworth, A.E. "*Tom Jones*: Dowdy." *Notes and Queries*,
Eleventh Series, 3 (1911), 289.

Asks who the Dowdy is to whom Fielding refers in *Tom
Jones* (VI.ix).

*   Allen, Walter. *The English Novel*. (See item 441.)

764. Allot, Miriam. "A Note on Fielding's Mr. Square."
Modern Language Review, 56 (1961), 69-72.

The notion advanced by Cross in his *History of Henry
Fielding* (item 126) that Square is based on the real
person of Thomas Chubb (1649-1747) is a misapprehension.
Square's beliefs are a composite of Christian and non-
Christian Deist principles current among many thinkers
of the early eighteenth century, including Samuel Clarke

and Bishop Hoadly. Square is an object of derision because he neglects both religion and the "natural goodness of the heart." That neglect is not typical of
Chubb or of any other single Deist of the time.

*   ————. *Novelists on the Novel.* (See item 636.)

*   Alter, Robert. "On the Critical Dismissal of Fielding:
         Post-Puritanism in Literary Criticism." (See item 445.)

765.   ————. "The Picaroon Domesticated," in his *Rogue's
         Progress: Studies in the Picaresque Novel.* Cambridge,
         Mass.: Harvard University Press, 1964. Pp. 80-105.

         Links *Tom Jones* with the picaresque tradition. The
         original picaresque came out of a period of social
         disintegration, but the relative stability of the
         eighteenth century forced Fielding and others to modify
         that tradition. Specifically, the hero is transformed
         from the rogue to the reformed rogue or moral man who
         does not really belong with the lower elements of
         society; the diction is made more elegant; and the nar-
         rative voice is shifted from first person to omniscient.
         The episodic plot and the satiric intention in *Tom Jones*
         survive from the original mode.

         Review: Dale B.J. Randall, *College English*, 26 (1964),
         65.

766.   Amory, Hugh. "*Tom Jones* Among the Compositors: An
         Examination." *Harvard Library Bulletin*, 26 (1978),
         172-92.

         Critiques the approach taken by the Wesleyan editors
         of *Tom Jones* in deciding on the definitive text. Oc-
         casionally, Professor Bowers, the general editor, errs
         in his selection of spellings and other emendations
         for the text, and these errors are a result of Bowers'
         critical approach. However, the errors—several of
         which are listed—are few, and the edition is an ex-
         tremely valuable one.

767.   ————. "*Tom Jones* Plus or Minus: Towards a Practical
         Text." *Harvard Library Bulletin*, 25 (1977), 101-13.

         Reports on the Harvard Library copy of the third edition
         of *Tom Jones*. The third edition is probably a reworking
         of the first edition that preserves the first edition
         "cancellandum."

768.   Anderson, Howard. "Answers to the Author of *Clarissa*:
       Theme and Narrative Technique in *Tom Jones* and *Tristram
       Shandy*." *Philological Quarterly*, 51 (1972), 859-73.

       Tom Jones is a rejection of the costly self-reliance
       apparent in *Clarissa*; through narrative method, Fielding
       demonstrates the necessity of interaction and mutual
       trust. Fielding's technique is to fully develop his
       narrator as a character and to force the reader to rely
       on the narrator's judgment and good-nature for an accu-
       rate presentation and interpretation of the materials
       of the story. Sterne follows the same method in *Tristram
       Shandy*.

*   Atkins, J.W.H. "Critical Cross Currents." (See item
       81.)

*   Baker, Ernest A. *History of the English Novel*. (See
       item 448.)

769.   Baker, John Ross. "From Imitation to Rhetoric: The
       Chicago Critics, Wayne C. Booth, and *Tom Jones*."
       Novel, 6 (1973), 197-217. Reprinted in *Towards a
       Poetics of Fiction*, ed. Mark Spilka, item 957.

       Compares Wayne C. Booth's treatment of the narrator of
       Tom Jones (see *The Rhetoric of Fiction*, item 456) with
       that of R.S. Crane (item 808). Crane, holding to a
       view of mimesis, finds Fielding's introductory essays
       intrusive and unassimilated into the whole of the novel.
       Booth, on the other hand, emphasizes the "didactic" and
       finds it necessary to search for norms within the work;
       he locates these norms in the introductory essays.
       Baker tries to reconcile these two views by arguing
       that the narrator is inside the "form" of the work but
       outside the "imitation," the story of Tom's adventures,
       and that the novel is best read in terms of the tension
       between Tom's world and the narrator's constant re-
       minder that he created that world.

770.   Baker, Sheridan. "Bridget Allworthy: the Creative
       Pressures of Fielding's Plot." *Papers of the Michigan
       Academy of Science, Arts, and Letters*, 52 (1966), 345-
       56. Reprinted in *Tom Jones*, ed. Sheridan Baker, item
       57.

       All novelists must conceive of both a plot and a way to
       convey that plot; these two elements often create con-
       flicting demands on the artist. In *Tom Jones*, Fielding

brilliantly resolves such a conflict with his conception of Bridget Allworthy. His plot calls for an ille-
gitimate child, which in turn requires a mother with a
passionate nature. However, the exigencies of conveying
the plot require a prudish old maid. Fielding is able
to fuse the characteristics of the passionate, lonely
woman with those of the comic old maid in the figure of
Bridget, whose character reflects the conflicts and
ambiguities of real human personality.

771.   ————. "Fielding and the Irony of Form." *Eighteenth
Century Studies*, 2 (1968), 138-54.

Sees the form of *Tom Jones* as ironic rather than sup-
portive; that is, form contrasts with content in the
novel instead of emphasizing it. The form of *Tom Jones*
is dramatic and highly structured, while the contents
are the disorderly life of the eighteenth century.
Form in *Joseph Andrews*, on the other hand, is linear
and emphasizes rather than ironizes the action.

*   ————. "Henry Fielding's Comic Romances." (See item
637.)

772.   Barnes, John L. "Lady Bellaston: Fielding's Use of the
Charactonym." *South-Central Names Institute Publications*, 1 (1971), 114-16.

The compilers have not seen this item, listed in *The
Annual Bibliography of English Language and Literature
for 1971*, 46 (1973).

773.   Battestin, Martin C. "Fielding's Definition of Wisdom:
Some Functions of Ambiguity and Emblem in *Tom Jones*."
ELH: A Journal of English Literary History, 35 (1968),
188-217. Reprinted in *Tom Jones*, ed. Sheridan Baker,
item 57. Also reprinted as Chapter 6 of Battestin's
Providence of Wit, item 776.

Views the definition of "wisdom" as the most important
theme in *Tom Jones*, but Fielding's use of the term is
difficult to determine because of the way in which he
ambiguously employs its ethical correlative, "prudence."
According to its context, prudence can be either "the
fundamental vice" or the "essential virtue." Prudence
is the main attribute of such self-seekers as Blifil,
Honour, and Lady Bellaston, but it is also seen as in-
dispensable for such moral figures as Allworthy, Sophia,
and Tom. The ambiguity of the term forces the reader to

make ethical distinctions between real and apparent
virtue. The attainment of prudence is necessary if one
is to gain true wisdom. Thus Tom must learn prudence
to win Sophia, whose name is the Greek for wisdom;
therefore, Sophia becomes an emblematic and "quasi-
allegorical" figure. Ambiguity, emblem, and allegory
all function to define Fielding's view of true wisdom.

*   ————. "Fielding's Novels and the Wesleyan Edition."
(See item 449.)

774.   ————. "General Introduction" to *The History of Tom
Jones, a Foundling* by Henry Fielding, 2 vols. Middle-
town, Conn.: Wesleyan University Press and Oxford:
The Clarendon Press, 1975. Pp. xvii-lxi.

Reviews the personal circumstances in which Fielding
wrote the novel; defines the period of its composition;
traces the publication history of the first four editions; and outlines the early reception of the book.
This erudite essay draws upon an extremely wide range
of scholarship to provide the best short account of
the publication history of *Tom Jones*.

775.   ————. "Osborne's *Tom Jones*: Adapting a Classic."
Virginia Quarterly Review, 42 (1966), 378-93. Reprinted in Compson, item 804.

Compares John Osborne and Tony Richardson's adaptation
of *Tom Jones* to the cinema with the original novel.
The film stands in relation to its original like Pope's
free imitations of Horace stand in relation to their
original, and it captures Fielding's spirit and his depiction of the sweep and quality of eighteenth-century
life. It also captures Fielding's thematic ridicule
of vanity and hypocrisy. The film, however, is unable
to convey the high moral seriousness which underlies
Fielding's humor and which makes the novel not only a
comic romp through the eighteenth century but also a
symbolic expression of its author's Christian vision of
a balanced and ordered universe. Nevertheless, the
film is a brilliant achievement and a masterpiece in
its own medium.

776.   ————. *The Providence of Wit: Aspects of Form in
Augustan Literature and the Arts*. Oxford: The Clarendon
Press, 1974.

Devotes two chapters——one of which was originally published as "*Tom Jones*: The Argument of Design" (item 778)

--to Fielding, whose *Tom Jones* is called "the last and
the consummate literary achievement of England's Augustan Age because it conceives of the work of art as
mimetic of cosmic order and design." The novel's symmetry and its manipulating, intrusive narrator make it
a symbol of the Universe, a microcosm of the harmonious
cosmos with its benevolent God directly supervising His
creation. Operating within the Christian humanist
tradition, Fielding recommends the attainment of true
wisdom, a combination of the speculative (*sophia*, sym-
bolized by the heroine) and the practical (*prudentia*,
embodied in Tom's experiences and growth toward maturity).
The culmination of this theme is the marriage of Tom
and Sophia, symbolizing the individual's attainment of
true wisdom.

777. ————. "Tom Jones and 'His Egyptian Majesty': Fielding's Parable of Government." *Publications of the
Modern Language Association of America*, 82 (1967), 68-77.

Argues that the episode of the gypsies in *Tom Jones*
(XII.xi-xii) serves as an emblem of England's condition
in 1745 and allows Fielding to present through historical
allusion his denunciation of an absolute monarchy. The
enlightened despotism of the Gypsy king offers a political moral for the reader. On the gypsy episode, also
see Bloch, "Bampflyde-Moore Carew," item 787; Fraser,
item 845; and Greene, item 851.

778. ————. "*Tom Jones*: The Argument of Design," in
The Augustan Milieu: Essays Presented to Louis A. Landa,
ed. Henry Knight Miller. Oxford: The Clarendon Press,
1970. Pp. 289-319.

Appears as the first of the two chapters on Fielding
in Battestin's *Providence of Wit*, item 776.

779. ————, ed. *Twentieth Century Interpretations of "Tom
Jones."* Englewood Cliffs, N.J.: Prentice-Hall, 1968.

The lengthy introduction sees *Tom Jones* as the major
literary achievement of Augustanism and discusses the
historical background of the novel and the ethical
stance of its author. Battestin argues that the art
of the novel--its use of chance and coincidence--re-
flects Fielding's conception of "the art of God." The
following essays are included in this collection: F.R.
Leavis, "Tom Jones and 'The Great Tradition': A Negative
View," item 879; Ian Watt, "Fielding as Novelist: *Tom
Jones*," item 977; William Empson, "*Tom Jones*," item 839;

Andrew Wright, "*Tom Jones*: Life as Art," item 983; R.S. Crane, "The Plot of *Tom Jones*," item 808; Wayne C. Booth, "'Fielding' in *Tom Jones*," item 789; Robert Alter, "Fielding and the Uses of Style," item 444.

Review: J.D. O'Hara, *Modern Language Journal*, 53 (1969), 207-08.

*   Bell, Michael. "A Note on Drama and the Novel." (See item 336.)

780.   Bennett, James O. "Fielding's *Tom Jones*," in his *Much Loved Books*. New York: Liverwright Publishing Corp., 1927. Pp. 236-42.

Praises Fielding's ability to present to posterity the real people and real life of his time. Because of *Tom Jones*, we know our ancestors better than we know ourselves.

781.   Bensly, Edward. "Fielding Queries: Sack and 'The Usual Words.'" *Notes and Queries*, Eleventh Series, 10 (1914), 392.

Replies to Dickson's request for information on sack and toasting, referred to several times in *Tom Jones*. Sack-whey is made by combining equal parts of sherry and milk and sugaring; the "usual words" for the toast are probably commonplace (like "to your health"). Also see de Castro, "Fielding Queries," item 814.

782.   ————. "Fielding's *Tom Jones*: Its Geography." *Notes and Queries*, Eleventh Series, 10 (1914), 292-93.

A reference to the miller with three thumbs (*Tom Jones*, VIII.ix) probably is derived from Mother Shipton's prophecies. The reference in the same novel to Greenland (XV.vi) is possibly a comment on Western's unfitness to carry out diplomacy with civilized people. Also see the following, all under the title listed for this item: Bensly, items 783 and 784; de Castro, items 817 and 818; and Dickson, item 824.

783.   ————. "Fielding's *Tom Jones*: Its Geography." *Notes and Queries*, Eleventh Series, 10 (1914), 372.

The Battle of Tannières refers to the engagement in Taisnières Woods, a part of the Battle of Malplaquet. "Greenland" might be a taunt, referring to Western's "greenness." Also see the following, all under the title of this item: Bensly, items 782 and 784; de Castro, items 817 and 818; and Dickson, item 824.

784. ————. "Fielding's *Tom Jones*: Its Geography." *Notes and Queries*, Eleventh Series, 11 (1915), 12.

Two possible references to the Battle of Malplaquet appear in *Tom Jones* (V.vii and VI.xii). Also see the following, all under the title given this article: Bensly, items 782 and 783; de Castro, items 817 and 818; and Dickson, item 824.

* Bissell, Frederick Olds. *Fielding's Theory of the Novel*. (See item 453.)

785. Blake, W.B. "*Tom Jones* in France." *South Atlantic Quarterly*, 8 (1909), 222-33.

French translators, critics, and imitators unwittingly treated Fielding badly in the eighteenth century. The critics often attributed truly terrible novels to Fielding; the translators attempted the "spirit" of the novels (and, misunderstanding that spirit, missed it entirely); and the imitators used Fielding's name to attempt to strengthen forgettable fictions.

* Bland, D.S. "Endangering the Reader's Neck." (See item 455.)

786. Bliss, Michael. "Fielding's Bill of Fare in *Tom Jones*." *ELH: A Journal of English Literary History*, 30 (1963), 236-43.

Views the eighteen introductory chapters in *Tom Jones* as an integral part of the novel which functions to provide a set of values with which the reader comes to identify closely. The theme of these chapters is the interdependence—or, "mutuality"—of creation and criticism. The "mutuality" theme also is reflected in the love story of the narrative proper.

787. Bloch, Tuvia. "Bampfylde-Moore Carew and Fielding's King of the Gypsies." *Notes and Queries*, n.s. 14 (1967), 182-83.

Argues that the King of the Gypsies (*Tom Jones*, XII.xii) was not, as Cross (item 126) and Dudden (item 171) believed, modeled on Bampfylde-Moore Carew, the notorious King of the Beggars; in fact, Fielding's gypsy king bears not the slightest resemblance to Carew's portrait in his

autobiography of 1745. The *Apology for the Life of
Bampfylde-Moore Carew* (1750) is a "dishonest" book be-
cause it is based on Fielding's gypsy king and not on
Carew's life at all. See Battestin, "Tom Jones and 'His
Egyptian Majesty,'" item 777; Fraser, item 845; and
Greene, item 851.

788. Bloom, Edward A. "The Paradox of Samuel Boyse." *Notes
and Queries*, n.s. 1 (1954), 163-65.

Mentions Fielding's praise in the *Champion* (February 12,
1740) of Boyse's long poem, "Deity," and points out
that Fielding also cites twelve lines from it in *Tom
Jones* (VII.i). These two references support Cross's
claim (item 126) that Fielding's journalistic essays
became analogues for the novel's critical and philosophical chapters.

789. Booth, Wayne C. "'Fielding' in *Tom Jones*," in *Twentieth
Century Interpretations of "Tom Jones*," ed. Martin C.
Battestin. Englewood Cliffs, N.J.: Prentice-Hall, 1968.
Pp. 94-96. Reprinted in *Tom Jones*, ed. Sheridan Baker,
item 57. This material originally was published as
part of Chapter VIII of the author's *Rhetoric of Fiction*,
item 456.

Although Fielding's intrusions into *Tom Jones* often
serve specific functions, many of them refer to nothing
but the reader and himself and therefore appear to be
extraneous to the action. A close reading of these passages, however, reveals a running account of a growing
intimacy between the narrator and reader which is essential in building the trust necessary to maintain Fielding's comic tone.

790. Bort, Barry D. "Incest Theme in *Tom Jones*." *American
Notes and Queries*, 3 (1965), 83-4.

Believes that the incest theme in *Tom Jones* is intended
as a burlesque of *Oedipus*.

791. Bosker, A. "Henry Fielding. Laurence Sterne," in his
Literary Criticism in the Age of Johnson. New York:
Hafner, 1953. Pp. 130-36. Originally published Gronin-
gen, 1930.

Derives Fielding's critical views from *The Covent-Garden
Journal* and *Tom Jones*. In spite of his reverential
attitude toward classical authors, Fielding did not
always accept their standards for modern writers. Truth,

"nature," and common sense should guide the artist, who must record matters realistically.

792. Bowers, Fredson. "Remarks on Eclectic Texts." *Proof*, 4 (1975), 31-76.

Uses *Tom Jones* as one of several examples of the difficulty an editor faces in compiling an "authorized" text. Bowers discusses the various forms through which *Tom Jones* passed in the four editions published in Fielding's lifetime, and notes what techniques are necessary to produce a standard, albeit eclectic, text of the novel.

793. ————. "Textual Introduction" to *The History of Tom Jones, a Foundling* by Henry Fielding, 2 Vols. Middletown, Conn.: Wesleyan University Press and Oxford: The Clarendon Press, 1975. Pp. lxii-lxxxiv.

Outlines the principles and procedures followed in preparing the text and its apparatus. The discussion is broken down into sections on the copy-text, the methods and purposes of each of the six appendices, and the collation procedure.

* Boyce, Benjamin. *The Benevolent Man: A Life of Ralph Allen of Bath*. (See item 100.)

* Bradbury, Malcolm. "Fielding, Sterne, and the Comic Modes of Fiction." (See item 647.)

* Braudy, Leo. "Fielding: Public History and Individual Perception." (See item 648.)

794. Brogan, Howard O. "Fiction and Philosophy in the Education of Tom Jones, Tristram Shandy, and Richard Feverel." *College English*, 14 (1952), 144-49.

Locke's theory of educational "procedures" influences Fielding: Tom Jones does not go to school but is educated at home under the watchful eyes of adults; he is gently reared; and he is encouraged for successes and not punished for failures. Fielding deviates from Locke, however, when he emphasizes the importance of birth, environment, and experience in Tom's growth toward maturity.

* Brooks, Douglas. *Number and Pattern in the Eighteenth-Century Novel*. (See item 652.)

795.   Burns, Wayne. "The Panzaic Principle." *Paunch*, No. 22
        (1965), 2-28.

        Defines the "Panzaic Principle" (named after Sancho
        Panza in *Don Quixote*) as the view that "the guts are
        always right," that one's senses are better guides to
        truth and reality than "the most profound abstractions
        of the noblest thinker." The author argues that idealist
        critics, ignoring the Panzaic Principle, distort works
        of art. Ian Watt, for example, attempts to subordinate
        the sensual and carnal in *Tom Jones* in order to present
        a distorted reading of the novel's moral significance.

*   Butt, John. *Fielding*. (See item 462.)

796.   Carroll, John J. "Henry Fielding and the 'Trunkmaker.'"
        Notes and Queries, n.s. 6 (1959), 213.

        In *Tom Jones* (IV.vi), Fielding makes an obscure reference
        to the "famous Trunk-maker in the Playhouse." This al-
        lusion, explained in Spectator 235, is to an unidentified
        playgoer who loudly hammered on the benches in the play-
        house whenever he thought a scene was particularly well
        performed.

797.   Carswell, John. "Kubla Khan." *Times Literary Supple-
        ment* (March 16, 1962), p. 185.

        Coleridge's poem may be indebted to the description of
        the landscape surrounding Allworthy's house in *Tom Jones*.
        Also see Maxwell, item 900, who points out that Fleiss-
        ner, item 843, had already noted the resemblance.

798.   Carver, Wayne. "The Worlds of Tom and Tristram."
        Western Humanities Review, 12 (1958), 67-74.

        Sees the worlds of Sterne and Fielding as diametrically
        opposed. The world of *Tom Jones* is finite and ordered,
        and it is a world of high seriousness. The world of
        Tristram Shandy is infinite and chaotic, and it is with-
        in the chaos that the comedy lies. Reason holds Field-
        ing's world together; nothing holds Sterne's world to-
        gether, but sentiment provides a kind of tenuous "glue"
        for it.

799.   Chandler, S. Bernard. "A Shakespeare Quotation in
        Fielding and Manzoni." *Italica*, 41 (1964), 323-25.

        In Manzoni's *I Promessi Sposi*, the quotation from Shake-
        speare's *Julius Caesar* comes from an Italian edition of

Tom Jones, based on de la Place's French edition, and not from Shakespeare directly.

800. Chesterton, G.K. "Tom Jones and Morality," in *All Things Considered*. New York: John Lane, 1916. Pp. 259-66. Originally published London: Methuen, 1908. Partially reprinted in Rawson, item 272.

An informal essay which asserts that Fielding was neither an immoral nor an offensive writer; he simply portrayed Tom Jones realistically, showing both his good and bad sides.

* Child, Harold H. "Fielding and Smollett." (See item 110.)

* Churchill, R.C. "Fielding: To the Novel from the Drama." (See item 111.)

801. Cleary, Thomas R. "Jacobitism in *Tom Jones*: The Basis for an Hypothesis." *Philological Quarterly*, 52 (1973), 239-51.

Inconsistencies in the development of the political backgrounds and characters of *Tom Jones* indicate that it was significantly revised, probably between late 1747 and early 1748. One such inconsistency is the reference (VII.ix) to the "Forty-five," which places the action in the last week of November or the first week of December 1745; however, the chapter headings of Books VI and VII indicate that exactly three weeks and one day have elapsed between the reference and All-worthy's recovery, which is said to be in late June. Fielding apparently wished to impose the political back-ground of the "Forty-five" on the novel, and did so after his first writing of the work, which accounts for the inconsistent time scheme and the fact that highly political figures like Sophia's aunt and father are consistently unaware of the rebellion.

802. Coley, William B., and John B. Shipley. "Fielding and the Cabal 'Against Amigoni': 'A Rebuttal' and 'A Reply.'" *Eighteenth Century Studies*, 2 (1969), 303-11.

See Shipley, item 294.

* ————. "Fielding, Hogarth, and Three Italian Masters." (See item 114.)

* ————. "Gide and Fielding." (See item 467.)

803.   Combs, William W. "The Return to Paradise Hall: An
        Essay on *Tom Jones*." *South Atlantic Quarterly*, 67
        (1968), 419–36.

        Argues that the story of *Tom Jones*, like the story of
        Paradise Lost, traces the "fortunate fall" from innocence
        to experience. Prudence, which Fielding emphasizes
        throughout the novel, is the link between initial inno-
        cence and life in a world fraught with evils.

804.   Compson, Neil, ed. *Henry Fielding: "Tom Jones."* Lon-
        don: Macmillan, 1970.

        A casebook with an introduction by Compson, a section
        of pre-1920 criticism, a section of modern criticism,
        and a brief bibliography. In his introduction, Compson
        argues that no other English novel, including *Ulysses*,
        is as elaborately plotted as is *Tom Jones*. Fielding's in-
        trusions into the novel are similar to Bernard Shaw's pres-
        ence in the prefaces and stage directions to his plays an
        show Fielding to be a novelist with the instincts of a
        playwright. The eighteenth- and nineteenth-century com-
        mentators on the novel are Lady Mary Wortley Montagu, Ar-
        thur Murphy, Lord Monboddo, Samuel Johnson, Samuel Taylor
        Coleridge, Sir Walter Scott, William Hazlitt, and
        William Makepeace Thackeray. The twentieth-century
        essays are: G.K. Chesterton, "Tom Jones and Morality,"
        item 800; Arnold Kettle, "*Tom Jones*," item 874; Dorothy
        Van Ghent, "On *Tom Jones*," item 975; J. Middleton Murry,
        "In Defence of Fielding," item 540; Ian Watt, "*Tom Jones*
        and *Clarissa*," item 978; William Empson, "*Tom Jones*,"
        item 839; C.J. Rawson, "Professor Empson's *Tom Jones*,"
        item 937; A.E. Dyson, "Satire and Comic Irony in *Tom
        Jones*," item 833; Martin C. Battestin, "Osborne's *Tom
        Jones*: Adapting a Classic," item 775; Ronald Paulson,
        "Lucianic Satire in *Tom Jones*," item 922; Robert Alter,
        "On the Critical Dismissal of Fielding," item 445; John
        Preston, "Plot as Irony: The Reader's Role in *Tom Jones*,"
        item 930.

805.   Cook, Albert. *The Dark Voyage and the Golden Mean: A
        Philosophy of Comedy*. Cambridge, Mass.: Harvard Uni-
        versity Press, 1949.

        Includes some unusual, if not downright eccentric, dis-
        cussions of *Tom Jones* and *Jonathan Wild*. Cook calls
        Tom Jones a "probable" character whose actions and
        physical features make him inseparable from the rest of
        his society. The norms of that society provide the
        reasons that Tom can be accepted back into it after his

transgressions. In passing, Cook notes that the plot of *Tom Jones* is identical to the plot of *Oedipus* with Laius represented by Partridge and Fitzpatrick.

806. Cowley, Malcolm, and Howard E. Hugo. *The Lesson of the Masters: An Anthology of the Novel from Cervantes to Hemingway.* New York: Charles Scribner's Sons, 1971.

Contains brief comments on excerpts from twenty-seven novels, including *Tom Jones*. A brief biography of Fielding is followed by the first seven chapters of Book X of the novel; the remarks on this excerpt point out the use of authorial intrusion and note that Fielding successfully adapted stage techniques of dialogue and characterization to the novel form.

807. Crane, R.S. "The Concept of Plot and the Plot of *Tom Jones*," in *Critics and Criticism: Ancient and Modern,* ed R.S. Crane. Chicago: University of Chicago Press, 1952. Pp. 616-47. Originally published as "The Plot of *Tom Jones*," item 808.

See under "The Plot of *Tom Jones*."

808. ————. "The Plot of *Tom Jones*." *Journal of General Education*, 4 (1950), 112-30. Reprinted in Battestin, item 779; Sepctor, item 584; and *Tom Jones*, ed. Sheridan Baker, item 57. Also reprinted as "The Concept of Plot and the Plot of *Tom Jones*" in *Critics and Criticism*, item 807, and Iser, item 507.

Conceives of "plot" as involving all elements of a novel, not just a narrow series of actions. If such a conception of plot is applied to *Tom Jones*, Fielding's achievement is impressive because all aspects of the novel combine to associate Tom with Sophia, separate him from her, and then to unite him with her. This formula subsumes everything in the work and is made coherent through the characters' believably motivated actions and a consistent comic tone that never allows a noncomic response from the reader.

*   Cross, Wilbur L. "Henry Fielding." (See item 472.)

809. ————. "The Secret of *Tom Jones*." *The Bookman*, 48 (1918), 20-9.

Analyzes the reasons for the continued popularity of *Tom Jones* (called "the *Hamlet* of English fiction") and concludes that the secret of its success lies in Fielding's universality, particularly in characterization.

His characters are always individuals, but each one also is representative of a type. The result is that *Tom Jones* is "an epic of human nature."

*   Crothers, George D., Maurice Dolbier, and Glenway West-
        cott. "Henry Fielding: *Tom Jones*," in *Invitation to
        Learning: English and American Novels*, ed. George D.
        Crothers. New York: Basic Books, 1966. Pp. 36-43.

        See under Dolbier, item 829.

810.   D. "*Tom Jones* in France." *Notes and Queries*, Ninth
        Series, 1 (1898), 175.

        Notes that the first translation of *Tom Jones* into
        French was that of de la Place in 1750. Also see Blake,
        item 785; Jones, "Was There a Temporary Suppression,"
        item 871; Roberts, item 371; and Shaw, item 952.

811.   Davis, Earle R. *The Flint and the Flame: The Artistry
        of Charles Dickens*. Columbia, Mo.: University of
        Missouri Press, 1963.

        See pp. 158-60, which argue that in *David Copperfield*,
        Dickens consciously imitated those aspects of *Tom Jones*
        which he particularly liked: the detailed observation
        of eccentrics; the panoramic view of the life of its
        era; the use of a "common" hero; the defense on the
        basis of good intentions of the hero's moral lapses.

812.   DeBruyn, John. "Tom Jones and Arthur Pendennis: A
        Tale of Two Heroes." *Literature in Transition*, 7 (1966),
        81-88.

        Thackeray's *Pendennis* was modeled on *Tom Jones*; it
        represents a technical advance, but is less successful
        because Pendennis is less interesting than Jones and
        Thackeray's world is less comprehensive than Fielding's.

813.   de Castro, J. Paul. "A Cryptic Utterance of Fielding's."
        Notes and Queries, Eleventh Series, 10 (1914), 85.

        Fielding's footnote reference to "the well-wooded forest
        of Hampshire" in *Tom Jones* (V.ii) is probably ironic
        because the forest had been stripped of nine-tenths of
        its usable timber by 1703.

814.   ———. "Fielding Queries: Sack and 'The Usual Words.'"
        Notes and Queries, Eleventh Series, 10 (1914), 293.

        Responds to Dickson's request, item 823, for information
        about a toast in *Tom Jones* (IX.iv): the toast referred

to is probably simply, "Hip-hip-hurrah," a common army toast. Also see Bensly, "Fielding Queries," item 781.

* ————. "Fieldingiana." (See item 138.)

* ————. "Fieldingiana." (See item 140.)

815. ————. "Fielding's Invocation to Fame." *Times Literary Supplement* (November 10, 1927), p. 818.

Asks what connection Milton might have with Hampstead or Highgate and who Mnesis might have been (referring to Fielding's invocation to love of fame in Book XIII of *Tom Jones*). He is answered by "Hibernicus," item 858.

816. ————. "Fielding's *Tom Jones*." *Notes and Queries*, Eleventh Series, 9 (1914), 507-08.

In *Tom Jones* (VIII.viii), Fielding refers to a pettifogging lawyer from Lidlinch in Somersetshire. There is a Lydlinch in Dorsetshire, but not in Somersetshire. It is possible that Fielding was attacking a real person and that he attempted to avoid a libel suit by moving the village from one county to another and thereby "fictionalizing" it.

817. ————. "Fielding's *Tom Jones*: Its Geography." *Notes and Queries*, Eleventh Series, 10 (1914), 253.

Responds to Dickson, "Fielding's *Tom Jones*," item 824, by identifying the "Noyle" in *Tom Jones* as West Knoyle in Wiltshire. Also see Bensly, items 783 and 784; and de Castro, item 818.

818. ————. "Fielding's *Tom Jones*: Its Geography." *Notes and Queries*, Eleventh Series, 11 (1915), 56-7.

Edmund Fielding, Henry's Father, probably did not serve at the Battle of Malplaquet because the births of three children between July 1708 and November 1710 indicate that he was at home during this period. Also see Bensly, items 783 and 784; de Castro, item 817; and Dickson, item 824.

819. ————. "Gravelot." *Notes and Queries*, 180 (1941), 87.

Identifies "Gravelot," the designer of sixteen plates for the French translation of *Tom Jones*, as H.F. Bourguignon.

* ————. "Portrait of Miss Sarah Andrew as Sophia Western." (See item 148.)

*   ————. "Ursula Fielding and *Tom Jones*." (See item
           153.)

820.   Dickson, Frederick S. "The Chronology of *Tom Jones*."
       Notes and Queries, Eleventh Series, 9 (1914), 425-26.

       In spite of Keightly's contention to the contrary (item
       222), the geography and chronology of *Tom Jones* is
       almost perfectly consistent. Keightly's objections to
       all but the date of Jones's battle with Thwackum can be
       disposed of with a few maps and an almanac. See "Cor-
       rigendum," item 122.

821.   ————. "The Chronology of *Tom Jones*." *The Library*,
       Third Series, 8 (1917), 218-24.

       Dates each major event from Allworthy's illness on by
       using political events mentioned in the novel to con-
       struct a chronology. The only weakness in the carefully
       worked out chronology is Fielding's failure to recognize
       Sundays; several inappropriate events take place on
       days that would be Sunday in the novel's time scheme.

822.   ————. "Errors and Omissions in *Tom Jones*." *Library*,
       Third Series, 9 (1918), 18-26.

       Lists twenty-four errors and omissions, concluding that
       they are all minor and do not seriously weaken *Tom Jones*.
       Examples of Fielding's mistakes include calling Mrs.
       Western "Di" at one point and "Bell" at another; saying
       Mrs. Miller was married for five years but making her
       daughters seven years apart; failing to mention a
       Sunday even when he tells his story day by day.

823.   ————. "Fielding Queries: Sack and 'The Usual Words.'"
       Notes and Queries, Eleventh Series, 10 (1914), 209.

       Requests information about sack, its preparation, the
       words used on the occasion of "treaty ceremonies," and
       the "libation" (*Tom Jones*, IX.iv). See responses, both
       under the above title, by Bensly, item 781, and de
       Castro, item 814.

824.   ————. "Fielding's *Tom Jones*: Its Geography." *Notes
       and Queries*, Eleventh Series, 10 (1914), 191-92.

       Refers to Fielding's use of non-existent geographical
       places in *Tom Jones*: Little Baddington, Noyle, the "Red
       Lion," Ox-cross, Aldergrove, Westerton, and Mazard Hill.
       The Battle of Tannières, to which he refers, is probably
       the engagement at Tavières, part of the Battle of

Ramillies. The reference to Greenland (XV.vi) is un-
clear, as is the mention of Bellisle, near Lisbon, in
the *Voyage to Lisbon*. Also see the following, all under
the title, "Fielding's *Tom Jones*: Its Geography": Bensly,
items 783 and 784; and de Castro, items 817 and 818.

825. ————. *An Index to "The History of Tom Jones, a Foundling" by Henry Fielding*. 1913.

The Library of Congress holds this unpublished manuscript
which contains sections on bibliography, characters,
persons mentioned, places mentioned, and chronology.
All references to the novel are to the first edition of
1749.

826. ————, collector. [Maps.] Library of Congress: Fielding Collection, Tray 19.

A collection of 38 maps, mostly from the *London Magazine*,
selected as illustrative of *Tom Jones*.

827. ————. "Tom Jones and His Sword." *Notes and Queries*,
Twelfth Series, 1 (1916), 506-07.

Shows Fielding's mastery of plot detail by noting that
although Tom purchases his sword in Book VII, he does
not use it until Book XVI.

*   Dilworth, E.N. "Fielding and Coleridge: 'Poetic Faith.'"
(See item 157.)

828. Dobson, Austin. *Samuel Richardson*. New York and London:
Macmillan, 1902.

Contends that the publication of *Tom Jones* probably
annoyed Richardson more than did either *Shamela* or *Joseph
Andrews*, for it was with *Tom Jones* that Fielding firmly
established himself as Richardson's foremost rival for
the position as England's most popular fiction writer.
Richardson's animosity toward Fielding possibly is based
more on psychological jealousy than on Richardson's
distaste for Fielding's morality and "indelicacy" of expression.

829. Dolbier, Maurice, George D. Crothers, and Glenway West-
cott. "Henry Fielding: *Tom Jones*," in *Invitation to
Learning: English and American Novels*, ed. George D.
Crothers. New York: Basic Books, 1966. Pp. 36-43.

A discussion taken from the tapes of the CBS radio show,
Invitation to Learning, which begins by comparing the

movie version of *Tom Jones* with the novel and moves on
to generalize about the novel's plot, morality, and intrusive narrator. Westcott views the latter device as
negative because it is digressive.

830.   Drew, Elizabeth. "Henry Fielding: *Tom Jones*," in her
        The Novel. New York: Norton, 1963. Pp. 59-74.

        Raises several objections to Fielding's methods: (1) the
        constant authorial intrusions become "wearisome"; (2) the
        denouement relies too heavily on coincidence; (3) the
        mock-heroic and classical allusions are boring for modern
        readers; (4) the "violent uproars" are repetitious; and
        (5) the stock comedy characterizations, like Western's
        tantrums and Partridge's cowardice, have become clichés
        by now. In spite of these faults, Fielding is a greater
        novelist than Defoe or Richardson because of his warmth,
        humor, and irony and because of the wide range of his
        fiction, which presents a panorama of the human scene
        never before achieved in the novel.

831.   Duff, L. "*Tom Jones*." *Notes and Queries*, Twelfth
        Series, 5 (1919), 327.

        Identifies Gibbon's comment about *Tom Jones* outlasting
        Austria as coming from the *Memoirs of My Life and
        Writings* (1817), Vol. I, p. 5.

832.   Dyson, A.E. *The Crazy Fabric: Essays in Irony*. London:
        Macmillan, 1965.

        The material on Fielding is reprinted in Compson, item
        804, as "Satire and Comic Irony in *Tom Jones*." For
        annotation see item 833.

833.   ————. "Satire and Comic Irony in *Tom Jones*," in *Henry
        Fielding: "Tom Jones*," ed. Neil Compson. London: Mac-
        millan, 1970. Pp. 182-92. This material originally ap-
        peared in Dyson's *The Crazy Fabric*, item 832. An ex-
        tract is reprinted in Rawson, item 272.

        On one level, the reader of *Tom Jones* is given three
        moral philosophies to choose from: Butler's, Shaftesbury's,
        and Fielding's own. On another level, the novel deals
        with the choice between "Reputation" and "Real Worth."
        These concerns are presented through comic irony and all
        conflicts are resolved through the marriage of Tom and
        Sophia.

*   ————. "Satiric and Comic Theory in Relation to Field-
        ing." (See item 172.)

834. Eaves, T.C. Duncan. "The Publication of the First Trans-
      lations of Fielding's *Tom Jones*." *Library*, Fourth Series,
      26 (1945), 189-90.

      A close study of the engraving plates proves that the
      French edition of *Tom Jones* had to have appeared before
      the Dutch version.

835. Edgar, Pelham. "Henry Fielding and *Tom Jones*," in his
      The Art of the Novel: From 1700 to the Present Time.
      New York: Macmillan, 1933. Pp. 52-67.

      Refutes the "myths" about Fielding propagated by Arthur
      Murphy's eighteenth-century biography, particularly the
      notion that Fielding's novels reflect their author's own
      immorality. Fielding is too frank for the overly sensi-
      tive moralist, but he survives because of his narrative
      vigor, his witty commentary, and his "rich and racy
      humanity." He is a pioneer in the novel because his
      Preface to *Joseph Andrews* is important theoretically
      and because he invented the comic epic in prose.

836. Edwards, P.D. "Education and Nature in *Tom Jones* and
      The Ordeal of Richard Feverel." *Modern Language Review*,
      63 (1968), 23-32.

      Sees a close resemblance between *Tom Jones* and *Richard
      Feverel* in that both novels are based on the implicit
      assumption that "the closer a man remains to his natural
      state, the better a man he will be." Tom is educated
      by his "father," and thus is not tainted by the "scien-
      tific humanism" of Thwackum and Square; therefore, he
      can come to terms with his natural sexuality. Richard's
      education follows a strict course of scientific humanism,
      which prevents him from dealing with his natural
      sexuality.

837. Ehrenpreis, Irwin. *Fielding: Tom Jones*. Studies in
      English Literature, No. 23. London: Edward Arnold,
      1964. An extract from this work is reprinted in Rawson,
      item 272.

      Divides the study into five sections: author, story,
      doctrine, meaning and form, and comedy. The first sec-
      tion discusses Fielding's narrative technique as well
      as the tone, rhetoric, and style of the novel. The
      second section notes the strengths and weaknesses in the
      plot and action of the work. Under "Doctrine," Ehren-
      preis considers Fielding's moral and religious views
      and his conception of "good nature." In the section on
      meaning and form, the author shows the novel's relation-

ship to other literary forms, especially the drama, and
relates the structure (highly ordered) to the meaning
of the novel (which depicts a highly ordered universe).
Finally, under comedy, Ehrenpreis discusses the various
comic methods employed by Fielding.

Review: Pierre Legouis, *Etudes anglaises*, 18 (1965),
315-16.

*   Elwin, Whitwell. "Fielding." (See item 177.)

838.   Empson, William. "Great Writers Rediscovered: The
Grandeur of Fielding's *Tom Jones*." *Sunday Times* (March
30, 1958), p. 13.

This item was not seen by the compilers prior to the
publication of this bibliography.

839.   ————. "*Tom Jones*." *The Kenyon Review*, 20 (1958),
217-49. Reprinted in Battestin, item 779; Compson, item
804; Iser, item 507; Paulson, item 258; Rawson, item
272; and *Tom Jones*, ed. Sheridan Baker, item 57.

Believes that *Tom Jones* has been consistently misin-
terpreted because Fielding's critics have missed his
"double irony." Often he poses alternatives and then
ironically ridicules both of them, thus confusing
critics like Dr. Johnson who look for one straight-
forward moral statement. For example, Tom's good impulses are often treated ironically because he lacks
prudence, and his sale of his body to Lady Bellaston is
ridiculed because he thinks his "honor" demands that he
sleep with her. Although many readers feel that Fielding accepts Tom's sexual escapades as morally justifia-
ble, the opposite is true. A close reading of the novel
shows that Fielding consistently bemoans Tom's imprudent
behavior. Fielding, however, confuses his moralist
critics because, unlike most of them, he recognizes that
there is more than one ethical code, and he explores--in
the gypsy episode, for instance--several of them. His
moral relativism confuses or irritates many readers.
See Rawson, "Professor Empson's *Tom Jones*, item 937.

Review: Eleanor N. Hutchens, *Philological Quarterly*, 38
(1959), 324-25.

840.   Evans, James E. "Fiction Rather than Fact: A New Look
at the King of the Beggars." *Library Chronicle*, 36
(1970), 110-14.

The compilers were unable to read this item before their manuscript went to the publisher.

841. Feil, J.P. "Fielding's Character of Mrs. Whitefield." *Philological Quarterly*, 39 (1960), 508-10.

Fielding's reference to Mrs. Whitefield of the Bell in *Tom Jones* provoked a dissenting comment from a contemporary, Lewis Thomas, who knew Mrs. Whitefield and found her far different from Fielding's portrait. Thomas saw her as a coquette, not as Fielding's model of virtue.

842. Ferguson, Oliver W. "Partridge's Vile Encomium: Fielding and Honest Billy Mills." *Philological Quarterly*, 43 (1964), 73-78.

Argues that the actor playing Claudius in the performance of *Hamlet* witnessed by Partridge in *Tom Jones* (XVI.v) is William Mills, widely known in Fielding's day for his mediocre performances.

843. Fleissner, Robert F. "'Kubla Khan' and 'Tom Jones': An Unnoticed Parallel." *Notes and Queries*, n.s. 7 (1960), 103-05.

Notes that the description of the landscape surrounding Allworthy's house (*Tom Jones*, I.iv) parallels some descriptive passages in Coleridge's "Kubla Khan," especially 11, 13, 19, 24-26, and 35-6. Also see Carswell, item 797, and Maxwell, item 900.

844. Folkenflik, Robert. "Tom Jones, The Gypsies, and the Masquerade." *University of Toronto Quarterly*, 44 (1975), 224-37.

Regards the gypsy feast episode in *Tom Jones* as an integral part of the novel designed to contrast with the masquerade that follows later. Fielding shows how the naturalness of the gypsies, their sylvan existence and joy in simplicity, is superior to the artifice of the high characters at the masquerade, who live a life in which appearance and actuality have little in common.

* Ford, Ford Madox. *The English Novel*. (See item 480.)

* ————. *The March of Literature*. (See item 481.)

* Forsyth, William. *The Novels and Novelists of the Eighteenth Century*. (See item 483.)

845. Fraser, Angus M. "Bampfylde-Moore Carew and Fielding's
      King of the Gypsies." *Notes and Queries*, n.s. 14
      (1967), 424.

      In the gypsy episode in *Tom Jones* (XII.xii), Fielding
      shows some knowledge of gypsy speech, but his view of
      gypsy life owes more to imagination than to fact. Also
      see Battestin, "Tom Jones and 'His Egyptian Majesty,'"
      item 777; Bloch, "Bampfylde-Moore Carew," item 787; and
      Greene, item 851.

*   Garnett, David. "Samuel Richardson, Henry Fielding,
      and Tobias Smollett." (See item 488.)

*   Gerould, Gordon Hall. *The Pattern of English and Ameri-
      can Fiction*. (See item 489.)

846. Gide, André. "Notes for a Preface to Fielding's *Tom
      Jones*," in *Fielding: A Collection of Critical Essays*,
      ed. Ronald Paulson. Englewood Cliffs, N.J.: Prentice-
      Hall, 1962. Pp. 81-83. These notes are taken from the
      "Feuillets" in *Oeuvres complètes*, Vol. 13. Paris: La
      Nouvelle Revue Française, Librairie Gallimard, 1937.
      Pp. 412-16. Translated by William H. McBurney. Ex-
      tracts reprinted in Rawson, item 272.

      A series of unconnected notes, mostly on the morality
      of *Tom Jones*. Gide comments that Jones' misdeeds never
      hurt anyone and are designed to help others. He also
      remarks that Allworthy is not a successful character
      because of the difficulty of creating a figure who is
      perfectly good. See Coley, "Gide and Fielding," item
      467.

847. Goldknopf, David. "The Failure of Plot in *Tom Jones*."
      Criticism, 11 (1969), 262-74. Reprinted in the author's
      The Life of the Novel. Chicago: University of Chicago
      Press, 1972. Pp. 125-42. Also in *Tom Jones*, ed.
      Sheridan Baker, item 57.

      Argues that the superstructure of authorial interpreta-
      tion which Fielding imposes on *Tom Jones* is designed to
      overcome the deficiencies of its often-admired but
      nonetheless weak plot. The plot fails because Fielding
      attempted to yoke two disparate elements, the picaresque
      and the classical. It is further weakened by the in-
      clusion of such irrelevancies as the Man of the Hill
      episode, the frequent use of coincidence, forced paral-
      lelisms (Bellaston hides when Honour visits Tom and

Honour hides when Bellaston visits), and gratuitously withheld information. The city scenes of the last third of the book are particularly contrived. It is therefore incorrect to say that *Tom Jones* contributed plot struc- ture to the development of the novel.

848. Grabo, Carl H. *The Technique of the Novel.* New York: Charles Scribner's Sons, 1928.

Regards *Amelia* as the first non-picaresque realistic novel, although its realism is marred by a contrived ending. *Tom Jones* is a more successful artistic whole and contributes to the development of the novel by realistically depicting the social background of the times.

849. Graham, W.H. "Fielding's *Tom Jones." Contemporary Re- view*, 169 (1946), 164-68.

Finds *Tom Jones* "coarse and vulgar" but a faithful record of eighteenth-century life. The article out- lines the novel's major characters and concludes that it is "a truly human book."

* Grant, Damian. *Tobias Smollett: A Study in Style.* (See item 492.)

850. Greenberg, Bernard L. "Fielding's 'Humane Surgeon.'" *Notes and Queries*, n.s. 9 (1962), 456-57.

The "humane surgeon" mentioned in The Man of the Hill's Tale in *Tom Jones* may have been Etienne Ronjat rather than John Ranby as is usually supposed.

851. Greene, J. Lee. "Fielding's Gypsy Episode and Sancho Panza's Governorship." *South Atlantic Bulletin*, 39 (1974), 117-21.

Most discussions of Fielding's gypsy episode in *Tom Jones* center on its source in the career of Bampfylde- Moore Carew (see Bloch, "Bampfylde-Moore Carew," item 787; Cross, item 126; Dudden, item 171; and Fraser, item 845). A better source for the episode, however, is Sancho Panza's governorship in *Don Quixote.* Both episodes present an ideal political, civil, and social system through the judgment of a supposed rape and in- dicate that reason and true nobility are not dependent on any particular social or political system. Also see Battestin, "Tom Jones and 'His Egyptian Majesty,'" item 777.

852.   Guthrie, William B.   "The Comic Celebrant of Life in
       Tom Jones."   *Tennessee Studies in Literature*, 19 (1974),
       91-105.

       Proposes that *Tom Jones* be read not as an endorsement
       of the value of prudence, but as a celebration of the
       virtues inherent in the comic spirit. Tom is a comic
       character in the sense that he represents the comic
       celebration of life. His sexual misdeeds can be ex-
       cused as part of that celebration.

853.   Harrison, Bernard.   *Henry Fielding's "Tom Jones": The
       Novelist as Moral Philosopher*.   London: Sussex University
       Press, 1975.

       Finds *Tom Jones* an impressive, well-reasoned philosophi-
       cal treatise as well as a great novel. Fielding deals
       with the nature of goodness, and by carefully defining
       his terms he builds a detailed argument against Mande-
       ville and others, finding in man a great deal of poten-
       tial for goodness. *Tom Jones* is not a watered down,
       and hence naive, Shaftesburian statement, but rather
       presents a reasonable argument, based on Locke, for
       a virtue which allies native good-heartedness with pru-
       dence. A close reading of the novel reveals that Field-
       ing defines his terms—such as "good nature"—in philo-
       sophical rather than emotional terms.

854.   Hassall, Anthony J.   "Garrick's *Hamlet* and *Tom Jones*."
       Notes and Queries, n.s. 24 (1977), 247-49.

       Notes that the two major scenes in Act III of *Hamlet*
       are reversed in Fielding's description of the version
       that Partridge and Tom attended in *Tom Jones*. The re-
       versal is probably inadvertent, caused by Fielding's de-
       sire to emphasize the effect of the ghost on Partridge.

*   Hatfield, Glenn.   *Henry Fielding and the Language of
       Irony*.   (See item 197.)

855.   ————.   "The Serpent and the Dove: Fielding's Irony
       and the Prudence Theme of *Tom Jones*."   *Modern Philology*,
       65 (1967), 17-32. Reprinted in his book, item 197.

       Throughout his literary career, Fielding was concerned
       with "corrupt language," especially with terms that ex-
       press contrary ideas or values. Consequently, many of
       his essays, most of his plays, and all of his novels
       attempt to redefine abstract social and moral terms in
       order to "restore" them to their proper meanings.

Jonathan Wild treats "goodness" and "greatness" to show "how empty a moral term can be when separated from one of its essential meanings." *Joseph Andrews* redefines "virtue," which is based on benevolence. *Tom Jones* defines "prudence" (a combination of wisdom, charity, and virtue) by using Sophia as a model from whom even Allworthy and Tom can learn.

856. "Henry Fielding." *Times Literary Supplement* (8 October 1954), p. 641.

An anonymous columnist remarks that the most important element in *Tom Jones* is the implicit statement that life has a total moral structure. Fielding also indicates that past actions cannot be run away from--their consequences are always with us. See the attack on this essay in Murry, item 540.

857. Herman, George. "Fielding Defends Allworthy." *Iowa English Yearbook*, 10 (1965), 64-70.

Argues that Fielding mitigates Allworthy's mistakes in judgment by showing how artfully various characters deceive him. Fielding sometimes steps in to point out how plausible the arguments are which Allworthy accepts, especially those in the hearings of Partridge and Jenny and those which Blifil uses to convince Allworthy to banish Tom.

858. "Hibernicus." "Fielding's Invocation to Fame." *Times Literary Supplement* (November 24, 1927), p. 888.

Responds to de Castro's question about Mnesis in Tom Jones ("Fielding's Invocation," item 815) by reporting that Mnesis is Fielding's fabrication.

859. Hilles, Frederick W. "Art and Artifice in *Tom Jones*," in *Imagined Worlds: Essays on Some English Novels and Novelists in Honour of John Butt*, eds. Maynard Mack and Ian Gregor. London: Methuen, 1968. Pp. 91-110. Reprinted in *Tom Jones*, ed. Sheridan Baker, item 57.

Justifies, in spite of much adverse criticism directed toward it, the artificiality of plot in *Tom Jones*. Although the plot is contrived and symmetrical, its artificiality is symbolic of Fielding's balanced view of mankind and is necessary for his purpose of keeping the reader detached so that he can clearly see and reflect upon the serious subject matter that underlies the comedy.

860.   ———. "Fielding Unmodernized." *Yale Review*, 65 (1975), 128-33.

A review-article of the Wesleyan editions of *The Jacob-ite's Journal and Related Writings* (item 63) and *Tom Jones* (item 58). Although Hilles questions some of the archaisms allowed to remain in *Tom Jones*, his review is quite favorable.

*   Hobbes, John Oliver [Mrs. Craigie]. "Letters from a Silent Study." (See item 998.)

861.   Hooker, Edward N. "Humour in the Age of Pope." *Hunting-ton Library Quarterly*, 11 (1948), 361-85.

Outlines the changing conception of humor in the eigh-teenth century, and remarks on *Tom Jones*. Tom is a comic figure in a very specialized sense: he is a figure of passion, which makes him humorous, but he is also sympa-thetic. Therefore, the reader may laugh at the ridicu-lous situations into which his passions lead him without ever losing sympathy for him as an individual.

862.   Hutchens, Eleanor Newman. *Irony in Tom Jones*. Univer-sity: University of Alabama Press, 1965.

Defines Fielding's irony as verbal and substantial. Verbal irony, the choice or arrangement of words, is produced through an emphasis on denotation or connota-tion and often is a result of tone or an implied refer-ence. Substantial irony, which is irony that arises from action or symbol, is produced through the events of the story. Both kinds of irony are applied to the theme of prudence. For example, when Blifil releases Sophia's bird and schemes to discredit Tom, it is ap-parent that his actions are devious and self-serving, but they are referred to as "prudent" actions. Field-ing's ironic techniques influenced Austin, Thackeray, Dickens, and Joyce.

863.   ———. "O Attic Shape! The Cornering of Square," in *A Provision of Human Nature: Essays on Fielding and Others in Honor of Miriam Austin Locke*, ed. Donald Kay. University: University of Alabama Press, 1977. Pp. 37-44.

Perceives a geometrical pattern in *Tom Jones* which is employed to underscore error and crime. This pattern often takes the form of balancing pairs like Square and Thwackum, both of whom represent the error of abstract

morality. Even normally good characters--like Tom and
Allworthy--are shown to be in error when they are seen
as one of a pair. Usually, however, the good figures
are portrayed as "asymmetrical," as ungeometric, in
order to emphasize their *natural* goodness.

864.   ———. "'Prudence' in *Tom Jones*: A Study of Connota-
        tive Irony." *Philological Quarterly*, 39 (1960), 496-
        507.

        "Prudence," which Fielding normally uses positively, is
        used ironically in *Tom Jones* to refer to "scheming."
        This connotative irony is the source of much of Field-
        ing's comedy of incongruity and produces the effect of
        "urbanity" in his style.

865.   ———. "Verbal Irony in *Tom Jones*." *Publications of
        the Modern Language Association of America*, 77 (1962),
        46-50.

        Contends that Fielding is the first English novelist to
        use verbal irony in a realistic work for both comic and
        moral purposes. Fielding's moral view is, in part,
        presented through such devices as the ironic use of
        "prudent" (also see Hutchens, "'Prudence' in *Tom Jones*,"
        item 864). The comic perspective of *Tom Jones* is main-
        tained through verbal irony, too: for example, without
        the ironic descriptions of Blifil as a "prudent" youth,
        his darkness of character would alter the comic tone
        of the novel.

*   Iser, Wolfgang. "The Role of the Reader in Fielding's
        Joseph Andrews and *Tom Jones*." (See item 677.)

866.   Iyengar, K.R. "Fielding's *Tom Jones*." *Journal of the
        University of Bombay*, 8 (1939), 29-44.

        The compilers were unable to read this article prior to
        publication.

*   Jackson, Holbrook. "Henry Fielding." (See item 508.)

867.   Jackson, Thomas A. "*Pamela* and *Tom Jones*," in his *Old
        Friends to Keep*. London: Lawrence and Wishart, 1950.

        Listed by Battestin in *The New Cambridge Bibliography
        of English Literature*, but the compilers have not seen
        the item.

*   Jaggard, William. "Revivals of Fielding's Plays." (See
        item 397.)

868.   James, Henry. *The Art of the Novel: Critical Prefaces
        by Henry James*. Ed. Richard P. Blackmur. New York:
        Charles Scribner's Sons, 1934.

        Includes James's fine tribute to Fielding and *Tom Jones*
        in the preface to *The Princess Casamassima*. James
        praises the quality of Fielding's mind and says that
        although Tom Jones does not have a reflecting mind, his
        sense of life (as it creates comedy) amounts to the
        same thing.

869.   Jensen, Gerard E. "Proposals for a Definitive Edition
        of Fielding's *Tom Jones*." *Library*, Fourth Series, 18
        (1937), 314-30.

        A definitive edition of *Tom Jones* can be based only on
        the first four editions, published during Fielding's
        lifetime. Of these, the third edition appears to be
        the author's definitive edition. Many of the correc-
        tions made in the fourth edition were probably made by
        someone other than Fielding. However, the extensive
        revisions of editions one and two which appear in the
        third edition seem to be almost entirely Fielding's.
        See Battestin's denial that the third is Fielding's
        "definitive edition," item 794.

870.   Johnson, Maurice. "The Device of Sophia's Muff in *Tom
        Jones*." *Modern Language Notes*, 74 (1959), 685-90.

        Sees the muff both as a symbol and a structural device.
        Symbolically, it represents the physical attraction be-
        tween Sophia and Tom; each uses it as a substitute for
        the other's person, kissing it and sleeping with it.
        Structurally, it parallels the symmetrical plot, being
        mentioned four times in the early country scenes, where
        it is in Sophia's possession, and four times on the road,
        where it passes into Tom's possession.

*   —————. *Fielding's Art of Fiction: Eleven Essays on
        "Shamela," "Joseph Andrews," "Tom Jones," and "Amelia."*
        (See item 511.)

871.   Jones, B.P. "Was There a Temporary Suppression of *Tom
        Jones* in France?" *Modern Language Notes*, 76 (1961),
        495-98.

        Replies to E.P. Shaw, item 952, arguing that there are
        doubts as to whether the *Arrêt du Conseil* of February
        24, 1750, directed at Paris bookseller Jacques Rollins,
        was really intended to suppress Rollins' edition of *Tom*

Jones or whether it was designed to frighten him into
compliance with government printing regulations. Since
the *Arrêt* was never implemented, the latter seems likely.

872. Kaplan, Fred. "Fielding's Novel about Novels: The 'Prefaces' and the 'Plot' of *Tom Jones*." *Studies in English
Literature*, 13 (1973), 535-49.

Contends that *Tom Jones* has a "second plot" contained
in the prefaces to the novel's eighteen books. This
"plot" treats "the nature of art and the relationship
between art, artist, and audience" and is always related to the main action.

*   Karl, Frederick R. "Henry Fielding: The Novel, the
Epic, and the Comic Sense of Life." (See item 514.)

*   Kaul, A.N. "The Adjudication of Fielding's Comedy."
(See item 515.)

873. Kearney, Anthony. "Tom Jones and the Forty-Five."
Ariel: A Review of International English Literature,
4 (1973), 68-78.

From Book VII on, *Tom Jones* becomes an allegory of the
rising of the forty-five, with Tom representing the
patriots and Blifil and others representing Jacobites.
See the negative review in *Philological Quarterly*, 53
(1974), 706. Also see Greason, "Fielding's *The History of the Present Rebellion*," item 1110, and Jarvis,
"Fielding and the Forty-Five," item 1037.

*   Kermode, Frank. "Richardson and Fielding." (See item
517.)

874. Kettle, Arnold. "*Tom Jones*," in *Fielding: A Collection
of Critical Essays*, ed. Ronald Paulson. Englewood
Cliffs, N.J.: Prentice-Hall, 1962. Reprinted in Compson,
item 804, and Iser, item 507.

For annotation, see Kettle, *An Introduction to the
English Novel*, item 518.

875. Klein, DeWayne. "A Fowl Tom Jones." *Bulletin of the
West Virginia Association of College English Teachers*,
2 (1975), 29-33.

Discovers several bird images that are associated with
Tom, including song-birds, partridges, ducks, and hawks.
The latter is most closely associated with Tom, who, by

the novel's end, seems to have combined its qualities
with those of the partridge and of song-birds in order
to become a more admirable "human creature."

876. Knight, Charles A. "Multiple Structures and the Unity
of 'Tom Jones.'" *Criticism*, 14 (1972), 227-42.

Suggests that a way of accounting for the coherence of
Tom Jones, particularly in the middle six books, lies
in perceiving and responding to "multiple structures"
rather than viewing the novel in Aristotelian terms or
reading it as having a single concept of plot. There
are four main structuring patterns: (1) the linear pattern of causal sequence which parallels the characters'
geographical movements in the middle books; (2) a non-
linear pattern of causation, which is concerned with
the hidden causes of events; (3) a symmetrical pattern,
based on the alteration of Tom and Sophia as central
figures; (4) a symmetrical pattern of corresponding
events, arranged around the Upton scenes and pointing
backwards and forwards towards the Somerset and London
scenes.

*   Knowles, A.S. "Defoe, Swift, and Fielding." (See item
521.)

877. Kronenberger, Louis. "Fielding: *Tom Jones*," in his *The
Republic of Letters*. New York: Alfred Knopf, 1955.
Pp. 74-80.

Views *Tom Jones* as a prose epic not a "modern novel."
It presents the multiplicity of life but lacks depth.
The book remains popular because of Fielding's "sound
values" in caring more about motives than behavior.

878. Lavin, Henry St. C. "Rhetoric and Realism in *Tom Jones*."
University Review, 32 (1965), 19-25.

Feels that the formal rhetoric of Tom, Allworthy, and
Sophia undercuts their realism as characters; often the
three give formal speeches rather than engaging in natural and realistic conversation.

879. Leavis, F.R. "*Tom Jones* and 'The Great Tradition': A
Negative View," in *Twentieth Century Interpretations of
Tom Jones*, ed. Martin C. Battestin. Englewood Cliffs,
N.J.: Prentice-Hall, 1968. This material appears as pp.
2-4 of the author's *The Great Tradition*, item 524.

For annotation, see item 524.

880. Ledlie, J.M.A. "Hard At It." *Notes and Queries*, n.s. 17 (1970), 93-94.

The occurrence of the term "hard at it" in *Tom Jones* (VII.v) antedates by 120 years the earliest occurrence recorded by Eric Partridge in his *Dictionary of Slang*.

881. Lockwood, Thomas. "Matter and Reflection in *Tom Jones*." *ELH: A Journal of English Literary History*, 45 (1978), 226-35.

Sees *Tom Jones* as linked to the essay form through Fielding's conversational style. Fielding's method is to identify the novel's subject matter in chapter headings and then to reflect on that matter in a chatty and highly personal way. The narrative proper only serves to organize the reader's attention in reading the book. Although *Tom Jones* has "no affinity with the formal conventions of modern narrative realism," Fielding himself emerges as the most realistic aspect of the novel.

*   Lodge, David. *Language of Fiction*. (See item 525.)

882. Longhurst, John E. "Fielding and Swift in Mexico." *Modern Language Journal*, 36 (1952), 186-87.

Cites two 1803 letters from the files of the Mexican Inquisition which recommend *Gulliver's Travels* and *Tom Jones* as being free from heretical doctrines.

883. Longmire, Samuel E. "Allworthy and Barrow: The Standards for Good Judgment." *Texas Studies in Literature and Language*, 13 (1972), 629-39.

The standards for right judgment, apparently adhered to by Fielding, are set forth in the latitudinarian divine Isaac Barrow's sermon, "Against Rash Censuring and Judging." Barrow's standards provide a yardstick with which Allworthy's shortcomings can be measured. The sermon, while it may not have directly influenced Fielding's thinking, certainly illuminates that part of Allworthy's character that allows him to be duped by Blifil and others.

884. ———. "The Critical Significance of *Rambler* 4." *The New Rambler*, 11 (1971), 40-47.

Attributes Johnson's dislike of *Tom Jones* to his view that vice is always detestable and should always be portrayed as such. Fielding, immorally according to

Johnson, excuses Tom's vices on the basis of the hero's good nature.

885.   ————. "Fielding's *Tom Jones*." *Explicator*, 33, no. 6 (1975), item 52.

Contradicts Robert Alter's statement (p. 165 of *Fielding and the Nature of the Novel*, item 443) that Fielding is ironic in marrying off the "timorous" Partridge to the lusty Molly by citing several passages in *Tom Jones* which indicate that Partridge is quite virile.

886.   ————. "Partridge's Ghost Story." *Studies in Short Fiction*, 11 (1974), 423-26.

Sees Partridge's ghost story in *Tom Jones* as a foil to the Man of the Hill's Tale, revealing certain things about Partridge, the Man of the Hill, and Fielding's narrative theory. The legal satire in the story shows Partridge's comic ability to rebound from adversity, while at the same time it demonstrates the Man of the Hill's misanthropy. The narrator's statement that ghosts should be avoided in a story, as they are likely to be met with laughter, is echoed in Tom's laughter. Fielding may be satirizing Clarendon's serious ghost story in the latter's *History of the Rebellion*, pointing out that a serious ghost story is a contradiction in terms.

887.   Loomis, Roger S. "*Tom Jones* and Tom-Mania." *Sewanee Review*, 27 (1919), 478-95.

Although *Tom Jones* has many admirable qualities, such as its moralistic attacks on hypocrisy and seduction, its plot is hackneyed and its characterization, especially that of Allworthy and Blifil, is weak. Fielding also was unable to recreate natural settings; he was more at home with the town than with the country. In addition, his conception of women in society is almost medieval.

888.   Lynch, James J. "'Evil Communications.'" *Notes and Queries*, n.s. 3 (1956), 477.

Corrects Fielding's mistake in *Tom Jones* and *The Journal of a Voyage to Lisbon* in attributing Menander's statement "evil communications corrupt good manners" to Solomon.

889.   ————. "Structural Techniques in *Tom Jones*." *Zeitschrift für Anglistik und Amerikanistik*, 7 (1959), 5-16.

Also published in *Stil und Formprobleme in der Literatur*,
ed. Paul Böckmann. Heidelberg: Carl Winter, 1959.

Finds two different methods used to structure *Tom Jones*.
The first runs throughout the narrative and consists
of the symmetrical plot division, spatial and temporal
verisimilitude, and parallel characters and events.
The second appears sporadically and consists of "the
planned reappearance, the undisclosed motive, the
blurred consequence, the minute cause, and the alternative interpretation." These latter devices serve as a
means for selecting, ordering, and integrating detail
in order to establish tight causal relationships in the
action.

*   Macallister, Hamilton. *Fielding*. (See item 528.)

890.   McCullough, Bruce. "The Novel of Manners, Henry Fielding: *Tom Jones*," in his *Representative English Novelists:
Defoe to Conrad*. New York: Harper and Row, 1946. Pp.
42-57.

Emphasizes Fielding's development of the omniscient
point of view and his methods of characterization. His
point of view is superior to the first person narration
used by Defoe and Richardson because it gives him more
ways to summarize, interpret, and explain than his predecessors had at their disposal. Whereas Defoe and
Richardson were concerned with what their characters
do, Fielding is concerned with what his characters are.
Although Fielding uses "type" characters, he presents
them in a variety of situations and from a variety of
perspectives, so that the reader comes to a thorough
understanding of them; that understanding, however, is
external and not psychological. This technique results
in the rich variety of scenes in *Tom Jones*, necessary
for Fielding's purpose of "revealing human nature" and
"exploring human foibles."

891.   McCutcheon, Roger P. *"Amelia, or the Distressed Wife."*
Modern Language Notes, 42 (1927), 32-3.

Notes that six months before Fielding's *Amelia* was published, there appeared an anonymous novel, *Amelia, or
the Distressed Wife*. A careful reading of these two
works reveals little in common between them and reveals
the title similarities to be merely coincidental.

*   McDowell, Alfred. "Fielding's Rendering of Speech in
Joseph Andrews and *Tom Jones*." (See item 687.)

892.   McKee, John B. *Literary Irony and the Literary Audience:*
       Studies in the Victimization of the Reader in Augustan
       Fiction. Amsterdam: Rodopi, 1974.

       Considers *Tom Jones*, *Gulliver's Travels*, and *Tristram*
       Shandy as examples of "reader-victimization irony," de-
       fined as the author's deliberate attempt to warp or
       obstruct his reader's understanding by shifting the
       narrator's position. Fielding shifts from historian
       to artist, from controller of information to "victim"
       of events as they "actually" happened. In the process,
       the reader often becomes the victim of Fielding's irony
       for failing to understand thoroughly the meaning of
       events or from failing to understand Fielding's objects
       of irony.

893.   McKenzie, Alan T. "The Processes of Discovery in *Tom*
       Jones." *Dalhousie Review*, 54 (1974-75), 720-40.

       Essential to the plot and structure of *Tom Jones* is the
       "process of discovery"; the novel is a series of real
       and false discoveries, of things hidden and things re-
       vealed at critical times. Three kinds of discoverers
       exist in the novel: the manipulative, like Blifil, who
       often tell lies or disclose truths at inopportune times;
       the instinctual, like Squire Western, who misconstrue
       what has been discovered to them; and the self-confi-
       dent, like Di Western, who seek discovery, but who can-
       not interpret it once found. Suspicion is the hallmark
       of all three groups.

894.   McKillop, Alan D. "An Iconographic Poem on *Tom Jones*."
       Philological Quarterly, 17 (1938), 403-06.

       A poem entitled "The Fan," which imitates "The Rape of
       the Lock," contains a long panegyric to *Tom Jones*. The
       fan of the title is decorated, like the Shield of
       Achilles, with scenes from life--in this case, with
       scenes from *Tom Jones*. The poem is one more indication
       of the contemporary popularity of Fielding's novel. Ex-
       cerpts from "The Fan" are reprinted in Paulson and Lock-
       wood (item 18), pp. 155-58.

895.   ————. "Some Recent Views of *Tom Jones*." *College*
       English, 21 (1959), 17-22.

       Surveys the *Tom Jones* scholarship of the 1950's, with
       particular attention paid to Wayne Booth, "The Self-
       Conscious Narrator," item 457; R.S. Crane, "The Concept
       of Plot," item 807; Dorothy Van Ghent, "On *Tom Jones*,"
       item 975; and Ian Watt, *The Rise of the Novel*, item 608.

896. Malone, Kemp. "Fielding's *Tom Jones*," in *Literary Mas-
      terpieces of the Western World*, ed. Francis H. Horn.
      Freeport, N.Y.: Books for Libraries Press, 1968. Pp.
      242-55. Originally published Baltimore: The Johns
      Hopkins Press, 1953.

      Rates *Tom Jones*, along with *The Bible*, *The Iliad*, *Hamlet*,
      Faust, and eight others, as a book which has "changed
      men's minds." It is a unique work in that it derives
      from the romance and combines the novel of manners with
      the novel of adventure. It is a masterpiece because it
      is "a treatise on human nature," touching upon all as-
      pects of eighteenth-century life.

897. Mandel, Jerome. "The Man of the Hill and Mrs. Fitz-
      patrick: Character and Narrative Technique in *Tom Jones*."
      Papers on Language and Literature, 5 (1969), 26-38.

      The ways in which the Man of the Hill and Mrs. Fitz-
      patrick tell their tales reveal their characters. The
      latter tells a digressive story through dialogue; she
      generalizes, interrupts herself, and blames society for
      her problems, revealing herself to be an illogical
      social creature unwilling to accept responsibility.
      The Man of the Hill delivers a monologue; he is specific,
      intolerant of interruption, and willing to accept respon-
      sibility for his actions, revealing himself to be logical
      but misanthropic.

898. Maugham, W. Somerset. "Henry Fielding and *Tom Jones*,"
      in his *Great Novelists and Their Novels*. Philadelphia:
      John C. Winston, 1948. Pp. 61-75.

      Presents a brief biography of Fielding and defends him
      against charges of immorality; praises the realism of
      Tom Jones but deplores Fielding's digressions.

899. ————. "The Ten Best Novels: *Tom Jones*." *Atlantic
      Monthly*, 180 (December 1947), pp. 120-26.

      The greatness of *Tom Jones* lies in its accurate portrayal
      (with the exceptions of Allworthy and Blifil) of real
      life. Moral reservations about the novel are immaterial;
      Fielding wrote not for a moral purpose but to reflect
      nature. The novel's primary weakness is the digressions;
      the interpolated stories and essays get in the way of
      the main action of the novel.

900. Maxwell, J.C. "Kubla Khan." *Times Literary Supplement*
      (March 23, 1962), p. 201.

Notes that Carswell's point about the similarities between "Kubla Khan" and *Tom Jones* (see item 797) had
already been made by R.F. Fleissner, item 843.

901. Maynadier, G.H. "Introduction" to *The History of Tom
Jones, a Foundling* by Henry Fielding. Cambridge, Mass.:
Harvard University Press, 1903. Pp. xxv-xlvi.

Because Fielding sought to set forth his "theory of
life" in *Tom Jones*, he was forced to construct a novel
on an epic scale. His accomplishment in so doing was
brilliant, and he gave to the novel the well-constructed
plot (marred only by the Man on the Hill and the gypsy
episodes) and total realism in characterization. *Tom
Jones* presents "the whole of life," and no novel has
ever surpassed it in terms of plot, realism, vigor, and
honesty.

902. Milburn, D. Judson. "The Psychology of Wit in Henry
Fielding's *Tom Jones* and in Laurence Sterne's *Tristram
Shandy*," in his *The Age of Wit: 1650-1750*. New York:
Macmillan and London: Collier-Macmillan, 1966. Pp.
106-19.

It is evident from the introductory essays to *Tom Jones*
that Fielding did not have that respect for wit and
fancy that characterized the century before the novel's
publication. Instead of "wit" and "fancy," Fielding
emphasized "genius," "invention," and "judgment." This
emphasis is reflected in the careful, logical ordering
of the plot of the novel.

903. Mildmay, Henry A. St. John. "Fielding's Parson Thwackum.
Notes and Queries, Eleventh Series, 6 (1912), 470.

Sir Paulet St. John, Bart., was the original for
Thwackum in *Tom Jones*. Also see "L.E.T.," item 965.

904. Miller, Henry Knight. "The 'Digressive' Tales in Fielding's *Tom Jones* and the Perspective of Romance." *Philological Quarterly*, 54 (1975), 258-74.

There are two important interpolated tales in *Tom Jones*:
the Man of the Hill's story and Mrs. Fitzpatrick's history. The first of these is artfully contrived to
parallel parts of Tom's own story as well as to enrich
the novel by alluding to and drawing upon some well-
known romantic materials. The Old Man takes a circular
journey (Departure, Initiation, and Return) which parallels Tom's adventures; he is cheated by a brother as Tom

is, his father turns against him as Allworthy turns
against Tom, he is betrayed by his mistress as Tom is
betrayed by Lady Bellaston, and he is jailed just as
Tom is. The Old Man, however, is embittered by his
experience, unlike Tom, who learns from it and attains
prudence and a belief in divine providence. There are
numerous romantic parallels for the Old Man's tale,
among them *Huon of Bordeaux*, Greene's *Arbasto*, Lyly's
Euphues, and the *Odyssey*. Mrs. Fitzpatrick's story, on
the other hand, is reminiscent of Restoration Comedy
with its sexual machinations, disappointing marriage,
and persecution of female innocence; moreover, like
Restoration Comedy, her story is a city story that prepares the reader for the London setting of the last
third of the book. Like the Old Man's tale, it is a
cautionary story which offers parallels to Sophia's
situation and which warns against imprudent behavior.
Thus, these two interpolated tales are not digressive
but rather are parallels and counterpoints to the main
action of the novel.

905.   ———. *Henry Fielding's "Tom Jones" and the Romance
Tradition*. English Literary Studies Series, No. 6.
Victoria, B.C.: University of Victoria, 1976.

Distinguishes between "novel" and "romance" in the introduction and argues that *Tom Jones* is "thoroughly in
the epic-romance tradition of Ariosto, Cervantes, and
Sidney." The rest of the book is divided into chapters
on plot and structure, setting, character, theme, and
style; each chapter focuses on the influence of romance
conventions on Fielding's art. For example, Fielding
employs the typical romance structure of "Departure (or
Exile), Initiation, and Return." His use of setting
is "a continuation of the romance mode" in that place
and time are focused on only when they are significant
for the narrative and not to present a realistic picture
of "life-by-the-clock" or to pursue the sociological
emphasis on the influence of environment. Like the
romance writers, Fielding uses "type" characters. *Tom
Jones*, also like traditional romances, demonstrates a
universal "body of truths that are assumed à *priori*"
rather than presenting "a personal and individual truth"
through induction. Stylistically, Fielding uses the
"high style" of Heliodorus, Lyly, and Sidney and employs all the devices of rhetoric associated with romance. Although Fielding sometimes "modernizes" romance
conventions, he still accepts "the fundamental cosmic,

metaphysical, and social assumptions that had for so
long sustained the romance."

906.   ———. "Some Functions of Rhetoric in *Tom Jones*."
Philological Quarterly, 45 (1966), 209-35.

Internal evidence demonstrates that Fielding was con-
sciously aware of the three major areas of rhetoric
(the *genera causarum*) and that he consistently uses
the terminology of rhetoric and oratory. The novel's
"deliberative rhetoric" concerns itself with the central
theme of Prudence and the entire work advances through
a series of rhetorical devices. Also see Sherbo, "Some
Aspects of Fielding's Style," item 577.

907.   ———. "The Voices of Henry Fielding: Style in *Tom
Jones*," in *The Augustan Milieu: Essays Presented to
Louis A. Landa*, eds. Henry Knight Miller, Eric Rothstein,
and G.S. Rousseau. Oxford: The Clarendon Press, 1970.
Pp. 262-88.

Analyzes the complex narrative method of *Tom Jones*. Although Fielding presents himself in the novel *as* himself, he emphasizes certain aspects of his character and
"fixes them for all time in the unchanging world of his
completed fiction." He alters his style to fit his
many guises and many voices: he uses the plain style
for direct narration; the middle style for more involved
narration and low-key commentary; the "elegant" middle
style for significant commentary of a moral nature; and
the "sublime" style to identify a particular occasion
as a special one. The wide range of tones and points-
of-view that Fielding employs in his narration enable
him to invite both detachment and involvement from his
readers. Also see Alter, "Fielding and the Uses of
Style," item 444, and Sherbo, "Some Aspects of Fielding's
Style," item 577, and "The Narrator in Fielding's
Novels," item 576.

908.   Miller, Susan. "Eighteenth-Century Play and the Game
of *Tom Jones*," in *A Provision of Human Nature: Essays
on Fielding and Others in Honor of Miriam Austin Locke*,
ed. Donald Kay. University: University of Alabama
Press, 1977. Pp. 83-93.

Contends that most critics take Fielding too seriously
and ignore the importance of "play" in his novels.
Recreation was an important aspect of eighteenth-century
life, providing individuals with a social context and

class mobility, and this view of "play" is reflected in *Tom Jones*, in which the plot, characters, setting, and narration all employ characteristics of actual or meta- phoric games. Tom's growth toward maturity is defined by his participation in games, poaching, fighting, tree- climbing, hunting, masquerades, among others. There is also a "game" for the reader, who tests his perception of Tom against the narrator's presentation of the story.

*   Monteser, Frederick. *The Picaresque Element in Western Literature*. (See item 537.)

909. Moore, George. *Avowals*. London: [privately printed], 1919. Reprinted New York: Boni and Liveright, 1926.

Describes *Tom Jones* as "an empty book without a glimpse of the world without or a hint of the world within." Allworthy is "transparently conventional," Sophia is passionless, and Western is little more than a "rough sketch." See I.A. Richards' remarks on this appraisal (item 941.)

*   Muir, Edwin. *The Structure of the Novel*. (See item 538.)

910. Mundy, P.D. "Fielding's *Tom Jones*." *Notes and Queries*, 169 (1935), 456.

Joseph Stratton's letter of April 15, 1749, claims that 2,500 copies of *Tom Jones* were sold before the novel's official publication date of February 10.

911. Murray, Peter B. "Summer, Winter, Spring, and Autumn in *Tom Jones*." *Modern Language Notes*, 76 (1961), 324- 26.

Associates Tom, his father and mother, Sophia, and Lady Bellaston with nature's seasons in order to clarify their relationships to one another. For example, Tom and Sophia both are associated with Spring, which em- phasizes their love for each other, and Lady Bellaston is identified with Autumn, indicating that she is too old and "used up" for Tom and will therefore lose him.

912. Murry, John Middleton. "Fielding's 'Sexual Ethic' in *Tom Jones*," in *Fielding: A Collection of Critical Essays*, ed. Ronald Paulson. Englewood Cliffs, N.J.: Prentice- Hall, 1962. Pp. 89-97. Reprinted in Compson, item 804.

The complete version of this article originally appeared as "In Defense of Fielding"; see item 540.

913. Nassar, Eugene Paul. "Complex Irony in *Tom Jones*," in
      his *The Rape of Cinderella: Essays in Literary Continu-
      ity*. Bloomington: Indiana University Press, 1970. Pp.
      71-84.

      Treats the tone of *Tom Jones*, which, though complex be-
      cause of unresolved ironies, is "continuous." Fielding
      directs his irony at the sentimentalist, the rationalist,
      and, on occasion, the narrator, but this very inconsis-
      tency and irresolution supply continuity to the tone of
      the novel.

914. "News for Bibliophiles." *Nation*, 87 (1908), 624.

      Notes that two six-volume editions of *Tom Jones* appeared
      in 1749. The type of the first edition is set differ-
      ently than that of the second; also, the first edition
      contains a page of errata not found in the second.

915. Noyes, Robert Gayle. "Shakespeare in the Eighteenth-
      Century Novel." *The Journal of English Literary History*,
      11 (1944), 213-16.

      Briefly notes that the *Hamlet* scene in *Tom Jones* (XVI.v.)
      gave other novelists the idea of describing actual plays
      as seen through the eyes of their characters.

916. ————. *The Thespian Mirror: Shakespeare in the Eigh-
      teenth-Century Novel*. Brown University Studies No. 15.
      Providence, R.I.: Brown University Press, 1953.

      Mentions several references to Shakespeare in Fielding's
      novels. Notes that the famous passage on Garrick's
      Hamlet in *Tom Jones* may have influenced other novelists
      to use actual performances in their novels.

917. Palmer, Eustace Taiwo. "Fielding's *Tom Jones* Recon-
      sidered." *English*, 20 (1971), 45-50.

      Finds in *Tom Jones* a Christian allegory of the Fall.
      Tom is driven from Paradise, is corrupted by the devil
      (Blifil), succumbs to sin, and finally repents.

918. ————. "Irony in *Tom Jones*." *Modern Language Review*,
      66 (1971), 497-510.

      Lists and analyzes the various kinds of irony in *Tom
      Jones*, which include "praise/blame" irony, tonal irony,
      linguistic irony, rhetorical irony, and dramatic irony.
      These forms of irony are used to make simple statements
      about social hypocrisy and the value of benevolence.

When Fielding wishes to criticize both the evils of the
world and the wrongdoings of one of his positive characters, he employs double irony, which is a combination
of two of the simple forms of irony. Recognition of
this use of double irony is essential to the understanding of Fielding's moral position in regard to the incorrect behavior of such admirable characters as Tom,
Sophia, and Allworthy.

919. Park, William. "Tom and Oedipus." *Hartford Studies
in English*, 7 (1975), 207-15.

Contends that an Oedipal pattern runs throughout *Tom
Jones*. Tom is rumored to be the lover of his mother,
Mrs. Blifil, and he sleeps with Mrs. Waters, who is al-
leged to be his mother. He also is suspected of desiring
the death of Allworthy, who acts as his father and who
is accused of being so. Other hints of incest and
patricide abound in the novel.

920. Parker, A.A. "Fielding and the Structure of *Don Quixote*."
Bulletin of Hispanic Studies, 33 (1956), 1-16.

Proposes that Fielding is incorrect when he writes in
the *Covent Garden Journal* of March 24, 1752, that the
episodes in *Don Quixote* are unconnected and may be re-
ordered without changing the story. In fact, there is
a logic underlying Don Quixote's adventures; it is not
a cause and effect pattern, but rather an expanding re-
iteration of theme that links Quixote's fortunes to his
own actions. In *Tom Jones*, on the other hand, there is
no causal connection between Tom's moral conduct and
his social fortunes, although the incidents of the plot
are linked logically.

921. Passler, Susan Miller. "Coleridge, Fielding, and
Arthur Murphy." *The Wordsworth Circle*, 5 (1974), 55-8.

Views the river metaphor that Murphy uses in his discussion of *Tom Jones* in his *Life of Fielding* as an analogue
for Coleridge's "Kubla Khan." In the latter, the river
is a metaphor for creative genius, and it is in this way
that Murphy applies it to Fielding. Moreover, Coleridge's
admiration for Fielding is well-documented, so perhaps
he turned Murphy's figure to his own uses.

922. Paulson, Ronald. "Lucianic Satire in *Tom Jones*," in
Henry Fielding: Tom Jones, ed. Neil Compson. London:
Macmillan, 1970. Pp. 209-17.

Traces Lucian's influence on Fielding. Highly influential were Lucian's use of a mobile protagonist and his focus on exposing the lies and frauds perpetuated by relatives, legal figures, philosophers, and priests. Most influential of all, however, was Lucian's use of a commentator-narrator, a device Fielding employs to good effect in both *Joseph Andrews* and *Tom Jones*. This material is excerpted from *Satire and the Novel*, item 545. Also see Lind, item 231, and Miller, item 1042.

923.   ————. "The Pilgrimage and the Family: Structures in the Novels of Fielding and Smollett," in *Tobias Smollett: Bicentennial Essays Presented to Lewis M. Knapp*, eds. G.L. Rousseau and P.G. Bouce. New York: Oxford University Press, 1971. Pp. 57-79.

In both *Tom Jones* and *Peregrine Pickle*, the family is used as a context to explain the protagonist's character and as a structuring device. The novels are built around the hero's expulsion from the family, "fortunate fall," pilgrimage to knowledge, and eventual reunion with his family unit.

924.   Payen-Payne, De V. "Tom Jones." *Notes and Queries*, Twelfth Series, 5 (1919), 268.

Requests information about Gibbon's comment that *Tom Jones* would outlive the Austrian eagle. See the responses by Duff, item 831, and White, item 980.

925.   Pierce, Robert B. "Moral Education in the Novel of the 1750's." *Philological Quarterly*, 44 (1965), 73-87.

Says that Fielding's handling of Tom's moral growth in *Tom Jones* influenced a number of other novelists in the following decade; however, few of them handled the moral growth of their protagonists as well as did Fielding. Usually, they saw "moral growth" as just a last-minute reformation of character, unlike Fielding, who developed his characters naturally.

926.   Poovey, Mary. "Journeys from This World to the Next: the Providential Promise in *Clarissa* and *Tom Jones*." *ELH: A Journal of English Literary History*, 43 (1976), 300-15.

Explains the difference between Fielding and Richardson in terms of their views of the world. Clarissa attains perfection through a growing understanding of her own heart and of the world around her; yet, this world is too base to contain that perfection. Tom, on the other hand, is a static character, who, instead of attaining perfection, gains wisdom through an understanding of the baseness of the world. In Fielding's view, perfection and wisdom can coexist in this world.

927. Porter, Katherine Anne, Allen Tate, and Mark Van Doren. "Fielding: *Tom Jones*," in *New Invitation to Learning*, ed. Mark Van Doren. New York: New Home Library, 1944. Pp. 194-205. Originally published New York: Random House, 1942.

Presents a transcript of a wide-ranging discussion of *Tom Jones* by Porter, Tate, and Van Doren. The three agree that the best qualities of the book are its style and plot. Fielding's minor characters are very much alive, but his major figures are incredibly so. His comedy is effective because he is self-assured enough to laugh at the foibles of his age.

928. Powers, Lyall H. "*Tom Jones* and Jacob de la Vallée." *Papers of the Michigan Academy of Sciences, Arts, and Letters*, 47 (1962), 659-67. Reprinted in *Tom Jones*, ed. Sheridan Baker, item 57.

Locates a pattern for Tom's character development in Marivaux's *Le Paysan parvenu*. There is a good deal of similarity between the characters themselves, their women, and the incidents in their educations.

929. Preston, John. *The Created Self: The Reader's Role in Eighteenth-Century Fiction*. London: Heinemann, 1970.

Explores the various ways in which eighteenth-century novelists sought to relate to their readers. Fielding "translates the lonely process of reading into a friendly encounter." In *Tom Jones*, he ironically offers the reader a number of ways in which he may be a bad reader so that eventually he comes to realize what is needed (judgment) to be a good reader. By making the reader conscious of himself as a reader, Fielding forces him to exercise his critical faculties and to learn to judge with knowledge and sympathy, which is the ultimate theme of the novel.

930. ————. "Plot as Irony: The Reader's Role in *Tom Jones*." *ELH: A Journal of English Literary History*, 35 (1968), 365-80. Reprinted in Compson, item 804, and *Tom Jones*, ed. Sheridan Baker, item 57.

The plot of *Tom Jones* is highly ironic in that it "faces two ways": from one perspective it looks arbitrary and contrived, but from the other it makes the reader guess at what has happened. The first perspective gives the reader a feeling of objectivity, but Fielding ironically undermines that feeling by not allowing the reader to understand more of what has happened than do the characters. The reader, thereby, is drawn into the confusion of the action and becomes aware of "history" as a process in which we all are involved but the effects of which we cannot predict. Fielding's ironic plot creates "a reader wise enough to create the book he reads."

931.   ————. "*Tom Jones* and the 'Pursuit of True Judgment.'" *ELH: A Journal of English Literary History*, 33 (1966), 315-27. Reprinted in Rawson, item 272.

The "moral sense" of *Tom Jones* seems ambiguous because it is not conveyed as we expect, by the novel's action, but by the narrator's commentary. Because the plot centers on Fortune, the "moral weight" of the story is lifted from the characters and placed on the narrator, who must develop a positive relationship with the reader in order to present and to have accepted the moral point. The narrator tries to teach the reader to accurately evaluate and judge the action, and the reader's responsibility to do so becomes part of the subject of the book. The idea of proper judgment is mirrored in the novel's action when we see Allworthy judging poorly because he lacks experience and, later, when we see Tom, especially with Nightingale, judging correctly because he has learned from his experience.

932.   Price, John V. "Sex and the Foundling Boy: The Problem in *Tom Jones*." *Review of English Literature*, 8 (1967), 42-52.

Tom's sexual transgressions are treated ironically in order to justify them because Fielding wishes to show the reader that unchaste behavior, in most circumstances should not be regarded as a sin of the same magnitude as, for example, murder. It should also be remembered that the only two major figures who are chaste are Sophia and, ironically, Blifil, the latter of whom is hardly to be viewed as a model for human behavior.

933.   Prideaux, W.F. "*Tom Jones* in French." *Notes and Queries*, Tenth Series, 12 (1909), 407-08.

Lists French translations of the novel. The La Place
edition of 1751 is the classical translation, although
it is abridged. The best translation is Bédoyère's
of 1833. Other translations are Cheron's (1804) and
Dufauconpret's (1836).

934. Priestley, J.B. "*Tom Jones*," in *A Book of Prefaces*, ed.
Van Wyck Brooks *et al*. New York: n.p., 1941.

Not listed in the National Union or British Museum
catalogs, but cited by Battestin in *The New Cambridge
Bibliography of English Literature*. The compilers have
not been able to locate the work.

935. Randall, David A., and John T. Winterich. "Fielding,
Henry: *The History of Tom Jones*." *Publisher's Weekly*,
141 (1942), 1200-02.

Notes the distinguishing characteristics of the first
and second editions and gives the novel's later publishing history, including mention of its imitations and
translations.

936. Rawson, C.J. "The Phrase 'Legal Prostitution' in Fielding, Defoe, and Others." *Notes and Queries*, n.s. 11
(1964), 298.

Traces the history of the stock phrase "legal prostitution" from *Tom Jones* (XVI.viii) back to Defoe's *Conjugal
Lewdness; Or, Matrimonial Whoredom* (1727).

937. ————. "Professor Empson's *Tom Jones*." *Notes and
Queries*, n.s. 6 (1959), 400-04.

Finds Empson's essay on *Tom Jones*, item 839, misleading
because it argues that Fielding's attitude toward Tom's
sexual morals is expressed through an evasive irony,
whereas it is actually stated emphatically and explicit-
ly.

938. ————. "*Tom Jones* and *Michael*: A Parallel." *Notes and
Queries*, n.s. 14 (1967), 13.

Lines 448-50 in Wordsworth's *Michael* recall a passage in
Tom Jones (VII.ii).

939. Reichert, John F. "'Organizing Principles' and Genre
Theory." *Genre*, 1 (1968), 1-12.

Concerned with the difficulties of classifying literature according to its aims; by placing a work such as

Tom Jones, for example, in a particular genre, a critic runs the risk of either excluding particular characteristics of the book that are important to it or assigning characteristics to it (overtly or by implication) which it does not possess. See Sacks, *Fiction and the Shape of Belief*, item 566.

940.   Rexroth, Kenneth. "*Tom Jones*." *Saturday Review* (July 1, 1967), p. 13. Reprinted in *Tom Jones*, ed. Sheridan Baker, item 57.

Although the minor characters are stereotyped, Tom--who resembles Fielding in many ways--is not. Through Tom, Fielding defines a gentleman. Tom is Fielding's conception of "optimum man," but he is seen entirely from the outside.

941.   Richards, I.A. *Coleridge on Imagination*. Bloomington: Indiana University Press, 1960. Originally published London, 1934.

Responds to George Moore's appraisal of *Tom Jones* (item 909).

942.   Roberts, W. "A Shelf of Eighteenth-Century Novels." *Book Collector's Quarterly* (July 1934), pp. 17-33.

Itemizes the many novels spawned in the eighteenth century by *Tom Jones*, *Pamela*, and *Tristram Shandy*.

943.   ————. "*Tom Jones* in France." *Notes and Queries*, Ninth Series, 1 (1898), 147.

Reports that *Tom Jones* was suppressed in France in 1750 as an immoral work. On this subject, see "D," item 810; Jones, "Was There a Temporary Suppression," item 871; and Shaw, item 952.

*   Robinson, Roger. "Henry Fielding and the English Rococo." (See item 562.)

*   Rogers, Pat. "Fielding." (See item 565.)

*   ————. "Fielding's Parody of Oldmixon." (See item 1095.)

944.   Røstvig, Maren-Sofie. "*Tom Jones* and the Choice of Hercules," in *Fair Forms: Essays in English Literature from Spenser to Jane Austen*, ed. Maren-Sofie Røstvig. Totowa, N.J.: Rowman and Littlefield, 1975. Pp. 147-77. Also published Cambridge: D.S. Brewer, 1975.

Compares Tom to Hercules. In the first part of the
novel, Tom is the comic Hercules, addicted to wine,
food, and women. In the latter part of the novel, he
is the Gallic Hercules, a wise man and an accomplished
orator. Tom's choice between virtue, represented by
Sophia, and pleasure is made at Upton, where he rejects
Mrs. Waters for Sophia. The Man of the Hill also parallels the Herculean choice in that his story shows how
he has chosen wrongly.

945. Rothschild, N.M.V. *The History of Tom Jones, a Changel-
ing.* Cambridge: Privately Printed for Lord Rothschild,
1951.

Cited by Battestin in *The New Cambridge Bibliography of
English Literature*, but the compilers have not been able
to locate a copy of the work.

946. Roy, G. Ross. "French Stage Adaptations of *Tom Jones*."
Revue de Littérature Comparée, 46 (1970), 82-94.

Several theatrical adaptations of *Tom Jones* appeared in
France in the eighteenth century, indicating Fielding's
popularity there. The first (rather unsuccessful) version was Poinsenet's, which opened February 27, 1765.
It was followed by Sedaine's version in January 1766
(revived in 1795). Choudard's *Tom Jones à Londres*
opened successfully in October 1782. In addition, at
least four plays were loosely based on Fielding's characters, and at least one dealt with Fielding himself.

947. Rundus, Raymond J. "*Tom Jones* in Adaptation: A Chronology and Criticism." *Bulletin of the New York Public
Library*, 77 (1974), 329-41.

An annotated list of adaptations of the novel.

948. Ruthven, K.K. "Fielding, Square, and the Fitness of
Things." *Eighteenth Century Studies*, 5 (1971), 243-55.

Finds Square's character rooted in that of Samuel Clarke.
Many of Square's cant phrases are traceable to Clarke's
writings, and even the name "Square" is a play on
Clarke's shallow use of mathematics for proof of God's
existence. Like Clarke, Square is a Deist. It should
not be assumed, however, that Fielding satirizes Clarke's
rational supernaturalism, because he only attacks
Clarke's shallowness and ineptness.

* Saintsbury, George. "The Four Wheels of the Novel Wain."
(See item 568.)

949.   Schneider, Daniel L.   "Sources of Comic Pleasure in *Tom Jones*." *The Connecticut Review*, 1 (1967), 51–65.

Theorizes that comedy results in the triumph of life-affirming forces over life-denying forces. In *Tom Jones*, the comic pleasure of the novel comes from the struggle of Tom and Sophia (the life-affirming forces) with Blifil and societal pressures (the life-denying forces), resulting in the victory of the young lovers.

*   Scholes, Robert, and Robert Kellogg. *The Nature of Narrative*. (See item 570.)

950.   Schonhorn, Manuel. "Fielding's Digressive-Parodic Artistry: *Tom Jones* and The Man of the Hill." *Texas Studies in Literature and Language*, 10 (1968), 207–14.

Views the Man of the Hill episode as an integral part of *Tom Jones* which is used in three ways: as an ironic allusion to the Wilson story in *Joseph Andrews*; as an ironic doubling of Tom's character; and as an ironic inversion of Aeneas's descent into hell.

951.   ————. "Heroic Allusion in *Tom Jones*: Hamlet and the Temptations of Jesus." *Studies in the Novel*, 6 (1974), 218–27.

Associates Tom with Hamlet as eighteenth-century playgoers viewed the Prince—a paragon of filial piety. Tom also resembles Christ in several ways, including his temptation by the Devil, represented by the Man of the Hill.

952.   Shaw, E.P.   "A Note on the Temporary Supression of *Tom Jones* in France." *Modern Language Notes*, 72 (1957), 41.

Because Jacques Rollins, a Paris bookseller, did not receive official permission to print *Tom Jones*, his 1750 edition was banned and he was fined five hundred livres. For a reply to this article, see B.P. Jones, item 871. Also see "D," item 810, and Roberts, item 371.

*   Sherbo, Arthur.   "'Inside' and 'Outside' Readers in Fielding's Novels." (See item 575.)

*   ————.   "The Narrator in Fielding's Novels." (See item 576.)

953.   Sherburn, George.   "Introduction" to *Tom Jones* by Henry Fielding. New York: Random House, 1950. Pp. v–xiv.

Discusses Fielding's use of topical allusion and current events as a backdrop for the novel. The popularity
of the novel is due to its "neat intercalation" of the
episodes, its genial morality which is not oppressive,
and its good humor and high spirits.

* Sherwood, Irma Z. "The Novelists as Commentators."
(See item 1022.)

954. Shesgreen, Sean. "The Moral Function of Thwackum,
Square, and Allworthy." *Studies in the Novel*, 2 (1970),
159-67.

Thwackum and Square represent, in a negative manner,
two of the three principles--sympathy, philosophic love
of virtue, and inducements of religion--necessary for
"good-nature" or benevolence. Thwackum ironically
represents the inducements of religion (sans sympathy
and love of virtue) while Square, again ironically,
represents love of virtue (sans sympathy and inducements
of religion). Allworthy, representing the middle path,
combines a true love of virtue and religion with sympathy and thus is the embodiment of benevolence.

* Slagle, K.C. *The English Country Squire in English
Prose Fiction.* (See item 582.)

955. Solomon, Stanley J. "Fielding's Presentational Mode in
Tom Jones." *CEA Critic*, 31 (1969), 12-13.

Disagrees with Ian Watt's view that Tom Jones is psychologically unrealistic (see Watt's *Rise of the Novel*,
item 608). Fielding succeeds in capturing Tom's inner
life by suspending the novel's irony whenever Tom
moralizes; he expects the reader to take Tom's words at
face value, even when there is a disparity between what
Tom says and what he does. The hero's moralizing also
is intended to mitigate the seriousness of his sexual
escapades.

956. Spacks, Patricia Meyer. *Imagining a Self: Autobiography
and Novel in Eighteenth-Century England.* Cambridge,
Mass.: Harvard University Press, 1976.

Compares Fielding's attitudes and fictional techniques
with Boswell's views and autobiographical methods (see
pp. 227-99). The latter's *London Journal* and Fielding's
Tom Jones both concentrate on youth rather than maturity
as a subject and are preoccupied with the relationship
between imagination and real life. *Boswell for the*

Defence and *Amelia* both use the legal system as symbols
of general social values and both Boswell and Booth
demonstrate similar attitudes toward sexuality.

*   Speaight, George. *The History of the English Puppet
         Theatre*. (See item 387.)

957.   Spilka, Mark. *Towards a Poetics of Fiction*. Blooming-
         ton: Indiana University Press, 1977.

         Includes John Ross Baker, "From Imitation to Rhetoric,"
         item 769.

958.   Stanzel, Franz. "The Authorial Novel: *Tom Jones*," in
         his *Narrative Situations in the Novel: "Tom Jones,"
         "Moby-Dick," "The Ambassadors," "Ulysses,"* translated
         by James P. Pusack. Bloomington: Indiana University
         Press, 1971. Pp. 38-58.

         Uses *Tom Jones* as his main example of the authorial
         novel in which "the author himself seems to enter as
         narrator." The authorial narrator "guarantees" the
         authenticity of the narrated material, although he re-
         mains outside the story he tells and functions to arouse
         and maintain the reader's interest and to evaluate the
         narrative for him. Also see Booth, items 457 and 789.

*   Steeves, Harrison R. "A Manly Man (Henry Fielding)."
         (See item 587.)

*   Stevenson, Lionel. *The English Novel*. (See item 715.)

959.   Stevick, Philip. "On Fielding Talking." *College Litera-
         ture*, 1 (1974), 19-33.

         Analyzes the complexity of the voice established by
         the narrator in *Tom Jones*. That voice combines the
         emotional and intellectual, the personal and the uni-
         versal. Most of all, through Fielding's intimacy and
         immediacy, it appears to be a spoken voice rather than
         a literary one. The speaker always anticipates the pos-
         sibility of alienating the listener in the "conversa-
         tion" that he conducts and therefore he reinforces his
         intimacy with the listener by frequently making familiar
         comments.

960.   Stitzell, Judith G. "Blifil and Henry Fielding's Con-
         cept of Evil." *West Virginia University Philological
         Papers*, 17 (1970), 16-24.

         The basis of Blifil's evil is his unnatural attitude

toward love and passion. Fielding shows Blifil as a
person who perverts the sanctity of married love into
unhealthy sexual appetite.

961. Strachan, L.R.M. "Fielding Query: 'At Home.'" *Notes
and Queries*, Thirteenth Series, 1 (1923), 337.

Responds to H. C___n's request for help in defining an
"at home," item 108, by pointing out that Walpole also
mentions an "at home" in his correspondence.

962. Streeter, Harold Wade. *The Eighteenth Century English
Novel in French Translation: A Bibliographical Study*.
New York: Benjamin Blom, 1970. Originally published
New York: Columbia University Press, 1936.

Contains a section on "English Realism" which discusses
the French reception of *Tom Jones*. Although the novel
was successful in France, it was criticized for its vul-
garity, its discursiveness, and its excessive length.
A few critics agreed with Mme. de Staël, however, that
in spite of minor blemishes, the novel was moral and a
masterpiece.

963. Stumpf, Thomas A. *"Tom Jones* from the Outside," in *The
Classic British Novel*, eds. Howard M. Harper, Jr., and
Charles Edge. Athens: The University of Georgia Press,
1972. Pp. 3-21.

Defines Fielding's method of characterization as "anti-
psychological" due to his rather typical eighteenth-
century distrust of contemplation and his belief that
too much self-consciousness is delusive because it
divorces one from the "real" world which exists outside
the mind. To Fielding, "judicious observation" is more
important than psychological speculation. Thus, he does
not try to get into the minds of his characters. Moreover, his good characters are those, like Sophia in
Tom Jones, who read appearances accurately and his
wicked characters are those, like Blifil, who are preoccupied with the workings of their own minds and who
are always searching for hidden motives in others.

964. Item deleted.

965. T., L.E. "Fielding's Parson Thwackum." *Notes and
Queries*, Eleventh Series, 6 (1912), 348.

Identifies the Reverend Richard Hele, canon of Salisbury,
as the model for Thwackum in *Tom Jones*. Also see Mildmay, item 903.

966.   Tannenbaum, Earl. "A Note on Tom Jones and the Man on
        the Hill." *College Language Association Journal*, 4
        (1961), 215-17.

        Compares and contrasts Tom and the Man of the Hill.
        The similarities between the two argue that Fielding
        meant for them to be considered corresponding charac-
        ters, but the differences imply that the Man of the
        Hill is to be seen as Tom's foil.

*   Tate, Allen, Mark Van Doren, and Katherine Anne Porter.
        "Fielding: *Tom Jones*," in *New Invitation to Learning*,
        ed. Mark Van Doren. New York: New Home Library, 1944.
        Pp. 194-205. Originally published New York: Random
        House, 1942.

        See under Porter, item 927.

967.   Taube, Myron. "*Tom Jones* with French Words and Music."
        Southern Speech Journal, 26 (1960), 109-17.

        Analyzes the French comic opera version of *Tom Jones*
        (acted in 1764), discovering the characters and theme
        of the novel to be altered radically to fit contemporary
        French tastes. In the altered version, most of the
        characters are weakened and made pathetic.

968.   Taylor, Duncan. *Fielding's England*. London: Dobson
        and New York: Roy Publishers, 1966.

        Uses places and events in *Tom Jones* as a starting point
        for presenting a detailed picture of life in early
        eighteenth-century England. For example, the author
        describes--often using photographs and drawings--the
        various neighborhoods in London mentioned in the novel,
        and he discusses such aspects of English life as educa-
        tion, employment, religion, and crime.

969.   Tillett, Nettie S. "Is Coleridge Indebted to Fielding?"
        Studies in Philology, 43 (1946), 675-81.

        Compares Chapters XIV and XXII of the *Biographia Liter-
        aria* with the Introduction to Book VIII of *Tom Jones*
        and discovers similarities in the two authors' atti-
        tudes towards probability, possibility, and the willing
        suspension of disbelief.

970.   Tillyard, E.M.W. "*Tom Jones*," in his *The Epic Strain in
        the English Novel*. London: Chatto and Windus, 1958. Pp.
        51-58. Also published Fair Lawn, N.J.: Essential Books,
        1958.

        Argues that *Tom Jones* is a romance and not an epic

because it lacks epic scope, the narration lacks epic intensity, and Tom lacks the stature of an epic hero. Also see Baker, "Henry Fielding's Comic Romances," item 637; Miller, *Henry Fielding's "Tom Jones" and the Romance Tradition*," item 905; and Thornbury, *Henry Fielding's Theory of the Comic Prose Epic*, item 598.

Reviews: Listener, 59 (1958), 949-50; *Times Literary Supplement* (May 2, 1958), 242; J.M.S. Tompkins, *London Magazine*, 5 (1958), 75-78.

*   Todd, William B. "Three Notes on Fielding." (See item 309.)

971.   Item deleted.

972.   Item deleted.

973.   V., E.H. "A Curious Double Parallel Between Milton and Fielding." *Notes and Queries*, 176 (1939), 260.

Notes a statement in *Tom Jones* that combines two widely separated quotations from Milton.

974.   Van Doren, Carl. "Tom Jones and Philip Carey." *Century*, 110 (1925), 115-20.

Regards Tom Jones and Philip Carey as representing the prevailing philosophical views of their respective centuries. Tom is a type, not an individual, and he faces an ordered universe to which he must, eventually, conform. Philip is an individual, and his universe is internal, with no governing order.

*   Van Doren, Mark, Katherine Anne Porter, and Allen Tate. "Fielding: *Tom Jones*," in *New Invitation to Learning*, ed. Mark Van Doren. New York: New Home Library, 1944. Pp. 194-205. Originally published New York: Random House, 1942.

See under Porter, item 927.

975.   Van Ghent, Dorothy. "On *Tom Jones*," in her *The English Novel: Form and Function*. New York: Rinehart and Co., 1953. Pp. 65-81. Reprinted in Iser, item 507, and Compson, item 804. An extract reprinted in Rawson, item 272.

Like *Don Quixote*, *Tom Jones* is characterized by a systematic organization of contrasts, the most important of which are contrasts of character. The contrasts

between Tom and Blifil and between Allworthy and
Deborah Wilkins are among the most important because
these contrasts make the moral point of the novel,
demonstrating Tom and Allworthy's good nature and Blifil
and Deborah's hypocrisy. Furthermore, such contrasts
illuminate Fielding's positive view of human nature--
Tom is "natural" and therefore good, but Blifil is "unnatural" (hypocritical and self-serving) and therefore
bad. Such a conception of life is oversimplified but
justified by its intelligibility.

976.   Vopat, James B. "Narrative Technique in *Tom Jones*: The
        Balance of Art and Nature." *Journal of Narrative Tech-
        nique*, 4 (1974), 144-54.

        The narrator-historian of *Tom Jones* attempts to improve
        upon nature with his art by constructing his novel so
        that its structure, erected upon a careful selection
        of details and a careful ordering of events, always re-
        flects "the sense of his discourse."

*   Warner, John M. "The Interpolated Narrative in the
        Fiction of Fielding and Smollett." (See item 605.)

977.   Watt, Ian. "Fielding as Novelist: *Tom Jones*," in *Twen-
        tieth Century Interpretations of Tom Jones*, ed. Martin
        C. Battestin. Englewood Cliffs, N.J.: Prentice-Hall,
        1968. Pp. 19-32. Originally published as Chapter IX,
        sections ii and iv, of Watt's *The Rise of the Novel*,
        item 608.

        Because Fielding's avowed purpose is to show "not men,
        but manners; not an individual, but a species," he makes
        no attempt to individualize his characters. The result
        of his method of characterization, his use of stilted
        diction, and his constant intrusions into the narrative
        is an emotional artificiality that derogates from the
        reality of his work and prevents him from fully conveying
        its larger moral significance.

*   ————. *The Rise of the Novel*. (See item 608.)

978.   ————. "*Tom Jones* and *Clarissa*," in *Fielding: A Col-
        lection of Critical Essays*, ed. Ronald Paulson. Engle-
        wood Cliffs, N.J.: Prentice-Hall, 1962. Pp. 98-122.
        This material originally appeared in a slightly differ-
        ent form as pp. 260-89 of Watt's *Rise of the Novel*,
        item 608. It is also reprinted in Compson, item 804.

        Examines Dr. Samuel Johnson's reasons for preferring
        Richardson over Fielding because Johnson has to be taken

seriously since he was the authoritative voice of neo-
classicism and yet rejected Fielding, the last, full
embodiment of the Augustan spirit. Johnson liked the
"moral" of Richardson's *Pamela*, whereas he found Fielding "low," but he also preferred Richardson's technique
over Fielding's. Watt's assessment of the two writers
is that Richardson is interested in character, Fielding
in plot; Richardson focuses on human psychology, Fielding on the panorama of society. Richardson is more
realistic than Fielding and his realism became a permanent element in the tradition of the novel, whereas
Fielding's unrealistic and eclectic approach precludes
him from what F.R. Leavis (see item 524) calls "the
great tradition" of the English novel.

979. Wess, Robert V. "The Probable and the Marvellous in
Tom Jones." *Modern Philology*, 68 (1970), 32-45.

Reviews briefly the criticism of plot in *Tom Jones* and
notes that it is sometimes censured because it does not
always have "a plausibly connected sequence of events."
In his own theory of fiction, however, Fielding does
not stress the relationship of incidents but rather the
agents involved; if the actions that occur "are plausible consequences of the characters involved, the bounds
of probability have not been exceeded." The "peculiar
quality" of *Tom Jones* is due to the feeling that what
happens to Tom is neither impossible nor probable but
"merely possible," and so at the end of the novel, the
reader is aware that all is not necessarily well with
the world and that one cannot rely on Fortune to help
the good.

* Weston, Harold. *Form in Literature: A Theory of Technique and Construction*. (See item 721.)

980. White, Thomas. "Tom Jones." *Notes and Queries*, Twelfth
Series, 5 (1919), 303.

Responds to Payen-Payne's request, item 924, for information on Gibbon's remark in his *Memoirs of My Life and
Writings* that *Tom Jones* would outlive the Austrian
eagle. (Incidentally, no one has ever proven that
Fielding was related to the Hapsburgs.)

* Whittuck, Charles A. *The Good Man of the Eighteenth
Century*. (See item 722.)

* Williams, Murial Brittain. *Marriage: Fielding's Mirror
of Reality*. (See item 325.)

981.   Williams, Orlo. *"Tom Jones* (Fielding)," in his *Some Great English Novels: Studies in the Art of Fiction.* St. Clair Shores, Mich.: Scholarly Press, 1970. Pp. 1-25. Originally published London: Macmillan, 1926.

Prefers *Joseph Andrews* (for its portrait of Adams), *Jonathan Wild* (for its sustained irony), and *Amelia* (for its psychological realism) over *Tom Jones*. Yet, on the basis of its comprehensiveness, its range and variety, *Tom Jones* must be regarded as a masterpiece, even if it does not match the particular strengths of the other novels.

*   Willy, Margaret. "Portrait of a Man: Henry Fielding." (See item 327.)

982.   Woodcock, George. *"Colonel Jack* and *Tom Jones*: Aspects of a Changing Century." *Wascana Review,* 5 (1970), 67-73.

Defoe's writing reflects the turbulence of the Restoration period and Fielding's the stability of the Augustan Age. Defoe's figures fight hard to succeed in a harsh world and thus the picaresque tradition and a terse journalistic style are ideal for him. Fielding's characters already have places in the social order, and after he mocks their follies and "educates" them, they return to their rightful places. His irony and smooth, confident, formal style fit his world view.

*   Wright, Andrew. *Henry Fielding: Mask and Feast.* (See item 612.)

983.   ————. *"Tom Jones*: Life as Art," in *Twentieth Century Interpretations of "Tom Jones,"* ed. Martin C. Battestin. Englewood Cliffs, N.J.: Prentice-Hall, 1968. Pp. 56-67. Originally published as part of Chapter I of the author's *Henry Fielding: Mask and Feast,* item 612.

Fielding deliberately makes *Tom Jones* artificial through his images of mask and feast because only festive art, which celebrates life, can redeem Tom's world of hypocrites and fools.

*   Yardley. E. "Fielding and Shakespeare." (See item 330.)

F. *Amelia*

*   Allen, Walter. *The English Novel*. (See item 441.)

984.   Amory, Hugh. "Magistrate or Censor? The Problem of
       Authority in Fielding's Later Writings." *Studies in
       English Literature*, 12 (1972), 503-18.

       In the *Enquiry into the Causes of the Late Increase
       of Robbers* (1751), Fielding shifts between the tradi-
       tional role of the Roman censor, who attempts to cure
       luxury without legislation, and the role of the magis-
       trate, who attempts to cure vice through imposition of
       legal restitution. The conflict between these roles,
       as well as society's refusal to heed either the censor
       or the magistrate, creates a "problem of authority"
       which Fielding tries to overcome in *Amelia* through the
       figure of Dr. Harrison, who, as clergyman/censor, can
       propose solutions for social ills which Fielding, in
       his role of magistrate, could not plausibly propound.

*   Baker, Ernest A. *History of the English Novel*. (See
       item 448.)

985.   Baker, Sheridan. "Fielding's *Amelia* and the Materials
       of Romance." *Philological Quarterly*, 41 (1962), 437-
       49.

       The comedy of *Joseph Andrews* and *Tom Jones* successfully
       mediates between realism and romance, but the serious-
       ness of *Amelia* renders Fielding's romantic techniques
       sentimental. Without comic controls, sentimentality
       and romantic improbability overwhelm the attempt at
       realism and cause the novel to fail.

986.   Battestin, Martin C. "The Problem of *Amelia*: Hume,
       Barrow, and the Conversion of Captain Booth." *ELH: A
       Journal of English Literary History*, 41 (1974), 613-48.

       Hypothesizes that *Amelia* is disappointingly different
       from Fielding's earlier novels because of its didacti-
       cism; Fielding sought to defend the Christian humanist
       view of the coherence of the world against the skepti-
       cism of David Hume. In the novel, Dr. Harrison repre-
       sents Fielding's views, based on the theology of Isaac
       Barrow, and Booth's "philosophic errors," particularly
       his doubts about religion due to his doctrine of "neces-
       sity arising from the impulse of the passions," are all
       derived from Hume.

987. Bensly, Edward. "Fielding Query: 'At Home.'" *Notes and Queries*, Thirteenth Series, 1 (1923), 319.

   Answers H. C___n's request for information, item 108, by noting that in *Amelia* (XI.iii) Fielding defines an "at home" as "to keep an assembly."

988. Bevan, C.H.K. "The Unity of Fielding's *Amelia*." *Renaissance and Modern Studies*, 14 (1970), 90-110.

   Conjectures that *Amelia* may have been intended to refute the "happiness through property" emphasis in Mandeville's *Fable of the Bees* through a dramatic presentation of benevolist ideals. Fielding's attacks are weakest when he presents them through philosophical disputation, mostly in the speeches of Dr. Harrison. He is more effective when he embodies his principles in the action as he does when he associates pleasure with altruistic impulses and domestic bliss through the character of Amelia and when Booth's troubles are dramatized as results of his beliefs. Throughout most of the novel, Fielding argues through example not precept, and this technique makes *Amelia* morally coherent.

   Review: C.J. Rawson, *Notes and Queries*, n.s. 20 (1973), 38.

989. Bloch, Tuvia. "*Amelia* and Booth's Doctrine of the Passions." *Studies in English Literature*, 13 (1973), 461-73.

   Booth's view that men are controlled by passion reflects Fielding's acceptance of the doctrine of the "ruling passion."

990. ————. "The Prosecution of the Maidservant in *Amelia*." *English Language Notes*, 6 (1969), 269-71.

   Justifies Booth's actions in prosecuting Betty, the maid, for stealing the heroine's garments in *Amelia* (XI.v, vii). Booth reflects Fielding's own views when he charges Betty with ingratitude, a crime of a "black dye," and when he argues that compassion for individuals at the expense of public good is criminal.

*   Braudy, Leo. "Fielding: Public History and Individual Perception." (See item 648.)

*   Brooks, Douglas. *Number and Pattern in the Eighteenth-Century Novel*. (See item 652.)

*   Butt, John. *Fielding*. (See item 462.)

991. C., T.C. "Fielding and Bentley." *Notes and Queries*, 186 (1944), 245-46.

In *Amelia* (X.i), Fielding introduces an emendation of Horace by Bentley, probably to show the erudition of Dr. Harrison.

*   Child, Harold H. "Fielding and Smollett." (See item 110.)

*   Churchill, R.C. "Fielding: To the Novel from the Drama." (See item 111.)

*   Coolidge, John S. "Fielding and 'Conservation of Character.'" (See item 470.)

*   Cross, Wilbur L. "Henry Fielding." (See item 472.)

*   de Castro, J. Paul. "Fieldingiana." (See item 139.)

*   ————. "Fieldingiana." (See item 140.)

992. ————. "A Forgotten Salisbury Surgeon." *Times Literary Supplement* (13 January 1927), p. 28.

Among the many biographical details Fielding uses in *Amelia* is the incident in which the heroine breaks her nose. Charlotte Cradock also broke her nose, which was probably set by her old neighbor, an eminent surgeon named Goldwyre. Also see Dubois, item 170.

993. Dickson, Frederick S. *Index to "Amelia"* by Henry Fielding. 1911.

Identifies persons mentioned in *Amelia* and lists the novel's characters. An unpublished manuscript in The Library of Congress.

994. Dodds, M.H. "Phrases." *Notes and Queries*, 193 (1948), 64.

Asks for the source of Fielding's phrase, "one fool at least in every married couple," in *Amelia* (IX.iv).

995. Eaves, T.C. Duncan. "Amelia and Clarissa," in *A Provision of Human Nature: Essays on Fielding and Others in Honor of Miriam Austin Locke*, ed. Donald Kay. Univer-

sity: University of Alabama Press, 1977. Pp. 95-110.

Attempts to determine why Fielding in *Amelia* chose to
be more serious than in his earlier novels and finds
the answer in Fielding's admiration for Clarissa. He
wished to emulate Richardson by creating a model character, but his novel failed because he employed his old
narrative method which is at variance with his more
serious subject matter. He also failed because he did
not allow his idealized heroine to have any flaws and
thus created a character who could not develop.

*   Elwin, Whitwell. "Fielding." (See item 177.)

996.   Folkenflik, Robert. "Purpose and Narration in Field-
       ing's *Amelia*." *Novel*, 7 (1974), 168-74.

       A response to Anthony Hassall's "Fielding's *Amelia*:
       Dramatic and Authorial Narration" (item 997). Although
       Amelia is a comic novel, "near-tragic elements" play
       just beneath its surface. The serious aspects of the
       novel force Fielding to abandon constant authorial in-
       trusion, used in *Joseph Andrews* and *Tom Jones* for
       comic distancing, in favor of a more dramatic narrative
       method.

*   Forsyth, William. *The Novels and Novelists of the
       Eighteenth Century*. (See item 483.)

*   Foster, James R. *History of the Pre-Romantic Novel in
       England*. (See item 484.)

*   Gerould, Gordon Hall. *The Patterns of English and
       American Fiction*. (See item 489.)

*   Grabo, Carl H. *The Technique of the Novel*. (See item
       848.)

997.   Hassall, Anthony J. "Fielding's *Amelia*: Dramatic and
       Authorial Narration." *Novel*, 5 (1972), 225-33.

       Argues that *Amelia* is weakened by its alternation be-
       tween authorial and dramatic narration; Fielding could
       not decide whether to tell or to show, and as a result,
       he does neither well. For a response to this argument,
       see Folkenflik, "Purpose and Narration," item 996.

998.   Hobbes, John Oliver [Mrs. Craigie]. "Letters from a
       Silent Study." *The Academy and Literature* (16 July
       1904), p. 51.

Tom Jones and *Amelia* should "be given to every girl on
her eighteenth birthday" because they are highly moral
works which could "save women from innumerable mistakes
and tears." Women can learn from Fielding the truth
about domestic life and the social scene because, unlike modern moralists, he is honest and direct.

999. Humphreys, A.R. "Introduction to 'Amelia,'" in *Amelia*
by Henry Fielding. London: Dent and New York: Dutton,
1962. Pp. vi-xiv.

Reviews the reactions to *Amelia* from its publication
to the mid-twentieth century. Humphreys' own views,
which conclude the Introduction, are extremely positive: the writing is Fielding's best because he avoided
the facetiousness of his earlier works, and the psychology of the characters (Booth, Amelia, and Harrison)
is utterly realistic.

1000. Hunter, J. Paul. "The Lesson of *Amelia*," in *Quick
Springs of Sense: Studies in the Eighteenth Century*,
ed. Larry S. Champion. Athens: University of Georgia
Press, 1974. Pp. 157-82.

Lists and discusses several flaws in Fielding's last
novel: (1) it is dull; (2) coincidence, which works
well in an artificial comedy like *Tom Jones*, only
cheapens a realistic and serious work like *Amelia*;
(3) the intensive moralizing is excessive; (4) a lack
of irony makes the novel too "stark"; (5) characterization is weak because in the book guilt is assigned to
a class or an institution, thus relieving evil characters of part of their responsibility for their actions;
(6) the morality is simplistic for such a serious work
--"virtue rewarded" is acceptable in comedies like
Joseph Andrews and *Tom Jones* but not in realistic fiction like *Amelia*. Fielding's talent was in comedy,
and when he went outside the borders of his comic
world, he was not nearly as successful. (This material
is reprinted in his *Occasional Form*, item 209.

1001. Johnson, E.D.H. "*Vanity Fair* and *Amelia*: Thackeray in
the Perspective of the Eighteenth Century." *Modern
Philology*, 59 (1961), 100-13.

Notes that commentators have stressed the influence of
Fielding's *Jonathan Wild* on Thackeray's *Catherine* and
Barry Lyndon and goes on to demonstrate that the lat-
ter's *Vanity Fair* has even closer affinities with
Amelia. For example, Thackeray's Amelia Osborne is

clearly patterned after Fielding's Amelia Booth; both
George Osborne and Booth take up with a scheming woman;
and Fielding's unnamed nobleman debaucher closely resembles Thackeray's Lord Steyne. In spite of such
similarities, however, *Amelia* ultimately affirms marriage and society, whereas *Vanity Fair* is more negative in its viewpoint.

*   Johnson, Maurice. *Fielding's Art of Fiction: Eleven
        Essays on "Shamela," "Joseph Andrews," "Tom Jones,"
        and "Amelia."* (See item 511.)

*   Karl, Frederick R. "Henry Fielding: The Novel, the
        Epic, and the Comic Sense of Life." (See item 514.)

*   Kaul, A.N. "The Adjudication of Fielding's Comedy."
        (See item 515.)

1002.   Le Page, Peter V. "The Prison and the Dark Beauty of
        Amelia." *Criticism*, 9 (1967), 337-54.

        Sees *Amelia* as Fielding's most carefully constructed
        work; at its center, and giving it unity, is the
        prison, in or around which all the important action
        takes place. The prison, like the city which contains
        it, becomes a symbol of the tyranny and injustice of
        "the social will" and is contrasted with the country,
        which represents freedom and the "individual will."

1003.   Loftis, John E. "Imitation in the Novel: Fielding's
        Amelia." *Rocky Mountain Review of Language and Litera-
        ture*, 31 (1977), 214-29.

        The power of *Amelia* is derived from its conscious par-
        allels with the *Aeneid*. While the novel is not an
        epic, its moral statements are elevated to epic propor-
        tions by the echoes of Virgil. In *Amelia*, the family
        functions as the "epic hero," and the moral values
        that Fielding believes are central to an ideal society
        are embodied in Booth's family.

1004.   Longmire, Samuel E. "*Amelia* as a Comic Action."
        Tennessee Studies in Literature, 17 (1972), 69-79.

        Challenges the critical commonplace that the happy
        ending of *Amelia* does not logically conclude the
        novel. (See Alter, *Fielding and the Nature of the
        Novel*, item 443, p. 165; Dudden, item 171, pp. 811-12;
        and Wright, *Henry Fielding: Mask and Feast*, item 612,

p. 120.) By reminding the reader that Booth is capable
of active virtue and is intrinsically good and by in-
serting episodes, such as the domestic conflict between
James and his wife, which force the reader to laugh at
the tormentors of Booth and Amelia, Fielding lightens
the seriousness of the novel and prepares for its happy
ending.

1005. ————. "Booth's Conversion in *Amelia*." *South Atlantic Bulletin*, 40 (1975), 12-17.

Explains Booth's conversion, which seems too abrupt to
some, as being a natural outcome of his reading of
Isaac Barrow. Barrow stressed an intellectual Christianity, and Booth, who is essentially a good man,
needs only the intellectual assurance of the rightness
of Christianity to redeem himself.

1006. McCusher, H. "First Editions of Fielding." *More Books:
The Bulletin of the Boston Public Library*, 13 (1938),
114.

Records the library's acquisition of first editions of
Amelia and *The Journal of a Voyage to Lisbon*.

1007. Malhotra, K.K. "The Art of Life—A Study of Fielding's
Amelia." *Panjab University Research Bulletin*, 2 (1971),
29-38.

Regards Amelia as the personification of the eighteenth-
century ideals of virtue, innocence, and prudence.
These qualities, dramatized in Amelia, provide an example for the "art of living" and give the novel its
thematic unity.

1008. Maynadier, G.H. "Introduction" to *Amelia* by Henry
Fielding. Cambridge, Mass.: Harvard University Press,
1903. Pp. xv-xxviii.

When Fielding came to write *Amelia*, he was physically
exhausted and deeply aware of the seriousness of life;
thus the novel lacks the vigorous high spirits of *Tom
Jones* and moves much more slowly. Yet the background
of the novel and the portraits of Miss Matthews, Booth,
and Amelia are as successful as anything else Fielding
wrote.

1009. Nathan, Sabine. "The Anticipation of Nineteenth Century Ideological Trends in Fielding's *Amelia*." *Zeit-*

schrift für Anglistik und Amerikanistik, 6 (1958), 382–409.

Because of his experience as a magistrate, Fielding had grown more serious and more aware of social problems when he came to write *Amelia*. In his search for solutions to these problems, he anticipated remedies proposed by nineteenth-century reformers. The social and religious views of Dr. Harrison in *Amelia*, for example, resemble those of William Wilberforce's Evangelical Party of 1797. The character of Amelia, too, is similar to the nineteenth-century ideal of the passive domesticated matron whose "protectors" are married security and religion.

1010.   Oakman, Robert L. "The Character of the Hero: A Key to Fielding's *Amelia*." *Studies in English Literature*, 16 (1976), 473–89.

Discusses the various functions of Booth, whose character is complex but limited by his role in building the structure of the novel. Booth, who functions as a counterpoint to the perfect Amelia, represents a false philosophy of life, against which Fielding displays a proper philosophy through Dr. Harrison and authorial intrusion. Booth also is used as a tool to show the corruption of contemporary society.

1011.   Palmer, Eustace. "*Amelia*--The Decline of Fielding's Art." *Essays in Criticism*, 21 (1971), 135–51.

The "moral outline" of *Amelia*, which attempts to show the results of a husband's lack of virtue, is a variation of the love/marriage theme which dominates Fielding's fiction. The novel seems more didactic and less interesting than the previous work because it is artistically flawed. Its main weakness is the "over-obvious didacticism" which comes about whenever Fielding states a thesis without fully demonstrating it in the action of the novel. Other flaws include a lack of variety in style and subject and a digressive plot.

1012.   Poston, Charles D. "The Novel as Exemplum: A Study of Fielding's *Amelia*." *West Virginia University Philological Papers*, 18 (1970), 23–29.

Regards *Amelia*, which does not represent a decline in Fielding's art, as a different *kind* of novel. Like Wilson's story in *Joseph Andrews* and the Man of the Hill's Tale in *Tom Jones*, *Amelia* is an *exemplum*. All

three stories deal with the imprudent decisions of a
central male figure who is essentially benevolent and
who learns from his mistakes. The lesson of all three
exempla is that a good heart combined with experience
leads to practical wisdom and discretion.

1013. Powers, Lyall H. "The Influence of the *Aeneid* on
Fielding's *Amelia*." *Modern Language Notes*, 71 (1956),
330-36.

Lists a series of parallels between the *Aeneid* and
Amelia in order to demonstrate how closely Fielding
followed his classical model, which he selected because its theme is close to that of his novel--"to
depict the development or reformation of a good man."
Fielding deviates from his model, however, at the conclusion of the novel because he wished to provide a
Christian denouement for it. Also see Sherburn, "Fielding's *Amelia*," item 1021.

1014. Purton, Valerie. "James's *The Turn of the Screw*, Chapter 9." *Explicator*, 34 (1975), item 24.

The governess's reading of *Amelia* before her third
encounter with Peter Quint may inform the whole mystery
since the governess apparently identifies with Amelia's
struggles.

1015. Rader, Ralph W. "Ralph Cudworth and Fielding's *Amelia*."
Modern Language Notes, 71 (1956), 336-38.

Replies to A.R. Towers, "Fielding and Dr. Samuel
Clarke," item 1026b, arguing that Cudworth and not
Clarke was the source for Fielding's refutation of
Robinson's atheism in *Amelia*.

1016. Rawson, C.J. "Nature's Dance of Death, Part II: Fielding's *Amelia* (With Some Comments on Defoe, Smollett,
and George Orwell)." *Eighteenth Century Studies*, 3
(1970), 491-522.

In *Amelia*, Fielding's confronts "unnaturalness" to a
far greater extent than he does in his earlier novels.
He tries to create an artistic form for the unnatural,
showing formal balance in life through style in art.

* Robinson, Roger. "The Influence of Fielding on Barnaby
Rudge." (See item 563.)

1017.   Rogers, Winslow. "Thackeray and Fielding's *Amelia*."
        Criticism, 19 (1977), 141-57.

        Traces the influence of *Amelia* on Thackeray, especially
        on *Vanity Fair*. Thackeray's theme in the latter novel
        --the confusion of values in the contemporary world--
        parallels Fielding's theme in *Amelia*. Thackeray's
        self-conscious narrator owes much to Fielding's narra-
        tive method, but the narrative uncertainty that weak-
        ens *Amelia* becomes a strength in *Vanity Fair* because
        Thackeray pegs his irony firmly to it.

1018.   Rothstein, Eric. "*Amelia*," in his *Systems of Order and
        Inquiry in Later Eighteenth-Century Fiction*. Berkeley
        and Los Angeles: University of California Press, 1975.
        Pp. 154-207.

        Because the narrator of *Amelia* has "retreated" from the
        novel, creating a "quasi-theatrical" method of presen-
        tation, the reader is put on the same level as the
        characters, who must "fumble" for the truth. This
        search for the truth is exemplified in the way the
        novel unfolds: first Booth sees the world as he wishes
        to see it; next, the world is shown as it really is;
        and finally, Booth must disregard his unrealistic views
        and accept the real world. Without authorial guidance,
        the reader often is confused; he is unable to really
        care for the weak characters, concern for whom lies at
        the center of the novel, and he is unable to fully
        assess in psychological depth the true nature of Booth
        and Amelia who are supposed to deeply love each other.
        Also see Booth, items 456 and 457.

*   Saintsbury, George. "The Four Wheels of the Novel
        Wain." (See item 568.)

*   Shepperson, Archibald B. "Additions and Corrections
        to Facts About Fielding." (See item 288.)

1019.   Sherbo, Arthur. "Fielding's *Amelia*: A Reinterpreta-
        tion," in his *Studies in the Eighteenth Century English
        Novel*. East Lansing: Michigan State University Press,
        1969. Pp. 85-103.

        Reviews the major criticism on *Amelia*, paying particu-
        lar attention to Murry, item 540; Sherburn, items 1021
        and 579; and Wright, item 612. The latter is viewed
        as the best treatment of the novel. Sherbo concludes
        that Fielding is still "playful" in *Amelia* and that his

powers did not fail at the end of his career: "there is no infirmity, hidden or revealed, in the narrator of *Amelia*."

*   ———. "The Narrator in Fielding's Novels." (See item 576.)

1020.   ———. "The Time-Scheme in *Amelia*." *Boston University Studies in English*, 4 (1960), 223-28.

Shows that Fielding is unusually accurate in his calendar references in *Amelia*; the dramatic action of the novel takes place in 1750, and the dates correspond precisely to days of the week for that year.

1021.   Sherburn, George. "Fielding's *Amelia*: An Interpretation." *ELH: A Journal of English Literary History*, 3 (1936), 1-14. Reprinted in Iser, item 507, and Paulson, item 258.

The unfavorable reception of *Amelia* in 1751 was in great part due to its serious tone which surprised and disappointed readers who had liked Fielding's earlier and lighter works. There also are other reasons why the book was not popular: (1) it was too learned for a wide audience; (2) Booth's conversion is not psychologically motivated; (3) Booth's character is too weak to merit his role as hero; and (4) the happy ending is contrived and not in keeping with the narrative premises of the story.

1022.   Sherwood, Irma Z. "The Novelists as Commentators," in *The Age of Johnson: Essays Presented to Chauncey Brewster Tinker*, ed. F.W. Hilles. New Haven: Yale University Press, 1949. Pp. 113-25. Reprinted in Iser, item 507.

Eighteenth-century novelists felt it was their duty to offer their readers morally edifying comments. Unfortunately, this practice often causes their novels to languish. Such is the case with *Amelia*, in which Fielding is unable to link Dr. Harrison's "edifying" conversations to the plot and the fortunes of the heroine. He is more successful in *Tom Jones*, but even there the moralizing often intrudes itself between the reader and the imaginative world of the novel.

*   Spacks, Patricia Meyer. *Imagining a Self*. (See item 956.)

1023.   Stephens, John C., Jr. "The Verge of the Court and
         Arrest for Debt in Fielding's *Amelia*." *Modern Lan-
         guage Notes*, 63 (1948), 104-09.

         Explains the eighteenth-century legal code pertaining
         to imprisonment for debt and contends that in part
         Amelia--through Booth's indebtedness--is a humanitarian
         tract designed to foster legal reform.

1023a.   Swain, Corinne R. "Amelia Booth and Lucy Feverel."
         Nation, 91 (1910), 440-41.

         Compares Fielding's heroine with Meredith's and dis-
         covers several similarities: both have a taste for
         "real" sentiment but scorn "artificial" sentimentalism;
         both have senses of humor; both are robust and vigor-
         ous. The main difference between them is that Amelia
         is not portrayed with the psychological depth of Lucy.

1024.   Thomas, D.S. "Fortune and the Passions in Fielding's
         Amelia." *Modern Language Review*, 60 (1965), 176-87.

         Fielding accepts both the ordering of Divine Providence
         and the random workings of Fortune (or Chance) in the
         universe. Providence provides order in the physical
         universe, in which Chance exists but can be overcome
         by Christian humility and resignation. The passions,
         which belong to (and are controlled by) Fortune, can
         be overcome by reason and submission to Providence.

1025.   ————. "The Publication of Henry Fielding's *Amelia*."
         Library, Fifth Series, 18 (1963), 303-07.

         Studies the type faces and contemporary publishing
         accounts to reveal that only one edition of *Amelia* was
         ever printed in the 1750's. See Todd, item 1026.

1026.   Todd, William B. "Press Figures." *Library*, Fifth
         Series, 7 (1952), 283.

         Amelia was printed on four presses, two in Strahan's
         shop and two in that of an unidentified printer.

1026a.   Towers, A.R. "*Amelia* and the State of Matrimony."
         Review of English Studies, 5 (1954), 144-57.

         Finds in *Amelia* "the conventional but enlightened opin-
         ion of the age" about marriage. Throughout the novel,
         Booth provides the problems of marriage and Amelia,
         with the help of Dr. Harrison, provides the solutions.
         For example, Booth's infidelity is met with Amelia's

quiet forgiveness, showing, according to the views of
the time, her wifely wisdom and charity.

1026b. ————. "Fielding and Dr. Samuel Clarke." *Modern
Language Notes*, 70 (1955), 257-60.

Classifies Fielding with the Latitudinarian divines
by showing how closely he follows the terminology of
Dr. Clarke, an influential Latitudinarian, when he re-
viles Robinson in *Amelia* for being a free-thinker and
atheist. For an opposing view, see Sherbo, *Studies
in the Eighteenth Century English Novel*, p. 119, note
16 (item 578) and Rader, item 1015.

1027. Wendt, Allan. "The Naked Virtue of *Amelia*." *ELH: A
Journal of English Literary History*, 27 (1960), 131-
48.

Amelia is both a symbol of "naked human virtue" and a
flesh and blood woman unable to stand alone and un-
aided in an imperfect world. Therefore, Fielding
adds Dr. Harrison to his moral scheme to help Amelia
by providing "absolute values." Booth is reformed
through Amelia's example and Dr. Harrison's articulated principles.

* Williams, Murial Brittain. *Marriage: Fielding's Mirror of Reality*. (See item 325.)

1028. Woolf, Cynthia Griffin. "Fielding's *Amelia*: Private
Virtue and Public Good." *Texas Studies in Literature
and Language*, 10 (1968), 37-55.

Presents a reading of *Amelia* in which the novel is
viewed as a statement of the necessity of strong laws,
sternly enforced, for the protection of the innocent
in society. The novel, however, is unsatisfying in
the presentation of this theme because Fielding is
unable to bridge the gap between private and public
morality. Amelia, as a good person, is forgiving, but
the law, as a good institution, cannot forgive.

VI

MISCELLANEOUS WRITINGS

A. General

1029.   Baker, Sheridan W. "Fielding and 'Stultus Versus
        Sapientem.'" *Notes and Queries*, 198 (1953), 343-44.

        "Stultus Versus Sapientem" (1749) should be removed
        from the Fielding canon; its style is not Fielding's
        and its pro-Irish political views are vastly different
        from his. See Coolidge, item 1033.

*   Banerji, H.K. *Henry Fielding: Playwright, Journalist,
        and Master of the Art of Fiction, His Life and His
        Works*. (See item 86.)

1030.   Bowers, Fredson. "Textual Introduction" to *Miscellanies
        by Henry Fielding, Esq*. Middletown, Conn.: Wesleyan
        University Press and Oxford: The Clarendon Press,
        1972. Pp. 1-lv.

        Offers technical commentary on the copy-text and its
        treatment, the early editions, the textual apparatus,
        and the collation of various editions to produce this
        one.

1031.   Carter, P.B., *et al*. "The Case of Elizabeth Canning."
        Police College Magazine, 7 (1961), 71-81.

        Reports on a modern jury of police officers which re-
        viewed the Canning case and vindicated Fielding's
        judgment that she was innocent.

1032.   Chandler, Knox. "Two 'Fielding' Pamphlets." *Philo-
        logical Quarterly*, 16 (1937), 410-12.

        Demonstrates that two 1742 pamphlets attacking Pope
        and popularly ascribed to Fielding were written by

other essayists. *The Cudgel* is a reprint of *A Playn Satyr*, published first in 1728 and probably written by Edward Ward, and *Blast Upon Blast* is a reprint of *Dean Jonathan's Parody*, first published in 1729 and probably written by Edward Roome.

1033.   Coolidge, Archibald C. "A Fielding Pamphlet?" *Times Literary Supplement* (May 9, 1936), p. 400.

Attributes the pamphlet, "Stultus Versus Sapientum," assigned by Cross (item 126) to Fielding, to William Chaigneau. The style is more Chaigneau's than Fielding's, the subject would not have interested Fielding as it would have Chaigneau, and publication evidence shows that all editions were published in Dublin, Chaigneau's home city. See Baker, item 1029.

1034.   Eddy, Donald D. "The Printing of Fielding's *Miscellanies* (1743)." *Studies in Bibliography*, 15 (1962), 247–56.

Determines the order of printing the first and second editions of the *Miscellanies* by a study of the printers' marks. There is very little variance between the first and second editions, which indicates that the same type and the same procedures were used for both.

*   Elton, Oliver. "Fielding and Smollett." (See item 175.)

1035.   Gerould, Gordon Hall. "Introduction" to *Selected Essays of Henry Fielding*. Boston: Ginn and Co., 1905.

Defends Fielding as a healthy, moral man who repented of his early vices. Fielding's essays are uneven in quality, but the best of them rank with the best of the more noted essayists.

*   Goad, Caroline. *Horace in the English Literature of the Eighteenth Century*. (See item 185.)

1036.   Graham, Walter. *English Literary Periodicals*. New York: Thomas Nelson & Sons, 1930. Reprinted New York: Octagon Books, 1966.

Covers Fielding's various journalistic endeavors: *The Champion* (1739–43) was distinguished from other newspapers of the time because its social and literary criticism was "of real value"; the *Jacobite's Journal*

(1747-48) was a work of "ingenuity" with clever and insightful observations on *Clarissa*, *The Castle of Indolence*, and the theatrical performances of the day; *The Covent-Garden Journal* (1752) has merit only because of Fielding's well-written essays.

1037. Jarvis, R.C. "Fielding and the 'Forty-Five.'" *Notes and Queries*, n.s. 3 (1956), 391-94; 479-82; continued in n.s. 4 (1957), 19-24.

Between 1745 and 1749, Fielding was deeply engaged in the anti-Jacobite cause, writing several pamphlets and editing his pro-ministry newspaper, *The True Patriot*. The author lists editions of works on the '45 written during this period and locates several listed as lost by Cross and Dudden. He also provides a bibliographic history of Fielding's *The History of the Present Rebellion in Scotland*. See Greason, "Fielding's *History of the Present Rebellion*," item 1110.

1038. Jones, Claude. "Henry Fielding as Translator." *Langue et Littérature*, 21 (1961), 212-13.

Discusses Fielding's translations from the French and Latin. His most important translation is his annotated edition of Ovid's *Art of Love*, a "free" translation falling somewhere between Dryden's "paraphrase" and "imitation."

1039. Leslie-Melville, A.R. "Henry Fielding." *Times Literary Supplement* (July 27, 1933), p. 512.

Notes that Fielding was probably author of a series of letters recommending various social reforms published in the *Gentleman's Magazine* and the *London Daily Advertiser* (1751-53). The letters are signed "Philanthropos."

1040. McCue, Lillian Bueno. "Elizabeth Canning in Print," in *Elizabethan Studies and Other Essays in Honor of George F. Reynolds*. University of Colorado Studies in the Humanities, V. 2, No. 4, 1945. Pp. 223-32.

Lists publications from 1753 to 1945, including Fielding's pamphlet, *A Clear State of the Case of Elizabeth Canning*, on the famous Canning case.

1041. Marr, George S. *The Periodical Essayists of the Eighteenth Century*. New York: D. Appleton, 1924. Originally published London, 1923.

Places Fielding's essays in the context of eighteenth-century periodical literature and sees him as a follower of Addison and Steele. Marr believes that Fielding's finest "periodical" essays appear in his novels, but that the novel eventually sucked the vitality out of the essay from.

1042. Miller, Henry Knight. *Essays on Fielding's "Miscellanies": A Commentary on Volume I.* Princeton, N.J.: Princeton University Press, 1961.

Views the first volume of the *Miscellanies* as a "microcosm" of Fielding's intellectual world. Chapters on poetry, essays, satires, translations, and Lucianic sketches concentrate on Fielding's "endless" experiments in a variety of genres and on his extensive background in classical rhetoric and Greek literature. The central topics of Good-Nature, true Greatness, Liberty, Marriage, Conversation, Human Nature, and so on, are placed in context, and the Lucianic influence on Fielding is stressed. Miller also emphasizes Fielding's growth as a comic writer and argues that the comic epic in prose was ideally suited to his active imagination. His comedy has the unique quality of embracing life's sadder truths but still accepting life with enthusiasm and hope. The apparent inconsistencies in his work are due to his fair-mindedness, which compelled him to weigh and consider both sides of issues.

Reviews: John Carroll, *University of Toronto Quarterly*, 32 (1962), 98-101; Donald D. Eddy, *Modern Philology*, 60 (1963), 290-93; Bernhard Fabian, *Archiv für das Studium der Neueren Sprachen und Literaturen*, 201 (1964), 461-65; L.P. Goggin, *Philological Quarterly*, 41 (1962), 590-91; Ronald Paulson, *Journal of English and Germanic Philology*, 61 (1962), 413-16; C.J. Rawson, *Review of English Studies*, 14 (1963), 88-90; Andrew Wright, *Modern Language Review*, 57 (1962), 422.

1043. ————. "General Introduction" to *Miscellanies by Henry Fielding, Esq.* Middletown, Conn.: Wesleyan University Press and Oxford: The Clarendon Press, 1972. Pp. xi-xlix.

Divides the discussion into four parts: circumstances of publication, contents of the *Miscellanies*, date of composition, and history of publication. The longest and most detailed section is the one on the contents;

here Miller provides background material for most of
the items printed and outlines Fielding's attitudes
towards his subject matter.

* Rogers, Pat. *Grub Street*. (See item 279.)

1044. Shipley, John B. "Fielding and 'The Plain Truth'
(1740)." *Notes and Queries*, 196 (1951), 561-62.

The British Museum lists the pamphlet, "The Plain
Truth," as a 1741 publication; the actual date is
1740 and the work should be ascribed to Fielding.

1045. Walker, Hugh. *The English Essay and Essayists*. London: J.M. Dent and New York: E.P. Dutton, 1915.

Views Fielding as an essayist of considerable skill
and power. Especially well-done are the essays in
Tom Jones, the Hercules Vinegar pieces in *The Champion*,
and the moral discussions in *The Covent-Garden Journal*.
Fielding was heavily influenced by Addison and Steele
and his essays are superior to most of their followers,
including Dr. Johnson.

1046. Wells, John E. "Fielding's *Miscellanies*." *Modern
Language Review*, 13 (1918), 481-82.

Makes several points about the *Miscellanies*: (1) the
first edition appeared on April 7, 1743; (2) the
second edition was published on April 23 of the same
year; (3) some copies, but not all, of the second
edition contain a list of subscribers; (4) some of
the poems in the *Miscellanies* were altered after
their first appearance. For a fuller discussion of
these matters, see Miller, item 1042.

1047. ———. "Henry Fielding and the 'History of Charles
XII.'" *Journal of English and Germanic Philology*,
11 (1912), 603-13.

Records an autograph receipt of Fielding which indicates that he received forty-five pounds on March 10,
1739/40 for translating *The History of Charles XII*
from French into English.

1048. ———. "News for Bibliophiles." *The Nation*, 96
(1913), 53-4.

A pamphlet advertised in several journals in July
1731 and entitled "An Answer to One Part of a Late

Infamous Libel, Reflecting on Captain Vinegar and the
Late Worthy Jonathan Wild" probably was a parody of
existing pamphlets in the Pulteney controversy.

1049.   Williams, Ioan. "Introduction" to *The Criticism of
        Henry Fielding*. London: Routledge and Kegan Paul and
        New York: Barnes and Noble, 1970.

        Although Fielding's criticism is scattered throughout
        numerous writings over a long period, his essays are
        all related through the medium of wit and the repeated
        subjects of judgment, charity, and good nature.

1050.   Woods, Charles B. "Fielding's Epilogue for Theobald."
        Philological Quarterly, 28 (1949), 419-24.

        Although Fielding's biographers and critics mention
        his prologue to Lillo's *Fatal Curiosity* and his epi-
        logues to Boden's *The Modish Couple* and Johnson's
        Caelia, they somehow overlooked a third epilogue,
        published in April 1731 in the only edition of Lewis
        Theobald's *Orestes: A Dramatic Opera*. The epilogue
        is undoubtedly Fielding's; not only does his name ap-
        pear as author in the *Orestes* edition, that edition
        was printed by John Watts, who printed most of Field-
        ing's plays. Moreover, the epilogue contains a charac-
        teristically slighting reference to Fielding's own
        Tom Thumb.

B. Letters

1051.   Amory, Hugh. "Fielding's Lisbon Letters." *Huntington
        Library Quarterly*, 35 (1971), 65-83.

        At various times, three different letters (called by
        Amory the "Dobson," "de Castro," and "Solly" letters)
        have been said to be Fielding's last letter. Through
        internal evidence, Amory determines that the "Solly"
        letter, which turned up at Sotheby's in 1962, is the
        real "last letter." All three of the "Lisbon letters"
        show Fielding to have been heavily in debt at the time
        of his death, and they all indicate that Fielding's
        health was improving just before he died. Thus, he
        must have died suddenly and not after a gradual decline
        as Cross claimed (item 126). See MacLaurin (item 240),
        who supports Cross's view.

*   Battestin, M.C. with R.C. Battestin. "Fielding, Bed-
         ford, and the Westminster Election of 1749." (See
         item 88.)

1052.   de Castro, J. Paul. "Fielding's Last Letter." *Times
Literary Supplement* (15 January 1920), p. 35.

         Prints two-thirds of a "short Lisbon letter" from
Fielding to his brother (which was written after the
"long Lisbon letter" which Dobson--item 1055--assumed
was Fielding's last letter). Part of the letter is
omitted by de Castro because it contains "confidential
information" meant only for John Fielding's eyes.

1053.   ————. "Fielding's Letters." *Notes and Queries*,
Eleventh Series, 10 (1914), 214-15.

         Responds to Digeon, "Fielding's Letters," item 1054,
who asks for information regarding a lost book entitled
H. Fielding's Letters. The "lost" book is probably
Sarah Fielding's *Familiar Letters between the Principal
Characters in David Simple*, to which Henry contributed.

1054.   Digeon, Aurélien. "Fielding's Letters." *Notes and
Queries*, Eleventh Series, 10 (1914), 91.

         Asks for information on a lost book of Fielding let-
ters listed in *The Catalog of English Books Published
1700-1767*. See de Castro's conjectural reply, item
1053.

1055.   Dobson, Austin. "A Fielding Find." *National Review*,
57 (1911), 983-92. Reprinted in Dobson's *At Prior
Park and Other Papers*. London: Oxford University
Press, 1912. Pp. 128-49.

         Prints two previously undiscovered letters from Field-
ing to his brother, John (July 12, 1754, and July 22,
1754). The letters, annotated by Dobson, are important
biographically because they cover a period of Fielding's life about which little was previously known.
See de Castro, "Fielding's Last Letter," item 1052.

*   Godden, G.M. "Henry Fielding: Some Unpublished Letters
and Records." (See item 187.)

1056.   McAdam, E.L., Jr. "A New Letter from Fielding." *Yale
Review*, 38 (1948), 300-10.

         Cites Fielding's praise of *Clarissa* in a letter he
wrote to Richardson (October 15, 1748). Fielding liked

the tragic scenes, the comedy, and the character por-
trayals of the novel. He denies that he is envious
of Richardson or that they should be considered rivals.
He concludes by wishing Richardson success and signs
his letter, "affectionately."

*   Nichols, Charles W. "Fielding Notes." (See item 430.)

1057.   Stewart, Mary M. "Henry Fielding's Letter to the Duke
         of Richmond." *Philological Quarterly*, 50 (1971), 135-
         40.

         This letter (dated April 8, 1749) is biographically
         significant in that it demonstrates that Fielding kept
         in contact with the Duke as late as 1749; it indicates
         that Fielding expected patronage from Richmond; and
         it connects Fielding with three famous murder trials
         in 1749.

                                C. Verse

1058.   Battestin, Martin C. "Pope's 'Magus' in Fielding's
         Vernoniad: the Satire of Walpole." *Philological
         Quarterly*, 46 (1967), 137-41.

         Pope's satire on Walpole in *The Dunciad* (IV.515-28)
         finds its source in a Scriblerian note to a couplet in
         Fielding's own mock epic, *The Vernoniad*.

1059.   Goggin, L.P. "Fielding's Masquerade." *Philological
         Quarterly*, 36 (1957), 475-87.

         Re-examines Fielding's first published work, *The Mas-
         querade* (1728), and concludes that, in spite of weak-
         nesses--attributed to "youth" and "inexperience"--the
         poem is a readable and effective satire which demon-
         strates Fielding's wit and learning at an early age.

1060.   Grundy, Isobel M. "New Verse by Henry Fielding." *Pub-
         lications of the Modern Language Association of
         America*, 87 (1972), 213-45.

         Prints almost 800, extensively annotated, lines of
         recently discovered poetry by Fielding, written be-
         tween 1729 and 1733, and analyzes its content. The
         poetry is highly significant because it clearly
         demonstrates Fielding's early partisanship in favor

of Walpole and his opposition to Pope and his circle.
Also see: Battestin, "Fielding's Changing Politics,"
item 638; Coley, "Henry Fielding and the Two Walpoles,"
item 116; and Goldgar, *Walpole and the Wits*, item 190.

1061.   ————. "Some Unpublished Early Verse of Henry Fielding." *New Rambler*, 7 (1969), 2-18.

Fielding attacked Pope in an early, unfinished parody
of *The Dunciad* and in a finished, but unpublished,
epistle. The attacks were stimulated by Pope's attacks on Lady Mary Wortley Montague, Fielding's cousin.

1062.   Hughes, Helen Sard. "A Dialogue—Possibly by Henry
Fielding." *Philological Quarterly*, 1 (1922), 49-55.

Attributes "A Dialogue Between a Beau's Head and His
Heels," published in Watts' *The Musical Miscellany*,
to Henry Fielding rather than the actor Timothy Fielding. Watts had published three of Fielding's plays
in toto and included in the *Musical Miscellany* songs
from each of Fielding's plays, so it is likely that
the "Dialogue," identified only as by "Mr. Fielding,"
was also written by Henry Fielding. Besides, Timothy
Fielding is not known to have written anything whatso-
ever.

*   Roberts, Edgar V. "Henry Fielding and Richard Leveridge: Authorship of 'The Roast Beef of Old England.'"
(See item 368.)

1063.   St. J.S., H.K. "Poem by Fielding." *Notes and Queries*,
Tenth Series, 5 (1906), 446.

Attributes "An Extempore in the Pump-Room, at Bath,"
a short poem in Samuel Rogers' *Poems on Various Occasions* (1782), to Fielding.

*   Sherbo, Arthur. "Fielding and Chaucer—and Smart."
(See item 1096.)

1064.   Shipley, John B. [A Query.] *Book Collector*, 7 (1958),
417.

Seeks copies of a work advertised as "The Coronation.
A Poem. And an Ode on the Birth-day. By Mr. Fielding.
Printed for B. Creake in Jermayn-street; and sold by
J. Roberts near Warwick-lane" (1727). If the poem
should prove to be by Fielding, it would be his ear-
liest published work.

1065. Vincent, Howard P. "Early Poems by Henry Fielding."
       Notes and Queries, 184 (1943), 159-60.

       Prints two early poems which he attributes to Fielding:
       "An Original Song on the *Beggar's Opera*" and "A Dia-
       logue Between a Beau's Head and His Heels."

1066. Wells, John E. "Fielding's First Poem to Walpole and
       His Garret in 1730." *Modern Language Notes*, 29 (1914),
       29-30.

       Notes that there are two versions of Fielding's "Letter
       to Walpole": a sixty verse version published in the
       Miscellanies and a forty-one verse version published
       in Dodsley's 1763 *Collection of Poems*. The longer ver-
       sion is probably the first, with the shorter version
       an emasculation of it. A reference to Fielding's
       garret in the longer version indicates that he lived
       on Picadilly Road in 1730, but later commentators do
       not read the poem so literally.

1067. ————. "Fielding's Signatures in *The Champion* and the
       Date of His 'Of Good Nature.'" *Modern Language Review*,
       7 (1912), 97-8.

       Locates a *Champion* essay (November 27, 1739), signed
       "C," which quotes from Fielding's "Of Good Nature."
       The reference implies that Fielding was the "C" of the
       Champion and that he composed this poem long before it
       appeared in the *Miscellanies*.

                        D. *Address to the Electors*
                           of Great Britain

1068. Cleary, Thomas R. "The Case for Fielding's Authorship
       of *An Address to the Electors of Great Britain* (1740)
       Reopened." *Studies in Bibliography*, 28 (1975), 308-
       18.

       Refers to articles by Jensen, item 1071, and Greason,
       item 1070, which support Fielding's authorship of the
       Address, and to Coley's argument, item 1069, which
       questions it. Cleary, who finds Coley's view uncon-
       vincing, believes that Fielding was, in fact, the auth-
       or because two contemporary writers name him as such
       and because the style closely resembles his. Cleary
       conjectures that possibly Fielding rewrote the *Address*

hurriedly when the original writer failed to complete it on time; this haste would explain the patches of awkward writing.

1069.   Coley, William B. "The Authorship of *An Address to the Electors of Great Britain* (1740)." *Philological Quarterly*, 36 (1957), 488-95.

Disputes the arguments by Jensen, item 1071, and Greason, item 1070, for Fielding's authorship of the *Address*, concluding that neither style nor content proves that he wrote it. Also see Cleary, item 1068.

1070.   Greason, A. LeRoy, Jr. "Fielding's *An Address to the Electors of Great Britain*." *Philological Quarterly*, 33 (1954), 347-52.

Supports Jensen's view (see item 1071) that Fielding wrote the anonymously published *Address*. A large portion of the *Address* appeared in *The Champion*; its content is similar to several of Fielding's signed leaders in the newspaper; the historical approach taken was a popular method with Fielding; and stylistically the pamphlet bears a close resemblance to Fielding's other work. Also see Cleary, item 1068, and Coley, item 1069.

1071.   Jensen, Gerard E. "*An Address to the Electors of Great Britain....* Possibly a Fielding Tract." *Modern Language Notes*, 40 (1925), 57-58.

Identifies Fielding as the author of the *Address* on the basis of style, allusion, and references to Walpole. The forms "hath," "doth," and "shew," among others, are consistent with Fielding's normal practice. Also consistent are the allusions to other authors. In addition, the tract attacks Walpole and uses the "Great Man" appellation, typical of Fielding's political position at this time. See Cleary, item 1068; Coley, item 1069; and Greason, item 1070.

E. *An Attempt Towards a Natural History of the Hanover Rat*

1072.   Jensen, Gerard E. "A Fielding Discovery." *Yale University Library Gazette*, 10 (1935), 23-32.

Attributes to Fielding a pamphlet entitled *An Attempt Towards a Natural History of the Hanover Rat* (London:

Cooper, 1744). Fielding used the term "Hanover rat" twice in *Tom Jones*; many of his idiosyncratic word usages are prevalent; the political ideas are similar to his; and Cooper, who published the tract, published other of his works.

F. *The Champion*

*   Bloom, Edward A. "The Paradox of Samuel Boyse." (See item 788.)

1073.   Coley, William B. "The 'Remarkable Queries' in the *Champion*." *Philological Quarterly*, 41 (1962), 426-36.

Discusses the authorship of the "Remarkable Queries," which began in the October 7, 1740 *Champion* (instead of the June 14 issue as generally believed), and suggests that they may have been written by Ralph, Fielding's partner, and not by Fielding himself.

*   Goldgar, Bertrand A. "Fielding, the *Champion*, and Cibber," in his *Walpole and the Wits*, pp. 189-96. (See item 190.)

1074.   Graham, Walter. "The Date of the *Champion*." *Notes and Queries*, 163 (1932), 150-51.

The last recorded date for the *Champion* is April 3, 1744. No copy of that issue exists, but it is referred to in *The Gentleman's Magazine*, 14 (1744).

1075.   ————. "The Date of the Champion." *Times Literary Supplement* (4 February 1932), p. 76.

A reference in the *Gentleman's Magazine*, Vol. 14, 1744, to an April 3, 1744 issue of the *Champion* proves that the *Champion* was published at least that late.

1076.   Kishler, Thomas C. "Fielding's Experiments with Fiction in the *Champion*." *Journal of Narrative Technique*, 1 (1971), 95-107.

In the *Champion* essays, Fielding creates a fictional circle of editor and character-commentators which he later transports, in form at least, to the novels. His fictional circle allows him to comment ironically on contemporary mores and to expose contemporary foibles.

1077. McCrea, Brian. "Fielding's Role in *The Champion*: A Reminder." *South Atlantic Bulletin*, 42 (1977), 19-24.

The political views that Fielding expresses in *The Opposition* do not represent a complete reversal of the views that he supposedly expresses in *The Champion*. Fielding wrote very few political essays in *The Champion*; he was more columnist than editorialist. What political comments he does make are in the minority of his *Champion* essays.

1078. Sackett, S.J. "Introduction" to *The Voyages of Mr. Job Vinegar from "The Champion" (1740)*. Augustan Reprint Society Publication No. 67. Los Angeles: Clark Memorial Library, 1958. Pp. i-iv.

Perceives the *Voyages* as an imitation of Swift which satirically attacks falsified travel narratives, prudes, and marriages for money instead of love. Many of the subjects treated foreshadow later treatments in the novels. (The argument against debtors' prisons in the *Champion* numbers 108 and 120, for example, is developed further in *Amelia*.) Sackett also discusses Fielding's views of "good breeding," which is satirized in the *Champion*, number 120.

1079. Shipley, John B. "Essays from Fielding's 'Champion.'" *Notes and Queries*, 198 (1953), 468-69.

Discovers seven essays from the *Champion* reprinted in the *York Courant* between December 2, 1740 and April 28, 1741.

1080. ————. "Fielding's *Champion* and a Publisher's Quarrel." *Notes and Queries*, n.s. 2 (1955), 25-28.

Covers the part the *Champion* played, with its articles of March 14 and April 18, 1741, in the debate over the relative merits of the John Torbuck and Richard Chandler volumes of Parliamentary proceedings.

1081. ————. "The 'M' in Fielding's *Champion*." *Notes and Queries*, n.s. 2 (1955), 240-45; 345-51.

Determines, on the basis of style and content, that the *Champion* articles signed with "M" are probably Fielding's.

1082. ————. "A New Fielding Essay from the *Champion*." *Philological Quarterly*, 42 (1963), 417-22.

Argues that an unsigned article in the Dublin *Evening Post* for Tuesday, December 30, 1740, may be a missing Fielding essay from the *Champion*. (No issues of the *Champion* between November 15, 1740, and the first half of 1741 are known to exist.) Shipley presents six parallels between the essay and Fielding's known work to support the probable attribution of the article to Fielding.

1083.   ————. "On the Date of the 'Champion.'" *Notes and Queries*, 198 (1953), 441.

Says that after June 1741, Fielding no longer wrote for the *Champion*.

1084.   Wells, John Edwin. "Fielding's Choice of Signature for 'The Champion.'" *Modern Language Review*, 7 (1912), 374-75.

Offers some possible reasons for Fielding's use of "C" and "L" as "signatures" for his *Champion* essays. He was probably copying Addison, who signed his *Spectator* essays with one of the letters making up "CLIO."

1085.   ————. "*The Champion* and Some Unclaimed Essays by Henry Fielding." *Englische Studien*, 46 (1912-13), 355-66.

Attributes to Fielding those *Champion* essays signed "C" and "L." In addition, several unsigned essays written in Fielding's style and dealing with the same subjects as some of the signed essays may also be attributed to Fielding. He probably did not write any *Champion* papers after June 1741. Also see Shipley, "The 'M' in Fielding's *Champion*," item 1081.

1086.   ————. "Fielding's *Champion* and Captain Hercules Vinegar." *Modern Language Review*, 8 (1913), 165-72.

There was a real Hercules Vinegar, a prizefighter "of considerable notoriety" in the 1740's. Fielding probably chose his name as a satirical gesture.

1087.   ————. "Fielding's *Champion*--More Notes." *Modern Language Notes*, 35 (1920), 18-23.

The publishing difficulties of *The Champion* are reflected in its various name changes--from *The Champion, or British Mercury* to *The Champion, or the Evening Advertiser* to *The British Champion, or the Impartial Advertiser*. Several essays in *The Champion* and other contemporary journals outline Fielding's publishing problems with his paper.

1088. Item deleted.

* ————. "Fielding's Signatures in *The Champion* and the Date of His 'Of Good-Nature.'" (See item 1067.)

1089. Wolfe, George H. "Lessons in Evil: Fielding's Ethics in *The Champion* Essays," in *A Provision of Human Nature: Essays on Fielding and Others in Honor of Miriam Austin Locke*, ed. Donald Kay. University: University of Alabama Press, 1977. Pp. 65–81.

In *The Champion* essays, which began in the fall of 1739, Fielding organized and articulated the ethical system which he later dramatized in his novels. At the core of this system is an emphasis on "good nature," good works instead of faith alone, and benevolence.

G. *Charge to the Jury*

1090. Liljegren, S.B. "Fielding's 'Charge to the Jury,' 1745." *Times Literary Supplement* (4 March 1926), p. 168.

Records the sale on February 15, 1926, of a copy of the *Charge to the Jury*, attributed here to Fielding on the basis of an advertisement in the second edition of Sarah Fielding's *Cleopatra and Octavia* (1758). The pamphlet was part of a long pamphlet war over the death of Walpole, but Fielding used the controversy as an excuse to attack quack physicians.

* Shepperson, Archibald B. "Additions and Corrections to Facts About Fielding." (See item 288.)

H. *The Covent Garden Journal*

* Baker, Ernest A. *History of the English Novel*. (See item 448.)

* Bosker, A. "Henry Fielding. Laurence Sterne." (See item 791.)

1091.   Coley, William B.   "Fielding and the Two *Covent Garden Journals*."   *Modern Language Review*, 57 (1962), 386-87.

Notes that although Fielding had nothing to do with the publication of the 1749 *Covent Garden Journal*, he was accused of publishing it by the hostile journal, *Old England*. It is probable that he took the title of the short-lived publication for his own *Covent Garden Journal* in 1752 as an ironic joke on his enemies at *Old England*.

1092.   Dobson, Austin.   *"The Covent Garden Journal*," in his *Sidewalk Studies*. London: Oxford, 1924. Pp. 63-92. Originally published London: Chatto and Windus, 1902. This article was originally printed in *The National Review*, 37 (1901), 383-96.

A brief history of Fielding's fourth, and last, newspaper, launched in 1752. Dobson focuses on Fielding's attacks on Smollett, his praise of Charlotte Lenox, and his reporting of criminal activity.

1093.   Jensen, Gerard E.   "The Covent Garden Journal Extraordinary."   *Modern Language Notes*, 34 (1919), 57-59.

Locates a copy of the above-named pamphlet in the collection of Fielding materials donated to Yale by F.S. Dickson. The pamphlet attacks Fielding by burlesquing his *Covent Garden Journal*. Several individuals could have written the work, but Jensen conjectures that either Bonnell Thornton or Tobias Smollett wrote it.

1094.   ————.   "Introduction" to *The Covent Garden Journal* by Henry Fielding, Vol. 1. New Haven: Yale University Press, 1915. Pp. 1-129.

Includes sections of the origins of the *Journal*, its general character, the newspaper war of 1751-52, Fielding's style, and texts and editions. The discussion of the newspaper war (pp. 29-98) goes into great detail identifying Fielding's enemies and the reasons for their animosity.

1095.   Rogers, Pat.   "Fielding's Parody of Oldmixon."   *Philological Quarterly*, 49 (1970), 262-66.

In addition to the derogatory references to the historian, John Oldmixon, in *Tom Jones* and the *Covent Garden Journal*, no. 3, Fielding wrote a parody of him in the *Covent Garden Journal*, no. 11, in which he appears as Humphrey Newmixon, an incompetent historian who misinterprets his materials and wilfully misreads texts.

1096. Sherbo, Arthur. "Fielding and Chaucer--and Smart." *Notes and Queries*, n.s. 5 (1958), 441-42.

Presents both external and internal evidence to show that Christopher Smart and not Fielding wrote the poem, "A Pleasant Balade, or Advice to the Fayre Maydens: Written by Dan Jeffry Chaucer," which appeared in the *Covent Garden Journal* of June 23, 1752, and which is ascribed to Fielding by Jensen in his 1915 edition of the *Covent Garden Journal* (item 1094).

I. *The Crisis*

1097. Jensen, Gerard E. "The Crisis: A Sermon." *Modern Language Notes*, 31 (1916), 435-37.

Although Fielding's archaisms appear throughout *The Crisis*, the work lacks his wit and epigrammatic style. There is no conclusive evidence that he wrote the sermon. See Wells, item 1098.

1098. Wells, John E. "Henry Fielding and *The Crisis*." *Modern Language Notes*, 27 (1912), 180-81.

According to some of his contemporaries, Fielding wrote *The Crisis*. It is likely that he did since the subject and form of the address would have appealed to him and since its printers, A. Dodd and Chappelle, had published other pieces of his. See Jensen, previous item.

J. *A Dialogue Between A Gentleman from London ... and an Honest Alderman*

* Bowers, Fredson. "Textual Introduction" to *The Jacobite's Journal*. (See item 1113.)

* Coley, W.B. "General Introduction" to *The Jacobite's Journal*. (See item 1114.)

*   Todd, William B. "Three Notes on Fielding." (See
        item 309.)

                    K. *An Enquiry into the Causes*
                    of the Late Increase of Robbers

*   Amory, Hugh. "Magistrate or Censor? The Problem of
        Authority in Fielding's Later Writings." (See item
        984.)

*   Shepperson, Archibald B. "Additions and Corrections
        to Facts about Fielding." (See item 288.)

1099.   Zirker, Malvin R., Jr. "Fielding and Reform in the
        1750's." *Studies in English Literature*, 7 (1967),
        453-65.

        Analyzes Fielding's two pamphlets, *An Enquiry Into the*
        Causes of the Late Increase of Robbers (1751) and *A*
        Proposal for Making an Effectual Provision for the
        Poor (1753). These works have led to speculation,
        especially by Cross (item 126) and Jones (item 219),
        that Fielding was behind much of the criminal reform
        of the 1750's; actually, Fielding's proposals were
        often at odds with those of the Committee of 1750,
        which instituted the period's major reforms, and he
        was not a major influence on the reform movement.
        Also see Amory, "Henry Fielding and the Criminal
        Legislation of 1751-52," item 73, and Radzinowicz,
        item 267.

1100.   ———. *Fielding's Social Pamphlets: A Study of "An*
        Enquiry into the Causes of the Late Increase of Rob-
        bers" and "A Proposal for Making an Effectual Pro-
        vision for the Poor." English Studies No. 31.
        Berkeley and Los Angeles: University of California
        Press, 1966.

        Provides detailed background material on the condition
        of the poor in the eighteenth century and the various
        projects for their relief. An analysis of Fielding's
        opinions in the *Enquiry* and the *Proposal* shows that he
        uncritically accepted the views of his age in accepting
        the hierarchical social order and in regarding the
        poor as an element in that order "to be used, coerced,
        managed, for the sake of the metaphysical social whole."

Even though these pamphlets deal harshly with the
poor as a class, Fielding treats the individual poor
with sympathy and envisages a moral reform of society.

Reviews: Ronald Paulson, *Journal of English and Germanic Philology*, 67 (1968), 161-65; *Philological Quarterly*, 46 (1967), 346.

L. *Epistles to Walpole*

1101. Amory, Hugh. "Henry Fielding's *Epistles to Walpole*:
A Reexamination." *Philological Quarterly*, 46 (1967),
236-47.

The second of the epistles was actually written in
1743, and not in 1730 as some critics apparently believe, as a response to a libel against Fielding
printed in 1740. See Goldgar, *Walpole and the Wits*,
item 190.

M. *Essay on Conversation*

1102. Miller, Henry Knight. "Benjamin Stillingfleet's
Essay on Conversation, 1737, and Henry Fielding."
Philological Quarterly, 33 (1954), 427-28.

Notes that Stillingfleet's poetic *Essay on Conversation*, because of its title, is often confused with
Fielding's prose "Essay on Conversation," published
in his *Miscellanies* (Vol. I, 1743). Fielding had no
connection with the 1737 poem.

N. *Essay on Nothing*

1103. Miller, Henry Knight. "The Paradoxical Encomium."
Modern Philology, 53 (1956), 145-78.

Defines the "paradoxical encomium" as "praise of un-
worthy or trifling objects" and traces its history
from ancient Greece through eighteenth-century England,
noting Fielding's use of the device in his "Essay on
Nothing," published in the *Miscellanies*.

O. *The Female Husband*

1104.   Baker, Sheridan W.   "Fielding's 'Female Husband': A
        Correction." *Notes and Queries*, n.s. 6 (1959), 404.

        Corrects a mistake in his "Henry Fielding's *The Female
        Husband*," item 1105; Mary Hamilton actually was arres-
        ted on a Saturday, not on a Tuesday.

1105.   ————. "Henry Fielding's *The Female Husband*: Fact
        and Fiction." *Publications of the Modern Language
        Association of America*, 74 (1959), 213-14.

        Argues for Fielding's authorship of *The Female Husband*,
        a 1746 pamphlet on Mary Hamilton, who, disguised as a
        man, married another woman. Mary Price and the widow
        Rusford of *The Female Husband* closely parallel Shamela
        and Mrs. Slipslop respectively both in speech and
        physical appearance. Mary Hamilton's voyage to Dublin
        seems to be a reworking of a scene from *Jonathan Wild*,
        and the anti-Methodist viewpoint of *The Female Husband*
        resembles that given to the Blifil family in *Tom Jones*.
        Fielding has taken a few facts from the Hamilton in-
        cident and turned them into his own fiction, often re-
        working old material to do so.

1106.   "Books in the Sale Rooms." *Bookman's Journal*, 12
        (August 1925), 205.

        Notes the sale at Sotheby's of a previously unknown
        first edition of Fielding's *The Female Husband*.
        Also see item 1107.

1107.   "Books in the Sale Rooms." *Bookman's Journal*, 12
        (September 1925), 245.

        Reports on the appearance and sale of a second copy
        of Fielding's *The Female Husband*. See item 1106.

1108.   de Castro, J. Paul. "Fielding's Pamphlet, 'The Female
        Husband.'" *Notes and Queries*, Twelfth Series, 8 (1921),
        184-85.

        Conjectures that Fielding sat among counsel at the
        trial of the infamous Mary Price, which gave him the
        inspiration for "The Female Husband." See Sheridan
        Baker, "Henry Fielding's *The Female Husband*," item
        1105.

1109. Green, Emanuel. *Bibliotheca Somersetensis*. 3 vols.
Taunton: Barnicutt and Pearce, 1902.

Mentions (II.463-64) *The Surprising Adventures of a
Female Husband* (1813), a racy nineteenth-century version of Fielding's *Female Husband* by J. Bailey.

P. *The History of the Present
Rebellion in Scotland*

1110. Greason, A. LeRoy, Jr. "Fielding's *The History of
the Present Rebellion in Scotland*." *Philological
Quarterly*, 37 (1958), 119-23.

Accepts Fielding's authorship of the pamphlet (see
Jarvis, item 1037) and lists its five printings to
show its popularity.

* Jarvis, R.C. "Fielding and the Forty-Five." (See
item 1037.)

* ————. "Fielding, Dodsley, Marchant, and Ray: Some
Fugitive Histories of the '45." (See item 216.)

1111. Seymour, Mabel. "Fielding's History of the Forty-
Five." *Philological Quarterly*, 14 (1935), 105-25.

Discusses four versions of Fielding's history of the
rebellion of 1745. The first version, the *History of
the Present Rebellion in Scotland* (1745), contains a
good deal of Hanoverian propaganda. This version was
expanded in 1746 under the title, *A Succinct History
of the Rebellion* and appeared in *Museum*. In 1747, an
edited version entitled *A Compleat and Authentick
History* was published by Cooper, and the following
year another version, edited by Richardson, was published as part of Defoe's *A Tour Through the Whole
Islands of Great Britain*. Much of the same material
is contained in Seymour's "Henry Fielding," item 1112.
For a discussion of Fielding's authorship of these
works, see Jarvis, item 1037.

1112. ————. "Henry Fielding." *London Mercury*, 24 (1931),
160.

Notes three versions of Fielding's history of the rebellion of 1745: the four part version in the *Museum*

for March 29, April 12, April 26, and September 13,
1746; the April 1747 pamphlet; and the edited version
in Defoe's *Tour Through the Whole Islands of Great
Britain*. Much of the same material, somewhat expanded,
appears in Seymour's "Fielding's History of the Forty-
Five," item 1111. For doubts about Fielding's authorship of some of these works, see Jarvis, item 1037.

Q. *The Jacobite's Journal*

1113. Bowers, Fredson. "Textual Introduction" to *The Jacob-
ite's Journal and Related Writings* by Henry Fielding.
Middletown, Conn.: Wesleyan University Press, and
Oxford: The Clarendon Press, 1975. Pp. lxxxiii-lxxxix.

Discusses the copy-text and its treatment, the apparatus, and the collation of the three texts included,
which are *A Dialogue Between a Gentleman from London
... and an Honest Alderman of the Country Party*; *A
Proper Answer to a Late Scurrilous Libel*; and *The
Jacobite's Journal*.

1114. Coley, William B. "General Introduction" to *The
Jacobite's Journal and Related Writings* by Henry
Fielding. Middletown, Conn.: Wesleyan University
Press and Oxford: The Clarendon Press, 1975. Pp.
xvii-lxxxii.

Breaks his discussion into four parts: (1) a biographical section on Fielding's activities in 1747-48;
(2) an analysis of *A Dialogue Between a Gentleman of
London ... and an Honest Alderman of the Country
Party*; (3) a discussion of *A Proper Answer to a Late
Scurrilous Libel*; and (4) a long essay on *The Jacobite's Journal*. Throughout, Coley outlines the political events of the 1740's and discusses Fielding's
involvement in them.

*   Hilles, Frederick W. "Fielding Unmodernized." (See
item 860.)

R. *The Journal of a Voyage to Lisbon*

*   Baker, Ernest A. *History of the English Novel.* (See
        item 448.)

1115.   de Castro, J. Paul. "Derham." *Notes and Queries*, 180
        (1941), 123.

        The Mr. Derham to whom Fielding refers in the *Voyage
        to Lisbon* is Rev. William Derham, Rector of Upminster
        and author of *Physics-Theology*.

*   ————. "Fieldingiana." (See item 139.)

1116.   ————. "Henry Fielding's Last Voyage." *Library*,
        Third Series, 8 (1917), 145-59.

        Points out that Fielding had a great deal of experience
        at sea and therefore is accurate in his use of nautical
        terms and descriptions of the ocean. The author goes
        on to side with Dickson ("The Early Editions," item
        1118) against Pollard (items 1128 and 1129) in their
        dispute over the first two editions of the *Journal
        of a Voyage to Lisbon*; de Castro concludes that the
        earlier version (January 1755) of the *Journal* was
        edited by John Fielding, Henry's brother, and that
        the later version (December 1755) is Henry Fielding's
        unedited text. Also see Prideaux, "Fielding's *Jour-
        nal*," item 1130, and St. Swithin, item 1132.

1117.   ————. "Queries from Fielding's *Voyage to Lisbon*."
        Notes and Queries, 179 (1940), 461.

        Responds to A.E.N., item 1126: "wind" was made by
        mixing the juice of thoroughly boiled turnips with
        wild berries and beer and letting the whole ferment.

1118.   Dickson, Frederick S. "The Early Editions of Fielding's
        Voyage to Lisbon." *Library*, Third Series, 8 (1917),
        24-35.

        Covers biographical details of Fielding's trip to
        Lisbon in 1754 and discusses the first two editions
        of *The Journal of a Voyage to Lisbon*. Dickson argues
        that Mrs. Fielding took the manuscript of the *Journal*
        to Andrew Millar, Fielding's publisher, and that Mil-
        lar, in turn, sent the galley proofs to Sir John
        Fielding, Henry's brother, who made "innumerable
        changes" in them. When Millar published a second

edition late in 1755, he ignored Sir John's changes
and printed the work as Fielding had written it.
Also see de Castro, "Henry Fielding's Last Voyage,"
item 1116; Pollard, items 1128 and 1129; Prideaux,
item 1130; and St. Swithin, item 1132.

1119.   ————. "Henry Fielding: Two Corrections." *Notes
and Queries*, Twelfth Series, 2 (1916), 515.

Notes Dobson's correction of the assumed date of
Fielding's arrival in Portugal (see item 165) and
points out that the corrected date confirms the internal chronology of the *Voyage to Lisbon*.

1120.   ————. *An Index to "The Journal of a Voyage to Lisbon"* by Henry Fielding. 1915.

Indexes both editions of 1755 and has sections on persons mentioned, places mentioned, words, "obscurities,"
and bibliography. An unpublished manuscript in the
Library of Congress.

1121.   Dobson, Austin. "Fielding's Voyage to Lisbon," in
his *18th Century Vignettes*, Series 1. London: Chatto
and Windus, 1892. Reprinted London: Oxford University
Press, 1951.

Traces Fielding's fatal illness from its inception
through his journey to Portugal, using extracts from
the *Voyage to Lisbon* to show that although Fielding's
body was racked with pain, his mind remained incisive
and clear throughout the voyage.

*   ————. "Henry Fielding: Two Corrections." (See item
165.)

1122.   Dodds, M.H. "Queries from Fielding's *Voyage to Lisbon*." *Notes and Queries*, 180 (1941), 50.

Responds to A.E.N., "Queries from Fielding's *Voyage
to Lisbon*," item 1126. A lady in "dishabille" wore
her hair uncurled and under a mob cap and was dressed
in a straight gown sans hoops and stays.

*   Humphreys, A.R. "Introduction" to *"Jonathan Wild the
Great" and "The Journal of a Voyage to Lisbon."* (See
item 740.)

1123.   Itzkowitz, Martin E. "A Fielding Echo in 'She Stoops
to Conquer.'" *Notes and Queries*, n.s. 20 (1973), 22.

A reference to bad inns in Act II of *She Stoops to Conquer* closely parallels a statement by Fielding in his *Voyage to Lisbon*.

*   Lynch, James J. "Evil Communications." (See item 888.)

1124.   M., E.F. "Queries from Fielding's *Voyage to Lisbon*." *Notes and Queries*, 180 (1941), 269.

Responds to A.E.N., item 1126. "Cornaro's Case" may refer to the Venetian centenarian Luigi Cornaro.

*   McCusher, H. "First Editions of Fielding." (See item 1006.)

1125.   Maynadier, G.H. "Introduction" to *"A Journey from this World to the Next" and "A Voyage to Lisbon"* by Henry Fielding. Cambridge, Mass.: Harvard University Press, 1903. Pp. xiii-xxii.

Surveys Fielding's minor works in the most general terms, concluding that the *Voyage to Lisbon* is by far the best of them. Not only is it stylistically superior, ranking next to his three great novels, but it vividly presents a picture of the age and of Fielding the family man.

1126.   N., A.E. "Queries from Fielding's *Voyage to Lisbon*." *Notes and Queries*, 179 (1940), 407.

Requests information about the superstition that said a drowned cat brought favorable wind; the drink, "wind"; what constituted "dishabille"; the story of Cornaro's Case; and the activities of Swiss seamen. For responses, see the following (all under the above title): de Castro, item 1117; Dodds, item 1122; and E.F.M., item 1124.

1127.   Pagliaro, Harold. "Editor's Introduction" to *The Journal of a Voyage to Lisbon* by Henry Fielding. New York: Nardon Press, 1963.

Explains Fielding's ethical and artistic principles by exploring his negative reaction to Cibber, Walpole, and Richardson, all three of whom misled the public in various ways. Fielding's preoccupation with appraising motives led him to reject Cibber's intellectual phoniness, Walpole's expedient political maneuverings, and Richardson's uncritical acceptance of Pamela's

false morality. Fielding's commitment to his principles is no where better seen than in the *Journal*.

1128.   Pollard, Alfred W. "The Two 1755 Editions of Fielding's *Journal of a Voyage to Lisbon*." *Library*, Third
Series, 8 (1917), 75-77.

Disagrees with Dickson's conclusion (see "The Early
Editions," item 1118) that the first edition of the
Journal is "brother John's version." Watermarks and
typography show that the January 1755 edition is
Henry's version and that the December 1755 version is
John's. (Pollard later admits that he erred in his
conclusion--see item 1129.) Also see de Castro,
"Henry Fielding's Last Voyage," item 1116; Prideaux,
item 1130; and St. Swithin, item 1132.

1129.   ———. "The Two 1755 Editions of Fielding's *Journal
of a Voyage to Lisbon*." *Library*, Third Series, 8
(1917), 160-63.

Admits his error (see item 1128) in regarding the
first edition of the *Journal* as Henry Fielding's and
the second as John Fielding's. Also see de Castro,
"Henry Fielding's Last Voyage," item 1116; Dickson,
"The Early Editions," item 1118; Prideaux, item 1130;
and St. Swithin, item 1132.

1130.   Prideaux, W.F. "Fielding's *Journal of a Voyage to
Lisbon*, 1755." *Notes and Queries*, Tenth Series, 6
(1906), 61-2.

Of the two editions of the *Voyage*, the shorter, larger
type edition is the first, while the longer version
is the second. Also see de Castro, "Henry Fielding's
Last Voyage," item 1116; Dickson, "The Early Editions,"
item 1118; and Pollard, items 1128 and 1129.

1131.   Rosenberg, Sondra. "Travel Literature and the Picaresque Novel." *Enlightenment Essays*, 2 (1971), 40-47.

Finds in Fielding's *Voyage to Lisbon* much satire of
contemporary travel literature, most of which Fielding
thought worthless. An example of this satire is the
seemingly irrelevant detail, which is, in fact, a
burlesque of the over-detailed writing of the lesser
travel writers.

1132.   St. Swithin. "Fielding's *Journal of a Voyage to Lisbon*, 1755." *Notes and Queries*, Tenth Series, 6 (1906),
115.

Notes that another, shorter version of *Voyage* was published in 1756. There is a lengthy, involved discussion of the early editions of the *Voyage* under various
titles. See the following: de Castro, item 1116;
Dickson, item 1118; Pollard, items 1128 and 1129; and
Prideaux, item 1130.

*   Wallace, Robert M. "Fielding Manuscripts." (See item
316.)

S. *A Journey from This World to the Next*

1133.   Dickson, Frederick S. *An Index to "A Journey from
This World to the Next"* by Henry Fielding. 1911.

An unpublished manuscript in the Library of Congress
identifying persons referred to in the *Journey*.

*   Esdaile, Katharine A. "Fielding's Danish Translator."
(See item 666.)

*   Hill, Rowland M. *"Jonathan Wild."* (See item 737.)

*   Maynadier, G.H. "Introduction" to *"A Journey from
this World to the Next" and "A Voyage to Lisbon."*
(See item 1125.)

1134.   Olshin, Toby A. "Form and Theme in Novels About
Non-Human Characters, a Neglected Sub-Genre." *Genre*,
2 (1969), 43-56.

Fielding's *A Journey from This World to the Next* belongs to a neglected sub-genre composed of novels
written by or about non-human characters with the in-
tention of commenting on human fallibility in a wide
range of circumstances. The common element of all
these books is the religious or moral commentary of
the narrator.

1135.   Rawson, C.J. "Introduction" to *A Journey from This
World to the Next* by Henry Fielding. London: Dent and
New York: Dutton, 1973.

The breaks in the manuscript of the *Journey* are crude
enough that it is probable Fielding had not finished
the work and was trying to disguise that fact by
adopting the familiar device of the incomplete manu-

script, often used by contemporary authors for verisimilitude. The *Journey*, which serves as a forerunner to the great later novels, contains much of
Fielding's moral philosophy, often couched in crude
irony.

1136. Robertson, Olivia. "Fielding as Satirist." *Contemporary Review*, 181 (1952), 120-24.

A Journey from this World to the Next is a satire
which, in its complexity, is worthy of Swift.

T. *The Opposition: A Vision*

*   Battestin, Martin C. "Fielding's Changing Politics
and *Joseph Andrews*." (See item 638.)

U. *A Proper Answer to a Late Scurrilous Libel*

*   Bowers, Fredson. "Textual Introduction" to *The Jacobite's Journal*. (See item 1113.)

*   Coley, W.B. "General Introduction" to *The Jacobite's
Journal*. (See item 1114.)

V. *A Proposal for Making an Effectual Provision for the Poor*

1137. Dircks, Richard J. "Some Notes on Fielding's *Proposal
for the Poor*." *Notes and Queries*, n.s. 9 (1962),
457-59.

Makes four observations on Fielding's *A Proposal for
Making an Effectual Provision for the Poor*: (1) Thomas
Gibson, a painter, drew up the plans for the buildings
suggested in the *Proposal*; (2) the plan was prepared
for presentation to the legislature in the form of a
law; (3) the "two learned persons" referred to as being
involved in poor-law reform are the Earl of Hills-

borough and Richard Lloyd; and (4) no accurate, scholarly edition of the *Proposal* exists.

* Zirker, Malvin R., Jr. "Fielding and Reform in the 1750's." (See item 1099.)

* ————. *Fielding's Social Pamphlets: A Study of "An Enquiry into the Causes of the Late Increase of Robbers" and "A Proposal for Making an Effectual Provision for the Poor."* (See item 1100.)

W. *Some Papers Proper to be Read Before the Royal Society*

1138. Miller, Henry Knight. "Henry Fielding's Satire on the Royal Society." *Studies in Philology*, 57 (1960), 72–86.

The "virtuosi" of the Royal Society were the victims of several satiric attacks by Fielding because, as a humanist, he distrusted what they stood for. One of these attacks, "Some Papers Proper to be Read before the Royal Society," is analyzed in this essay.

X. *The True Patriot*

1139. Jones, Claude. "Fielding's *True Patriot* and the Henderson Murder." *Modern Language Review*, 52 (1957), 498–503.

Fielding takes a rather sordid murder case and uses it as a text for an ironic sermon on the value of honesty to the poor.

Y. *The True State of Bosavern Penlez*

* Shepperson, Archibald B. "Additions and Corrections to Facts about Fielding." (See item 288.)

Z. *The Voyages of Mr. Job Vinegar*
See under *The Champion*.

VII

FOREIGN-LANGUAGE MATERIALS

1140. Alain, M. "En lisant Fielding." *La nouvelle revue française*, 52 (1939), 484-91.

1141. Appel, E. *Henry Fielding als Kritiker der englischen Literatur*. Dissertation. Breslau, 1922.

1142. Bachrach, A.G.H. "Eeen Leids Oud-Alumnus onder de Engelse Klassieken." *De Nieuwe Stern* (Arnheim), February 1957, pp. 84-95; March 1957, pp. 154-62.

1143. Becker, Gustav. "Die Bedeutung des Wortes *romantic* bei Fielding und Smollett," *Archiv für das studium der neueren Sprachen und Literaturen*, 110 (1903), 56-66.

1144. ———. "Der Einfluss des Don Quijote auf Fielding," in his *Die Aufnahme des Don Quijote in die englische Literatur, 1605-c.1770*. Berlin [Palaestra 13], 1906. Pp. 122-57.

1145. Berger, T.W. "Der Einfluss des Don Quixote auf Fieldings Roman," in his *Don Quixote in Deutschland und sein Einfluss auf den deutschen Roman, 1613-1800*. Heidelberg, 1908.

1146. Billi, Mirella Mancioli. *Strutture narrative nee roman 30 di Henry Fielding*. Milan: Bompiani, 1974.

1147. Binz-Winiger, Elisabeth. *Erziehungsfragen in den Romanen von Richardson, Fielding, Smollett, Goldsmith, und Sterne*. Weida: Druck von Thomas und Herbert, 1926.

1148. Birkner, Gerd. "Zum Verhältnis von äesthetischer Norm und Funktion in Fieldings *Tom Jones* und *Joseph Andrews*." *Anglia*, 95 (1977), 359-78.

1149. Böckmann, Paul, ed. *Stil und Formprobleme in der
       Literatur*. Vorträge des VII. Kongresses der Inter-
       nationalen Vereinigung fur moderne Sprachen und
       Literaturen in Heidelburg. Heidelberg: Carl Winter,
       1959.

       Includes James L. Lynch's "Structural Techniques in
       Tom Jones," item 889.

1150. Borinski, Ludwig. *Der englische Roman des 18. Jahr-
       hunderts*. Frankfort, 1968.

1151. Bosdorf, Erich. *Entstehungsgeschichte von Fieldings
       Joseph Andrews*. Weimar, 1908.

1152. Broich, Ulrich. "Fieldings *Shamela* und *Pamela or, The
       Fair Imposter*. Zwei Parodien von Richardsons *Pamela*."
       Anglia, 82 (1964), 172-90.

1153. Bruhn, Ernst. *Fieldings Gesellschafts- und Staats-
       auffassung*. Hamburg, 1940.

1154. Buck, Gerhard. "'Written in Imitation of the Manner
       of Cervantes.'" *Germanisch-romanische Monatsschrift*,
       29 (1941), 53-61.

1155. Caliumi, Grazia. *Il Romanzo di Henry Fielding*. Milan:
       Istituto Editoriale Cisalpino, 1959.

1156. Carrière, Martine. "Fielding dramaturge se veut-il
       moraliste?" *Caliban*, 3 (1967), 21-28.

1157. Cazenave, Michel. "A Propos de *Tom Jones*." *La
       Nouvelle Revue Française*, 12 (1964), 891-94.

       Reprinted in Iser, item 507.

1158. Cobb, Lillian. *Pierre-Antoine de la Place: sa vie et
       son oeuvre*. Paris: Boccard, 1928.

       Deals with Fielding's French translator.

1159. De Stasio, Clothilde. *Henry Fielding e il Giornalismo*.
       Bari: Adriatica, 1970.

1160. Deinhardt, M. "Beziehungen der Philosophie auf die
       Romane Fieldings," in her *Beziehungen der Philosophie
       zu dem grossen englischen Roman des achtzehnten
       Jahrhunderts*. Hamburg, 1925.

1161. Deppe, Wolfgang G. *History Versus Romance. Ein Beitrag zur Entwicklungsgeschichte und zum Verständnis der Literaturtheorie Henry Fieldings.* Münster: Aschendorf, 1965.

Review: Natascha Würzbach, *Die neueren Sprachen*, 67 (1967), 299-300.

1162. Dibelius, W. *Englische Romankunst. Die Technik des englischen Romans in achtzehnten und zu Anfang des neunzehnten Jahrhunderts.* 2 Vols. Berlin: Mayer and Müller, 1910. Published in shorter form in *Palaestra*, 92 (1911), 85-155, under the title "Englische Romankunst."

Review: J. Tieje, *Journal of English and Germanic Philology*, 11 (1912), 626-31.

1163. Digeon, Aurélien. "Autour de Fielding." *Revue germanique*, 11 (1920), 209-19; 353-62.

1164. ———. "La condemnation de *Tom Jones* à Paris." *Revue Anglo-Américaine*, 4 (1927), 529-31.

For a discussion on this subject, see B.P. Jones, item 871, and E.P. Shaw, item 952.

1165. ———. "Fielding a-t-il écrit le dernier Châpitre de *A Journey from This World Into the Next*?" *Revue Anglo-Américaine*, 8 (1931), 428-30.

1166. ———. "Une recente Biographie de Fielding." *Études anglaises*, 7 (1954), 402-04.

Reviews Dudden, item 171.

1167. ———. *Les Romans de Fielding.* Paris: Librairie Hachette, 1923.

Translated as *The Novels of Fielding.* London: Routledge and Kegan Paul, 1925. See item 474.

Reviews: F.T. Blanchard, *University of California Chronicles*, 28 (1926), 105-07; S.B. Liljegren, *Litteris*, 3 (1926), 103-04.

1168. ———. *Le Texte des Romans de Fielding: étude critique.* Paris: Librairie Hachette, 1923.

1169. Dolder, Ernst. *Henry Fieldings "Don Quixote in England."* Bern: Buchdruckerei Gebr. Leemann, 1907.

1170.   Düber, Rudolf. *Beiträge zu Henry Fieldings Roman-
        technik*. Halle: Kaemmerer, 1910.

1171.   Ducrocq, Jean. *Le Théâtre de Fielding: 1728-1737 et
        ses prolongements dans l'oeuvre romanesque*. Études
        Anglaises 55. Paris: Didier, 1975.

1172.   Dupas, Jean-Claude. *"Joseph Andrews*: L'Excentricité
        d'un discours carnavalisé," in *L'Excentricité en
        Grand-Bretagne au 18e siècle*, ed. Michèle Plaisant.
        Lille: Université de Lille, 1976. Pp. 59-82.

1173.   Elistratova, Anna. ["Fielding."] *Soviet Literature*,
        October 1954.

1174.   ———. ["Fielding's Realism,"] in *Iz Istorii Anglis-
        kogo Realizma*. Moscow, 1941.

1175.   Erämetsä, Erik. "Über den englischen Einfluss auf den
        deutschen Wortvorrat des 18. Jahrhunderts." *Neu-
        philologische Mitteilungen*, 59 (1958), 34-40.

1176.   Erzgräber, Willi. "Das Menschenbild in Henry Fieldings
        Roman *Amelia*." *Die neueren Sprachen*, 3 (1957), 105-16.

        Reprinted in *Henry Fielding und der Englische Roman
        des 18. Jahrhunderts*, ed. Wolfgang Iser. Darmstadt:
        Wissenschaftliche Buchgesellschaft, 1972. Pp. 145-61.

1177.   Ewald, Eugen. *Abbild und Wunschbild der Gesellschaft
        bei Richardson und Fielding*. Wuppertal, 1935.

1178.   Fernandez-Alvarez, J. "Un probable eco de Henry
        Fielding in La Fe de Armando Palacio Valdés." *Filo-
        logía moderna* (Madrid), Nos. 33-34, 101-08.

1179.   Fischer, Hildegard. *Das subjektiv Element in den
        Romanen Fieldings*. Ohlau: Eschenhagen, 1933.

1180.   Foltinek, Herbert. *Fieldings "Tom Jones" und das
        österreichische Drama*. Wien: Verlag der Wissen-
        schaften, 1976.

1181.   Fornelli, Guido. *Enrico Fielding e la sua epoca*.
        Pisa: Artigrafiche Pacini-Mariotti, 1928.

1182.   Frey, Bernhard. *Shaftesbury und Henry Fielding*.
        Bern, 1963. Originally published Bern, 1952.

1183. Fröhlich, R. Armin. *Fieldings Humor in seinen Romanen.* Leipzig: Druck von Robert Noske, 1918.

1184. Gide, André. *Oeuvres complètes.* Paris: La Nouvelle Revue Française, Librairie Gallimard, 1937.

See Gide, "Notes for a Preface to Fielding's *Tom Jones*," item 846.

1185. Glättli, W. *Die Behandlung des Affekts der Furcht im englischen Roman des 18. Jahrhunderts.* Zurich, 1949.

1186. Greiner, Walter F. *Studien zur Entstehung der englischen Romantheorie an der Wende zum 18. Jahrhundert.* Tübingen: Niemeyer, 1969.

1187. Haage, Richard. "Charakterzeichnung und Komposition in Fieldings *Tom Jones* in ihrer Beziehung zum Drama." *Britannica*, 13 (1936), 119-70.

1188. Habel, Ursula. *Die Nachwirkung des picaresken Romans in England, von Nash bis Fielding und Smollett.* Breslau: Priebatsch, 1930.

1189. Harris, Kathleen. *Beiträge zur Wirkung Fieldings in Deutschland (1742-92).* Göttingen, 1960.

1190. Haslinger, Adolf. "Die Funktion des Stadt-Land-Themas in Henry Fieldings *Tom Jones* und *Joseph Andrews*." *Die neueren Sprachen*, 14 (1965), 101-09.

1191. Homann, Wilhelm. *Henry Fielding als Humorist.* Marburg, 1900.

1192. Hornát, Jaroslav. "Pamela, Shamela, und Joseph Andrews." *Časopis pro Moderni Filologii*, 41 (1959), n.p.

1193. Hunter, Alfred C. "Les Opinions du Baron Grimm sur le Roman Anglais." *Revue de Littérature Comparée*, 12 (1932), 390-400.

1194. Imbert, Henri-François. "Stendhal et *Tom Jones*." *Revue de Littérature Comparée*, 30 (1956), 351-70.

1195. Iser, Wolfgang, ed. *Henry Fielding und der englische Roman des 18. Jahrhunderts.* Darmstadt: Wissenschaftliche Buchgesellschaft, 1972.

Contains essays in English, French, and German. For
complete table of contents, see item 507.

1196. ———. "Die Leserrolle in Fieldings *Joseph Andrews*
und *Tom Jones*," in *Henry Fielding und der englische
Roman des 18. Jahrhunderts*, ed. Wolfgang Iser. Darmstadt: Wissenschaftliche Buchgesellschaft, 1972. Pp.
282–318.

1197. ———. *Die Weltanschauung Henry Fieldings*. Tübingen:
Max Niemeyer, 1952.

Reviews: E.A.J. Honigmann, *Modern Language Review*, 49
(1954), 114; J.M.S. Tompkins, *Review of English Studies*,
n.s. 5 (1954), 302–05.

1198. Itkina, N.L. "Fil'ding i Sterne." *Moskovskii
gosudarstvennyi pedagogicheskii institut imeni Lenina*
(Moscow), 180 (1967), 140–54.

1199. Joesten, Maria. *Die Philosophie Fieldings*. Leipzig:
Bernard Tauchnitz, 1932.

Review: *Philological Quarterly*, 12 (1933), 116.

1200. Kayser, Wolfgang. *Die Entstehung und Krise der
modernen Romans*. Stuttgart, 1955.

Touches on Cervantes and Fielding (see pp. 16ff).

1201. Kluge, Walter. *Die Szene als Bauelment des Erzählers
im englischen Roman des achtzehnten Jahrhunderts*.
Munich, 1966.

Discusses the function of scene in Fielding and other
major eighteenth-century English novelists.

1202. Köhler, Friedrich. *Fieldings Wochenschrift "The
Champion" und das englische Leben der Zeit*. Munster,
1928.

1203. Koljevic, S. "Fildingov Tom Dzons i ljubavna etika
evropskog romana." *Izraz* (Sarajevo), 10 (1966).

1204. Krawschak, Regina. *Sprachstil und Charakter im Roman-
werk Henry Fieldings*. Berlin: Freie Universität,
1965.

1205. Krieg, Hans K.W. *J.J. Chr. Bode als Übersetzer des
Tom Jones von H. Fielding*. Greifswald, 1909.

On one of Fielding's translators.

1206. Lange, Victor. "Erzählformen im Roman des achtzehnten
       Jahrhunderts." *Anglia*, 76 (1958), 129-44.

       Reprinted in *Henry Fielding und der englische Roman
       des 18. Jahrhunderts*, ed. Wolfgang Iser. Darmstadt:
       Wissenschaftliche Buchgesellschaft, 1972. Pp. 474-
       90. (See item 507.)

1207. Leimbach, Burkard, and Karl H. Loschen. "Fieldings
       Tom Jones: Bürger und Aristokrat: Sozialethik als
       Indikator sozialgeschichtlicher Widersprüche." *Abhand-
       lungen zun Kunst-, Musik- und Literaturwissenschaft 154*.
       Bonn: Bouvier, 1974.

1208. Levidora, I.M. *[Fielding: A Bio-bibliographical Guide
       in Honour of the 250th Anniversary of his Birth.]*
       Moscow, 1957.

       Listed by Battestin in *The New Cambridge Bibliography
       of English Literature*.

1209. Lubbers, Klaus. "Aufgaben und Möglichkeiten der
       Rezeptionsforschung." *Germanisch-Romanische Monats-
       schrift*, 14 (1964), 292-302.

1210. Lücker, Heinz. *Die Verwendung der Mundart im englischen
       Roman des 18. Jahrhunderts*. Darmstadt: K.F. Bender,
       1915.

1211. Mandelkow, Karl Robert. "Der Deutsche Briefroman zum
       Problem der Polyperspektive im Epischen." *Neophilolo-
       gus*, 44 (1960), 200-08.

1212. Marion, Denis. "Lectures in actuelles: Tom Jones."
       Europe, 50 (1939), 665-69.

1213. Mathesius, V. *Henry Fielding a jeho dílo. Příběh
       malezencův*. Prague, 1932.

       An appendix to a new Czech translation of *Tom Jones*
       (English translated as "Henry Fielding and His Work").

1214. Mazza, A. "Coincidenze." *Vita e Pensiero*, Jan. 1965.

       On *I Promessi Sposi* and *Tom Jones*.

1215. Michon, Jacques. "Du *Beggar's Opera* au *Grub Street
       Opera*." *Études anglaises*, 24 (1971), 166-70.

1216.   Mitani, Norio. "The Narrator in *Tom Jones*." *Studies in English Literature* (English Literary Society of Japan), 49 (1973), 185-98.

Although the title is in English, this article is in Japanese.

1217.   "Numéro special pour le 200ᵉ anniversaire de la mort d'Henry Fielding." *Les Lettres françaises*, No. 536 (30 Sept. au 7 Octobre 1954).

Review: Charles B. Woods, *Philological Quarterly*, 34 (1955), 288.

1218.   Oesterreich, Helga. *Das Gesprach im Roman: Untersucht im Werke von Defoe, Fielding und Jane Austen*. Münster, 1964.

1219.   Ohnsorg, R. *John Lacys "Dumb Lady," Mrs. Centlivres "Love's Contrivance" und Henry Fieldings "Mock Doctor" in ihrem Verhältnis zu einander und zu ihrer gemein-schaftlichen Quellen*. Hamburg, 1900.

1220.   Orf, Rolf-Jürgen. *Die Rezeption Henry Fieldings in Frankreich 1744-1812 und ihre Auswirkung*. Inaugural Dissertation zur Erlangung der Doktorwürde der Philosophischen Fakultäten der Albert-Ludwigs-Univer-sität zu Freiburg i. Br. Baienfurt, 1974.

1221.   Oschinsky, Hugo. *Gesellschaftliche Zustände Englands während der ersten Hälfte des 18. Jahrhunderts im spiegel Fieldingscher Komodien....* Berlin: R. Gaertner, 1902.

1222.   Pálffy, István. "Fielding és a XVIII. század angol színpadi paródiái." *Kwartalnik Neofilologiczny* (Warsaw), 22 (1976), 47-55.

1223.   Papetti, Viola. "Amor sacro e amor profano in alcuni romanzi settecenteschi." *English Miscellany*, 24 (1973-74), 105-27.

1224.   Parfitt, G.E. *L'Influence française dans les Oeuvres de Fielding et dans le théâtre anglais contemporain de ses Comédies*. Paris: Presses universitaires, 1928.

1225.   Pastalosky, Rosa. *Henry Fielding y la tradición picaresca*. Buenos Aires: Solar, 1970.

1226. Philippide, Al. "Un strămos al romanului modern," in *Consideratti confortabile*. Bucureşti: Editura Eminescu, 2. Pp. 130-35.

1227. Pons, Émile. "Fielding, Swift, et Cervantes." *Studia Neophilologica*, 15 (1943), 305-33.

1228. Pracht, Erwin. "Bittere Enttäuschung und erschütterer Optimismus in Fieldings Spätwerk?" *Zeitschrift für Anglistik und Amerikanistik*, 7 (1959), 288-93.

1229. ————. *Die Gnoseologischen Grundlagen der Romantheorie Fieldings*. Berlin, 1957.

1230. ————. "Henry Fielding zu Fragen der Romantheorie." *Zeitschrift für Anglistik und Amerikanistik*, 3 (1955), 152-74.

1231. ————. "Probleme der Entstehung des Romans." *Zeitschrift für Anglistik und Amerikanistik*, 6 (1958), 283-96.

1232. Praz, Mario. "Hogarth e Fielding," in his *La Casa della Fama*. Milan, 1952.

1233. Prinsen, J. *De Roman in de 18e Eeuw in West Europa*. Groningen, 1925.

1234. Radnoti, Sándor. "Walpole-ok és Jonathan Wildok. Jegyzet a XVIII. századi angol ivodalom egy tipikus motivumához." *Filológiai Közlöny*, 15 (1969), 13-23.

1235. Radtke, Bruno. *Henry Fielding als Kritiker*. Leipzig: Mayer and Müller, 1926.

  Review: F.B.K., *Philological Quarterly*, 6 (1927), 180.

1236. Raynard, Martine. "Fielding et l'unité dramatique de *The Historical Register for the Year 1736*." *Caliban*, 8 (1972), 41-53.

1237. Reiter, Hildegard. *William Hogarth und die Literatur seiner Zeit*. Breslau, 1930.

1238. Robert, Frédéric. "*Tom Jones*. De Fielding à Philidor." In *Roman et Lumières au XVIIIe siècle. Colloque* (Centre d'Études et de Recherches Marxistes ...). Paris: Éditions Sociales, 1970. Pp. 360-65.

  Discusses Philidor's lyric comedy, *Tom Jones* (1765).

1239. Rojhan-Deyk, Barbara. *Henry Fielding: Untersuchungen zu Wesen und Funktion der Ironie in seiner frühen Prosa.* Nürnberg: Hans Carl, 1973.

1240. Rolle, Dietrich. *Fielding und Sterne: Untersuchungen über die Funktion des Erzählers.* Münster: Aschendorff, 1963.

1241. Ronte, Heinz. *Richardson und Fielding: Geschichte ihres Ruhms.* Leipzig: B. Tauchnitz, 1935.

   Reviews: Paul Goetsche, *Die neueren Sprachen* (1964), 254–55; George J. Worth, *Journal of English and Germanic Philology*, 64 (1965), 176–77.

1242. Sandmann, Manfred. "La Source Anglaise de *Candide* (I et II)." *Zeitschrift für Französische Sprache und Literatur*, 83 (1973), 255–59.

1243. Schacht, H.R. *Der gute Pfarrer in der englischen Literatur bis zu Goldsmiths "Vicar of Wakefield."* Berlin, 1904.

   Treats *Joseph Andrews* and *Amelia.*

1244. Schmidt, Karl Ernst. *Vorstudien zu einer Geschichte des Komischen Epos.* Halle (Saale): Max Niemeyer, 1953.

   Reviews: Anglia, 72 (1955), 493–95; *Modern Language Review*, 49 (1954), 385.

1245. Schmidt-Hidding, Wolfgang. *Sieben Meister des literarischen Humors in England und Amerika.* Heidelberg: Quelle und Meyer, 1959.

   Reviews: Martin Dolch, *Die neueren Sprachen*, 9 (1960), 100–02; Werner Habicht, *Anglia*, 78 (1960), 119–20.

1246. Schönzler, Heinrich. *Fieldings Verhältnis zu Le Sage und zu anderen Quellen.* Weimar: Wagner, 1915.

1247. Schröer, M.M.A. *Grundzüge und Hampttypen du Englischen Literatur-geschichte.* Berlin, 1922.

1248. Schumann, H. "Die Darstellung der gesellschaftlichen Wirklichkeit in Fieldings *Tom Jones*." *Zeitschrift für Anglistik und Amerikanistik*, 2 (1954), 42–65.

1249. Sokolyanskii, M.G. "Istorizm Fildinga: na Materiale 'Komicheskikh Epopei." *Nauchnye doklady vysshei shkoly*, 1 (1974), 34–42.

1250. ————. "Tvorčestvo Henri Fildinga: Kniga očerkov."
Kiev: IzD Kievskogo University, n.d.

1251. Solomon, Petre. *"Introduction" to Tom Jones. Poesta
unui copel gǒsit.* Bucureşti: Editura pentru litera-
turǎ, 1969.

1252. Stanzel, Franz. *"Tom Jones* und *Tristram Shandy:* Ein
Vergleich als Vorstudie zu einer Typologie des Romans."
English Miscellany, 5 (1954), 107-48.

Reprinted in Iser, item 507.

1253. ————. *Die typischen Erzählungssituationen im Roman.*
Vienna: Wilhelm Braumuller, 1971. Translated as
Narrative Situations in the Novel, item 958.

Review: B.Q. Morgan, *Comparative Literature*, 8 (1956),
251-62.

1254. Stapfer, Paul. *Humour et humoristes.* Paris: Fisch-
backer, 1911.

The first chapter treats Fielding.

1255. "Stendahl. Notes sur Son Exemplaire de *Tom Jones*, de
Fielding." *Litteratura*, April 1937.

1256. Studt, Annelise. "Fieldings Charakterromane."
Britannica, 13 (1936), 101-18.

1257. Suerbaum, Ulrich. "Das Gasthaus zu Upton: zur Struktur
von Fieldings *Tom Jones*," in *Festschrift für Edgar
Mertner*, eds. Bernhard Fabian and Ulrich Suerbaum.
Munich: Fink, 1969. Pp. 213-30.

1258. Takács, Ferenc. *Fielding Világa.* Budapest: Európa,
1974.

1259. Thomas, P.K. *Die literarische Verkörperung des
philanthropischen Zuges in der englischen Aufklärung.*
Breslau, 1929.

Touches on the relationship between Shaftesbury, the
Spectator, and Fielding, on natural goodness and practical philanthropy.

1260. Thomsen, Ejnar. *Studier i Fieldings Romaner.* Copen-
hagen, 1930.

1261. Waldschmidt, Carl. *Die Dramatisierungen von Fieldings
"Tom Jones."* Wetzlar: K. Waldschmidt, 1906.

1262. Weide, Erwin. *Henry Fieldings Komödien und die
       Restaurationskomödie.* Hamburg: Joachim Heitmann & Co.,
       1947.

1263. Weisgerber, Jean. "Nouvelle lecture d'un livre ancien:
       L'Espace dans l'Histoire de Tom Jones, enfant trouvé."
       Cahiers Roumains d'Études Littéraires, (1975), 69–86.

1264. Wicklein, E. *Das 'Ernsthafte' in dem englischen
       Komischen Roman des XVIII Jahrhunderts.* Dresden, 1908.

1265. Wolff, Erwin. "Fielding, Tom Jones," in *Der englische
       Roman,* ed. Franz Stanzel. Düsseldorf, 1969.

1266. ————. *Shaftesbury und seine Bedeutung für die
       englische Literatur des 18. Jahrhunderts: Der Moralist
       und die literarische Form.* Tübingen: Max Niemeyer,
       1960.

       See pp. 217–19 for comments on Fielding.

1267. Wolff, Max Ludwig. *Geschichte der Romantheorie.*
       Nuremberg, 1915.

1268. Zeller, Hildegard. *Die Ich-Erzählung im englischen
       Roman.* Breslau: Priebatsch, 1933.

       Says that Fielding displaced, as the leading form in
       English novels, the first-person narrative technique.

1269. Zimmermann, Heinz. "Henry Fielding: *The Tragedy of
       Tragedies.*" *Das englische Drama im 18. und 19. Jahr-
       hundert: Interpretationen.* Ed. Heinz Kosok. Berlin:
       Schmidt, 1975.

VIII

DISSERTATIONS

1270.   Allen, Louis David. "Prose Fiction as Symbolic Form."
        DAI, 36 (1976), 8029A-30A (University of Nebraska,
        1975).

1271.   Amory, Hugh. "Law and the Structure of Fielding's
        Novels." *DA*, 27 (1966), 451A-52A (Columbia University,
        1964).

1272.   Ashmore, Charles DeLoach. "Henry Fielding's 'Art of
        Life': A Study in the Ethics of the Novel." *DA*, 19
        (1959), 2610 (Emory University, 1958).

1273.   Bailey, Vern Dixon. "Fielding's Politics." *DAI*, 31
        (1971), 6588A (University of California, Berkeley,
        1970).

1274.   Baker, Myra M. "Satiric Characterizations in the
        Novels of Henry Fielding." *DA*, 27 (1967), 3033A-34A
        (Alabama State University, 1966).

1275.   Baker, Sheridan. "Setting, Character, and Situation
        in the Plays and Novels by Henry Fielding." Univer-
        sity of California, Berkeley, 1950.

1276.   Bassein, Beth Ann (Croskey). "Crime and Punishment
        in the Novels of Defoe, Fielding, and Godwin." *DA*,
        22 (1962), 2783 (University of Missouri, 1961).

1277.   Battestin, Martin C. "Fielding's *Joseph Andrews*:
        Studies Towards a Critical and Textual Edition." *DA*,
        19 (1959), 2080 (Princeton University, 1958).

1278.   Beasley, Jerry Carr. "The Minor Fiction of the 1740's:
        A Background Study of the Novels of Richardson, Field-
        ing, and Smollett." *DAI*, 32 (1971), 3242A (Northwestern
        University, 1971).

1279. Bennett, Robert C. "Fielding and the Satiric Dance."
       DAI, 30 (1970), 4397A (University of Pennsylvania,
       1969).

1280. Bissel, Frederick Olds. "Fielding's Theory of the
       Novel." Cornell University, 1931.

1281. Blanchard, Frederic Thomas. "Fielding's Reputation as
       a Novelist in English Literary History." Yale Uni-
       versity, 1922.

1282. Bolles, Edwin Courtlandt. "Sea Travelling from
       Fielding to Today." University of Pennsylvania, 1931.

1283. Borthwick, Sister Mary Charlotte, F.L.S.P. "Henry
       Fielding as Critical Realist: An Examination of the
       East German Estimate of Fielding." *DA*, 26 (1966),
       3945-46 (Fordham University, 1965).

1284. Bradley, Toby Snitkin. "The Relationship Between
       Satire and Sentimentality in the Works of Henry
       Fielding." *DAI*, 36 (1975), 2213A (University of Cali-
       fornia, Santa Barbara, 1975).

1285. Branch, Mary Elizabeth. "Fielding's Attitude Toward
       the Chief Religious Groups of His Time." University
       of Chicago, 1926.

1286. Braudy, Leo B. "The Narrative Stance: Problems on
       History and Methods of Fiction in David Hume, Henry
       Fielding, and Edward Gibbon." *DA*, 28 (1968), 4118A
       (Yale University, 1967).

1287. Brewerton, Marti J. "Henry Fielding's *The Mock Doctor,
       or The Dumb Lady Cur'd* and *The Miser*: A Critical
       Edition." *DA*, 33 (1972), 269A (University of North
       Dakota, 1971).

1288. Brown, Jack R. "Four Plays by Henry Fielding." North-
       western University, 1937.

1289. Bryant, Virginia M. "The Literary and Philosophical
       Background of Tom Jones." University of Cincinnati,
       1940.

1290. Burnette, Patricia L.B. "The Polemical Structure of
       Fielding's Plays." *DAI*, 32 (1972), 6921A (Indiana
       University, 1972).

1291. Burt, David James. "Henry Fielding's Attitudes
      Toward the Eighteenth Century Gentleman." *DAI*, 33
      (1973), 5114A (University of Kentucky, 1972).

1292. Capers, Connie. "From Drama to Novel: A Study of
      Fielding's Development." *DAI*, 31 (1971), 5353A
      (University of New Mexico, 1970).

1293. Carter, Charlotte A. "Personae and Characters in the
      Essays of Addison, Steele, Fielding, Johnson, Gold-
      smith." *DAI*, 30 (1970), 4938A (University of Denver,
      1969).

1294. Castillo Cofiño, Rosa. "Los Conceptos del Amor en la
      Novelística de Henry Fielding." University of Madrid,
      1973.

1295. Chandor, Kenneth Francis. "English Inns and Taverns:
      Their Structural and Thematic Function in Fielding's
      Novels." *DAI*, 37 (1977), 4364A (Tulane University,
      1976).

1296. Chaudhary, Awadhesh. "Henry Fielding: His Attitude
      Toward the Contemporary Stage." *DA*, 26 (1966), 1642-
      43 (University of Michigan, 1963).

1297. Clark, Charles Marston. "The Life of Mr. Jonathan
      Wild the Great by Henry Fielding, Edited with Intro-
      duction and Notes." Cornell University, 1942.

1298. Cleary, Thomas R. "Henry Fielding as a Periodical
      Essayist." *DA*, 31 (1971), 6544A (Princeton University,
      1970).

1299. Clements, Frances M. "Social Criticism in the English
      Novel: 1740-1754." *DA*, 28 (1968), 5011A (Ohio State
      University, 1967).

1300. Coley, William B., II. "Fielding's Comic: A Study of
      the Relation Between Wit and Seriousness in a Comic
      Augustan." *DA*, 30 (1970), 4403A (Yale University, 1954).

1301. Combs, William W., Jr. "Man and Society in Fielding's
      Works." Harvard University, 1962.

1302. Coolidge, A.C. "Henry Fielding, Critic of His Times."
      Trinity College (Dublin), 1937.

1303. Cooper, Frank B. "The Structure of the Novels of Henry
       Fielding." *DAI*, 30 (1970), 5404A (Claremont Graduate
       School and University Center, 1969).

1304. Crockett, Harold Kelly. "The Picaresque Tradition in
       English Fiction to 1770: A Study of Popular Back-
       grounds with Particular Attention to Fielding and
       Smollett." University of Illinois, 1953.

1305. Davis, Charles George. "Satire on the Reader in the
       Novels of Henry Fielding." *DAI*, 31 (1971), 6006A
       (University of North Carolina, Chapel Hill, 1970).

1306. DeBruyn, John R. "Tom Jones: A Genealogical Approach:
       Fielding's Use of Type Characters in *Tom Jones*." *DA*,
       15 (1955), 1070 (New York University, 1954).

1307. Demarest, David Porter, Jr. "Legal Language and Situa-
       tion in the Eighteenth Century Novel: Readings in
       Defoe, Richardson, Fielding, and Austen." *DA*, 24
       (1964), 2907 (University of Wisconsin, 1963).

1308. Derstine, Virginia. "Fielding's Shift in Instructional
       Method as Reflected in His Early Prose Fiction." *DA*,
       21 (1961), 3780 (University of Washington, 1960).

1309. Devine, Mary Elizabeth. "Fielding on Walpole: A
       Study of Henry Fielding's Major Political Satires."
       Loyola University of Chicago, 1964.

1310. Dircks, Richard Joseph, ed. "Henry Fielding's *A Pro-
       posal for Making an Effectual Provision for the Poor*:
       An Edition." *DA*, 23 (1962), 223 (Fordham University,
       1961).

1311. Doland, Virginia Marie. "Versions of Pastoral in Henry
       Fielding's Prose Fiction." *DAI*, 31 (1970), 1222A
       (University of Southern California, 1969).

1312. Drumwright, Charles M. "The Dramatic Burlesques of
       John Gay and Henry Fielding." University of Texas,
       Austin, 1955.

1313. Emery, Helene La Verne. "The Interrelationship of
       Literature and Sociology in the Explication of Three
       English Novels." Middle Tennessee State University,
       1973.

1314. Eubanks, Katherine L. "Fielding's Political Plays: A Study in Background and Allusions." University of Texas, Austin, 1937.

1315. Evans, James E. "Fielding's Community of Fiction: Fielding's Supporting Characters in *Joseph Andrews*, *Tom Jones*, and *Amelia*." *DA*, 32 (1972), 4560A–61A (University of Pennsylvania, 1971).

1316. Evans, William E. "Poetic Justice and the Endings of Henry Fielding's Novels." *DAI*, 34 (1973), 2555A–56A (Ohio University, 1973).

1317. Farringdon, M.G. "A Study of Quantitative Literary Analysis and Literary Data Processing by Computer, with Some Quantitative Analysis of the Prose Style of Henry Fielding and Some Writers Contemporary With Him." University of Bristol, 1974.

1318. Fenster, Alan Richard. "The Other Tradition: An Essay in Forms of Realism in the Novel." *DAI*, 38 (1977), 802A–03A (University of California, Berkeley, 1976).

1319. Fleming, John Paul. "The Classical Retirement Theme in the Fiction of Defoe, Fielding, Johnson, and Goldsmith." *DAI*, 38 (1977), 2840A–05A (Bowling Green State University, 1977).

1320. French, Robert D. "The True Patriot by Henry Fielding." *DA*, 33 (1972), 1140A (Yale University, 1920).

1321. Glenn, Sidney Erwin. "Some French Influences on Henry Fielding." University of Illinois, 1932.

1322. Gligor, Emil Peter. "A Study of Fielding's *The Opposition: A Vision*." *DAI*, 37 (1977), 7761A–62A (Case Western Reserve University, 1976).

1323. Goggin, Leo P. "The Development of Fielding's Technique as a Writer of Comedies." University of Chicago, 1950.

1324. Goldberg, Homer. "*Joseph Andrews* and the Continental Comic Romances." University of Chicago, 1962.

1325. Goldknopf, Irma. "Crime and Prison-Experience in the Early English Novel: Defoe, Fielding, Smollett." *DA*, 29 (1968), 1207A (Syracuse University, 1968).

1326.   Goyne, Arlie Vernon. "Defoe and Fielding: A Study of
        the Development of English Novel Technique." Uni-
        versity of Texas, Austin, 1954.

1327.   Grace, Matthew S. "Fielding in the Eighteenth Cen-
        tury." *DA*, 25 (1965), 6624 (University of Wisconsin,
        1965).

1328.   Graves, William Thomas. "National Characters in the
        Novels of Henry Fielding, Samuel Richardson, and
        Tobias Smollett." *DAI*, 31 (1971), 6549A (New York
        University, 1970).

1329.   Gravitt, Garland Jack. "Mockery of the Aesthetic
        Ideal of Organic Unity in Restoration and Eighteenth
        Century Literature." Southern Illinois University,
        1973.

1330.   Gray, Ernest W. "The Fielding-Smollett Tradition in
        the English Novel from 1750 to 1835." Harvard Uni-
        versity, 1931.

1331.   Greason, Arthur L., Jr. "The Political Journals of
        Henry Fielding." Harvard University, 1954.

1332.   Guthrie, William Bowman. "The Comic Celebrant of Life."
        DA, 29 (1969), 3098A (Vanderbilt University, 1968).

1333.   Hanes, Sara Louise. "Dialect in the Novels of Field-
        ing and Smollett." *DAI*, 35 (1975), 6694A (University
        of Georgia, 1974).

1334.   Harmen, Margaret M. Campbell. "Exposition in the
        Novels of Henry Fielding." *DAI*, 34 (1973), 1911A
        (Catholic University of America, 1973).

1335.   Harris, Elizabeth Wanning. "Fiction and Artifice:
        Studies in Fielding, Wieland, Sterne, Diderot." *DAI*,
        34 (1974), 7191A (Yale University, 1973).

1336.   Hatfield, Glenn Wilson, Jr. "Fielding's Irony and the
        Corruption of Language." *DA*, 25 (1964), 1194-95
        (Ohio State University, 1964).

1337.   Hemingson, Peter Harold. "Fielding and the '45: A
        Critical Edition of Henry Fielding's Anti-Jacobite
        Pamphlets." *DAI*, 34 (1974), 5174A (Columbia University,
        1973).

1338. Hessler, Mabel D. "The Literary Opposition to Sir Robert Walpole, 1721-1742: Fielding's Attacks on Walpole." University of Chicago, 1936.

1339. Hill, Rowland Merlin. "Realistic Descriptive Setting in English Fiction from 1550 through Fielding." Boston University, 1941.

1340. Hillhouse, James Theodore. "The Tragedy of Tragedies, A Dramatic Burlesque, by Henry Fielding, Edited with Introduction and Notes." Yale University, 1914.

1341. Holloway, Jean. "Law and Literature in the Age of Enlightenment: Blackstone and Fielding." University of Texas, Austin, 1950.

1342. Holly, Grant Innes. "Fielding's Enchanted Glass: A Study of the World as Language in Selected Comic Prose." *DAI*, 35 (1974), 2226A (University of Rochester, 1974).

1343. Honhart, Carol Taplett. "Fielding, Smollett, Sterne, and the Development of the Eighteenth-Century Travel Book." *DAI*, 35 (1975), 5348A-49A (Duke University, 1974).

1344. Horn, Robert Dewey. "The Farce Technique in the Dramatic Work of Henry Fielding and Samuel Foote and Its Influence on the 'Maerchensatiren' of Ludwig Tieck." University of Michigan, 1930.

1345. Howe, Jean Marie. "Studies in the Plays of Henry Fielding." University of Texas, Austin, 1938.

1346. Hubbard, Lester A. "Fielding's Ethics Viewed in Relation to Shaftesbury's Characteristics." University of California, Berkeley, 1934.

1347. Humphrey, Theodore Carl. "Henry Fielding: An Annotated Bibliography of Studies and Editions, 1895-1970." University of Arkansas, 1972.

1348. Hutchens, Eleanor N. "Verbal Irony in *Tom Jones*." *DA*, 17 (1957), 2611 (University of Pennsylvania, 1957).

1349. Irwin, William R. "The Making of 'Jonathan Wild': A Study in the Literary Method of Henry Fielding." Columbia University, 1942.

1350. Jacobson, Margaret Charlotte Kingsland. "Women in the
       Novels of Defoe, Richardson, and Fielding." *DAI*, 35
       (1975), 7256A (University of Connecticut, 1975).

1351. Jacobson, William Spencer. "The Rhetorical Structure
       of Fielding's Epic, Joseph Andrews." *DA*, 27 (1966),
       1057A-58A (Stanford University, 1966).

1352. Jennings, Edward Morton III. "Reader-Narrative Rela-
       tionships in *Tom Jones*, *Tristram Shandy*, and *Humphrey
       Clinker*." *DA*, 26 (1965), 3303-04 (University of Wis-
       consin, 1965).

1353. Jensen, Gerard Edward. "The Covent-Garden Journal,
       by Sir Alexander Drawcansir, Knt. Censor of Great
       Britain (Henry Fielding), Edited with Introduction and
       Notes." Yale University, 1913.

1354. Jobe, Alice Joyce Cushman. "Fielding Criticism: A
       Twentieth Century Selective Enumeration with Commen-
       tary." *DAI*, 31 (1970), 1761A (University of Texas,
       Austin, 1970).

1355. Johnson, Jeffrey L. "The Good-Natured Young Man and
       Virtuous Young Woman in the Comedies of Henry Field-
       ing." *DAI*, 30 (1970), 5411A-12A (Florida State Uni-
       versity, 1969).

1356. Jordan, Burt Arthur. "The Moral Code in Fielding's
       Novels: 'Jonathan Wild,' 'Joseph Andrews,' and
       'Amelia.'" University of South Carolina, 1969.

1357. Kaiser, John Irving. "A Study of the Plays by Henry
       Fielding as a Commentary on the Early 18th Century
       Theatre." St. John's University, 1962.

1358. Kalpakgian, Mitchell A. "The Idea of the Marvellous
       or Wonderful in Fielding's Novels." *DAI*, 35 (1974),
       2227A (University of Iowa, 1974).

1359. Keller, Ellen Holland. "*L'Enfant trouvé: Tom Jones* as
       an Eighteenth-Century French Novel." *DAI*, 38 (1977),
       307A (Case Western Reserve University, 1976).

1360. Kiehl, James Millinger. "Epic, Mock-heroic, and
       Novel, 1650-1750." Syracuse University, 1972.

1361. Kinder, Marsha. "Henry Fielding's Dramatic Experimentation: A Preface to His Fiction." *DA*, 28 (1967), 633A-34A (University of California, Los Angeles, 1967).

1362. Kishler, Thomas Charles. "The Satiric Moral Fable: A Study of an Augustan Genre with Particular Reference to Fielding." *DA*, 20 (1959), 1352-53 (University of Wisconsin, 1959).

1363. Krause, Lothar P. "The Conflict Between Social Communities and Individuals in the Novels of Henry Fielding." *DAI*, 30 (1970), 4991A (University of Pittsburgh, 1969).

1364. Kreutz, Irving William. "A Study of Henry Fielding's Plays." *DA*, 16 (1956), 2165-66 (University of Wisconsin, 1956).

1365. Kurtz, Eric W. "Fielding's Thoughtful Laughter." *DA*, 28 (1967), 234A (Yale University, 1967).

1366. Lepage, Peter V. "Fielding's Immanent Symbology." *DA*, 25 (1965), 5282 (Bowling Green State University, 1964).

1367. Levine, George Richard. "The Techniques of Irony in the Major Early Works of Henry Fielding." *DA*, 22 (1962), 4005-06 (Columbia University, 1961).

1368. Locke, Miriam A. "An Edition of 'The True Patriot' by Henry Fielding, with an Introduction and Critical Notes." Northwestern University, 1945.

1369. Loftis, John E., III. "The Moral Art of Henry Fielding." *DA*, 32 (1972), 6382A-83A (Emory University, 1971).

1370. Longmire, Samuel E. "The Narrative Structure of Fielding's *Amelia*." *DA*, 29 (1969), 3103A-04A (Indiana University, 1968).

1371. MacAndrew, Mary E. "The Debate Between Richardson and Fielding." *DAI*, 34 (1973), 280A (Columbia University, 1970).

1372. McCrea, Brian Richard. "Fielding's Political Writings." *DAI*, 36 (1976), 4514A (University of Virginia, 1975).

1373. McKee, John B. "Literary Irony and the Literary
       Audience: Studies in the Victimization of the Reader
       in Early English Fiction." *DAI*, 33 (1973), 5132A–33A
       (Syracuse University, 1972).

1374. McNamara, Susan P. "Paradox in the Novels of Henry
       Fielding." *DAI*, 36 (1975), 2222A–23A (New York
       University, 1975).

1375. McWilliams, David J. "The Technique of Henry Field-
       ing." University of Texas, Austin, 1933.

1376. Meeker, Richard K. "Experiments in Point of View:
       Animal, Vegetable, and Mineral Narrators in the Eigh-
       teenth Century English Novel." University of Penn-
       sylvania, 1955.

1377. Mellen, Joan. "Morality in the Novel: A Study of
       Five English Novelists, Henry Fielding, Jane Austen,
       George Eliot, Joseph Conrad, and D.H. Lawrence." *DA*,
       29 (1968), 1543A (City University of New York, 1968).

1378. Meredith, Robert Chidester. "Henry Fielding and the
       Idea of Benevolence: A Study of the Structure of *Tom
       Jones*." University of Wisconsin, 1956.

1379. Miller, Henry K., Jr. "Fielding's *Miscellanies*: A
       Study of Volumes I and II of *Miscellanies, by Henry
       Fielding, Esq.; in Three Volumes*, 1743." *DA*, 14
       (1954), 821–22 (Princeton University, 1953).

1380. Nagourney, Peter Jon. "Law in the Novels of Henry
       Fielding." University of Chicago, 1971.

1381. Nelson, Judith Kay. "Fielding and Molière." *DAI*, 32
       (1971), 2064A (Rice University, 1971).

1382. Neuendorf, Mary Margaret Schulge. "The 'Great Man'
       in the Works of Henry Fielding." *DA*, 25 (1964), 2498
       (Rice University, 1964).

1383. Newhouse, Edward B. "Poetic Theory and Practice in
       the Novels of Henry Fielding." *DA*, 32 (1972), 5194A
       (Ball State University, 1971).

1384. Nichols, Charles W. "Fielding's Satirical Plays of
       1736 and 1737: *Pasquin, Tumble-Down Dick, The Historical
       Register for the Year 1736*, and *Eurydice Hiss'd*. Edited

with a Historical Introduction and Explanatory Notes."
DA, 33 (1973), 731A (Yale University, 1918).

1385. Nielsen, Elizabeth E. "Attitudes of English Writers
(1690-1750) towards the English Poor." Northwestern
University, 1944.

1386. Nisbet, Janice Ann. "The Art of Life As Represented
in Henry Fielding's Amelia." *DAI*, 35 (1974), 1057A
(Ball State University, 1974).

1387. Oden, Richard L. "Fielding's Drama in Relation to
Restoration Comedy and to *Tom Jones*." *DA*, 29 (1969),
3106A-07A (Tulane University, 1968).

1388. Ormond, Jeanne Dowd. "The Knave with a Hundred Faces:
The Guises of Hermes in Nashe, Fielding, Melville,
and Mann." *DAI*, 35 (1975), 7320A-21A (University of
California, Irvine, 1974).

1389. Parker, Alice. "Views of Crime and Punishment in
Fielding and Smollett." Yale University, 1939.

1390. Passler, Susan M. "Theatricality, the Eighteenth Century and Fielding's *Tom Jones*." *DA*, 32 (1972), 6941A
(University of North Carolina, 1971).

1391. Penner, Allen Richard. "Fielding and Cervantes: The
Contribution of *Don Quixote* to *Joseph Andrews* and *Tom
Jones*." *DA*, 26 (1966), 6720-21 (University of
Colorado, 1965).

1392. Persky, Charles. "The Comic Alternative: A Study of
Henry Fielding and His Novels from 'Shamela' to 'Tom
Jones.'" Harvard University, 1968.

1393. Pykare, Nina Coombs. "The Female Part of the Species:
A Study of Women in Fielding." *DAI*, 37 (1976), 991A-
92A (Kent State University, 1976).

1394. Rader, Ralph Wilson. "Idea and Structure in Fielding's
Novels." *DA*, 19 (1958), 1367 (Indiana University,
1958).

1395. Rence, Robert J. "The Burlesque Techniques Employed
by James Robinson Planché in His Dramatic Works and
Their Relationship to the English Burlesque Tradition
Between Henry Fielding and W.S. Gilbert." *DA*, 28
(1967), 2376A (University of Minnesota, 1967).

1396. Rinehart, Hollis, III. "Fielding's 'Jonathan Wild':
       Form and Intention." University of Chicago, 1966.

1397. Rizvi, S.M.J.Z. "Political Satire in the Plays of
       Henry Fielding." University of Edinburgh, 1967.

       Goldgar, *Walpole and the Wits* (item 190), draws upon
       this dissertation.

1398. Roberts, Edgar V. "The Ballad Operas of Henry Field-
       ing, 1730-1732: A Critical Edition." *DA*, 21 (1961),
       3451-52 (University of Minnesota, 1960).

1399. Rosenblood, Bryan N. "Some Aspects of Henry Field-
       ing's Heroes." *DAI*, 30 (1969), 695A (University of
       Pittsburgh, 1968).

1400. Rudolph, Valerie Christine. "Theatrical Verisimilitude
       and Political Belief in the Plays of Henry Fielding."
       DAI, 32 (1971), 1485A (University of Iowa, 1971).

1401. Rundus, Raymond J. "The History of *Tom Jones* in
       Adaptation." *DAI*, 30 (1969), 1535A (University of
       Nebraska, 1969).

1402. Ryan, Marjorie. "The Tom Jones Hero in Plays and
       Novels, 1750-1800: A Study of Fielding's Influence."
       DA, 19 (1958), 815-16 (University of Minnesota, 1957).

1403. Sackett, Samuel John. "The Place of Literary Theory
       in Henry Fielding's Art." University of California,
       Los Angeles, 1956.

1404. Sacks, Sheldon. "From Artistic Judgment to Ethical
       Statement: The Shape of Belief in Fielding's Novels."
       University of Chicago, 1960.

1405. Seamon, Roger G. "The Rhetorical Pattern of Neo-
       classical Mock-Heroic Satire." *DA*, 28 (1968), 1058A-
       59A (Claremont Graduate School and University Center,
       1966).

1406. Sells, Larry Francis. "Fielding's Central Triad:
       Repetition and Variation in the Novels." *DAI*, 32
       (1971), 932A (Pennsylvania State University, 1970).

1407. Seltman, Kent Daniels. "Henry Fielding, the Preacher:
       A Study of the Layman's Sermons in Historical and

Rhetorical Context." *DAI*, 35 (1975), 5425A-26A
(University of Nebraska, 1974).

1408. Sharp, Ruth Marian McKenzie. "Rational Vision and the
Comic Resolution: A Study in the Novels of Richardson,
Fielding, and Jane Austen." University of Wisconsin,
1969.

1409. Shea, Bernard. "Classical Learning in the Novels of
Henry Fielding." Harvard University, 1952.

1410. Shepperson, Archibald Bolling. "Types of the Burlesque Novel from Fielding to Thackeray." University
of Virginia, 1928.

1411. Sherwood, Irma Z. "The Influence of Digressive
Didacticism on the Structure of the Novels of Richardson and Fielding." *DAI*, 30 (1970), 3436A (Yale University, 1945).

1412. Shesgreen, Sean Nicholas. "The Literary Portraits in
the Novels of Henry Fielding." *DAI*, 31 (1971), 3564A
(Northwestern University, 1970).

1413. Shoup, Louise. "The Use of the Social Gathering as a
Structural Device in the Novels of Richardson, Fielding, Smollett, and Sterne." Stanford University, 1950.

1414. Siegel, Shirley F. "Chivalric Comedies: A Study of
Romance Elements in *Tom Jones* and *Joseph Andrews*."
DAI, 36 (1975), 911A-12A (Southern Illinois University,
1974).

1415. Sieker, Don W. "Henry Fielding as Playwright: A Study
of Relationships between Comic Drama and Moral Purpose." *DAI*, 36 (1975), 2224A-25A (University of California, Davis, 1975).

1416. Skinner, Mary L. "The Interpolated Story in Selected
Novels of Fielding and Smollett." *DA*, 29 (1969),
4020A-21A (University of Tennessee, 1968).

1417. Slevin, James Francis. "Morals and Form: A Study of
Tradition and Innovation in *Joseph Andrews*." *DAI*, 36
(1976), 4517A-18A (University of Virginia, 1975).

1418. Smith, Leroy W. "The Doctrine of the Passions as It
Appears in the Works of Henry Fielding, Particularly
in *Amelia*." Duke University, 1956.

1419. Solon, John James. "Fielding in the Twentieth Century." University of Wisconsin, 1956.

1420. Speer, John Forbes. "A Critical Study of the *Champion*." University of Chicago, 1951.

1421. Stephenson, William Alva, Jr. "Henry Fielding's Influence on Lord Byron." *DAI*, 35 (1974), 478A (Texas Technical University, 1973).

1422. Stern, Guy. "Fielding, Wieland, and Goethe: A Study in the Development of the Novel." *DA*, 14 (1954), 1731-32 (Columbia University, 1954).

1423. Stevick, Philip Thayer. "Fielding: The Novelist as Philosopher of History." *DA*, 24 (1964), 2912-13 (Ohio State University, 1963).

1424. Stewart, Maaja A. "The Artifice of Comedy: Fielding and Meredith." *DA*, 27 (1967) 2163A (University of Michigan, 1966).

1425. Stitzel, Judith G. "Comedy and the Serious Moralist: The Concept of Good-Nature in the Novels of Henry Fielding." *DA*, 29 (1969), 2686A (University of Minnesota, 1968).

1426. Stuart, Walter Harding. "The Role of the Narrator in the Novels of Fielding." *DA*, 24 (1963), 2489-90 (University of Wisconsin, 1963).

1427. Sullivan, William Arnett. "Fielding's Dramatic Comedies: The Influence of Congreve and Molière." *DAI*, 32 (1972), 3966A (Louisiana State University, 1972).

1428. Swann, G.R. "Philosophical Parallelism in Six English Novelists." University of Pennsylvania, 1929.

1429. Swanson, Gayle Ruff. "Henry Fielding and the Psychology of Womanhood." *DAI*, 38 (1977), 291A (University of South Carolina, 1976).

1430. Tabbs, Bernard Linden. "Fielding's Oedipal Fantasy: A Psychoanalytic Study of the Double in Tom Jones." *DAI*, 37 (1976), 1524A (American University, 1976).

1431. Thoms, Jerrald Phillip. "Henry Fielding's Comedies of Manners: A Study in the Eighteenth-Century Problem Play." *DAI*, 35 (1975), 5369A (Kansas State University, 1974).

1432. Thornbury, Ethel Margaret. "Henry Fielding's Theory of the Comic Prose Epic." University of Wisconsin, 1928.

1433. Towers, A.R. "An Introduction and Annotations for a Critical Edition of *Amelia*." *DA*, 14 (1954), 351-52 (Princeton University, 1952).

1434. Van Loon, Nelles Hart. "The Comic and the Sentimental in the Novels of Henry Fielding." *DAI*, 38 (1977), 3461A (University of Toronto, 1976).

1435. Varcoe, George. "The Intrusive Narrator: Fielding, Thackeray, and The English Novel." Upsala University, 1972.

1436. Wallace, Robert Marsden. "Henry Fielding's Narrative Method, Its Historical and Biographical Origins." University of North Carolina at Chapel Hill, 1946.

1437. Ward, John Chapman. "The Tradition of The Hypocrite in Eighteenth-Century English Literature." University of Virginia, 1972.

1438. Warren, Leland Eddie. "Henry Fielding and the Search for History: The Historiographical Context of *Tom Jones*." *DAI*, 37 (1976), 2705A-06A (University of Illinois, 1976).

1439. Wendt, Allan E. "Richardson and Fielding: A Study in Eighteenth Century Compromise." *DA*, 17 (1957), 859 (Indiana University, 1956).

1440. Wess, Robert Victor. "Modes of Fictional Structure in Henry Fielding and Jane Austen." University of Chicago, 1970.

1441. Wieczorek, Anthony Paul. "Henry Fielding's Role as Moral Arbiter and Teacher in the *Champion*: 1739-1741." *DAI*, 35 (1975), 6687A (Northwestern University, 1974).

1442. Wilbur, Frederick. "Henry Fielding's Life in the Theatre and the New Species of Writing." *DAI*, 35 (1975), 6115A (Duke University, 1974).

1443. Williams, Murial Brittain. "Henry Fielding's Attitudes Toward Marriage." *DA*, 24 (1964), 4204 (University of Alabama, 1963).

1444. Wilner, Arlene Fish. "Henry Fielding and the Uses of
       Language: A Study of *Joseph Andrews* and *Tom Jones*."
       DAI, 37 (1976), 3656A-57A (Columbia University, 1976).

1445. Wilson, Robin Scott. "Henry Fielding and the Passionate
       Man." *DA*, 20 (1959) 3285-86 (University of Illinois,
       1959).

1446. Winterowd, Walter Ross. "The Poles of Discourse: A
       Study of Eighteenth Century Rhetoric in *Amelia* and
       Clarissa." *DA*, 26 (1965), 360-61 (University of Utah,
       1965).

1447. Wolfe, George Hubert. "Lessons in Virtue: Fielding
       and the Ethical Imperative." *DAI*, 38 (1977), 814A
       (University of North Carolina, 1976).

1448. Wood, David C. "The Dramatic Tradition of Henry Field-
       ing's Regular Comedies." *DAI*, 30 (1970), 4428A (Bowl-
       ing Green University, 1969).

1449. Woods, Charles Burton. "Studies in the Dramatic Works
       of Henry Fielding." Harvard University, 1935.

1450. Wright, Kenneth Daulton. "Henry Fielding and the
       London Stage, 1730-1737." *DA*, 21 (1960), 1293-94
       (Ohio State University, 1960).

1451. Yskamp, Claire E. "Character and Voice: First Person
       Narrators in *Tom Jones*, *Wuthering Heights*, and *Second
       Skin*." *DA*, 32 (1972), 6948A (Brandeis University,
       1972).

1452. Zakaras, Laura V. "Love and Morality in *Tom Jones*."
       DAI, 34 (1973), 2585A-86A (University of Washington,
       1973).

1453. Zirker, Malvin Ralph, Jr. "Henry Fielding's Social
       Attitudes: A Study of 'An Enquiry into the Causes of
       the Late Increase of Robbers' and 'A Proposal for
       Making an Effective Provision for the Poor.'" *DA*, 21
       (1962), 456A (University of California, Berkeley,
       1962).

AUTHOR INDEX

Included in this index are the names of authors of articles
and books on Fielding, editors of collections of essays, and
authors and editors of general works which include material
on Fielding. The numbers following each name refer the reader
to item numbers in the bibliography.

TITLE INDEX

Titles listed are those of primary books and articles on Fielding, of collections in which essays on or information about Fielding appear, and of general series containing volumes including information on Fielding. Like English items, foreign-language items are indexed according to the first substantive (non-article) word in the title--e.g., *Die Aufnahme des Don Quijote* appears under the A's, not the D's. Numbers following the title refer the reader to item numbers, not page numbers.